D0555351

Counseling African American Males

A volume in
African American Male Series:
Guiding the Next Generation Through Mentoring, Teaching and Counseling
William Ross, *Series Editor*

Counseling African American Males

Effective Therapeutic Interventions and Approaches

edited by

William Ross
Prairie View A&M University

INFORMATION AGE PUBLISHING, INC.
Charlotte, NC • www.infoagepub.com

Library of Congress Cataloging-in-Publication Data

A CIP record for this book is available from the Library of Congress
http://www.loc.gov

ISBN: 978-1-68123-549-3 (Paperback)
      978-1-68123-550-9 (Hardcover)
      978-1-68123-551-6 (ebook)

Printed in the United States of America

CONTENTS

INTRODUCTION

William Ross

African American males today face a myriad of challenges that significantly impact their development. Therefore, effective measures to provide therapeutic counseling interventions must be based on sensitivity to their historical, social, and cultural development. It is vital for committed therapists to acquire attitudes and behaviors that will enable them to intervene with African American males at a level that will assist this group in functioning at an optimal psycho-social and academic level in this ever-changing world.

Therapists that work with African American males must recognize that traditional therapeutic theories, strategies, and interventions may not be effective in addressing the problems and concerns presented by these boys and men. One reason for this ineffectiveness as outlined by Sue and Sue (2013) is an understanding of the scholars who developed these theories, and the populations on which they were normed. Our historical therapy models are based primarily on Eurocentric assumptions, which do not consider the influence and impact of racial and cultural socialization (APA, 2003). These counseling strategies do not incorporate the unique historical, cultural, and social influences common to African American males. The developmental psychologist Urie Bronfrenbrenner (2005) championed

Counseling African American Males, pages vii–xvi
Copyright © 2016 by Information Age Publishing

the development of the ecological systems theory and the importance of environmental and societal influences on psychological development. Toldson and Toldson (1998) surmised that "the psychosocial development of African American males is complicated by an intricate system of ecological factors that have been neglected by many mental health professionals" (p. 71). It is an ethical obligation that counselors develop sensitivity to cultural differences if they hope to craft interventions that are consistent with the values and beliefs of African American males. The therapist's role is to assist clients in making decisions that are congruent with the clients' worldview, not to live by the therapist's values (Corey, 2013).

These societal and environmental influences mentioned by Bronfrenbrenner (2005) are dramatically different for African American males. Corey said,

> the postmodern approaches: social constructionism, solution-focused brief therapy, and narrative therapy challenge the basic assumptions of most of the traditional approaches by assuming that there is no single truth and that reality is socially constructed through human interaction. Both the postmodern and the systemic theories focus on how people produce their own lives in the context of systems, interactions, social conditioning, and discourse. (Cory, 2013, p. 24)

If therapists want to be successful providing psychological services to African American males they must embrace these postmodern therapeutic approaches.

A second concern fundamental to traditional theories applied to counseling African American males and their ineffectiveness is the understanding that these theories do not incorporate the effects of racism and discrimination on psycho-social development. The field of research on racial identity development and psycho-social functioning in African American males unequivocally support the negative impact of racism and discrimination on all areas of development (Bobo, 2011; Harper, Davis, Jones, McGowan, Ingram, & Plat, 2011; Pieterse & Carter, 2010; Stevens, Eagle, Kaminer, & Higson-Smith, 2013). However, there have been in the last few decades attempts by the profession to address multicultural awareness in counselor training programs in this country. Among these approaches, three prominent ones have emerged: (a) separate course approach, (b) integration and infusion approach, and (c) area of concentration approach (Chae, Foley, & Chae, 2006). When considering these multicultural training approaches, the separate course model is the one most commonly used by counselor training programs. However, based on the research of Banks (2012) these single course approaches are inadequate because they lack the level of commitment necessary to systematically combat counselor cultural encapsulation and generations of racial discrimination. Treatment for

African American males must not only embrace the impact of racism and discrimination, the contemporary concerns of African American people, but also must reflect aspects of African heritage, cognitive styles, and psychological defenses. All African American men, regardless of educational achievements, and socioeconomic, have to some degree been traumatized by pervasive racism and discrimination.

Considering the historical fact of the issues that are unique to the African American male, which includes racism and discrimination, an unusual level of sensitivity and appreciation for the contextual meaning of being in their position (culture) is required of the counselor to make an actual impact in the lives of these boys and men. Vereen, Hill, & Butler (2013) bring to the reader's attention the fact that multiculturalism (recognizing non-Eurocentric cultural backgrounds) is a new phenomenon and that counselors are therefore charged with the responsibility of finding methods that will positively impact the African American male in the therapeutic process, while putting into consideration the distrust they have had for the counseling process.

In a world in which there continues to be negative views and statistics about African American males, there are several techniques that can be utilized by therapist when working with this population. The clinical treatment for African American men can be improved by using nontraditional treatment approaches. This text offer approaches in which clinical treatment strategies can be incorporated into both environmental (microaggressions, oppression, etc.) and cultural forces when working with African American males. Finally, the authors of this text offer both African centered and traditional counseling techniques that mental health counselors can use to improve the effectiveness of their strategies and interventions.

In African-centered counseling groups, group counseling rules are based on the traditional African values of (a) respect, (b) responsibility, (c) reciprocity (good deeds come back to you), (d) restraint (the group before selfish needs), (e) reason (resolving disputes through the group), and (f) reconciliation (forgiveness). Peer mediation is also a strategy in which two student mediators sit down to mediate conflict resolution between two individuals or groups. These are their peers so there is a sense of comfort in being able to relate to someone their age to diffuse conflict and arising tension. This is most helpful in situations that involve gang violence, interracial conflict, and other arguments (Harper, Terry, & Twiggs, 2009).

This text is opened with the work of Owens, Stewart, and Queener who propose that the clinical treatment for African American men can be improved by using nontraditional treatment approaches. The chapter offers ways in which clinical treatment can incorporate both environmental (microaggressions, oppression, etc.) and cultural forces. Finally, the authors offer both African centered and traditional counseling techniques that mental health counselors can use.

It is the work of Dr. Kniffley that concludes that African American men are engaged in an internal conflict in regards to their own beliefs about the negativity of African American manhood that is inconsistent with their historical and lived experience. This conflict is significantly influenced by the chronic experience of racial discrimination. Previous research has documented the negative effect of racial discrimination on the mental health of African American males. In addition, racial discrimination has been found to have a significant impact on African American masculinity development. His chapter introduces a model of African American male psychopathology that discusses the relationship between social oppression (via the experience of racial discrimination) and cultural identity suppression (via the internalization of socially constructed negative stereotypes of African American masculinity), and their influence on the development and maintenance of mental illness.

In the Sawyer, DeLapp, and Williams's chapter, they surmise that African American males may experience a disproportionate amount of barriers to treatment, such as financial limitations, concern about the treatment process, lack of mental health literacy, or a mistrust of psychotherapy. Although these barriers alone are significant, African American males also face higher levels of community violence exposure and experiences of racial discrimination. Due to traumatic experiences as a result of chronic community violence exposure, many issues may arise when treating African American male clients, such as potential blunted reactions due to trauma or a reluctance to report events as distressing. In addition, racial discrimination faced by African American males may further perpetuate a reluctance to report symptoms, as well as make establishing a strong therapeutic alliance difficult. Understanding the unique and complex experiences of African American males may help clinicians establish better rapport, more accurately assess symptoms, and attain positive therapeutic outcomes.

The work of Wilson and Williams confirm that the health status of the African American males continues to be challenged by a society that deems them to be less than human. The effect of dealing with this dehumanization challenges African American male college students' personality development. Having a healthy African American personality can be located within an African cultural mental health model of connectedness, competency, and consciousness. Existing models are inadequate in capturing the African grand narrative of the African American male college student. Ubuntu model of mental health provides a proper framework for locating healthy African American personality around African narratives that speaks to authentic behavioral expressions of their humanity. Their chapter will introduce Ubuntu model of mental health and reveal how this African concept can be used to identify healthy African American personality functioning through African narratives.

Yolanda Hamilton identifies that African American men have been underrepresented in empirical research. Scientists in their quest for information and knowledge about human behavior have predominately used White males. African American men have been disregarded from academic research for centuries, and when included African American males have been used solely to demonstrate a negative or adverse point of human condition. The large influx of other cultures have compelled U.S. counseling governing entities to become more conscious of this anomaly and more open and inclusive in its future research on understanding human behavior. Therefore, counseling African American men advocate research in gaining effective therapeutic interventions and approaches in counseling this underrepresented population. This chapter examines African American men vulnerabilities to ask for counseling and examined through a lens of valuing them as whole persons, needing a promotive environment in which they are accepted and allowed to express their inner feelings. This empathetic style should begin to permeate effective approaches in counseling African American males.

"The Empathy Wheel: The Needs of African American Male Students" by David Ford discusses the needs of African American male students and how counselors in various settings can assist these students in meeting these educational and emotional needs. It begins by the author discussing a conversation he had counselor while in high school. During his senior year, he, an African American male was applying to colleges and asked his high school counselor (who was also African American) for assistance. He was applying to several universities, all of which were Predominantly White Institutions (PWIs). His counselor recommended he apply to Historically Black Colleges/Universities instead of the PWIs he wanted to attend. Because the school counselor did not validate his choices, she did not assist him, and thought she knew what schools were best for him; he never had any more conversations with her. African American males benefit from counselors in various settings showing them a deeper level of empathy. Being empathic results in getting to know the history of African American males, getting to know them as individuals, getting to know their needs, showing that you care and are interested in their success, valuing their presence and experiences, validating their experiences, and fostering a sense of belonging among them.

Ahmad Washington suggests that professional school counselors should seriously entertain the idea of utilizing certain socially conscious rap artists to engage African American male youth in conversation about socioeducational institutional and systemic injustices they encounter. The author supports this position by addressing the following points. First, there are myriad ways African American males are criminalized, such that criminal behavior and African American maleness become synonymous. Second, a brief historical overview is conducted of hip-hop and socially conscious rap music. Particular attention will be paid to the sociopolitical context in which hip-hop developed. Third, the author connects the work of particular socially conscious rap artists (e.g., Common, Shad, etc.) to the idea of social and political empowerment against injustice within counseling (Hipolito-Delgado, & Lee, 2007) and how it can be applied to African American males. Finally, the author provides actual strategies on how to integrate socially conscious rap lyrics into various secondary education settings.

The author Darron Garner confirms that suicide remains the third leading cause of death for youth aged 15 to 24 (CDC, 2010). Among African American males aged 15 to 44, suicide is the third, fifth, and sixth leading cause of death, respectively, when categorizing the age groups as follows: 15–24, 25–34, and 35–44 (CDC, 2010). While it is true that suicide was not a leading cause of death for African Americans 40 years ago, this recent decade has shown an increase in the rate of suicide completion and nonfatal suicidal behavior among adolescent and young adult African American males between the ages of 15 and 24 (Garlow, Purselle, & Heninger, 2005). This chapter focuses on strategies and techniques to intervene with suicidal African American males.

Struggs and Harris believe that depression is often overlooked and left untreated in African American males. Their study examined how certain demographic variables predict depression in a sample of African Americans males 18 to 54 years of age in a rural area. Results from multiple regression analysis showed that level of education, age when diagnosed with depression, and level of functioning were statistically significant predictors of depression for participants in this study. The chapter addresses how principles of the health belief model and resilience theory can be integrated to develop effective therapeutic interventions for this population of individuals.

Ratliff, Finch, and Davis examine African American male graduate and undergraduate students. They conclude that this group does not utilize counseling services on their college campus. The researchers conducted an exploratory study examining male students' attitudes (trust, stigma, socialization, and open to counseling) toward seeking professional counseling. Four regression models were computed to determine the predictability of age, classification, marital status, and prior counseling (factors) on students' attitudes. Neither factor was found to be independent predictors in seeking professional counseling. Implications for university based therapists and university counseling centers are presented.

Karla Sapp looked at the Sentencing Project report in 1990, and found that African American males accounted for 23% of the population between the ages of 20 and 29, who were currently under the supervision of a criminal justice system to include parole, probation, prison, and/or jail (Mauer & Huling, 1995). It has also been reported that more than one third of African American males not enrolled in college were incarcerated by the early 2000s, and that nearly twice of those younger than 40 years of age had a bachelor's degree. This chapter focuses on counseling strategies and approaches that can be effective with this population.

Moss, Land, and Rozzi said African American male students have an increased potential of encountering obstacles to education when compared to their White peers (Holcomb-McCoy, 2007; Losen, 2011). White school counselors, therefore, are professionally charged and trained to advocate with and on behalf of African American male students in order to break down barriers hindering the academic experiences of the African American male students with whom they work (American School Counselor Association, 2012), including negative academic experiences, feelings of isolation, power differences, increased discipline referrals, low retention rates, and decreased graduation rates (Holcomb-McCoy, 2007; Losen, 2011). This chapter highlights specific skills, strategies, and behaviors that White school counselors can utilize as they strive to become allies with African American male students who navigate cumbersome and often racist academic settings (Taylor, Gillborn, & Ladson-Billings, 2009). Accordingly, sections of this chapter include: (a) the effects of school counselor identities on the student-counselor relationship, (b) culturally responsive school counseling interventions, (c) assessing school counselors' multicultural competence, (d) a social justice approach to school counseling, (e) the influence of race and culture on intervention planning, and (f) the student-counselor relationship and theoretically sound practices.

Donald Grant looked at a variety of factors that negatively impact the trajectories of African American males through the life span. Understanding the details of these factors can support culturally competent engagement and ecological enhancement with and for African American males from community stakeholders and policymakers in addition to clinical and academic professionals across a myriad of domains. The synergistic effects of stereotype threat and disidentification along with their associated factors are implicated in this solution based discourse on ecologies that limit optimal success for African American men and boys.

Josephine Olson in her chapter concludes that there is little that compares to the contagious laughter and the spontaneous energy of a child immersed in play. Play is defined as "a set of behaviors that are freely chosen, personally directed, and intrinsically motivated" (Wilson, 2009, p. 3). Play is a naturally occurring process that stimulates creativity and fosters the imagination. Play in its purest form is not sanctioned by adults but directed by the child himself (Frost 2010). As the emergent child engages in play, the child interacts with his surroundings in a way that is mutually beneficial to both the environment and the child. Play enhances a child's development on several dimensions (Ginsburg, 2007). In fact, play fosters the assimilation of the developmental domains and promotes overall healthy development (Lemcke, 2014). This chapter examines the developmental attributes associated with play. Specifically the author will explore the physical, cognitive, emotional, and social domains of development as it pertains to the developing child. The author will explore the ramifications for the absence of play experiences or what was first recognized as "play deprivation" by Stuart Brown (Brown, 2009). The author concludes with practical trauma-informed play therapy techniques as a remedy for the deficits associated with play deprivation among the African American male youth population.

Wilson and Williams in their chapter broaden the discussion of mental health functioning to include the psychological implications of significant social (identity) processes for African American males that are directly linked to outcomes. Because African American males are disparately criminalized and dehumanized (this identity negatively constructed by and for others) within American society, structure confronts the African American male existence in ways that impact his ability to maintain healthy functioning—to develop healthy self-concepts, to cope with daily challenges to his identity, to be mentally healthy and productive. A direct challenge to the popular notions of identity within American society, the discussion herein highlights the inability of traditional western theory/treatment to appropriately produce positive outcomes for African Americans because these structures do not significantly consider the reality of Black identity and functioning. As a result, its theoretical paradigms—and subsequent recommendations based upon such theorizing—do not/cannot effectively evaluate or accurately reflect the reality of African American identity.

The authors Gadsden and Howard attempt to deconstruct the prevailing negative archetypes and complexes of African American male masculinity. They begin by briefly summarizing the predominant organizing discourse on racial identity development and socialization as it pertains to African American males. The discourse provides a basis for understanding the process of identity development and socialization. Next, Jungian personality theory is explicated with particular attention to personality constructs that facilitate an understanding of the production and internalization of negative racial stereotypes, archetypes, and complexes of African American male masculinity. Finally, they conclude by positing clinical strategies informed by Jungian theory for supporting positive racial identity development among African American males, as mediated through the development and praxis of mental health therapists and counselors.

REFERENCES

American Psychological Association. (2003). *Ethical principles of psychologists and code of conduct.* Washington, DC. Retrieved from http://www.apa.org/ethics/code2002.html

American School Counselor Association. (2012). *The ASCA national model: A framework for school counseling programs.* Alexandria, VA: Author. doi:10.1037/e504812012-001

Banks, J. A. (2012). Multicultural and citizenship education in diverse societies. In N. Palaiologou, & G. Dietz (2012), *Mapping the broad field of multicultural and intercultural education worldwide: Towards the development of a new citizen.* Newcastle upon Tyne, England: Cambridge Scholars.

Bobo, L. D. (2011). Somewhere between Jim Crow & post-racialism: Reflections on the racial divide in America today. *Daedalus, 140*(2), 11–36.

Boykin, A. W., Jagers, R. J., Ellison C. M., & Albury, A. (1997). Communalism: Conceptualization and measurement of an Afrocultural social orientation. *Journal of Black Studies, 27,* 409–418.

Bronfenbrenner, U. (2005). *Making human beings human: Bioecological perspectives on human development.* Thousand Oaks, CA: Sage.

Brown, S. (2009) *Play: How it shapes the brain, opens the imagination, and invigorates the soul.* London, England: Penguin.

Centers for Disease Control and Prevention. (2010). *Suicide facts at a glance.* National Center for Injury Prevention and Control. Retrieved from www.cdc.gov/violenceprevention/pdf/Suicide_DataSheet-a.pdf

Chae, M., Foley, P. F., & Chae, S. Y. (2006). Multicultural competence and training: An ethical responsibility. *Counseling and Psychology Journal, 3,* 71–80.

Corey, G., (2013). *Theory and practice of counseling and psychotherapy.* Australia: Brooks/Cole /Cengage Learning.

Frost, J. (2010). *A history of children's play and play environments: Toward a contemporary child-saving movement.* New York, NY: Routledge.

Garlow, S. J., Purselle, D., & Heninger, M. (2005). Ethnic differences in patterns of suicide across the life cycle. *American Journal of Psychiatry, 162,* 319–323.

Ginsburg, K. R. (2007). The importance of play in promoting healthy child development and maintaining strong parent-child bonds. *Pediatrics, 119*(1), 182–191.

Harper, F., Terry, L., & Twiggs, R. (2009). Counseling strategies with Black boys and Black men: Implications for policy. *Academic Success for School-age Black Males, 78*(3), 216–232.

Harper, S. R, Davis, R. J., Jones, D. E., McGowan, B. L., Ingram, T. N., & Platt, C. S. (2011). Race and racism in the experiences of Black male resident assistants at predominantly White universities. *Journal of College Student Development, 52*(2), 180–200.

Hipolito-Delgado, C., & Lee, C. (2007). Empowerment theory for the professional school counselor: A manifesto for what really matters. *Professional School Counseling, 10*(4), 327–332.

Holcomb-McCoy, C. (2007). *School counseling to close the achievement gap: A social justice framework for success.* Thousand Oaks, CA: Sage.

Lemcke, S. (2014). *The neurological benefits of play.* Retrieved from http://prezi. com/296ho36h2in/theneorologicalbenefitsofplay

Losen, D. J. (2011). *Discipline policies, successful schools, and racial justice.* Boulder, CO: National Education Policy Center. Retrieved from http://nepc.colorado. edu/publication/dicipline-policies.

Mauer, M., & Huling, T. (1995). *Young Black Americans and the criminal justice system: Five years later.* Retrieved from https://www.ncjrs.gov/App/Publications/ abstract.aspx?ID=157929

Pieterse, A. L., & Carter, R. T. (2010). The role of racial identity in perceived racism and psychological stress among Black American adults: Exploring traditional and alternative approaches. *Journal of Applied Social Psychology, 40*(5), 1028–1053. doi:10.1111/j.1559-1816.2010.00609.

Stevens, G., Eagle, G., Kaminer, D., & Higson-Smith, C. (2013). Continuous traumatic stress: Conceptual conversations in contexts of global conflict, violence and trauma. *Journal of Peace Psychology, 19*(2), 75–84. doi.org/10.1037/a0032484

Sue, D. W., & Sue, D. (2013). *Counseling the culturally diverse: Theory and practice* (6th ed.). Hoboken, NJ: John Wiley.

Taylor, E., Gillborn, D., & Ladson-Billings, G. (2009). *Foundations for critical race theory in education.* New York, NY: Routledge.

Toldson, I. A., & Toldson, I. L. (1999). Esoteric group therapy: Counseling African American adolescent males with conduct disorder. *Journal of African American Men, 4*(3), 73–88.

Trahan, D.P., & Lemberger, M. E. (2014). Critical race theory as a decisional framework for the ethical counseling of African American clients. *Counseling & Values, 59*(1), 112–124.

Vereen, L. G., Hill, N. R., & Butler, K. S. (2013). The use of humor and storytelling with African American men: Innovative therapeutic strategies for success in counseling. *International Journal for the Advancement of Counseling, 35*(1), 57–63. doi:http://dx.doi.org/10.1177/s10447-012-9165-5

Wilson, P. (2009). The playwork primer. *Alliance for Childhood.* Retrieved from: http://www.ultimateblockparty.com/download/Playwork_Primer.pdf

CHAPTER 1

COUNSELING AFRICAN AMERICAN MALES UTILIZING NONTRADITIONAL CLINICAL TREATMENT APPROACHES

Delila Owens, John Queener, and Tiffany Stewart

CLINICAL TREATMENT OF BLACK MEN

The experiences of African American men are significantly different from men of other racial and ethnic backgrounds. It is essential for therapists to understand the longitudinal effects of the period of enslavement (Marbley, 2011), African Americans being one of the few involuntary (ancestors brought to America because of slavery) minority in America, the development of cultural mistrust, and how the above factors into African American men's worldviews. In addition to historical discrimination (Bell, 1992) and the daily stressors of life, African American men's worldviews are also affected by discriminatory macro- and microaggressions (Bonhomme, 2004; Erguner-Tekinapl, 2009; Marbley, 2011; Pieterse & Carter, 2007). Robinson (1999) noted that sustained prejudices and discriminatory practices against African American men are in part responsible for the myths and

Counseling African American Males, pages 1–10
Copyright © 2016 by Information Age Publishing

1

misconceptions about them. Counselors must be aware of the stereotypes that permeate African American males in the United States. These generalized misconceptions contribute to society's aggressive behavior toward this population. These concerns are uniquely associated with African American men and other men of color who remain marginalized. It is critical that we have culturally competent therapists who can effectively understand and work with African American men. It is also important to note that the vast majority of African Americans reside in more female-headed families (Prince, 1997; Sarkisian & Gerstel, 2004). Thus, therapists must consider the cultural complexities and implications of African American boys being raised by single mothers.

Another critical aspect of providing culturally responsive mental health services is the therapist's ability to recognize the historical monocultural enthnocentric bias, microaggressions, systemic oppression, and racism in the lives of African American men. Therapists must have an awareness of the fundamental multicultural counseling dimensions (Roysircar, Hubbell, & Gard, 2003; Sue & Sue, 2016). These dimensions include the therapists' awareness of their own biases and beliefs toward specific cultural groups, knowledge of diverse populations, and the appropriate skills to effectively service specific populations (Sue & Sue, 2016). It is imperative that therapists understand historical cultural mistrust between African Americans and social services agencies. Cultural mistrust for African Americans developed as a result of years of historical oppression and racism (Marbley, 2011; Sue & Sue, 2016; Terrell, Terrell, & Taylor, 1981).

America's history of using African American bodies for medical experimentation has left a legacy of cultural mistrust for social service and mental health agencies (Achter, Parrott, & Silk, 2004; Marbley, 2011; Sue, 2015). In particular, three cases that are widely known are the Tuskegee Syphilis Study, which took place between the years of 1932 and 1972. The study was conducted by the United States Public Health Service (USPHS), which used 400 infected, impoverished Black men from Alabama for medical research. The men were under the impression that they were being treated for syphilis. However, the goal of the study was to test the effects of untreated syphilis on the human body. At the outset of the Tuskegee study, there was no known cure or treatment for syphilis. Researchers found a cure before the completion of the experiment, but the cure was not given to the men. In fact, the USPHS actively sought to withhold treatment from them. In the 1950s, penicillin was being used as a treatment for syphilis, but the men were not administered the treatment. More than 100 men passed away due to the advanced effects of syphilis.

Another case involved using enslaved Black women for surgical experimentation that led to the field of gynecology in the 1800s (Ojanuga, 1993). Dr. James Marion Sims, known as the father of American gynecology, bought and used enslaved Black women for medical experimentation between the years of 1845 and 1849. Dr. Sims was well known for treating vesicovaginal fistula or vaginal tears. This condition was a devastating effect of childbirth. He began designing surgical repair tools to aid in repair and used slave women to test these tools without an anesthetic (Ojanuga, 1993). His medical inventions at the expense of poor African American women led to the field of gynecology.

Perhaps one of the most disturbing cases is that of Henrietta Lacks. In 1951, a poor African American woman visited John Hopkins Medical Center complaining of pain and was later diagnosed with cervical cancer. John Hopkins was the only hospital that would service African Americans. In the most preemptive act, doctors seized parts of her tumor for medical research without her consent. She passed away on October 4, 1951, but her replicated cells have contributed substantially to the development of the polio vaccines, acquired immune deficiency syndrome, and cancer research, and her cells continue to be replicated. HeLa cells (coined after her name) have been used in more than 74,000 studies for six decades. They were the first cells to be commercialized and are still being used in 2016. The cells continue to be used for the improvement of medical research (Skloot, 2010). For more than 20 years Henrietta's family had no knowledge of her indescribable gift and how it has transformed medical research and millions of lives. These are a few of the countless medical experiments that were conducted using African Americans bodies for experimentation. The challenge for trained mental health professionals is to understand that these experiments have left a legacy of mistrust for both medical and mental health professionals.

Historical events and the lack of culture centered treatment approaches continue to influence the rate and underutilization of African Americans seeking mental health services (Marbley, 2011; Sue & Sue, 2016). More specifically, African Americans are less likely to seek mental health treatment and generally receive poorer quality services compared to their White counterparts (Brown & Keith, 2003; Schwartz & Feisthamel, 2009; Sue & Sue, 2016). One major concern in the field of mental health counseling is the racial bias and lack of culture-specific mental health approaches among therapists offering services (DHHS, 1999; Sue, 2015). As such, there are sizable implications for the mental health care of African American men (Watkins & Jefferson, 2013).

Research conducted by the National Institute of Mental Health estimates that in the United States nearly 6 million men suffer from depression (National Institute of Mental Health, 2009), and they are more likely to hold adverse attitudes toward seeking mental health treatment (Addis & Mahalik, 2003). While women generally internalize depression (Carr, Szymanski, Taha, West & Kaslow, 2014; Jones & Shorter-Gooden, 2003), men are more prone to aggressive acting out of their depressed mood. They often mask or minimize painful experiences (Jansz, 2000; Lisak, 2001). The task of seeking help, which includes a reliance on others and the admission that one could benefit from psychological services and the stigma that goes with seeking mental health services, goes against the rules of masculinity in the United States. This describes a concept known as the gendered nature of masculinity (Scher, 2001), which, in addition to male inexpressiveness (Balswick, 1982), is a vital part of manhood. It means that men are socialized in the larger society to not express their emotions.

Culturally responsive therapists must pay particular attention to both the gender and race related dynamics of counseling African American men. There is a scarcity of literature that addresses this topic. Thus, we offer our expertise as experienced researchers and counselors. The general purpose of this chapter is to introduce nontraditional strategies and techniques for counseling African American men.

Men can feel a sense of powerlessness in their lives despite their dominant position of power in United States culture (Kiselica & Woodford, 2007). Men historically have been taught in Western society to hide feeling and emotions. For the most part, men have been socialized to fear the core components of therapy (focusing on feelings, emotions, expression, etc.). Brannon and David (1976), described the blueprint of manhood in four components. They avoid appearing feminine, attempt to gain/maintain status and respect, try to appear invulnerable, and, finally, seek violence and adventure. The expression of emotion can be seen as unacceptable and not masculine. Men are less likely to seek help for both physical and emotional concerns (Addis & Mahalik, 2003; Sandman, Simantov & An, 2000). The fields of counseling and psychology were founded primarily by White men to assist White people (Sue, 2015). Specifically, for men of color, their levels of self-worth can decline due to high levels of daily racial microaggressions (Sue, 2015; Sue & Sue, 2016). What's more, men of color may enter counseling with a high external locus of control and feel as though environmental (racial microaggressions, oppression, and discrimination) forces outside of their control dictate the direction of their lives (Caldwell & White, 2001; Sue & Sue, 2016).

Research findings on mental health disorders for African American men are inconsistent. For instance, one study reported that fewer African American men develop depression as opposed to Whites (Breslau, Kendler, Su, Gaxiola-Aguilar, & Kessler, 2005), while others propose that mental health disorders are more often than not underdiagnosed in men of color (Dallas & Burton, 2004; Woodward, Taylor, Bullard, Aranda, Lincoln & Chatters,, 2011). Given the scope and negative impact that the underutilization of mental health services have on the lives of African American men, nontraditional approaches for clinical treatment are warranted.

NONTRADITIONAL THEORIES AND STRATEGIES

Some researchers and mental health therapists argue that one of the main reasons mental health disparities like underutilization, premature termination, and biases in diagnoses and treatment for African American men exist when compared to their White counterparts is the use of traditional theories and interventions that do not take into account culture and discrimination (Leach & Aten, 2010; Marbley, 2011; McAulifee & Associates, 2008; Sue & Sue, 2016; Sue, 2015). In fact, Griner and Smith (2006) conducted a meta-analysis of studies that used traditional interventions, general minority interventions, and culturally specific interventions. They found that the effect size was highest for culturally specific interventions, being four times higher than the effect size for traditional Western interventions. Thus, we outline nontraditional approaches to providing therapy to African American males. First, we discuss an African-centered perspective and how it could be used as adaptations of the traditional perspectives that fail to take into account culture and discrimination. This section is followed by a discussion on nontraditional techniques.

AFRICAN-CENTERED PERSPECTIVE

Based in ancient African culture, the African-centered perspective is based on the belief that traditional Western theories in psychology are based on assumptions and principles that are inconsistent with African American men. Most traditional theories were formed using monocultural ethnocentric bias. Therapists are guilty of imposing monocultural ethnocentrism when they attempt to apply White, Western, male, heterosexual, middle-class standards to the lived experiences of people of color. For instance, Western theories in psychology emphasize individualism as the unit of analysis, whereas ancient African culture emphasizes the collective, community, and spirituality. We believe that using theories such as Belief Systems Analysis (BSA) (Myers, 1988) in working with African American males provides the therapist with a conceptual framework that is consistent with the culture of African American males. Briefly, BSA is based on what Myers (1988) calls optimal psychology and is grounded on the principles of African philosophy. These include *spirit* as central to human development, intrinsic self-worth, and self-knowledge as the key to all knowledge and extended self-identity, which connects all humans to each other, and to those who came before (ancestors) and those who will come after. Two such principles are diunital logic or the union of opposites, and holistic analyses. Regardless of the presenting concerns, therapists using BSA principles help African American men change their world (Harrell, 2000; Neblett, Seaton,

Hammond & Townsend, 2010). The goal of BSA is for clients to develop inner peace by having faith, a positive belief system, and patience.

It is important for helping professionals to understand the psychological world of African American men. Therapists must also use culturally responsive counseling that considers their worldviews. The first strategies we introduce are directly from the African-centered perspective.

- Use rites of passage programs.
- Meditate and focus on being in union with God.
- Conduct nature and wellness activities to connect men with the creator and being one with nature.
- Use African Day names, which posits that the creator chooses a person to be born on a certain day based on characteristics that are needed in the community.
- Teach about the ancient African ethical code system of Ma'at. This system focuses on truth, justice, propriety, harmony, balance, reciprocity, and order.
- Teach about the seven principles of Ngzo Saba. These principles include unity, self-determination, collective work and responsibility, cooperative economics, purpose, creativity and faith.
- Use bibliotherapy with books on African American males such as *Visions for African American Men* by Naima Akbar, *Letters to a Young Brother, Manifest Your Destiny* by Hill Harper, *40 Black Men Speak on Living, Leading, and Succeeding* by Ben Jealous and Trabian Shorters, and *32 Ways to Be a Champion* by Earvin "Magic" Johnson.
- Therapists must help African American men develop a sense of collectiveness through connecting them with mentoring programs.
- Therapists should seek to strengthen community ties with African American men. One such effort might include speaking engagements for African American organizations. These organizations include but are not limited to community-based organizations, African American churches, social clubs, high schools, colleges, and universities.
- We believe in aspects of positive psychology. Traditional therapy has focused on the "problem" or what is not working in the lives of individuals. Therapists should take a *strength*-based approach with African American men. This approach focuses on both the client's strengths and community resources (Ivey, Ivey, & Zalaquett, 2014).
- Therapist should seek nontraditional ways to allow men to express their emotions. More specifically, traditional counseling theories use the "intrapsychic approach" which stresses that clients have the answers within and must be introspective at the onset of counseling. The African American men may not see immediate insight as relevant to their current situation. Oftentimes, when men of color

enter treatment, they have a high external locus of responsibility. This means that systemic forces are affecting their current present- ing problem (Sue & Sue, 2016). Thus, intrapsychic approach may not be initially beneficial at the onset of theory.

- In contrast to the intrapsychic perspective, allowing men to process systemic oppression at the onset of the counseling relationship is recommended. It validates their lived experiences. The exploration of those forces assists them with understanding personal power.
- Therapists must be creative with the re-story process or helping African American men imagine ideal solutions to their challenges. Therapist must explore nontraditional ways to open the dialogue for discussion. This could include but not be limited to therapy outside of the office, such as asking clients to pick a song, poem, or movie that best describes them.
- Develop interventions that focus on strengths, resources, and posi- tive change.
- Explore cultural beliefs about healing and spirituality/religion in the lives of African American men.
- Increase counselors' multicultural case conceptualization ability is crucial. Research has found that counselors with higher levels of case conceptualization ability exhibit higher ethnic tolerance at- titudes. (Constantine & Gushue, 2003).
- Become advocates and appreciate various worldviews and lived ex- periences is critical, that is, intentional cultural immersion (cultural interactions with diverse groups) will ultimately build the cross cultural competence of counselors.
- It is critical that therapists also take an ecological perspective in behavior analysis. This perspective emphasizes focusing on one's behavior in the context of the environment. Environmental effects on behavior must be reviewed as well as potential resources/support for positive change in behavior (Barker, 1965).
- Exploring racial identity is warranted. Racial identity can be defined as the way in which we view ourselves as racial beings (Sue, 2015). Being comfortable with one's racial group sets the tone for open discussion on race. Racial identity affects the way individuals view themselves and others.
- Therapists must seek to understand the dynamics of African Ameri- can families (Billingsley, 1968) and be comfortable with explicit race talk and open discussions about race and racism in America.

This chapter discussed several cases of African American bodies being used for medical experimentation. These experiments have led to historical mistrust for both medical and mental health professionals for many African

Americans. Thus, therapists must be aware of initial resistance and choose approaches that mirror the political and economic realities of African American men. Many of the traditional counseling theories remain ethnocentric in nature. Embedded in many traditional counseling theories is an assumed universal reality for all individuals. Western rationalization does not fit the lived experiences of African American men. The African-centered approach is more suitable. The approach focuses more on collectivism, service, community, and honor. To effectively service African American men, we must view the world through the lenses of their experiences and be mindful to choose strategies and techniques that reflect the socialization experiences of the cultures we serve.

REFERENCES

Achter, P., Parrot, R., & Silk, K. (2004). Blacks' opinions about human-genetics research. *Politics and the Life Sciences, 23*(1), 60–66.

Addis, M. E., & Mahalik, J. R. (2003). Men, masculinity, and the contexts of help seeking. *American Psychologist, 58*(1), 5–14.

Balswick, J. O. (1982). Male inexpressiveness: Psychological and social aspects. In K. Solomon & N. B. Levy (Eds.), *Men in transition: Theory and therapy.* New York, NY: Plenum.

Barker, R.G. (1965). Explorations in ecological psychology. *American Psychologist, 20,* 1–14

Bell, D. (1992). *Faces at the bottom of the well: The permanence of racism.* New York, NY: HarperCollins.

Billingsley, A. (1968). *Black families in White America.* Englewood Cliffs, NJ: Prentice Hall.

Bonhomme, J. J. E. (2004). The health status of African American men: Improving our understanding of men's health challenges. *Journal of Men's Health & Gender, 1,* 142–146.

Brannon, R., & David, D. S (1976). *The forty-nine percent majority: The male sex role.* Reading, MA: Addison-Wesley.

Breslau, J., Kendler, K., Su, M., Gaxiola-Aguilar, S., & Kessler, R. (2005). Lifetime risk and persistence of psychiatric disorders across ethnic groups in the United States. *Psychological Medicine, 35,* 317–327. doi:10.1017/S0033291704003514

Brown, D. R., & Keith, V. M. (2003). *In and out of our right minds.* New York, NY: Columbia University Press.

Caldwell, L. D., & White, J. L. (2001). African-centered therapeutic and counseling interventions for African American males. In G. Brooks & G. Good (Eds.), *A new handbook of counseling and psychotherapy approaches for men.* San Francisco, CA: Jossey-Bass

Carr, E. R., Szymanski, D. M., Taha, F., West, L., & Kaslow, N. (2014). Understanding the link between multiple oppressions and depression among low-income African American women: The role of internalization. *Psychology of Women Quarterly, 38,* 233–245.

Constantine, M. G., & Gushue, G. V. (2003). School counselors' ethnic tolerance attitudes and racism attitudes as predictors of their multicultural case conceptualization of an immigrant student. *Journal of Counseling & Development, 81*(2), 185–190.

Dallas, C., & Burton, L. (2004). Health disparities among men from racial and ethnic minority population. *Annual Review of Nursing Research, 22,* 77–100.

Erguner-Tekinapl, B. (2009). Daily experiences of racism and forgiving historical offenses: And Black experience. *International Journal of Human and Social Sciences, 4,* 1–9.

Griner, D. & Smith, T. B. (2006). Culturally adapted mental health interventions: A meta-analytic review. *Psychotherapy: Theory, Research, Practice, Training, 43,* 531–548.

Harrell, S. P. (2000). A multidimensional conceptualization of racism-related stress: Implications for the well-being of people of color. *American Journal of Orthopsychiatry, 70,* 42–57

Ivey, A. E., Ivey, M. B., & Zalaquett, C. P. (2014). *Intentional interviewing and counseling: Facilitating client development in a multicultural society* (8th ed.). Belmont, CA: Cengage Learning.

Jansz, J. (2000). Masculine identity and restrictive emotionality. In A. H. Fischer (Ed.), *Gender and emotion: Social psychological perspectives* (pp. 166–186). New York, NY: Cambridge University Press.

Jones, C., & Shorter-Gooden, K. (2003). *Shifting: The double lives of Black women in America.* New York, NY: HarperCollins.

Kiselica, M. S., & Woodford, M. S. (2007). Promoting healthy male development: A social justice perspective. In C. Lee (Ed.), *Counseling for social justice* (pp. 11–135). Alexandria, VA: American Counseling Association.

Leach, M. M., & Aten, J. D. (2010). *Culture and the therapeutic process.* London, England: Routledge.

Lisak, D. (2001). Homicide, violence, and male aggression. In G. Brooks & G. Good (Eds.), *A new handbook of counseling and psychotherapy approaches for men.* San Francisco, CA: Jossey-Bass.

Marbley, A. F. (2011). *Multicultural counseling: Perspectives from counselors as clients of color.* London, England: Routledge.

McAuliffe, G., & Associates (2008). *Culturally alert counseling.* Thousand Oaks, CA: Sage.

Myers, L. J. (1988). *Understanding an Afrocentric world view: Introduction to an optimal psychology.* Dubuque, IA: Kendall/Hunt.

National Institute for Mental Health. (2009). *Fact sheet on depression and other illnesses.* Retrieved from http://www.nami.org/Content/NavigationMenu/Mental_Illnesses/Depression/Depression_and_Men_Fact_Sheet.htm

Neblett, E. W., Seaton, E. K., Hammond, W. P., & Townsend, T. G. (2010). Underlying mechanisms in the relationship between Afrocentric worldview and depressive symptoms. *Journal of Counseling Psychology, 571*(1), 105–113.

Ojanuga, D. (1993). The medical ethics of father of gynecology, Dr. J. Marion Sims. *Journal of Medical Ethics, 19*(1), 28–31.

Pieterse, A. L., & Carter, R. T. (2007). An examination of the relationship between general life stress, racism-related stress, and psychological health among Black men. *Journal of Counseling Psychology, 54*, 101–109.

Prince, K. (1997). Black family and Black liberation. *Psych Discourse, 28*(1), 4–7.

Robinson, D. W. (1999). Sexual addiction as an adaptive response to post-traumatic stress disorder in the Black community. *Sexual Addiction & Compulsivity, 6*, 11–22.

Roysircar, G., Hubbell, R., & Gard, G. (2003). Multicultural research on counselor and client variables: A relational perspective. In D. Pope-Davis, H. L. K. Coleman, W. M., Liu, & R. I. Toporek (Eds.). *Handbook of multicultural competencies* (pp. 247–282). Thousand Oaks, CA: Sage.

Sandman D., Simantov E., & An, C. (2000). *Out of touch: American men and the health care system.* New York, NY: Commonwealth Fund.

Sarkisian N., & Gerstel, N. (2004). Kin support among Blacks and Whites: Race and family organization. *American Sociological Review, 69*, 812–837.

Scher, M. (2001). Male therapist, male client: Reflections on critical dynamics. In G. Brooks & G. Good (Eds.), *The handbook of counseling and psychotherapy approaches for men* (pp. 719–733). San Francisco, CA: Jossey-Bass.

Schwartz, R. C., & Feisthamel, K. P. (2009). Disproportionate diagnosis of mental disorders among Black versus Euro-American clients: Implications for counseling theory, research and practice. *Journal of Counseling & Development, 87*, 295–301.

Skloot, R. (2010). *The immortal life of Henrietta Lacks.* New York, NY: Broadway Books.

Sue, D. W. (2015). *Race talk and the conspiracy of silence.* Hoboken, NJ: John Wiley.

Sue, D. W., & Sue, D. (2016). *Counseling the culturally diverse: Theory and practice* (7th ed.). Hoboken, NJ: John Wiley.

Terrell, F., Terrell, S. L., & Taylor, J. (1981). Effects of race of examiner and cultural mistrust on the WAIS performance of Black students. *Journal of Consulting and Clinical Psychology, 49*, 750–751.

U.S. Department of Health and Human Services. (1999). *Mental health: A report of the surgeon general.* Rockville, MD: Author.

Watkins, D. C., & Jefferson, S. O. (2013). Recommendations for the use of online social support for Black men. *Psychological Services, 10*(3), 323–332.

Woodward, A. T., Taylor, R. T., Bullard, K. M., Aranda, M. P., Lincoln, K. D., & Chatters, L. M. (2011). Prevalence of lifetime DSM-IV affective disorders among older African Americans, Black Caribbeans, Latinos, Asians and non-Hispanic White people. *International Journal of Geriatric Psychiatry, 27*(8), 816–827. doi:10.1002/gps.2790

CHAPTER 2

BLACK MASCULINITY AND IDENTITY DEVELOPMENT AS FOUNDATION FOR COUNSELING AFRICAN AMERICAN MALES

Steven D. Kniffley

There is an old African proverb that states, "If there is no enemy within, the enemy without can do you no harm." Many Black men are engaged in an internal conflict in regards to their own beliefs about the negativity of Black manhood that is inconsistent with their historical and lived experience. This conflict is significantly influenced by the experience of chronic racial discrimination. Racial discrimination has contributed to the internalization of messages of Black men being viewed as dumb, deviant, and dangerous (Kniffley, 2014). These messages have impacted the creation of "an enemy within" in the form of hypermasculinity, endorsement of negative stereotypes, and cultural identity suppression. Furthermore, the messages associated with racial discrimination have influenced the development and maintenance of mental health issues for Black men (Ghafoori, Barragan, &

Palinkas, 2013). Black men presenting with these issues will pose significant challenges in a counseling setting in regards to the formation of a therapeutic alliance and the implementation of meaningful clinical interventions (Scott, McCoy, Munson, Snowden, & McMillen, 2011).

The current chapter will explore the etiology and manifestation of mental illness in Black men and how these factors have been impacted by the experience of racial discrimination. Furthermore, the current chapter will examine the process of Black masculinity development as a buffer against (and contributor to) the experience of mental health issues within the context of racial discrimination. Specifically, this section will explore the role of social construction and Black masculinity, the intergenerational transmission of trauma, alexithymia, the influence of messages related to anger and aggression, and racial/ethnic identity development. In addition, this section will introduce a model of Black male psychopathology that discusses the relationship between social oppression (via the experience of racial discrimination) and cultural identity suppression (via the internalization of socially constructed negative stereotypes of Black masculinity) and their influence on the development and maintenance of mental illness. This chapter will conclude with a discussion of a case example and the utilization of the model as a conceptualization framework.

BLACK MALES AND MENTAL HEALTH OVERVIEW

From the moment Black men are born into this world, the weight of social oppression weighs heavy upon their shoulders. The negative impact of this identity variable has been demonstrated across numerous studies, which have highlighted that Black men have the lowest life expectancy; highest death rate; highest likelihood to die by homicide, heart disease, and HIV/AIDS; and the most likely to be born preterm (Okwumabua, Okwumabua, Peasant, Watson, & Walker, 2014). From birth to death, these results suggest that every day is a fight against the odds for Black men. A significant hindrance in this fight is the experience and internalization of racial discrimination.

Racial discrimination is based on a socially constructed definition of Black masculinity as well as other factors (Robinson, Keating, & Robertson, 2011). This definition perpetuates both negative and positive stereotypes that have been created and maintained through social messages that have been formulated over hundreds of years. A social constructionist perspective here denotes that stereotypes associated with Black masculinity are not biologically defined, but instead manifest as a result of a socially defined and projected image of Black maleness that has been internalized as the norm (Parker & Moore, 2014).

For Black males, racial discrimination is a chronic part of their lived experience. Sellers and Shelton (2003) noted that this discrimination can be both overt (e.g., being called a racial slur) or covert (e.g., women clutching their purses when a Black male steps in an elevator). A study by Kessler, Mickelson, and Williams (1999) examined the prevalence of perceived discrimination and found that more than 60% of Black adults reported encountering racial discrimination in their daily lives. The experience of racial discrimination has been found to have important consequences for the mental health of Black men. The following section will explore the impact of racial discrimination on Black male mental health as well as facilitate a discussion related to the manifestation of specific mental health issues, including depression, anxiety, suicide, and substance use.

RACIAL DISCRIMINATION
AND BLACK MALE MENTAL HEALTH

Several studies have highlighted an increasing vulnerability for the development of mental illness for Black men (Ghafoori et al., 2013; Lincoln, Taylor, Chatters, & Joe, 2012; Ward, Wiltshire, Detry, & Brown, 2013; Utsey, Hook, & Standard, 2007). The literature has indicated that the experience of racial discrimination is a contributing factor to the manifestation of mental health issues for this population. Frequently, researchers have highlighted that for Black men, mental health problems may be a function of socially induced stress created by the intersection of racism and discrimination. For example, a study by Utsey, Payne, Jackson, and Jones (2002) found that racial discrimination was a significant predictor of psychological health in elderly African American females. In regards to Black males, a study by Landrine and Klonoff (1996) found that the experience of racial discrimination by Black males was related to symptoms of anxiety, depression, and somatization.

A more recent study by Watkins, Abelson, and Jefferson (2013) indicated that members within the Black community view the experience of psychopathology in Black males as being significantly influenced by social oppression and chronic struggles with identity. Considering the intersection between racial discrimination and mental illness and the indication that Black males are more likely to experience inequality and social exclusion related to racial discrimination, these men are at a heightened risk for the development of mental health issues. The following paragraph will explore the impact of this intersection on specific mental health issues related to depression, anxiety, suicide, and substance use in Black men.

Social oppression in the form of racial discrimination has significantly impacted the lives of Black men, in particular Black male mental health. Ghafoori et al. (2013) found social oppression contributed to the experience of increased mental health difficulties in Black men via traumatic stress exposure. Similarly, Robinson et al. (2011) also found the addition of social determinants such as social expectations and socioeconomic exclusion served as significant mental health factors for Black males. One mental disorder that has received some attention in the literature in relation to Black men is depression.

DEPRESSION AND BLACK MEN

Ward and Mengesha (2013a) conducted a meta-analysis of 18 studies related to the experience of depression, with the results highlighting an increasing vulnerability for the development of depressive symptoms for Black men. Specifically, the authors noted that the prevalence rates for depression in Black men ranges from 5% to 10%. In addition, the authors reported that the prevalence rates have increased significantly since the 1990s (2.5% to 6.5%). Furthermore, the authors indicated that the most vulnerable group was 18 to 29-year-old Black males, whose rates of depression had increased from 9.5% to 21.3% over the last 20 years.

Although there was a significant increase in rates of depression, Black males were still behind their White male counterparts. However, the reported role impairment of depressive symptoms is more severe for Black males when it comes to chronicity and disability (56.5% versus 38.6%), work (37.2% versus 28.9%) and social interactions (55.4% versus 34.2%). The study suggests Black men are increasingly struggling with depressive symptoms related to sadness and low self-worth. For many Black men, however, it is unsafe to express these feelings of sadness. In addition, indicating that one is struggling to manage depressive symptoms conflicts with the traditional masculine ideology many Black men endorse. The dual influence of limited safety and conflicting identities contributes to the experience of a phenomenon called "silent frustration" in Black males (Kniffley, 2014).

Silent frustration calls attention to the exhaustion of resources to combat the chronic experience of racism and discrimination (Kniffley, 2014). Black men's frustration stems from the guilt and shame associated with being unable to fulfill cultural expectations of masculinity within the context of the Black community (as well as hegemonic masculinity expectations) and feeling defenseless against the negative stereotypes placed upon them by society. Unable to fully express these feeling of shame and guilt, Black men turn to the default traditional masculine ideology emotions of anger and rage. This anger and rage is directed at the institutions that reinforce racial discrimination, the communities that the Black men are from, other Black men, and ultimately the Black male himself. As the Black male engages in this anger and rage, he significantly damages his interpersonal relationships, leaving him alone and isolated. With no support and with coping resources exhausted, Black men are left suffering in silence, frustrated with the impact of racism and discrimination and the chronic challenges related to managing this experience. As a final effort to cope with symptoms of depression and the subsequent impact of silent frustration, many Black men are turning toward suicide and suicidal behaviors.

Lincoln et al. (2012) report that the rates of suicide among Black males have increased significantly since the mid-1980s. Between 1980 and 1995, the rates of suicide more than doubled for Black male adolescents between the ages of 15 and 19. The current mortality rates for Black males indicate that suicide is the third leading cause of death for Black males aged 15 to 24 and fourth for those aged 10 to 15 and 25 to 34. Studies have indicated a lifetime prevalence rate of 5.4% for completed suicide in Blacks. In addition, a prevalence rate of 11.7% was noted for suicidal ideation and 4.1% for suicide attempts (Lincoln et al., 2012). What was thought of only as a "White" problem from the perspective of the Black community has become a significant issue for Black males. Many studies are now reporting that there is no longer a significant difference in the risk for suicide attempts between Blacks and Whites. These studies call attention to the increasing vulnerability that Black men (especially young Black men between the ages of 15 and 14) are experiencing related to suicide and suicidal behaviors.

SUBSTANCE USE AND ANXIETY IN BLACK MEN

Several studies have found that racial discrimination may contribute to substance use among Black people (Hurd, Varner, Caldwell, & Zimmerman, 2014; Lee, Mun, White, & Simon, 2010). Furthermore, researchers have noted that they are at the greater risk for substance use during emerging adulthood, a developmental period of significant identity expansion and identity reconciliation, during which youth move into socially defined adult roles. For Black individuals, this period is compounded by increased exposure to racial discrimination as they seek out jobs and educational opportunities, which may exacerbate the risk and negative consequences associated with substance use.

Hurd et al. (2014) explored the impact of racial discrimination on substance use among a sample of 607 Black emerging adults (47% male). They found that reported racial discrimination in emerging adulthood contributes to an increase in substance use across the transition of emerging adulthood for both Black men and women. Similarly, Lee et al. (2010) compared the substance use trajectories of Black adolescents and young adults and they found substance use increased as Black youth transitioned into emerging adulthood as compared to Whites. These studies highlight that although the rates of substance use for Black individuals is low compared to Whites, a significant period of vulnerability is noted during emerging adulthood that is influenced by the experience of chronic racism and discrimination.

According to the American Heart Association (AHA; Go et al., 2013), 44.4% of Black men 20-years-old and older suffer from cardiovascular disease. In addition, 43% of Black men were reported as suffering from high blood pressure with a death rate from high blood pressure that is nearly three times the national average at 51.6%. Furthermore, the AHA has indicated that for Black men, heart disease is the leading cause of death for all ages. Several studies have linked the experience of racism and discrimination with physical health in Black men (Sellers, Cherepanov, Hanmer, Fryback, & Palta, 2013). Symptoms of physical health such as heart related problems are influenced by the chronic worrying associated with navigating the role and meaning of negative stereotypes and how they relate to the experience of being a Black male (Cené et al., 2013). Mental health issues intersect this dynamic via the development of anxiety-related symptoms.

Faced with the chronic experience of negating and overcoming negative racial stereotypes, many Black men are in a constant state of hypervigilance with their radars on high alert for the possible presence of discriminatory acts. This hypervigilance manifests as symptoms of anxiety such as excessive worry, fear, racing thoughts, and challenges related to concentration and being distracted. For Black men, this hypervigilance originally served as a protective factor against social stress that has been passed down via generational messages associated with the experience of cultural traumas (e.g., the world is not a safe place for Black men). However, what was designed to protect the cultural identity of Black men has contributed to significant physical (e.g., heart disease, high blood pressure) and mental symptoms (e.g., anxiety).

Social oppression in the form of racial discrimination can significantly impact the experience of negative physical and mental health. For example, Bynum, Burton, and Best (2007) conducted a study to examine the effect of racism on the psychological health of Black men. Utilizing a sample of 107 Black men, they found experiences of racism were significantly associated with greater anxiety symptoms (e.g., nervousness, fearfulness, restlessness, and hypervigilance). Due to the chronic experience of racial discrimination, Black men are at an increased vulnerability for the development of mental health issues. This vulnerability is compounded by a number of factors, including challenges in developing and maintaining coping resources and reconciling cultural expectations for a traditional masculine ideology with a self-defined concept of Black masculinity. Consistent with the current discussion in this chapter, this study calls attention to the negative impact that racial discrimination can have on the mental health of Black men (with an emphasis on symptoms of anxiety).

The current section has explored the specific disorders of anxiety and depression as well as coping strategies in the form of substance use and suicide. This exploration has highlighted the following: (a) due to depression and the phenomenon of "silent frustration," Black men are at an increased risk for suicide completions and attempts; (b) the transitional period of emerging adulthood contributes to an increased vulnerability for Black men to use substances; and (c) factors such as hypervigilance, which provides protection against the experience of racism, have become a double edged sword contributing to symptoms of anxiety. Another factor that is important to consider in the discussion of the intersection between racial discrimination and Black men's health is the development of Black masculinity. The ways in which Black masculinity is defined, expressed, and reinforced can serve as a buffer against (as well as contribute to) the experience of racial discrimination and subsequent mental health challenges. The implications of this relationship are considered in the following section, which discusses the development of Black masculinity focusing on the impact of intergenerational transmission of trauma, emotional restriction, anger and aggression, and racial/ethnic identity development.

BLACK MASCULINITY DEVELOPMENT

Black manhood is a fluid process of masculinity evaluation within the relational context of community, family, and peer groups (Powell-Hammond & Mattis, 2005). In addition, Black masculinity is developed through the integration of sociohistorical and economically influenced expectations of masculinity. At its most basic level, Black masculinity development highlights the intersection between race and gender. These factors do not develop in isolation and are simultaneously impacted by the experience of social oppression (via racial discrimination), cultural expectations, and self-identification. An important component of this discussion is to understand the social messages that Black men receive within and outside their communities related to the meaning of Black masculinity (Parker & Moore, 2014). Many of these social messages (e.g., Black men don't cry and Black men must be tough and hyperaggressive) stem from cultural narratives that have been passed down through generations as guidelines for protecting oneself from the experience of cultural traumas (Carter et al., 2013).

On a daily basis, Black men are exposed to acts of racism and discrimination that reinforce negative perceptions of themselves as well as other Black men. These acts are overt (e.g., being denied a job based on having a "Black" name) as well as overt and trap Black men into stereotypical boxes, limiting their ability to put forth a self-defined Black masculinity. Chronic exposure to racial discrimination (e.g., cultural traumas) contributes to the development of trauma-related behaviors such as a chronic reliving of the trauma, hyper-vigilance, and emotional numbing (Carter et al., 2013). These behaviors stem from messages that have been passed down within the community and the family system that communicate hopelessness and despair. In addition, they create an expectation that racial discrimination will be an ongoing part of the Black male's experience and that coping resources should focus on survival instead of growth (Lowe, Okubo, & Reilly, 2012). This expectation, coupled with the reinforcement of maladaptive coping strategies, contributes to the experience of shame, guilt, rage, poor attachment, silence, and the development of confusing unspoken rules in the family (Kniffley, 2014). Furthermore, the expectation of chronic racial discrimination as part of the lived experience of Black men has significant implications for both the development of gender norms and racial/ethnic identity.

GENDER IDENTITY AND BLACK MASCULINITY DEVELOPMENT

Several studies have sought to quantify the cognitions, behaviors, and socialization processes that influence the development of gender identity. O'Neil and Carroll (1998) have created a model of gender identity development called gender role journey theory, which consists of five phases: (a) acceptance of traditional gender roles, (b) ambivalence about gender roles, (c) anger over gender roles, (d) personal-professional activism, and (e) celebration and integration of gender roles. According to O'Neil and Carroll (1998), this theory represents a transition from strict adherence to traditional gender stereotypes, to a period of cognitive dissonance influenced by an increased awareness of the impact of accepting rigid gender norms, to an integration of societal gender norms/expectations, the individuals lived experience, and the creation of a self-defined gender identity. Connecting this theory to the experience of gender identity development in men, beginning with this transitional period, demonstrates the endorsement of a traditional masculine ideology.

Masculine ideology is a socially defined set of standards of "maleness" that impact the performance, cognitions, and transmission of socialization messages related to gender expression in men. A masculine ideology develops as young men and boys internalize cultural norms related to gender as well as expectations around gender roles within the context of the family system, peer groups, and society. Within this context, the endorsement of a traditional masculine ideology represents the beginning stages of masculinity development as well as the stereotypical gender role expectations and gender norms society has for expressions of "maleness." Traditional masculine ideology is a strict adherence to stereotypical gender norms and gender expectations for men such as competiveness, propensity towards violence, emotional restriction, and the avoidance of feminine behavior as defined by peer groups and popular culture. Gender identity literature has demonstrated that Black men endorse the values of traditional masculine ideology more than other races. However, it has been speculated that this endorsement may serve as a coping factor for the experience of racism/ discrimination and the inherent conflicts in gender role expectation/expression influenced by this construct. This conflict is most evident in the hyper endorsement of the foundational constructs of traditional masculine ideology, emotional restriction, and anger/aggression.

Oftentimes, Black males receive conflicting messages around emotional expression. On the one hand, they are told that by their very nature of being Black men, they are emotionally invulnerable and above the experience of emotional states, that the display of emotions is not safe, and that the expression of emotions is a sign of weakness. However, they are concurrently asked to engage emotionally with their families and in intimate relationships, as well as positively cope with emotionally challenging situations. This conflict can be quantified in the concept of alexithymia (or emotional restriction).

Alexithymia, an emotionally restrictive posture, has been passed down through generations of the Black community serving as a coping resource in managing chronic experiences of racial discrimination (Reijntes, Kamphuis, Thomaes, Bushman, & Telch, 2013). However, emotional challenges have been created via the endorsement of this posture (Kniffley, 2014). First, the experience of alexithymia contributes to the underdevelopment of emotional awareness. Second, Black males have become disconnected from their emotional selves. Third, the endorsement of an emotionally restrictive posture contributes to the perception of an external locus of control (e.g., I can't impact my situation, so it is easier to not feel anything toward it). This perception also influences the development of a passive coping style for emotionally charged situations. Fourth, emotional restriction increases the likelihood of Black men engaging in impulsive behavior as a way to separate themselves from disagreeable emotional states. Lastly, emotional restriction contributes to chronic feelings of anxiety and anger in Black men that influences the experience of hostility toward self and other Black men. Emotional restriction does not denote the absence of an emotional experience; instead, it restricts the range of emotional states Black male's can express. Consequently, Black males are limited to anger and aggressive behaviors associated with its expression, which are deemed "acceptable," rather than a full range of emotional expression.

Black men have received conflicting messages about the use of anger and aggression (Cooper, 2013; Hunter & Davis, 1992). In the sports arena, the aggressive Black man is celebrated as a necessary component for athletic achievement. Anger is seen as the instrumental driving force for engaging in these aggressive acts and is internalized via social messages such as "fear is for the weak," or "a real man doesn't let anyone walk all over him." The challenging aspect of Black males' experience with anger and aggression is that, while such behavior is rewarded in various arenas, it simultaneously denigrates and characterizes Black men as "dangerous and scary." A culture is created, reifying the stereotypes of Black men being dangerous, deviant, and embodying uncontrollable aggressive behaviors.

Kniffley (2014), argues that a circular pattern of Black male aggression is co-created in which these men, representative of a chronically denigrated segment of the population, gain a sense of power through the use of aggression. An innate fear response is internalized by society as an integral component of the perception of Black males. This creates a conundrum for Black men, who are then forced to adhere to behaviors within the confines of a stereotype that provides a sense of power and intimidation in relation to other groups in society. Furthermore, Black males are reduced to angry automatons who utilize aggression as a blunt instrument to manage challenging emotional situations.

The use of anger and aggression are not just reinforced by society; oftentimes, they are endorsed by the Black male's peer group as well (Majors & Billson, 1993; Powell-Hammond & Mattis, 2005). To gain acceptance within their peer group, Black males must possess the ability to demonstrate that they can be aggressive as well as match the intragroup aggressiveness of their peer circle. Black men learn early in their development that the use of aggression is the most respected solution to problems. In addition, they learn that if they do not engage in aggressive behaviors, they are at risk for losing their membership within the peer group (which may serve as their only source of support and buffer against the experience of racial discrimination).

In summary, the experience and expression of anger and aggression represent a challenging conflict for Black men, in which their expression is simultaneously celebrated and denigrated by society. Due to an adherence to traditional masculine ideology, many Black men are socialized to view anger as the default feeling for managing emotionally charged situations, and aggression as the necessary extension for expressing this anger. Additionally, this concept is reinforced by the Black males' peer group and oftentimes serves as a prerequisite for intragroup membership. As noted previously in this section, the development of gender identity indicates a transition from a strict adherence to gender role expectations and stereotypical gender norms to the manifestation of an integrated gender identity that has resolved the conflict between societal and cultural expectations of gendered behaviors and cognitions with the individual's lived experience. However, when this gender identity conflict is not resolved, the individual experiences a phenomenon called gender role conflict (O'Neil, 1981). Gender role conflict has been defined as a psychological posture through which the individual endorses a strict adherence to gender role expectations and stereotypical gender norms that leads to negative consequences for the individual and others such as personal restriction and devaluation (O'Neil, Good, & Holmes, 1995). According to O'Neil (1990), gender role conflict significant contributes to the manifestation of maladaptive behaviors such as addiction and aggression. Given the research that has demonstrated the significant expression of a traditional masculine ideology by Black men, they are vulnerable to the experience of gender role conflict and its subsequent consequences (e.g., increased maladaptive behaviors and mental health challenges).

In examining the process of Black masculinity development, the previous section explored the following: (a) the construct of gender identity and its development, (b) the impact of cultural messages transmitted across generations, (c) the conflict between adhering to an emotionally restrictive posture, (d) the experience and expression of anger and aggression, and (e) how these concepts contribute to the experience of gender role conflict and its influence on mental health challenges for Black men. For many Black men, racial and ethnic identity is an important component of their Black masculinity due to its saliency. Furthermore, due to the sociohistorical overlap, it is challenging for these men to separate their racial experience from that of their gender. The following section will explore the constructs of racial and ethnic identity and their impact on Black masculinity development (as well as their influence on mental health in Black men).

RACIAL/ETHNIC IDENTITY AND BLACK MEN

According to Gardner-Kitt and Worrell (2007), racial identity represents a permanent set of biological characteristics such as skin color, hair texture, and ancestral origin. These characteristics have been given a sociohistorical context to indicate their relation to positive attributes associated with a particular racial standard. Ethnic identity represents a set of cultural norms such as language, food, dress, religion, and other cultural practices that stem from a particular national heritage or background (Phinney & Ong, 2007). According to Kirscheinman and Neckerman (1991), Black racial identity accomplishes two main tasks. First, it aids in the process of assembling a positive sense of self. Second, it works towards discrediting negative stereotypes attributed to Black men and women. Oyserman, Gant, and Ager (1995), further postulate that the Black racial identity also serves to make sense of the self as a member of the Black community, to find meaning and coherence in regards to current and historical racism and its influence on access to limited opportunities, and to organize a self-relevant knowledge about personal effort and its meaning as a Black individual.

Several studies have highlighted the impact of racial and ethnic identity on the mental health of Black men (Anglin & Wade, 2007; Utsey & Constantine, 2008; Utsey, Giesbecht, Hook, & Stanard, 2008). For example, Whittaker and Neville (2010) conducted a study examining the impact of racial attitudes and psychological distress with 317 Black college students. They found that individuals reporting a greater internalization of positive racial attitudes demonstrated higher levels of psychological well-being compared to those with less positive racial attitudes. Other researchers have found similar results related to Black men's endorsement of more progressive racial attitudes being associated with positive psychological well-being (Anglin & Wade, 2007; Utsey & Constantine, 2008; Utsey, Giesbecht, Hook, & Stanard, 2008).

Several studies have highlighted the influence of ethnic identity on the mental health of Black men (Gray-Little & Hafdahl, 2000; Utsey, Chae, Brown, & Kelly, 2002). For example, Walker, Wingate, Basi, and Joiner (2008) conducted a study to examine the influence of ethnic identity development on depression and suicide with 296 Black college students. They found Black students who reported more attachment to their ethnic group as African Americans reported less suicidal ideation.

Collectively, the aforementioned studies suggest that racial/ethnic identity development can serve as a buffer against racial discrimination experienced by Black men. An advanced racial identity helps Black men develop a multicultural perspective that serves as a bridge between one's Blackness and the greater community. In addition, an integrated ethnic identity provides an avenue for an increased understanding for Black men on how to be resilient in the face of constant threats to their group identity. An integrated ethnic identity involves the incorporation of cultural norms based on the Black male's ethnic background that intersects with the salience he places on his ethnic identity within the context of the dominant culture. Integration fosters a positive association with the Black male's membership within his ethnic group and provides the context on which he can build his unique ethnic identity expression (Phinney & Ong, 2007).

For many Black individuals, their racial identity is a significantly salient identity variable. For example, Croll (2007) surveyed Black Americans about their racial identity and found that more than 72% of their sample reported it to be important to them. As noted earlier in the chapter, the salience of racial identity can have a conflicting effect on Black males. On the one hand, identifying strongly with one's racial background can contribute to the chronic experience of racial discrimination, which has been demonstrated to have a deleterious impact of both physical and mental health in Black men. However, pride in one's racial identity and ethnic heritage may serve as a buffer against this impact via the development of an authentic cultural identity and the formation of an integrated Black masculinity.

Authentic cultural identity refers to the resolution of the conflict in the development of Black masculinity between the endorsement of hypermasculine traits/stereotypes and the Black males lived experience (that has been influenced by racial socialization messages, family/peer groups, and sociohistorical factors). The current chapter argues that the internalization of stereotypical hypermasculine traits/stereotypes that are inconsistent with the Black males lived experience (and the factors that influence this experience) contributes to the development of an inauthentic cultural identity. This identity variable influences the formation of an unintegrated Black masculinity and subsequently impacts the development of psychopathology in Black males. The following section will discuss how these components fit together to influence the development of psychopathology in Black men. In addition, the next section will present a clinical example of conceptualizing a mental health case related to a Black male utilizing this model.

MODEL OF BLACK MALE PSYCHOPATHOLOGY DEVELOPMENT

To understand the experience of Black male psychopathology, one must consider the dual influence of social oppression and identity development. As highlighted in the current chapter, these factors can significantly impact Black male mental health. With the chronic experience of racial discrimination, it is important to call attention to the fact that racial discrimination negatively impacts the etiology and contributes to mental illness experienced by Black men. Racial discrimination perpetuates stereotypes, which creates challenges for Black men, exposing them to chronic traumatic cultural stress along with the effects of the hyper endorsement of traditional masculine ideology and a reduced ability to fulfill community and societal expectations in regards to the stereotypical "male" role.

Several studies have highlighted how these factors have contributed to mental health symptoms in Black men (Neighbors, Jackson, Bowman, & Gurin, 1983; Robinson et al., 2011; Ward et al, 2013). The current chapter has focused on four main mental health issues: depression, anxiety, suicide, and substance use. The results from these studies demonstrated that although Black men are more likely to be diagnosed with a mental illness related to externalizing symptoms, the experience of depression among Black men is comparable to their White counterparts and has steadily increased over the last 20 years. In addition, the impact of depression is more detrimental for Black men, contributing to challenges in interpersonal relationships, work, and overall impairment (Ward & Mengesha, 2013).

Black males transitioning into emerging adulthood represent the most vulnerable age group for the experience of symptoms related to depression, suicide, and increased substance use. Researchers have called attention to the fact that, although, in general, emerging adulthood can be a stressful transition period, it is compounded by an increased exposure to racial discrimination for Black males as they seek out jobs and educational opportunities (Lee et al., 2010). Emerging adulthood is a period of identity expansion and reconciliation. For Black males, the chronic presence of racial discrimination presents significant challenges for fulfilling the stereotypical roles associated with this transition period. According to the literature, for Black males, the struggle of identity development is most evident during the formation of a Black masculinity.

As noted previously, the development of Black masculinity is a fluid process of evaluation that is created within the relational context of the Black males' community, family, and peer group (Powell-Hammond & Mattis, 2005). Black masculinity development helps Black males to make sense of the social messages received about the intersection of their racial background and gender (Kniffley, 2014). In addition, this construct helps Black men to integrate the sociohistorical and economically influenced expectations of Black masculinity. Studies have highlighted how Black men significantly endorse a traditional masculine ideology as a protective factor against the experience of racial discrimination and the subsequent reduction in fulfilling these expectations (Wade, 1998).

A traditional masculine ideology represents a strict adherence to the stereotypical cultural norms for men related to physical and sexual violence, restricted emotionality, and competitiveness (Kniffley, 2014). The endorsement of this ideology has created a conundrum for Black men where they are somewhat shielded from cultural traumas in the form of racial discrimination at the cost of being placed in a stereotypical box related to the use of anger/aggression and emotional restriction. This conundrum contributes to the development of gender role conflict that impacts the experience of maladaptive behaviors by Black men such as addiction and mental health challenges (O'Neil, 1990). The rigidity of this box has been influenced by social messages that have been passed down via generations of the Black community in regards to the accurate manifestation of Black masculinity.

The experience of chronic social oppression significantly influences the development of Black masculinity. Social oppression here refers to attitudes, thoughts, and behaviors created at the institutional level that are designed to limit access consciously and unconsciously to socioeconomic, educational, health, employment, etc. opportunities for the oppressed group (Scott et al., 2011). These attitudes, thoughts, and behaviors are reinforced through a variety of mediums including the media and popular culture (Cooper, 2013). Social oppression for Black males occurs in the form of racial discrimination. As previously noted, the concept of racial discrimination impacts Black men as well as the greater society by limiting the various forms that Black masculinity can be expressed, thus placing Black men in a rigid cultural identity box (Hunter & Davis, 1992). Here, the limits that social oppression places on Black masculinity expression contributes to a phenomenon called cultural identity suppression.

According to Parker and Moore (2014), cultural identity suppression refers to the internalization of racial misconceptions that fuel misperceptions and perpetuates misunderstandings between Black males and members of other cultures. Additionally, cultural identity suppression limits the Black males' ability to manage an "interior self" and an "exterior positive image" (Parker & Moore, 2014). Cultural identity suppression involves three components: the endorsement of an inauthentic cultural identity, conflict between self versus attributed identity, and the development of a false psychological consciousness.

According to Cooper (2013), an inauthentic cultural identity refers to Black men endorsing stereotypical masculine traits that are inconsistent with their cultural background (e.g., racial self-hate, individualism versus collectivism) or represents an overendorsement of particular traits (e.g., emotional restriction, aggression). This process is facilitated through the conflict between self-identity (Black men's internal perception of who they are) and attributed identity, which reflects Black men's identities as others see them (Cooper, 2013). Kniffley (2014) postulates that this conflict occurs because of the perceived threat of Black manhood and the competing benefits and consequences experienced by Black men when endorsing stereotypical behavior as a means of reconciling negative gender expectations, racism, and discrimination with their lived experience. For these Black men, the assumption of an identity that is inconsistent with their cultural background and is rooted in conflict between societal, cultural, and sociohistorical expectations of their intersecting gender and racial identities contributes to the formation of an unintegrated Black masculinity. The formation of an unintegrated Black masculinity, as postulated by the author, contributes to the development of a rigid (inability to navigate varying expression of Black masculinity based on context) or unstructured (inability to assume a self-generated Black masculinity that integrates historical context, media/popular culture influence and lived experience into a coherent sense of self) Black masculinity. Stuck between these limited expressions of Black masculinity, Black men remain in a chronic state of conflict related to their intersecting gender and racial identities. As noted throughout this chapter, this conflict can contribute to the experience of psychological challenges such as depression and anxiety as well as maladaptive behaviors (addiction and anger or aggression).

To summarize, social oppression (in the form of racial discrimination), combined with cultural identity suppression, contribute to the formation of an unintegrated Black masculinity. This unintegrated Black masculinity is impacted by the development of an inauthentic cultural identity and conflict in the Black males' self versus attributed racial identity. Consistent with the literature in regards to racial identity and Black masculinity development, the combination of this conflict and lack of integration contributes to the experience of Black male psychopathology. However, several studies have highlighted that an integrated Black masculinity (a) reduces the endorsement of traditional masculine ideology, (b) develops awareness of negative racial socialization messages, and (c) identifies societal expectations of gendered cognitions and performance influenced by their racial background. These factors contribute to Black men being less likely to be negatively impacted by the experience of racial discrimination and subsequently suffering mental health issues (Landrine & Klonoff, 1996; Utsey et al., 2008; Whittaker & Neville, 2010).

CASE EXAMPLE

James is a 19-year-old Black male who is presenting to a mental health clinic for symptoms related to increased irritability, anger, a diminished interest in things he found enjoyable, and his mother reports that "all he does is lay around the house and sleep all day." James indicates that he has been getting angry quicker and feeling "down" a lot. He also reports that he has been struggling with figuring out what to do with his life now that he is an adult because he doesn't feel that he has many opportunities to succeed. Additionally, James notes that he has been coping with the way he has been feeling by using drugs and hanging out with his friends. He mentioned that his friends "aren't exactly the best," that he has to do things that he doesn't necessarily like to fit in, but that "they are loyal and don't judge him." James grew up with his younger brother and sister in a single-parent home because his father died when he was three due to gang violence in his neighborhood. Lastly, he mentioned that his family "had it rough" because they didn't have much money.

Case Conceptualization

As a young Black male, James is at an increased vulnerability for the experience of symptoms related to depression as well as the utilization of maladaptive coping skills such as substance use. During the intake, James mentioned that after his father's death, he had to become "the man of the house" and took on pseudo-parental tasks such as taking care of his two siblings. With the absence of a male figure, ongoing exposure to popular media, the significant influence of his peer group, James grew up with two competing frameworks about what it means to be a Black male.

On the one hand, he learned from his community and his mother about concepts such as the importance of putting ones family over one's personal ambitions and concerns, the need to find a balance and flexibility between stereotypical male roles and varying expressions of Black masculinity, and the need to understand and integrate Black cultural history and its relationship to Black masculinity development. However, through his peer group and popular media, James learned about the perceived benefits of endorsing a traditional masculine ideology.

As noted in his intake, James is struggling with increased irritability, anger, and depression that he attributes to the perception of limited opportunities as he transitions into adulthood. This perception is influenced by the social messages that he received from his family (e.g., it is unsafe for Black men to show emotion, a Black male has to expect to work twice as hard to get half as much), peers, and popular culture in regards to the experience of racial discrimination and ways of coping. James noted that the way he has been coping is through the use of substances and increased expressions of anger. Traditional masculine ideology highlights the need for hyper restraint on emotional expression. The only acceptable emotion to express within this framework is anger and its behavioral component aggression.

James mentioned that he is experiencing feelings of being "down," which may suggest the presence of depressive symptoms that are an extension of feelings of shame, guilt, and frustration related to his perceived inability to fulfill stereotypical male roles. However, the only emotion that he feels he can express is anger, which is reinforced by the perceived limitation of Black masculinities available to him as well as expectations by his peer group to utilize anger and aggression as prerequisites for group membership. For James, this experience creates a posture of silent frustration where he is grappling with significant feelings of depression (e.g., anhedonia, tiredness, depressed mood) that he is unable to express and instead manifest as increased irritability.

To summarize, James appears to be struggling with a constellation of symptoms consistent with the experience of depression. These symptoms are intricately connected to his experience of racial discrimination (social oppression) as it relates to the value and potential of Black males and the messages he has received about his ability to cope. In addition, James's symptoms are also compounded by the conflicting messages that he has internalized related to the creation, role, and manifestation of Black masculinity. This conflict represents a struggle between his community's expectations and those of his peer group and popular culture (attributed identity) and his own expectations (self-identity).

The conflict in expectations contributes to the endorsement of masculine traits that are inconsistent with his cultural background (inauthentic cultural identity) such as James's restricted emotional expression and increased use of aggression. The endorsement of these restricted traits contributes to a limited expression of Black masculinity (unintegrated Black masculinity). The combination of these conflicts in identity and expectations coupled with the endorsement of a limited expression of Black masculinity can be quantified as cultural identity suppression. Social oppression (via the experience of racial discrimination) in tandem with the varying components of cultural identity suppression significantly contribute to James's current presentation of mental health symptoms.

James will benefit from a mode of therapy that helps him to integrate a self-defined Black manhood with the social messages that he has received from his community, peers, and popular cultural into a coherent sense of self that would increase his flexibility in exhibiting varying expressions of Black masculinity. This increased flexibility could influence the following: a wider range of emotional expression, more adaptive coping skills for the experience of racial discrimination, increased ability to facilitate dialogue around depressive symptoms, improved insight into the influence of peer groups and costs of membership, and greater fluidity in the fulfillment of role expectations.

REFERENCES

Anglin, D. M., & Wade, J. C. (2007). Racial socialization, racial identity, and Black students' adjustment to college. *Cultural Diversity & Ethnic Minority Psychology*, *13*(3), 207–215.

Bynum, M. S., Burton, E. T., & Best, C. (2007) Racism experiences and psychological functioning in African American college freshment: Is racial socialization a buffer? *Cultural Diversity & Ethnic Minority Psychology*, *13*(1), 64–71.

Carter, R. T., Mazzula, S., Victoria, R., Vazquez, R., Hall, S., Smith, S., Sant-Barket, S., Forsyth, J., Bazelais, K., & Williams, B. (2013). Initial development of the race-based traumatic stress symptom scale: Assessing the emotional impact of racism. *Psychological Trauma: Theory, Research, Practice, and Policy*, *5*(1), 1–9.

Cené, C. W., Dennison, C. R., Powell Hammond, W., Levine, D., Bone, L. R., & Hill, M. N. (2013). Antihypertensive medication nonadherence in black men: direct and mediating effects of depressive symptoms, psychosocial stressors, and substance use. *Journal of Clinical Hypertension, 15*(3), 201–209. doi:10.1111/jch.12056

Cooper, F. (2013). We are always already imprisoned: Hyper-incarceration and Black male identity performance. *Boston University Law Review, 93,* 1185–1204.

Croll, P. R. (2007). Modeling determinants of White racial identity: Results from a new national survey. *Social Forces 86*(2), 613–642.

Gardner-Kitt, D., & Worrell, F. (2007). Measuring nigrescence attitudes in school-aged adolescents. *Journal of Adolescence, 30*(2), 187–202.

Ghafoori, B., Barragan, B., & Palinkas, L. (2013). Gender disparities in the mental health of urban survivors of trauma. *Journal of Aggressive Maltreatment Trauma, 22*(9), 950–963.

Go, A. S., Mozaffarian, D., Roger, V. L., Benjamin, E. J., Berry, J. D., Borden, W. B., et al. (2013). Heart disease and stroke statistics—2013 update: A report from the American Heart Association. *Circulation, 127,* e6–e245.

Gray-Little, B., & Hafdahl, A. R. (2000). Factors influencing racial comparisons of self-esteem: A quantitative review. *Psychological Bulletin, 126,* 26–54.

Hunter, A. G., & Davis, J. E. (1992). Constructing gender: An exploration of African American men's conceptualization of manhood. *Gender & Society, 6,* 464–479.

Hurd, N., Varner, F. A., Caldwell, C. H., & Zimmerman, M. A. (2014). Does perceived racial discrimination predict changes in psychological distress and substance use over time? An examination among Black emerging adults. *Developmental Psychology, 50*(7), 1910–1918.

Kessler, R., Mickelson, K., & Williams, D. (1999). The prevalence, distribution, and mental health correlates of perceived discrimination in the United States. *Journal of Health and Social Behavior, 40,* 208–230.

Kirschenman, J., & Neckerman, K. (1991). "We'd love to hire them, but . . . ": The meaning of race for employers. In C. Jencks & P. E. Peterson (Eds.), *The urban underclass* (pp. 203–232). Washington, DC: Brookings.

Kniffley, S. (2014). *Knowledge of self: Understanding the mind of the Black male.* Lexington, KY: CreateSpace.

Landrine, H., & Klonoff, E. (1996). The schedule of racist events: A measure of racial discrimination and a study of its negative physical and mental health consequences. *Journal of Black Psychology, 22,* 144–168.

Lee, C., Mun, E. Y., White, H. R., & Simon, P. (2010). Substance use trajectories of Black and White young men from adolescence to emerging adulthood: A two-part growth curve analysis. *Journal of Ethnicity in Substance Abuse, 9*(4), 301–319.

Lincoln, K. S., Taylor, R. J., Chatters, L. M., & Joe, S. (2012). Suicide, negative interaction and emotional support among Black Americans. *Social Psychiatry & Psychiatric Epidemiology, 47*(12), 1947–1958.

Lowe, S. M., Okubo, Y., & Reilly, M. F. (2012). A qualitative inquiry into racism, trauma, and coping: Implications for supporting victims of racism. *Professional Psychology: Research and Practice, 43*(3), 190–198.

Majors, R., & Billson, J. M. (1993). *Cool pose: The dilemmas of Black manhood in America.* New York, NY: Simon & Schuster.

Neighbors, H., Jackson, J., Bowman, P., & Gurin, G. (1983). Stress, coping, and Black mental health. *Prevention in Human Services, 2*(3), 5–29.

Okwumabua, T., Okwumabua, J., Peasant, C., Watson, A., & Walker, K. (2014). Promoting health and wellness in African American males through rites of passage training. *Journal of Human Behavior in the Social Environment, 24*(6), 702–712.

O'Neil, J. M. (1981). Patterns of gender role conflict and strain: Sexism and fear of femininity in men's lives. *Personnel and Guidance Journal, 60,* 203–210.

O'Neil, J. M. (1990). Assessing men's gender role conflict. In D. Moore & F. Leaf-gren (Eds.), *Men in conflict: Problem solving strategies and interventions*. Alexandria, VA: American Association for Counseling and Development Press.

O'Neil, J. M., & Carroll, M. R. (1988). A gender role workshop focused on sexism, gender role conflict, and the gender role journey. *Journal of Counseling and Development, 67*, 193–197.

O'Neil, J. M., Good, G. E., & Holmes, S. (1995). Fifteen years of theory and research on men's gender role conflict: New paradigms for empirical research. In R. Levant & W. Pollack (Eds.) *The new psychology of men* (pp. 164–206). New York, NY: Basic Books.

Oyserman, D., Gant, L., & Ager, J. (1995). A socially contextualized model of African American identity: Possible selves and school persistence. *Journal of Personality & Social Psychology, 69*(6), 1216.

Parker, R., & Moore, J. (2014). Black male college students: Their perspective of media and its stereotypical angle of "Blackness and maleness." *Black History Bulletin, 77*(1), 10–15.

Phinney, J., & Ong, A. (2007). Conceptualization and measurement of ethnic identity: Current status and feature directions. *Journal of Counseling Psychology, 54*(3), 271–281.

Powell-Hammond, W., & Mattis, J. S. (2005). Being a man about it: Manhood meaning among African American men. *Psychology of Men and Masculinity, 6*(2), 114–126.

Reijntes, A., Kamphuis, J. H., Thomaes, S., Bushman, B. J., & Telch, M. J. (2013). Too calloused to care: An experimental examination of factors influencing youths' displaced aggression against their peers. *Journal of Experimental Psychology: General, 142*(1), 28–33.

Robinson, M., Keating, F., & Robertson, S. (2011). Ethnicity, gender and mental health. *Diversity in Health Care, 8*, 81–92.

Scott., L., McCoy, H., Munson, M., Snowden, L., & McMillen, J. (2011). Cultural mistrust of mental health professionals among Black males transitioning from foster care. *Journal of Child and Family Studies, 20*, 605–613.

Sellers, R., & Shelton, J. (2003). The role of racial identity in perceived racial discrimination. *Journal of Personality and Social Psychology, 84*(5), 1079–1092.

Sellers, S. L. Cherepanov, D., Hanmer, J., Fryback, D. G., & Palta, M. (2013). Erratum to: Interpersonal discrimination and health related quality of life among Black and White men and women in the United States. *Quality of Life Research, 22*(6), 1313–1318.

Utsey, S. O., Chae, M. H., Brown, C. F., & Kelly, D. (2002). Effect of ethnic group membership on ethnic identity, race-related stress and quality of life. *Cultural Diversity and Ethnic Minority Psychology, 8*(4), 366–377.

Utsey, S. O., & Constantine, M. (2008). Mediating and moderating effects of racism-related stress on the relation between poverty-related risk factors and subjective well-being in a community sample of African Americans. *Journal of Loss and Trauma, 13*, 186–204.

Utsey, S., Giesbrecht, N., Hook, J., & Stanard, P. (2008). Cultural, sociofamilial, and psychological resources that inhibit psychological distress in African

Americans exposed to stressful life events and race-related stress. *Journal of Counseling Psychology, 55*(1), 49–62.

Utsey, S., Hook, J., & Standard, P. (2007). A re-examination of cultural factors that mitigate risk and promote resilience in relation to African American suicide: A review of the literature and recommendations for future research. *Journal of Death Studies, 31*, 399– 416.

Utsey, S. O., Payne, Y. A., Jackson, E. S., & Jones, A. M. (2002). Race-related stress, quality of life indicators, and life satisfaction among elderly African Americans. *Cultural Diversity and Ethnic Minority Psychology, 8*(3), 224–233.

Wade, J. C. (1998). Male reference group identity dependence: A theory of male identity. *The Counseling Psychologist, 26*, 349–383.

Walker, R. L., Wingate, L. R., Obasi, E. M., & Joiner, T. E., Jr. (2008). An empirical investigation of acculturative stress and ethnic identity as moderators for depression and suicidal ideation in college students. *Cultural Diversity and Ethnic Minority Psychology, 14*, 75–82. doi:10.1037/1099-9809.14.1.75

Ward, E., & Mengesha, M. (2013). Depression in African American men: A review of what we know and where we need to go from here. *American Journal of Orthopsychiatry, 83*(2), 386–397.

Ward, E., Wiltshire, J. C., Detry, M. A., & Brown, R. L. (2013). African American men and women's attitude toward mental illness, perceptions of stigma, and preferred coping behaviors. *Nursing Research, 62*(3), 185–194.

Watkins, D., Abelson, J., & Jefferson, S. O. (2013). "Their depression is something different... It would have to be": Findings from a qualitative study of Black women's perceptions of depression in Black men. *American Journal of Men's Health, 7*(4), 465–475.

Whittaker, V., & Neville, H. (2010). Examining the relation between racial identity attitude clusters and psychological health outcomes in African American college students. *Journal of Black Psychology, 36*(4), 383–409.

CHAPTER 3

COMMUNITY VIOLENCE EXPOSURE AND RACIAL DISCRIMINATION AS BARRIERS TO TREATMENT

Implications for African American Males in Counseling

Broderick Sawyer, Ryan DeLapp, and Monnica Williams

There are many barriers to the treatment for African American males seeking psychotherapy. African American clients may have concerns about treatment seeking reflecting badly on their families (Alvidrez, Snowden, & Kaiser, 2008); have fears of being hospitalized involuntarily, being mistreated, or being used as "guinea pigs" (Ayalon & Alvidrez, 2007); and generally see psychologists as older White males who most likely do not understand their social or economic difficulties (Thompson, Bazile, & Akbar, 2004). In addition, African Americans are frequently overdiagnosed with psychosis, which may be a result of stereotypes suggesting that African Americans may have more severe psychopathology (Whaley & Hall, 2009). Furthermore,

Counseling African American Males, pages 33–60
Copyright © 2016 by Information Age Publishing

members of this ethnic group may not see as much symptom improvement when in treatment using empirically supported interventions (Pole, Gone, & Kulkarni, 2008). African Americans may also have a preference to be ethnically matched to their clinicians (Malat, Purcell, & van Ryn, 2010), which may not be possible, as African Americans only comprise about 5% of psychologists (U.S. Bureau of Labor Statistics, 2012).

African American males may also have less knowledge about particular disorders or mental illness, may deny a need for treatment, and have concerns about the treatment process (Williams, Gooden, & Davis, 2012). In interviews with six African Americans, Williams, Beckmann-Mendez, and Turkheimer (2013) uncovered that they were concerned with negative social consequences of disclosing psychopathology, as well as cultural mistrust of treatment providers. Overall, these findings suggest that among the African American community, there may be unfavorable views toward mental illness, and a mistrust of mental health providers may also contribute toward these negative views. This is consistent with previous research by Masuda, Anderson, and Edmonds (2012) in which the authors investigated mental health perceptions among African American undergraduates and found that participants held negative views toward mental illness. Help-seeking attitudes were related to mental health stigma, and subjects endorsed that the concealment of personal information was important to them. Furthermore, considering the role of religion in the African American community, these individuals tend to report more positive religious experiences when coping with anxiety in comparison to non-Hispanic Whites (Chapman & Steger, 2010; Himle, Taylor, & Chatters, 2012). Along with the taboo surrounding mental illness, the notion that African Americans may be more likely to use religion to cope with distress may further reduce the likelihood they would openly discuss mental illness.

Besides the numerous aforementioned barriers to psychotherapy, there are additional barriers unique to the African American male experience that may make it difficult to engage in treatment. Experiences with violence exposure and racial discrimination may significantly impact their engagement in therapy and overall therapeutic outcomes. Evidence has demonstrated that the impact of violence exposure in the African American community begins to take effect during childhood and adolescence. For instance, African American youth have greater exposure to abuse (Sedlak et al., 2010) relative to other ethnic groups and have been shown to experience higher rates of serious violent crimes as both victims and perpetrators in comparison to non-Hispanic Whites (Lauritsen & White, 2012). Furthermore, during this period (2002–2010), rates of serious violent crimes remained consistent for African American youth, while for non-Hispanic Whites it decreased by 26%. Furthermore, discrimination may produce poor mental health outcomes such as fear of negative judgment, anxiety, hypervigilance, self-blame, and lower overall well-being (Carter & Forsyth, 2010; Soto, Dawson-Andoh, & BeLue, 2011). In addition to these harmful effects, African Americans may experience racial discrimination in therapy, which may make it difficult to establish a strong therapeutic alliance, thereby producing negative therapeutic outcomes (Sue et al., 2007; Williams et al., 2014).

Given that violence exposure and racial discrimination may significantly impact treatment outcomes, it is essential to understand how these experiences may influence African American males overall, and where these issues may reveal themselves in therapeutic interactions. In the following sections, we will outline research illustrating these factors impacting treatment of African American males, and ways to reduce their potential effects in a therapeutic setting.

DISCUSSION

Community Violence Exposure

African Americans at Risk

During childhood and adolescence, African American males in urban communities are more likely to encounter interpersonal traumatic experiences (Richards et al., 2004), experience abuse (Sedlak et al., 2010), and rates of serious violence are higher among African American youth in comparison with non-Hispanic Whites (Lauritsen & White, 2012). Furthermore, these experiences may prompt African American males to engage in potentially harmful behaviors that can be detrimental to their personal health or the health of others (i.e., substance use, risky sexual behaviors, domestic abuse; Richardson & Robillard, 2012; Reed et al., 2009). For instance, evidence suggests that African American males who are involved in neighborhood violence or perceive their neighborhood to consist of violence are more likely to perpetuate intimate partner violence (Raiford, Seth, Braxton, & DiClemente, 2013; Reed et al., 2009). Along these lines, urban neighborhoods may also be impacted by poverty, unemployment, and substance use, which can all contribute to the rates of violence within this population (Reed et al., 2009). Additionally, chronic exposure to violence can be extremely stressful for African American males, thereby impacting their everyday functioning. For example, Patton, Woolley, & Hong (2012) found in a sample of 9th-grade African American males that exposure to violence predicted lower levels of perceived parental support, involvement in school, academic success, and self-esteem. Furthermore, students felt less safe in school and their neighborhoods. Although there is a dearth of studies that have examined the frequency of violence exposure among African American male adults, extant literature detailing the potentially detrimental effects of violence warrants a clear understanding of how to address this topic area with African American males of all ages.

Cumulative Trauma

Cumulative trauma (CT) is the accumulation of multiple traumatic experiences over time, and these experiences may include many types of trauma (i.e., sexual assault or natural disaster), which is known as polyvictimization (Kira, Lewandowski, Somers, Yoon, & Chiodo, 2012). If an individual endures CT, the impact of one experience cannot be isolated from the other traumas. The additive nature of CT may amplify PTSD symptoms, and polyvictims are more symptomatic in comparison with those having the same type of victimization (Finkelhor, Ormrod, & Turner, 2007). CT, polyvictimization, and intense adversities across the lifespan are shown to contribute to significant mental health outcomes (Kira et al., 2008; Richmond, Elliott, Pierce, Aspelmeier, & Alexander, 2009), and African American males may be more likely to encounter these experiences. For example, Jenkins and colleagues (Jenkins, Wang, & Turner, 2009) found that African American male children were more likely to endorse internalizing behaviors such as depression, somatization, and anxiety, after having family members or friends die or become injured in violent incidents. Furthermore, Kira et al. (2012) investigated a group of African American and Iraqi adolescents and found that while certain types of trauma (i.e., sexual assault, abandonment, survival, and community violence) had negative effects on certain components of IQ, CT dynamics had negative effects on all four components of IQ (perceptual reasoning, processing speed, verbal comprehension, and working memory). Specifically, sexual abuse had negative effects on perceptual reasoning and working memory, and abandonment had negative effects on perceptual reasoning, working memory, and processing speed. Further, survival traumas (i.e., getting shot at) had negative effects on processing speed, which may be relevant when considering African American males who are frequently exposed to community violence.

Negative Outcomes

For African American males, there may be several factors that can influence their experiences of traumatic stress. African Americans may be disproportionately exposed to more community violence in comparison to other ethnic groups; therefore, encountering or witnessing traumatic life events may be more likely. Consistent exposure to these events has been shown to produce adverse outcomes in African American youth. For example, Last and Perrin (1993) found that African American adolescents are more likely to have a history of PTSD compared to non-Hispanic Whites, which is consistent with research suggesting that they may be more likely to experience trauma.

After a traumatic event occurs, there may be a down-regulating of the hypothalamic-pituitary-adrenal axis, and this can cause a stress response to become suppressed due to negative feedback systems, which has been hypothesized as an evolved response to protect the brain (Hart, Gunnar, & Cicchetti, 1995; De Bellis, 2001). However, this psychological suppression may also be a reflection of traumatized individuals becoming habituated to trauma, in turn causing them to lack physiological reactivity. Either way, lacking appropriate cortisol levels may cause an inaccurate fight or flight response, which makes exposure to new, potentially life-threatening situations dangerous. Traumatized individuals who have habituated to traumatic experiences or suppressed stress reactions may act differently in dangerous situations, such that they may not perceive danger when they, in fact, should (Diseth, 2005).

When considering habituation to CT in African Americans, males may have a blunted reaction after a large amount of exposure. Traumatic experiences may produce cardiovascular responses assisting in fight or flight, such that the release of cortisol and epinephrine cause an increase in blood pressure (Perry, 1994). Consistent with Hart et al. (1995), Conner-Warren (2013) found that in a sample of African American adolescents experiencing significant levels of trauma, higher levels of blood pressure were not found, suggesting a reduced physiological response. This finding suggests that the normative physiological reaction to trauma is being disrupted, which has the potential to interrupt appropriate fight or flight responses when encountering dangerous situations. Similarly, Hunt, Martens, and Belcher (2011) linked community violence with PTSD symptoms in urban-dwelling African American youth. The authors also found that despite significant traumatic exposures, in comparison to other studies reporting 25% to 40% clinically significant PTSD symptoms (Fletcher, 1996), their sample had a 16% rate. When considering differences between these findings, aside from sample and methodological differences, Edlynn, Gaylord-Harden, Richards, and Miller (2008) suggest two explanations. It may be that African American youth may become habituated to frequent trauma exposure and are less likely to develop clinical symptoms, or there are resilience factors that prevent the development of clinically significant PTSD symptoms. Resilience factors such as social support, formal kinship, and spirituality have been shown to buffer against negative effects of trauma exposure in African American children (Jones, 2007). These protective factors are congruent with an Afrocentric perspective, a system of beliefs and core values within the African American community that have been shown to influence how members of this community approach life and cope with stressors (Daly, Jennings, Beckett, & Leashore, 1995).

EXPERIENCES OF RACIAL DISCRIMINATION

Racial Discrimination and the Treatment of African American Men

Racism can be defined as a categorization of people groups by phenotypical characteristics and a ranking of some racial groups as innately or culturally inferior to others based on these characteristics (Williams & Mohammed, 2009). At the foundation of racism, there is an ideology of inferiority that often fosters the development of prejudices and discrimination of certain people based upon their physical appearance or affiliation in a certain racial group (Soto et al., 2011; Williams & Mohammed, 2009). Based in racist ideology, the American society perpetuates a number of stereotypes about African American men and contributes to the disproportionate levels of discrimination against this population. Specifically, African American men are more likely to experience discrimination relative to African American women and other ethnic groups (Seaton, Caldwell, Sellers, & Jackson, 2009). They are often perceived as aggressive, angry, threatening, unintelligent, poor, lazy, or sexually deviant/predatory, which can have distinct implications for therapy when working with this population (Williams, Gooden, & Davis, 2012). Significantly, evidence has shown that the frequency, chronicity, and severity of perceived racial discrimination is associated with a multitude of mental health outcomes (e.g., depression, anxiety, psychological distress, well-being, substance use; Paradies, 2006; Soto et al., 2011; Williams & Mohammed, 2009). As such, the deleterious effects of perceived racial discrimination require mental health professionals to understand how the various forms of racial discrimination uniquely impact the lives of African American men.

What is Racial Discrimination?

Researchers have proposed that when compared to traditionally overt racial prejudices and hatred, racism in American society has evolved in ways that make it more difficult to pinpoint and are more ambiguously experienced by its victims. As such, racial discrimination can currently be understood as a continuum ranging from repeated yet covert microaggressions to blatant hate crimes and physical assaults (Williams et al., 2014). A microaggression characterizes a more modern form of racism and describes "subtle daily racial slights and insults" that racial minorities frequently encounter (Torres, Driscoll, & Burrow, 2010). Such race-based affronts are often brief verbal or nonverbal behaviors that communicate demeaning and condescending messages to the racial minority. Sue and colleagues (2007) proposed three categories of microaggressions: micro-assaults, microinsults, and microinvalidations, which will be used in this section to elucidate the various ways that racial discrimination can impact the lives of African American men.

Relative to the other categories of microaggression, microassaults are most similar to the traditional forms of racism as they characterize deliberate verbal or nonverbal attacks intended to racially degrade. Microassaults include racial slurs, messages or behaviors that discourage interracial interactions, or brandishing racially charged symbols (e.g., swastika, confederate flag) that hurt, threaten, or even isolate African American men from the dominant culture.

Similar to microassaults, ethnoviolence is another form of racial discrimination that can be more overt and blatant in nature. In particular, ethnoviolence is defined as "violence and intimidation directed at members of ethnic groups that have been marginalized and stigmatized by the dominant or host culture because of their inability to assimilate threatens the dominant group's entitlement to society or community resources" (Helms, Nicolas, & Green, 2012, p. 54). Based upon the description of ethnoviolence by Helms, Nicolas, and Green (2010), African American men who are subjected to this form of discrimination experience manipulative ploys from the dominant culture to control their behavior and coerce their assimilation into the dominant culture's preconceived roles for the Black man. Ethnoviolence can be experienced by African American men directly (e.g., hate crimes or violence) or indirectly by witnessing another African American man experiencing race-based stress (e.g., seeing a Black male wrongfully searched, arrested, or shot). Given its resemblance to other traumatic stressors, ethnoviolence (along with other forms of microaggressions) can be precursors to the development of trauma-like symptoms (e.g., loss of memory, somatic complaints, self-blame; Helms et al., 2010).

Microinsults are more subtle in nature and describe messages that debase the racial heritage or identity of African American men. This form of racial discrimination can include an African American man being skeptically questioned by a White peer regarding his ability to obtain a lauded achievement (e.g., college admission, job). This inadvertently communicates an underlying message that Black men are not typically qualified for such opportunities, or implies that Black men only receive certain achievements through affirmative action or a quota based program (Williams, Gooden, & Davis, 2012). Similarly, microinsults can be communicated nonverbally and unconsciously by prominent figures in the lives of African American men. For instance, a teacher who frequently overlooks an African American student or a supervisor/boss who appears distracted when a Black male is talking during a meeting may indirectly communicate that the learning or the intellectual contributions of the Black male are not important (Sue et al., 2007).

Similar to microinsults, microinvalidations are often subtly communicated and unconsciously committed against African American men. Sue and colleagues define this form of racial discrimination as messages that "exclude, negate, or nullify the psychological feelings, or experiential reality of people of color" (p. 274). To illustrate microinvalidations, the authors provide examples of ethnic minorities who are confronted with statements or social interactions that minimize the importance of their racial/ethnic heritage. Regarding African American men, Sue and colleagues propose that statements like, "I don't see color," convey that their racial/cultural experiences are insignificant or that a core element of their identity is irrelevant. This ideology that racial/cultural experiences are irrelevant is known as colorblind ideology, and Sue and colleagues propose that individuals who endorse these views are at risk of unconsciously minimizing or denying the relevance of an African American male's racial or experiential reality and they assert that this ideology provides an excuse for such individuals to believe they are not susceptible to holding prejudices or discriminating against others. Furthermore, Terwilliger, Bach, Brian, and Williams (2013) note that a colorblind approach is associated with negative outcomes.

Overall, the power of modern forms of racial discrimination lies in their frequently covert and seemingly invisible qualities. Specifically, racial discrimination can suddenly onset, occur chronically, be performed intentionally or unintentionally, and can appear vague or specific to the African American male (Helms, 2010, 2012). Often, the subtlety as well as the unconscious committal of racial discrimination can leave the perpetrator defensive and unaware of the harm they have caused, whereas the recipient is left uncertain if his uncomfortable encounter was due to their race/ethnicity (Sue et al., 2007).

Gender Role Strain: Being Black and a Man in America

When mental health professionals are working with African American males, it is imperative that there be an appreciation for the unique life experiences that result from the intersection of their racial and gender identities. Traditional masculine roles and norms in American society include restrictive emotionality, self-reliance, competitiveness, stoicism, physical strength, toughness, aggression, and an avoidance of femininity (Griffith, Ellis, & Allen, 2013; Hammond, 2012; Matthews, Hammond, Nuru-Jeter, Cole-Lewis, & Melvin, 2013; Orneles et al., 2009). Griffith and colleagues describe that the pursuit to fulfill such gender norms and societal expectations can impose substantial pressure on men to conform and can influence a man's ability to navigate these stresses, which is also known as gender role strain. Extant literature examining the gender role strain of African

American men have identified themes related to work stress (e.g., gaining employment, managing job responsibilities, and navigating interracial work relationships) and the management of multiple roles and responsibilities (e.g., balancing self-care and care for others, holding multiple jobs and community positions, being the family "breadwinner"; Griffith et al., 2013; Orneles et al., 2009). For example, Mong and Roscigno (2010) reviewed discrimination suits filed using the Ohio Civil Rights Commission dating from 1988 to 2003 and found that African American men disproportionately received discretionary sanctions, were unjustly policed within their work environments, and were not equally hired or awarded promotions. Such findings highlight work-related stress that may contribute to the gender role strain of African American men by fostering a chronic fear for their job security, which indirectly impacts their ability to meet their expectation to provide for their families.

An ambition to meet and fulfill various gender norms can be protective and harmful. For instance, Orneles and colleagues (2009) utilized a qualitative assessment method (i.e., photovoice) to capture the relationship between gender norms, such as an idealized male strength and self-reliance, and male attitudes toward health from the perspective of middle-aged African American men. A finding that elucidates a contributing factor to the limited help seeking behaviors of African American men was that many Black men do not prioritize their health due to expectations for men to be strong and healthy. Such attitudes demonstrate that gender norms and expectations imposed on men equate sickness and needing help to weakness and vulnerability, which is incongruent with the societal image of masculinity and creates pressures for Black men to appear strong and stoic. Also, the men in this study endorsed that a core element of Black male masculinity is to assume responsibility for the health of others (e.g., family and community). Though this gender role can be protective in that it provides Black men the opportunity to care for and share their wisdom with their loved ones, it can also represent a strain when one's perceived responsibility to the family and community overshadows the prioritizing of personal health. Moreover, Hammond (2012) found evidence that certain gender roles are related to depressive symptoms in this population. This study found that certain African American men (i.e., ages 18 to 29 and 30 to 39 years) who highly endorsed restrictive emotionality experienced higher depressive symptoms, whereas for certain Black males (i.e., ages 18 to 29 and 40+), the endorsement of self-reliance (e.g., seeking independence and autonomy) was inversely related to depressive symptoms. Altogether, these findings demonstrate that expectations linked with the masculinity roles that African American men seek to fulfill can have distinct implications for their health.

Extant literature has utilized the term *John Henryism* and conceptualized the cool pose to characterize how African American men attempt to cope with societal expectations placed upon them. Researchers propose that John Henryism reflects a perception that a hard work ethic and determination will yield a sense of mastery and will properly satisfy the demands of one's society (Lehto & Stein, 2013; Matthews et al., 2013). Though the characteristics associated with John Henryism (e.g., individualism, personal freedom, self-reliance) are often ideal for career achievement and personal gain, there can also be negative health implications when these characteristics are met with seemingly insurmountable obstacles that are rooted in social inequalities (e.g., disparities in social class, economic opportunities, racism). For example, African American male respondents emphasized in a study by Griffith et al. (2013) that there is a chronic, daily source of stress connected with being a Black man, which has infiltrated all domains of his life. These respondents highlighted life experiences where they had been treated differently because of their race, and they emphasized that, in American society, being a Black male "represents everything bad." As demonstrated by these responses, the chronic race-based stress and societal inequalities (e.g., racial disparities in educational opportunities and income levels) within one's environment can limit the ability of African American men to effectively meet personal and societal expectations. It is important to note that when African American men are equipped with the resources to cope with social inequalities in society, there are mixed findings describing whether the embodiment of a John Henryism mindset is protective enough to yield desired outcomes. For example, Lehto and Stein (2013) found positive buffering effects of John Henryism among African American men with higher levels of education and at higher socioeconomic statuses. However, when unable to meet personal goals through brute strength and hard work, African American men may be left with a sense of futility and despair. For instance, Hudson and colleagues (2012) found that as socioeconomic status increased, experiences of racial discrimination increased as well, thus increasing the odds of depression within African American men. Such findings illustrate that even with the opportunities provided by education and financial stability, experiences of discrimination can be extremely stressful.

The cool pose describes another "distancing coping mechanism that serves to counter, at least in part, the dangers that Black males encounter on a daily basis" (Majors & Mancini Billson, 1993, p. 3). In particular, it represents a "subcultural tradition" that attempts to resolve the conflict of societal barriers (e.g., decreased earning potential, labeled as socially inferior) that impede the ability of Black men to fulfill the gender norms placed on them (Hall & Pizarro, 2010). Moreover, this coping strategy characterizes the Black man's use of speech, attire, walk, and interpersonal dynamics that comprises an identity utilized to counteract the stress of racial discrimination and a defense mechanism to maintain their manhood (Aymer, 2010; Hall & Pizarro, 2010). Specifically, Hall and Pizarro (2010) describe that the cool pose coincides with a pursuit of respect, toughness, and self-reliance that is often accomplished by presenting oneself as more threatening and emotionally restricted. To an extent, the cool pose adaptively allows Black men to protect themselves from the pain associated with race-based stress, but also fosters a sense of avoidance of emotional expression, which can have profound consequences (e.g., diminished quality of life; Aymer, 2010; Hammond, 2012; Majors & Mancini Billson, 1993). Additionally, the cool pose can support the use of violence as a means to preserve a sense of masculinity primarily among Black males residing in more impoverished, urban settings. However, for Black males from middle to upper class social status, violence may not be a vital component of their cool pose mentality because they theoretically have more resources to fulfill masculinity norms (e.g., self-reliance, providing for one's family; Hall & Pizarro, 2010). It can be important to consider whether Black male clients have attempted to resolve the gender role strain with a cool pose mentality as this coping mechanism can influence their emotional expressiveness in treatment. Also, due to the variability in the endorsement of a cool pose mentality, African American males who do not fully embody a cool pose (e.g., males who display the language and dress, but do not ascribe to the use of violence for conflict resolution) may encounter social isolation and ridicule from their Black male peers, which can have implications for their sense of belonging to the Black male community.

Another dimension to the intersection between gender and racial identities is the dissonance between how Black men are perceived by society and how they wish to be perceived. The invisibility syndrome describes what African American men experience as an inner psychological struggle when their true talents, identity, and overall worth are undermined by the demeaning preconceptions and ill-treatment imposed upon them by society (Franklin, 1999). The chronic exposure to racial discrimination shapes their self-development by placing a greater emphasis on negative prejudices and lacking a healthy respect or acceptance for their true personal identity, thereby fostering a sense of invisibility across various domains of life (Franklin, 1999; Yen, 1999). As such, there is a struggle for African American men to maintain a sense of visibility (or a sense of self), which occurs by remaining vigilant to being misjudged based upon their race/racial heritage in attempt to avoid acting in ways that are inconsistent with their personal identity (e.g., confirming negative stereotypes; Franklin, 1999). A case study example of the invisibility syndrome offered by Franklin (1999) describes when a well-dressed African American male lawyer (called Sam) enters an elevator with a White woman who frighteningly asks him, "Are you going to hurt me," or behaves as such by clutching her purse.

Within this example, Sam's identity as a kind and respectful professional is eclipsed by negative stereotypes characterizing him as angry and aggressive. Black men are constantly confronted with similar situations that cause them stress, anger, disillusionment, and confusion (Franklin, 1999). Collectively, the invisibility syndrome provides a conceptual framework for understanding the battle between society and the self, which can be an inner and external struggle with distinct psychological consequences for African American men who lack the appropriate resources to actively cope with the unjust demands and expectations placed on them. Specifically, Yen (1999) encourages mental health professionals to avoid labeling reactions to racism (i.e., stress, anger, disillusionment, confusion) as indicative of dysfunctional mental health and maladaptive coping. Instead, these reactions can be understood within the context of attempting to balance personal definitions of their self with external definitions of the Black man. In a case example by Carr and West (2013), the authors illustrate the treatment of Xavier, a 32-year-old African American male experiencing depression with psychotic features, and also outline addressing the invisibility syndrome within a therapeutic setting. Xavier, although being hospitalized in the past for depression, was noncompliant with any medication and held negative views of mental health overall. He believed that medication was not for Black men, so the therapist began to explore his gender and racial identity to gain some insight into why he was so reluctant. The therapist uncovered that Xavier was in a caregiver role at a very young age, and expressed that he had some emotional avoidance. Furthermore, as a Black male he felt that he should not have a mental problem, and that if his mother were alive, she would be disappointed if he used psychiatric medications. Discussing his developmental context made him feel more comfortable and heard, which was an important step, allowing him to be more open to treatment. Aside from reluctance about treatment, another conversation concerning Xavier's feelings about working with a White female therapist allowed him to express his hesitancy and further bolster the therapeutic alliance. After Xavier was comfortable with the therapist, he began to discuss instances of discrimination that he received from his mother and other African American members of the community. For example, his mother told him he was "like a White person in a Black person's body" (p. 128) whenever he expressed interest in playing sports like running or skiing instead of "Black men sports" like basketball or football. These multiple instances of racism made him feel as if members from his own group had held him back, and lowered his self-worth. Through a discussion of his developmental history and cultural reframing, Xavier was able to see how his upbringing made it difficult for him to discuss any mental health problems or emotional needs. Furthermore, Xavier was provided a safe space to explore his racial identity and come to conclusions about the ways in which he was proud of his identity (Carr & West, 2013).

As demonstrated by Xavier's case study, it is important to examine how an African American male's identities as Black and a man conjoin to form a unified identity. Extant literature has demonstrated that at the intersection of their racial and gender identities lies a pursuit of independence, personal freedom, and the self-perceived responsibility to provide for their loved ones. However, within the context of racism and other social injustices, Black men may struggle to fulfill these roles, and they may experience emotional distress when confronted with obstacles to satisfy these demands and expectations.

THEORY

Community Violence Exposure

Cognitive processing therapy (CPT; Resick & Schnicke, 1993) involves clients discussing traumatic events to help them confront negative emotions associated with the events. Clients will often avoid negative emotions associated with the trauma, and this hinders natural recovery. Additionally, CPT aims to change the meaning of the event to the client, and decrease avoidance behaviors so that meanings and beliefs can be understood in the original context (i.e., during the experience). When working with African American males having experienced cumulative trauma, there may be several traumatic events that may be distressing the client. Further, they may be at risk of encountering community violence daily if they live in an impoverished neighborhood. Still being at risk to experience traumatic experiences within their own community may produce strong automatic thoughts about the safety of the world, as well as their own ability to cope with consistent stress brought on by potentially experiencing more traumatic events in the future.

African Americans are more likely to experience trauma (Richards et al., 2004; Sedlak et al., 2010; Lauritsen & White, 2012), and live in impoverished areas compared to non-Hispanic Whites (Current Population Survey, 2013). Inasmuch, when treating African American clients, it may be useful to provide them with cognitive techniques to buffer against the deleterious effects of frequent community violence exposure. If an individual is living in poverty, low finances may make it difficult to move their place of residence to escape community violence exposure.

However, without processing traumatic events, individuals may hold certain beliefs about the events that bring up strong negative emotions that promote emotional avoidance and prevent recovery. Emotional processing theory (Foa, Gillihan, & Bryant, 2013) states that cognitions resulting from a traumatic event may be difficult to overcome because of fear structures that cause general associations. These cognitions may impede normal functioning because they do not represent real situations. Generalizations like this may cause significant distress when afflicted individuals encounter stimuli that remind them of the trauma. Processing traumatic events and the resulting emotions can help individuals more realistically appraise traumatic events, as well as reduce negative emotions associated with the event (i.e., guilt, sadness, horror, shame, anger). As a client discusses the trauma and relevant emotions, they begin to habituate to strong emotions related to memories and reminders of the trauma; this helps clients to no longer associate emotions resulting from the trauma to everyday life. However, African Americans experiencing cumulative trauma may be less likely to endorse negative emotions due to protective factors, such as the aforementioned "cool pose." Although adaptive against race-based stress, it may prevent African American males from being emotionally expressive when processing traumatic experiences.

Racial Discrimination

According to cognitive theory, Beck (2005) conceptualized depression and anxiety as being influenced by a cognitive triad, which includes automatic cognitions about oneself, others, and the environment. Components of automatic cognition include how people give meaning to the event (e.g., their appraisal process) as well as how they explain the occurrence of the event (e.g., their attributional process). These cognitive components have been implicated as important factors in capturing how individuals respond to stress as well as how stressful events are connected to adverse outcomes (Brondolo, ver Halen, Pencille, Beatty, & Contrada, 2009; Harrell, 2000). Although cognitive theory often includes a focus on restructuring negative cognitive distortions, an African American male's response to discrimination may not be best characterized as a maladaptive form of thinking (or even be conducive to a restructuring of their cognitive response to discrimination; Yen, 1999). Instead, their cognitive processes related to racial discrimination may more appropriately represent a legitimate (potentially adaptive) form of making sense of and seeking to explain their experience. As such, we purport that cognitive theory provides a framework for understanding how cognition (e.g., appraisal and attributions) contributes to the adverse psychological consequences associated with experienced racial discrimination.

According to extant models of perceived discrimination, cognitive appraisals and attribution are cognitive processes that can influence the relationship between perceived discrimination and adverse psychological outcomes (Brondolo et al., 2009; Clark, Anderson, Clark, & Williams, 1999, Harrell, 2000). Within social psychology, evidence suggests that the likelihood of attributing negative events to discrimination varies across individuals and situations (Major, Quinton, & McCoy, 2002). Such variability can be influenced by a number of factors, including the African American male's ethnic/racial identity (Branscombe, Schmitt, & Harvey, 1999), their prototypes or exemplars for discrimination (Simon, Kinias, O'Brien, Major, & Bivolaru, 2013), and perceived social costs of endorsing judgments of discrimination (Stangor, Swim, Van Allen, & Sechrist, 2002). Although less studied within the context of racial discrimination, an individual's attribution style can influence the onset of harmful emotions in response to discrimination. African American males may seek to explain the onset of a stressor by deciding who was at fault for the event (i.e., internal versus external locus of control) and attempt to formulate future oriented expectations that project the likelihood the event will reoccur (Abramson, Seligman, & Teasdale, 1978). Such future-oriented expectations can consist of the perceived likelihood the stressor will reoccur within the same environment (stable attributions) and the perceived likelihood the stressor will occur across multiple life domains (global attributions). When individuals demonstrate a tendency to attribute negative events as internal, stable, and global, evidence suggests that such an attribution style can increase one's vulnerability to the onset of adverse psychological outcomes (Heimberg, Vermilyea, Dodge, Becker, & Barlow, 1987; Luten, Ralph, & Mineka, 1997; Mezulis, Abramson, Hyde, & Hankin, 2004). Regarding race-based stressors, the tendency to attribute discrimination as stable, global, and severe can be related to harmful outcomes (Burns, Kamen, Lehman, & Beach, 2012; Eccleston & Major, 2006; Paukert, Pettit, Perez, & Walker, 2006).

Aside from attributing experiences with discrimination as global and stable, emotional reactions to discrimination may also be elicited by how African American males appraise (or give meaning to) the event (Burns et al., 2012; Folkman, Lazarus, Dunkel-Schetter, DeLongis, & Gruen, 1986; Luten et al., 1997). Specifically, when race-based stress is appraised as harmful and posing a threat to one's self or other loved ones, individuals may be particularly susceptible to the adverse psychological outcomes associated with perceived racial discrimination (Eccleston & Major, 2006), especially if there are limited available resources for coping with the discriminatory event (Brondolo et al., 2009). Importantly, evidence suggests that when experiences with discrimination are perceived as harmful or threatening, African Americans are likely to implement coping strategies to manage the onset of harmful consequences associated with the stressor (Brondolo et al., 2009; Folkman et al., 1986).

TECHNIQUE

Community Violence Exposure: General Guidelines

When treating African American males, performing a more extensive trauma assessment may be useful (Malcoun, Williams, & Bahojb-Nouri, 2015). A cultural mistrust of mental health professionals may result in reluctance to disclose during psychotherapy (Hunter & Schmidt, 2010). Additionally, Black males may consider their violence exposure a part of their mundane social environment, thus decreasing the likelihood of reporting such experience because they may consider this information unimportant or irrelevant to their presenting issues. Furthermore, given that African Americans may habituate to traumatic encounters over time, clinicians need to be aware that clients that have experienced repeated trauma exposure may lack significant affective responses when discussing their traumas. Having an open dialogue about their experiences and gathering comprehensive background information about these experiences may help put them at ease if there is reluctance to report. Having a comprehensive list of potential traumatic experiences to inquire about may be a helpful approach (i.e., PDS parts 1&2, Foa, Cashman, Jaycox, & Perry, 1997).

Community Violence Exposure: Cognitive Processing

When cognitively processing traumatic experiences with African American male clients, clinicians should provide education regarding post-traumatic symptoms and the benefit of cognitively processing traumatic experiences, and an explanation of automatic thoughts and resulting emotions should be provided. The goal of this is to help clients make the connection between automatic thoughts and resulting negative emotions. When considering cumulative trauma, it may be useful to have a discussion about the most notable traumatic events that they can remember, given that they may have had several significant traumatic experiences. After identifying the most notable events, clinicians may then want to formally process the worst traumatic experiences in order to help clients habituate to strong emotional reactions. This can be done by writing down detailed accounts of the experiences and processing them while tolerating negative emotions brought up by recounting the trauma (Williams, Powers, & Foa, 2012). Through this, clients learn that negative emotions stem from reminders or memories of the trauma, and that these reminders and memories are not immediately harmful.

Modifying the meaning of the trauma and decreasing avoidance patterns may look different when treating African American males living in neighborhoods with high rates of community violence, as they may still be likely to encounter traumatic situations. Although they may be at risk of experiencing more trauma, clinicians should still help them to make sense about the safety of the world and their role in it. By using Socratic questioning to elicit and challenge negative cognitions related to the trauma (i.e., I could have stopped it, it was my fault, I cannot cope with the stress of my environment) clients can begin to reframe how they view the traumatic event(s), and also how they view the likelihood that they may encounter more. This not only helps them overcome negative thoughts pertaining to past experiences, but also cognitions related to their still being at risk within their communities.

When considering retraumatization after PTSD treatment, clinicians need to be cognizant of the reality that African American males who reside in violent communities may very likely experience trauma again. Considering that retraumatization may be realistic for this population, helping a client see a particular traumatic experience as an isolated event may be inaccurate, and this may risk them being retraumatized if they do experience another trauma post treatment (Williams et al., 2014). In addition to a discussion of the risks of retraumatization, helping clients formulate practical strategies about being safe in their community and potentially finding a safer place to live may be useful. Avoiding the likelihood of encountering traumas may not be possible for some clients due to financial difficulties or needing to live with one's family in a particular neighborhood. However, if there are ways to reduce the likelihood of encountering community violence, these options should be explored.

Racial Discrimination: General Guidelines

Mental health professionals should examine their own experiences with race to understand how racism within American society has influenced their view of the Black man. In doing so, it will generate greater awareness of prejudices and racial biases that are held toward this population, which may decrease the committal of microaggressions or, at least, allow the clinician to become aware of how these race-based messages have influenced the therapeutic alliance. Without exploring one's prejudices towards Black men, clinicians may unknowingly perpetuate negative stereotypes when treating this population, contributing to feelings of shame and stigma in these clients. Although clinicians may not consciously convey these stereotypes to African American men, such messages can be delivered unintentionally in their verbal dialogue or expressed nonverbally in their body language. And, without monitoring the endorsement of such stereotypes, it may cause Black males to feel unfairly treated, and decrease their trust and comfort within treatment (Constantine, 2007).

In addition to assuring that their racial biases are managed within therapy, mental health professionals should also avoid devaluing the significance of race when working with African American males. Particularly, clinicians should be hesitant to approach their client's using a colorblind ideological approach, as this increases the likelihood of committing microinvalidations (e.g., "I don't see color"; Sue et al., 2007; Terwilliger et al., 2013). In the event that an African American male client is expressing the impact of his experiences with race-based stress, it could be costly for a clinician to inadvertently question the subjective reality of their client's experiences and/or invalidate the relevance of such an experience. As a result, the client may perceive the clinician as uninterested in his experiences as a Black man and unappreciative of the importance of his racial identity, which can be detrimental to the therapeutic alliance. However, if it becomes clear that the clinician's use of microaggressions has created an impasse in the therapeutic process, it is imperative that the clinician acknowledge his/her mistake, seek to explore the client's reactions to this race-based stress, and ask for feedback on how to communicate in a more culturally-sensitive manner.

If a clinician were to encounter a client suffering from the experience of significant racial microaggressions, these feelings may make attaining positive therapeutic outcomes difficult; therefore, it is essential to establish strong rapport early in the therapeutic relationship. Taking time to understand an African American male's unique experience and taking a genuine interest will help to negate potential negative racial experiences they may have encountered in other settings (Williams et al., 2014). Additionally, a thorough assessment of an African American male's experiences of racial discrimination will provide useful information, and will alert a clinician to any particularly psychologically harmful instances of racism that require further exploration.

Racial Discrimination: Cognitive Techniques

Cognitive therapeutic techniques may be extremely useful when working with African American males presenting with significant difficulties brought on by racist experiences or ongoing ethnoviolence. Given that racism is out of their control and may not be something they can escape, focusing attention on how they view themselves and others may alleviate distress brought on by encountering discriminatory events. Similar to CPT, the goal of cognitive therapy is to identify automatic thought patterns and connect them to the client's uncomfortable emotions (Barlow et al., 2011). Understanding which emotions they feel and why they think they feel that way helps them identify precipitating thoughts before emotions become evident. Particularly, clinicians can help the client better understand their appraisal (e.g.,What about the event may have been threatening? Were coping strategies available to help manage the stress of the event?) and attribution (e.g., Does the client possess self-blame for the events? Is there an anticipation of future discrimination?) processes in order to highlight how their cognitive response to discriminatory events may help conceptualize their emotional reactions. For example, in light of the gender role strain described previously, the appraised stress of discrimination may be characterized by the client's perceived inability to reconcile the disparity between gender role expectations (e.g., being a breadwinner) and societal obstacles (e.g., race-based stress within work environments). Moreover, the appraisal process may be influenced by perceptions that experiences of discrimination will or have jeopardized their resources (e.g., loss of a job) or threatened themselves or loved ones.

In exploring their attributional processes, clinicians can learn how African American clients make sense of race-based stress (e.g., self-blame versus attributions to discrimination) and their future expectations for this stress. Consistent exposure to race-based stressors, like microaggressions, can produce symptoms such as hypervigilance and paranoia (Carter, 2007), especially when clients are in settings where these are realistic threats (i.e., settings in which they may encounter racism). For example, an African American male who has experienced significant microaggressions may be more likely to perceive a salesman at a department store asking them if they need help finding anything as racial profiling. Cognitive theory suggests that they may have flawed schemas about the environment, so they attribute a potentially nonthreatening question as racism. However, African American males are likely to encounter discrimination, so these schemas may not be flawed and instead may represent preparatory cognitive processes to help identify realistic threats in the environment. As such, if a client is attributing ambiguous events to discrimination and feeling distressed after the attribution, an exploration of a client's attribution style is warranted. This is similar to exploring automatic thoughts and resulting emotions, but therapists should use Socratic questioning to help clients better understand factors that influence the attributions they make.

In addition to helping African American male clients make these connections, clinicians should explore the settings in which these appraisals and attributions occur, which will help identify situational factors associated with the onset of such cognitions. Given that perceptions of discrimination and associated emotional responses characterize the subjective reality of the African American male, it is important that clinicians avoid discrediting their experiences by seeking to identify maladaptive cognitions as this traditional component of cognitive therapy may increase the likelihood of perceived microaggression by the client. Instead, a focus on cognitive appraisals and attributional patterns helps to better characterize the client's subjective reality and allows for an informed assessment of how such cognitive processes are associated with the coping strategies implemented by the African American male. Importantly, when a social encounter is cognitively appraised as meaningful or potentially threatening, then cognitive, emotional, and behavioral coping strategies are employed to "manage specific external and/or internal demands that are appraised as taxing or exceeding the [Black male's] resources" (Folkman et al., 1986, p. 993).

When an African American male client is experiencing significant racial microaggressions, coping attempts could include avoidance of settings in which the events occur, people who may be likely to perpetrate against them, or emotional experiences resulting from the events. It may be difficult for African American males to completely avoid settings where racism may occur, especially if they have experienced racism from a particular ethnic group and they are still surrounded by members of that ethnic group. Particularly, when avoidance is a prevalent coping mechanism employed by the client, it presents an opportunity for the clinician to see how the client's cognitive processing of discrimination and their gender role strain contribute to the implementation of this coping strategy. Avoidant coping strategies could be influenced by any combination of factors, including the gender norms endorsed by the client (e.g., restricted emotionality), a defense mechanism in response to societal barriers impeding their achievement of gender norms (e.g., cool pose), or simply a coping strategy implemented in response to the appraised stressfulness of discrimination. However, given that avoidant coping strategies have been associated with adverse psychological outcomes in African Americans experiencing discrimination (citations), it warrants that the clinician explore the client's perceived efficacy (e.g., does the client feel this avoidant strategy was effective in managing outcomes associated with discrimination) and whether he is aware of more effective strategies (if necessary).

Aside from avoidant coping, evidence suggests that there are a myriad of coping strategies employed by African Americans following experiences of discrimination. These strategies include confrontative coping (Pittman, 2011), problem solving (Barnes & Lightsey, Jr., 2005), religious coping (Gaylord-Harden & Cunningham, 2009; Hayward & Krause, 2015), substance use coping (Gerrard et al., 2012), and support seeking (Clark et al., 1999). Specifically, an important resource for some African American men may be the Black community, which offers a sense of belonging and acceptance by other Black men and women and provides a source of visibility (Yen, 1999). For example, in Franklin (1999), following his experience in the elevator, Sam was able to find support from a Black colleague or peer to offer validation for the illegitimacy of the women's negative reaction to him and provide an emotional outlet for him to express his frustration and anger for being misconceived in such a manner. Altogether, there still remains limited research outlining which coping strategies promote optimal health outcomes following experiences with discrimination; however, clinicians should help the client identify and evaluate the effectiveness of both current and potentially available coping strategies.

IMPLICATIONS FOR COUNSELORS AND THERAPISTS

Clinicians may not be familiar with the many stressors African American males face, and this may complicate the therapeutic process. The techniques provided in the current chapter reflect environmental stressors that uniquely impact the lives and psychological functioning of African American males. The suggested general guidelines increase the cultural sensitivity of empirically supported treatments, as clinicians can better understand how these unique environmental stressors impact their African American male clients. Cognitive and emotional processing theories were outlined and then applied to African American males, which aim to guide clinicians in providing treatment based on empirically supported treatment modalities. Within these theoretical models, therapists can effectively address the unique stressors faced by this population and resulting emotional distress. The current chapter also provides specific recommendations detailing important pitfalls to avoid when working with this population and highlights potential avenues for incorporating discussions that help the client explore and make sense of these unique stressors. Specifically, we have outlined how traditional coping mechanisms utilized by African American males, environmental stressors outside a client's control (e.g., residence), and race-related stressors all have the potential to impede the therapeutic process if not addressed appropriately. Through describing these mechanisms, clinicians may now better understand the African American male experience, which can assist in improving rapport building and attaining positive therapeutic outcomes.

CONCLUSION

African American males are disproportionately afflicted by community violence exposure and racism. Experiences of cumulative trauma can cause difficulties when treating African American male clients, such as potential blunted reactions and inaccurate assessment or diagnosis. Furthermore, racial discrimination may significantly impact therapeutic interactions, as well as put African American males at risk for experiencing microaggressions in therapy. To combat the unique barriers and complex experiences of African American males, clinicians need to be cognizant of the many issues that arise when treating members of this population.

REFERENCES

Abramson, L. Y., Seligman, M. E., & Teasdale, J. D. (1978). Learned helplessness in humans: Critique and reformulation. *Journal of Abnormal Psychology, 87*, 49–74.

Alvidrez, J., Snowden, L. R., & Kaiser, D. M. (2008). The experience of stigma among Black mental health consumers. *Journal of Health Care for the Poor and Underserved, 19*(3), 874–893. doi:10.1353/hpu.0.0058

Ayalon, L., & Alvidrez, J. (2007). The experience of Black consumers in the mental health system: Identifying barriers to and facilitators of mental health treatment using the consumers' perspective. *Issues in Mental Health Nursing, 28*(12), 1323–1340. doi:10.1080/01612840701651454

Aymer, S. R. (2010). Clinical practice with African American men: What to consider and what to do. *Smith College Studies in Social Work, 80*(1), 20–34.

Barlow, D. H., Farchione, T. J., Fairholme, C. P., Ellard, K. K., Boisseau, C. L., Allen, L. B., & Ehrenreich-May, J. (2011). Unified protocol for transdiagnostic treatment of emotional disorders: Therapist guide. New York, NY: Oxford University Press.

Barnes, P. W., & Lightsey, O. R. (2005). Perceived racist discrimination, coping, stress, and life satisfaction. *Journal of Multicultural Counseling and Development, 33*(1), 48–61.

Beck, A. T. (2005). The current state of cognitive therapy: A 40-year retrospective. *Archives of General Psychiatry, 62*(9), 953–959.

Branscombe, N. R., Schmitt, M. T., & Harvey, R. D. (1999). Perceiving pervasive discrimination among African Americans: Implications for group identification and well-being. *Journal of Personality and Social Psychology, 77*, 135.

Brondolo, E., ver Halen, N. B., Pencille, M., Beatty, D., & Contrada, R. J. (2009). Coping with racism: A selective review of the literature and a theoretical and methodological critique. *Journal of Behavioral Medicine, 32*(1), 64–88.

Burns, M. N., Kamen, C., Lehman, K. A., & Beach, S. H. (2012). Minority stress and attributions for discriminatory events predict social anxiety in gay men. *Cognitive Therapy and Research, 36*(1), 25–35. doi:10.1007/s10608-010-9302-6

Carr, E. R., & West, L. M. (2013). Inside the therapy room: A case study for treating African American men from a multicultural/feminist perspective. *Journal of Psychotherapy Integration, 23*, 120–133.

Carter, R. T. (2007). Racism and psychological and emotional injury: Recognizing and assessing race-based traumatic stress. *The Counseling Psychologist, 35*(1), 13–105.

Carter, R. T., & Forsyth, J. (2010). Reactions to racial discrimination: Emotional stress and help-seeking behaviors. *Psychological Trauma: Theory, Research, Practice, and Policy, 2*(3), 183.

Chapman, L., & Steger, M. F. (2010). Race and religion: Differential prediction of anxiety symptoms by religious coping in African American and European American young adults. *Depression and Anxiety, 27*(3), 316–322. doi:10.1002/da.20510

Clark, R., Anderson, N. B., Clark, V. R., & Williams, D. R. (1999). Racism as a stressor for African Americans: A biopsychosocial model. *American Psychologist, 54*(10), 805–816.

Conner-Warren, R. (2013). Effects of CT load on perceptions of health, blood pressure, and resting heart rate in urban African American youth. *Journal for Specialists in Pediatric Nursing, 19,* 127–138.

Constantine, M. (2007). Racial microaggressions against African American clients in cross-racial counseling relationships. *Journal of Counseling Psychology, 54*(1), 1–16.

Current Population Survey. (2013). Kaiser Family Foundation estimates based on the Census Bureau's March Current Population Survey. *Annual Social and Economic Supplements.*

Daly, A., Jennings, J., Beckett, J. O., & Leashore, B. R. (1995). Effective coping strategies of African Americans. *Social Work, 40,* 240–246.

De Bellis, M. D. (2001). Developmental traumatology: The psychobiological development of maltreated children and its implications for research, treatment, and policy. *Developmental Psychopathology, 13,* 537–561.

Diseth, T. H. (2005). Dissociation in children and adolescents as reaction to trauma: An overview of conceptual issues and neurobiological factors. *Nordic Journal of Psychiatry, 59*(2), 79–91.

Eccleston, C. P., & Major, B. N. (2006). Attributions to discrimination and self-esteem: The role of group identification and appraisals. *Group Processes and Intergroup Relations, 9*(2), 147–162.

Edlynn, E. S., Gaylord-Harden, N. K., Richards, M. H., & Miller, S. A. (2008). African American inner-city youth exposed to violence: Coping skills as a moderator for anxiety. *American Journal of Orthopsychiatry, 78,* 249–258.

Finkelhor, D., Ormrod, R. K., & Turner, H. A. (2007). Poly-victimization and trauma in a national longitudinal cohort. *Development and Psychopathology, 19*(1), 149–166.

Fletcher, K. E. (1996). Childhood post-traumatic stress disorder. In E. J. Mash & R. A. Barkley (Eds.), *Child psychopathology* (pp. 242–276). New York, NY: Guilford Press.

Foa, E. B., Cashman L., Jaycox L., & Perry, K. (1997). The validation of a self-report measure of posttraumatic stress disorder: The posttraumatic diagnostic scale. *Psychological Assessment, 9,* 445–451.

Foa, E. B., Gillihan, S. J., & Bryant, R. A. (2013). Challenges and successes in dissemination of evidence-based treatments for posttraumatic stress: Lessons learned from prolonged exposure therapy for PTSD. *Psychological Science in the Public Interest, 14,* 65–111.

Folkman, S., Lazarus, R. S., Dunkel-Schetter, C., DeLongis, A., & Gruen, R. J. (1986). Dynamics of a stressful encounter: Cognitive appraisal, coping, and encounter outcomes. *Journal of Personality and Social Psychology, 50*(5), 992–1003.

Franklin, A. J. (1999). Invisibility syndrome and racial identity development in psychotherapy and counseling African American men. *The Counseling Psychologist, 27*(6), 761–793.

Gaylord-Harden, N. K., & Cunningham, J. A. (2009). The impact of racial discrimination and coping strategies on internalizing symptoms in African American youth. *Journal of Youth and Adolescence, 38*(4), 532–543.

Gerrard, M., Stock, M. L., Roberts, M. E., Gibbons, F. X., O'Hara, R. E., Weng, C. Y., & Wills, T. A. (2012). Coping with racial discrimination: The role of substance use. *Psychology of Addictive Behaviors, 26*(3), 550–560.

Griffith, D. M., Ellis, K. R., & Allen, J. O. (2013). An intersectional approach to social determinants of stress for African American men: Men's and women's perspectives. *American Journal of Men's Health, 7*(4 suppl.), 19S–30S.

Hall, R. E., & Pizarro, J. M. (2010). Cool pose: Black male homicide and the social implications of manhood. *Journal of Social Service Research, 37*(1), 86–98.

Hammond, W. P. (2012). Taking it like a man: Masculine role norms as moderators of the racial discrimination–depressive symptoms association among African American men. *American Journal of Public Health, 102*(S2), S232-S241.

Harrell, S. P. (2000). A multidimensional conceptualization of racism-related stress: Implications for the well-being of people of color. *American Journal of Orthopsychiatry, 70*(1), 42–57.

Hart, J., Gunnar, M., & Cicchetti, D. (1995). Salivary cortisol in maltreated children: Evidence of relations between neuroendocrine activity and social competence. *Developmental Psychopathology, 7*, 26.

Hayward, R. D., & Krause, N. (2015). Religion and strategies for coping with racial discrimination among African Americans and Caribbean Blacks. *International Journal of Stress Management.* [Advance online publication.] Retrieved from http://dx.doi.org/10.1037/a0038637

Heimberg, R. G., Vermilyea, J. A., Dodge, C. S., Becker, R. E., & Barlow, D. H. (1987). Attributional style, depression, and anxiety: An evaluation of specificity of depressive attributions. Special issue: Anxiety: Cognitive factors and the anxiety disorders. *Cognitive Therapy and Research, 11*, 537–550.

Helms, J. E., Nicolas, G., & Green, C. E. (2010). Racism and ethnoviolence as trauma: Enhancing professional training. *Traumatology, 16*(4), 53–62.

Helms, J. E., Nicolas, G., & Green, C. E. (2012). Racism and ethnoviolence as trauma: Enhancing professional and research training. *Traumatology: An International Journal, 18*(1), 65–74.

Himle, J. A., Taylor, R., & Chatters, L. M. (2012). Religious involvement and obsessive compulsive disorder among African Americans and Black Caribbeans. *Journal of Anxiety Disorders, 26*(4), 502–510. doi:10.1016/j.janxdis.2012.02.003

Hudson, D. L., Bullard, K. M., Neighbors, H. W., Geronimus, A. T., Yang, J., & Jackson, J. S. (2012). Are benefits conferred with greater socioeconomic position undermined by racial discrimination among African American men? *Journal of Men's Health, 9*(2), 127–136.

Hunt, K. L., Martens, P. M., & Belcher, H. M. E. (2011). Risky business: Trauma exposure and rate of posttraumatic stress disorder in African American children and adolescents. *Journal of Traumatic Stress, 24*, 365–369.

Hunter, L.R. & Schmidt, N.B. (2010). Anxiety psychopathology in African American adults: Literature review and development of an empirically-informed, sociocultural model. *Psychological Bulletin, 21*, 211–235.

Jenkins, E. J., Wang, E., & Turner, L. (2009). Traumatic events involving friends and family members in a sample of African American early adolescents. *American Journal of Orthopsychiatry, 79*, 398–406.

Jones, J. M. (2007). Exposure to chronic community violence: Resilience in African American children. *Journal of Black Psychology, 33*(2), 125–149.

Kira, I., Lewandowski, L., Somers, C. L., Yoon, J. S., & Chiodo, L. (2012). The effects of trauma types, cumulative trauma, and PTSD on IQ in two highly traumatized adolescent groups. *Psychological Trauma: Theory, Research, Practice, and Policy, 4*(1), 128–139.

Kira, I., Lewandowski, L., Templin, T., Ramaswamy, V., Ozkan, B., & Mohanesh, J. (2008). Measuring cumulative trauma dose, types and profiles using a development-based taxonomy of trauma, *Traumatology, 14*(2), 62–87.

Last, C. G., & Perrin, S. (1993). Anxiety disorders in African-American and White children. *Journal of Abnormal and Child Psychology, 21*, 153–164.

Lauritsen, J. L., & White, N. (2012). Bureau of Justice Statistics: Violent crime against youth, 1994–2010. Retrieved from http://www.bjs.gov/index.cfm?ty=pbdetail&iid=4575

Lehto, R. H., & Stein, K. F. (2013). The impact of John Henryism on self-reported health behaviors in African American men. *Journal of Transcultural Nursing, 24*(3), 291–296.

Luten, A. G., Ralph, J. A., & Mineka, S. (1997). Pessimistic attributional style: Is it specific to depression versus anxiety versus negative affect? *Behaviour Research and Therapy, 35*(8), 703–719.

Major, B., Quinton, W. J., & McCoy, S. K. (2002). Antecedents and consequences of attributions to discrimination: Theoretical and empirical advances. *Advances in Experimental Social Psychology, 34*, 251–330.

Majors, R., & Mancini Billson, J. (1993). *Cool pose: The dilemmas of Black manhood in America.* New York, NY: Touchstone Books.

Malat, J., Purcell, D., & van Ryn, M. (2010). Factors affecting Whites' and Blacks' attitudes toward race concordance with doctors. *Journal of the National Medical Association, 102*(9), 787–793.

Malcoun, E., Williams, M. T., & Bahojb-Nouri, L. V. (2015). Assessment of posttraumatic stress disorder in African Americans. In L. T. Benuto & B. D. Leany (Eds.), *Guide to psychological assessment with African Americans.* New York, NY: Springer.

Masuda, A., Anderson, P. L., & Edmonds, J. (2012) Help-seeking attitudes, mental health stigma, and self-concealment among African American college students. *Journal of Black Studies, 43*(7), 773–786.

Matthews, D. D., Hammond, W. P., Nuru-Jeter, A., Cole-Lewis, Y., & Melvin, T. (2013). Racial discrimination and depressive symptoms among African-American men: The mediating and moderating roles of masculine self-reliance and John Henryism. *Psychology of Men & Masculinity, 14*(1), 35–46.

Mezulis, A. H., Abramson, L. Y., Hyde, J. S., & Hankin, B. L. (2004). Is there a universal positivity bias in attributions? A meta-analytic review of individual, developmental, and cultural differences in the self-serving attributional bias. *Psychological Bulletin, 130*(5), 711–747.

Mong, S. N., & Roscigno, V. J. (2010). African American men and the experience of employment discrimination. *Qualitative Sociology, 33*(1), 1–21.

Ornelas, I. J., Arnell, J., Tran, A., Royster, M., Armstrong-Brown, J., & Eng, E. (2009). Understanding African American men's perceptions of racism, male gender socialization, and social capital through photovoice. *Qualitative Health Research, 19*(4), 552–565.

Paradies, Y. C. (2006). Defining, conceptualizing and characterizing racism in health research. *Critical Public Health, 16*(2), 143–157. doi:10.1080/09581590600828881

Patton, D., Woolley, M. E., & Hong, J. (2012). Exposure to violence, student fear, and low academic achievement: African American males in the critical transition to high school. *Children and Youth Services Review, 34*(2), 388–395. doi:10.1016/j.childyouth.2011.11.009

Paukert, A. L., Pettit, J. W., Perez, M., & Walker, R. L. (2006). Affective and attributional features of acculturative stress among ethnic minority college students. *Journal of Psychology: Interdisciplinary and Applied, 140*(5), 405–419. doi:10.3200/JRLP.140.5.405-419

Perry B. (1994). Neurobiological sequelae of childhood trauma: PTSD in children. In M. Murberg (Ed.), *Catecholamine function in posttraumatic stress disorder: Emerging concepts* (pp. 233–255). Washington, DC: American Psychiatric Press.

Pittman, C. T. (2011). Getting mad but ending up sad: The mental health consequences for African Americans using anger to cope with racism. *Journal of Black Studies, 42*(7), 1106–1124. doi:10.1177/0021934711401737

Pole, N., Gone, J. P., & Kulkarni, M. (2008). Posttraumatic stress disorder among ethnoracial minorities in the United States. *Clinical Psychology: Science and Practice, 15*(1), 35–61. doi:10.1111/j.1468-2850.2008.00109.x

Raiford, J. L., Seth, P., Braxton, N. D., & DiClemente, R. J. (2013). Interpersonal- and community-level predictors of intimate partner violence perpetration among African American men. *Journal of Urban Health, 90*(4), 784–795.

Reed, E., Silverman, J. G., Welles, S. L., Santana, M. C., Missmer, S. A., & Raj, A. (2009). Associations between perceptions and involvement in neighborhood violence and intimate partner violence perpetration among urban, African American men. *Journal of Community Health, 34*(4), 328–335.

Resick, P. A., & Schnicke, M. K. (1993). *Cognitive processing therapy for rape victims: A treatment manual.* Newbury Park, CA: Sage.

Richards, M. H., Larson, R., Miller, B. V., Luo, Z., Sims, B., Parrella, D. P., & McCauley, C. (2004). Risky and protective contexts and exposure to violence in urban African American young adolescents. *Journal of Clinical Child & Adolescent Psychology, 33*, 138–148. doi:10.1207/S15374424JCCP330113

Richardson, J., & Robillard, A. (2012). The least of these: Chronic exposure to violence and HIV risk behaviors among African American male violent youth offenders detained in an adult jail. *Journal of Black Psychology, 39*(1), 28–62. doi:10.1177/0095798412447645

Richmond, J. M., Elliott, A. N., Pierce, T. W., Aspelmeier, J. E., & Alexander, A. A. (2009). Polyvictimization, childhood victimization, and psychological distress in college women. *Child Maltreatment, 14*(2), 127–147.

Seaton, E. K., Caldwell, C. H., Sellers, R. M., & Jackson, J. S. (2009). The prevalence of perceived discrimination among African American and Caribbean Black youth. *Developmental Psychology, 44*, 1288–1297.

Sedlak, A. J., Mettenburg, J., Basena, M., Petta, I., McPherson, K., Greene, A., & Li, S. (2010). *Fourth National Incidence Study of Child Abuse and Neglect (NIS–4): Report to Congress.* Washington, DC: U.S. Department of Health and Human Services, Administration for Children and Families.

Simon, S., Kinias, Z., O'Brien, L. T., Major, B., & Bivolaru, E. (2013). Prototypes of discrimination: How status asymmetry and stereotype asymmetry affect judgments of racial discrimination. *Basic and Applied Social Psychology, 35*(6), 525–533.

Soto, J. A., Dawson-Andoh, N. A., & BeLue, R. (2011). The relationship between perceived discrimination and generalized anxiety disorder among African Americans, Afro Caribbeans, and non-Hispanic Whites. *Journal of Anxiety Disorders, 25*(2), 258–265.

Stangor, C., Swim, J. K., Van Allen, K. L., & Sechrist, G. B. (2002). Reporting discrimination in public and private contexts. *Journal of Personality and Social Psychology, 82*(1), 69–74.

Sue, D. W., Capodilupo, C. M., Torino, G. C., Bucceri, J. M., Holder, A., Nadal, K. L., & Esquilin, M. (2007). Racial microaggressions in everyday life: Implications for clinical practice. *American Psychologist, 62*(4), 271–286.

Terwilliger, J. M., Bach, N., Bryan, C., & Williams, M. T. (2013). Multicultural versus colorblind ideology: Implications for mental health and counseling. In A. Di Fabio (Ed.), *Psychology of counseling.* Hauppauge, NY: Nova Science.

Thompson, V. L. S., Bazile, A., & Akbar, M. (2004). African Americans' perceptions of psychotherapy and psychotherapists. *Professional Psychology: Research and Practice, 35*(1), 19–26.

Torres, L., Driscoll, M. W., & Burrow, A. L. (2010). Racial microaggressions and psychological functioning among highly achieving African Americans: A mixed-methods approach. *Journal of Social and Clinical Psychology, 29*(10), 1074–1099.

U.S. Bureau of Labor Statistics. (2012). *Labor force characteristics by race and ethnicity, 2011: Report 1036.* Washington, DC: U.S. Department of Labor.

Whaley, A. L., & Hall, B. N. (2009). Effects of cultural themes in psychotic symptoms on the diagnosis of schizophrenia in African Americans. *Mental Health, Religion & Culture, 12*(5), 457–471.

Williams, D. R., & Mohammed, S. A. (2009). Discrimination and racial disparities in health: Evidence and needed research. *Journal of Behavioral Medicine, 32*(1), 20–47.

Williams, M., Powers, M., & Foa, E. (2012). Psychological treatment for obsessive-compulsive disorder, Chapter 13. In P. Sturmey & M. Hersen (Eds.), *Handbook of evidence-based practice in clinical psychology,* (Vol. 2). Hoboken, NJ: John Wiley.

Williams, M. T., Beckmann-Mendez, D., & Turkheimer, E. (2013). Cultural barriers to African American participation in anxiety disorders research. *Journal of the National Medical Association, 105*(1), 33–41.

Williams, M. T., Gooden, A. M., & Davis, D. (2012). African Americans, European Americans, and pathological stereotypes: An African-centered perspective. In G. R. Hayes & M. H. Bryant (Ed.), *Psychology of culture.* Hauppauge, NY: Nova Science.

Williams, M. T., Malcoun, E., Sawyer, B. A., Davis, D. M., Nouri, L. B., & Bruce, S. L. (2014). Cultural adaptations of prolonged exposure therapy for treatment and prevention of posttraumatic stress disorder in African Americans. *Behavioral Sciences, 4*, 102–124.

Yen, C. J. (1999). Invisibility and self-construal in African American Men: Implications for training and practice. *Counseling Psychologist, 27*(6), 810–819.

CHAPTER 4

UBUNTU

A Framework for African American Male Positive Mental Health

Derek Wilson, Seyi Olubadewo, and Veeda Williams

FRAMEWORK FOR BLACK MALE MENTAL HEALTH

Defining healthy mental functioning in Black males has been a major challenge for the field of psychology. African American males are disparately underrepresented in measures of healthy outcomes relative to other ethnicities in the population, and often underutilize access to health services. Racial and cultural explanations are typically offered to explain these negative patterns. Yet, prevailing models in clinical psychology inadequately address conditions of healthy functioning for the African American male. The paucity of conceptual models that expound on the experiences of African males requires much needed exploration from a different paradigm.

Ubuntu (uu-Boon-too), a positive mental health framework emanating out of an African worldview, addresses this deficiency in clinical psychology. It structures the behavioral expression of African American males' personality, wellness, and competency through its focus on African-centered connectedness, competency, and consciousness (Wilson, 2012; Wilson &

Counseling African American Males, pages 61–80
Copyright © 2016 by Information Age Publishing

Williams, 2013). It has the potential to inform clinicians', counselors', and therapists' practice of proper clinical assessment and intervention methods for African American males. In this chapter, the authors will contribute to the current body of psychological and or clinical research by establishing Ubuntu's impact on mental health functioning, and they will provide a contextual framework for assessment and intervention practices with African American males.

Black psychology continues to pioneer new theories of analysis in understanding different "ways of being" in the field of psychology. Lack of clinical understanding of African and African American well-being by most psychologists impedes our understanding of positive mental health practices in the African American community. While the goal is to advance the field of psychology by testing old and new models to build upon our existing body of knowledge, it is difficult for the Western psychological community to accept new models and epistemological paradigm shifts in the examination of positive mental health for African Americans. This challenge is best explained in the definition of *Black psychology* by Kambon (1998a):

> African (Black) Psychology is defined as a system of knowledge (philosophy, definitions, concepts, models, procedures, and practice) concerning the nature of the social universe from the perspective of African cosmology. Black psychology is nothing more or less than the uncovering, articulation, operationalization, and application of the principles of the African reality structure relative to psychological phenomena. (p. 242)

The African notion of being human (or "of humanity") is unique. The peculiarity of the African diaspora in locale often lends to intradiverse ethnic groups of African ancestry. Yet symbols of African culture continue to permeate and reflect authentic African cultural reality (Wilson et al., 2008; Wilson & Williams, 2013). The challenge for Black males is to change the popular consciousness of the African male, which invokes historical, social, and cultural prejudices (Nobles, 2006; Wilson & Williams, 2013). Popular consciousness is the recognition that a people's sense of awareness is influenced by an idea or set of ideas that society utilizes to award or deny value or self-esteem (Nobles, 1985). Unlike other cultural groups residing in the United States, America's popular consciousness regarding Black men has not been favorable. For example, an analysis of the popular consciousness of the African American male in White Americans (Wilson & Williams, 2014) reveals that before Whites know the name or anything of significance about Black men, they automatically construe them as criminals, threatening, violent, unintelligent, uneducated, lazy, poor, athletic, and musical (Goff, Eberhardt, Williams, & Jackson, 2008). If African American males decide to classify themselves differently, they can only do so in response to Whites' popular consciousness.

Because these stereotypes are so strong and enmeshed in the psyche of Whites in America, they come to influence the perception and behavior of Whites on other racial groups in the United States (Feagin & Cobas, 2008). Evidence now demonstrates that individuals who were not deemed worthy of social consideration on a neurological level are not even recorded in the brain functioning of Whites in a recent neuroimaging study (Harris & Fiske, 2006). This demonstrates that members of non-White races who are viewed to the extreme by Whites are not encoding the area of the brain that recognizes someone as a social being. For African American males, the region of the brain typically recruited for social perception (the medial prefrontal cortex) is not activated in the cognitive functioning of Whites; thus, Black males are not socially considered to be part of humanity (Goff, Eberhardt, Williams, & Jackson, 2008). This phenomenon was recently played out in the killings of Oscar Grant, Trayvon Martin, Jordan Davis, and Michael Brown, unarmed African American youth who were unjustly murdered in the name of lawfulness. America's response to these events, evinced by the unconditional release of the murderers, conveys an implicit meaning as to the identity, the innate nature, and how much value Black males have in this American society (Wilson & Williams, 2015). For the African American male, this illuminates the impact that psychosocial forces have on their psychological functioning. Thus, the improvement of African American male mental health requires a different cultural analysis.

Healthy psychological functioning through the lens of African-centered psychologists appear in many works (Adeola & Perry, 1997; Akbar, 1994; Hobfoll, Schroder, Well, & Malek, 2002; Kambon, 1998b; Azibo, 1998; Myers & Haggins, 1998; Nobles, 2006). This collective body of research and experience has established that the foundation of healthy psychological functioning is a pedigree of authentic African/Black personality. The examination of mental health and well-being within a framework of Ubuntu guides the present discussion. The following sections will explore Ubuntu as a positive mental health orientation around the themes of *connectedness, competency* and *consciousness* for robust African American male functioning (Wilson, 2012).

DEFINING UBUNTU FOR AFRICAN MALES

Recent discussion of Ubuntu proposes that the essence of being human is our connectedness to others' humanity (Wilson & Williams, 2013). Recognizing one's full possibility and infinite potential to impact the world requires a sense of oneness between being human and the authentic self (Nobles, 2012, 2015). The task to theoretically integrate the mental health functioning of African American males necessitates the consideration of cognitive appraisal, redefinition, and culture ecological analysis. Herein lays the shift for defining mental health for African American males. Thus for the Black male, Ubuntu defines the need to be human based on critical examinations of their: (a) *identity*: How is African humanity in males recognized? (b) *consciousness*: How are African males aware of that humanity? (c) *epistemological reflection*: How do African males make sense of their reality? (d) *African narrative*: How do African males record, acknowledge, and define their reality? And lastly, (e) *African voice*: How do African males express their sense of being? (Nobles, 2015). When the human spirit is fully integrated holistically as previously described, being human is then characterized by our feeling of connectedness, competence and consciousness (see Table 4.1).

Ubuntu informs us that the community we operate in is vital to our well-being. This concept of connectedness maintains that the utmost quality of life is predicated on the community's principles of interrelatedness and interdependence (Wilson, 2012; Wilson & Williams, 2013). Thus, African males' mental health and humanity is made possible through the humanity of others (Wilson & Williams, 2013). When examining African humanity, the first point of entry is the notion of feeling connected. Connectedness represents the link between an individual's need to establish and participate in some semblance of social bonds. The survival of the group holds the utmost importance. It is through our human connection that we identify reciprocal healthy bonds from our relationships, which serve the mutual interests of both the giver and receiver (Hammack, 2008). This mutual connectedness links us to our mental health. Clinicians' ability to evaluate the individual's ongoing evaluation of his social process allows for effective identification of levels of competency for African American males' psychological functioning.

The second general concept concerning positive mental health is that of competency, which provides direct access to cognitive processes and efficacy within psychological functioning. The concept of competency allows for epistemological reflection within the African American male, making sense of the reality they live and revealing their reality through discourse. Meaningful contextual competence (Zittoun, 2008) allows for the actor to construct healthy notions of functioning in the mastering of their environment (Khatib & Murray, 1998). Humans should appropriately utilize the

TABLE 4.1 Ubuntu: Three Cs Model of Mental Health	
African descent	**European descent**
Connectedness	Individuation
Social competency	Competency from self
Group consciousness	Personal consciousness

materials and resources around them. This power for the African male is his defined reality—and the most important reality to define is the meaning of his own human beingness (Nobles, 2012, 2015).

The final domain, consciousness, is captured by Nobles's statement, which defines consciousness as "the process of understanding, examining, and explicating the meaning, nature and functioning of being human for African people by conducting a deep, profound, and penetrating search, study, and mastery of the process of illuminating the human spirit." In essence, it is that which emanates from our collective human consciousness and prescribes meaningful solutions and balance for our material and spiritual deprivation. The individual self is complementary to others. This psychic energy for the African male makes him aware of his impact on the humanity of others and carries with it the expression for his behavioral possibilities (Wilson & Williams, 2013). The experience of consciousness or self-actualized capacity allows for one to grasp the process towards attaining positive mental health. There is concern over the decline of this collective consciousness, initiated and maintained by the negative stereotypes of the Black male in our Western culture (Hammack, 2008). Humanity is the conscious recognition of others. When a Black man's humanity is not recognized, he must risk life until recognized and adopts a strategy of conquest or death to gain his humanity and not adopt a slave strategy to just remain alive by submitting to oppression for fear of losing his life. One who attains recognition without reciprocating becomes the "master." One who recognizes the other but is not reciprocally recognized becomes the "slave" (Nobles, 2015).

Identity: Stereotypes and Dehumanization of the Black Male

Stereotypes are social-cognitive tools created from irrational, implicit motivational biases (fear/anxiety) that are embodied in the ideological structures of political, scientific, religious, and capitalist cultural ethos they represent (Tov & Diener, 2007). Stereotypes are pernicious and pervasive, resulting in implicit biases that are mechanically triggered and prejudgmental (Tov & Diener, 2007). The implicit biases we harbor in our subconscious regarding others affects our understanding, actions, decisions, and attitudes. Based on characteristics such as age, appearances, ethnicity, nationality, and race, these biases include both sympathetic and hostile appraisals absent of the individual's knowledge or intended power (Tov & Diener, 2007). Historically, society has aggressively and negatively stereotyped Black males. Perhaps these stereotypes emanate out of irrational anxiousness or fear (xenophobia) of the Black male (Nobles, 2015). Stereotypes have strong influences on our psychological processes such as limited internalized introspection, antipathy, unjust social practices, and gross oversimplification of trends when in the presence of the triggering stimulus (Perlin, 2001; Macrae & Bodenhausen, 2000). Through the use of stereotypes, we structure polarized, dichotomous social perceptions (Perlin, 2001) that are disproportionate to the existing data. Consequently, Black males' disparate levels of participation in varied societal structures remain evident. Psychologically, stereotypes restructure and impose epistemological reflections of order on the way we see the world; they reflect our internal and mental representations of reality. For the African male, this order has dehumanized him (the "denial of full humanness to others"; Haslam, 2006, p. 252). His presence produces a perceived sense of threat to others, inflicting false expectation of harm to the identity persona of Whites, which establishes immediate stereotype activation. Stereotype activation is the speed at which we apply bias judgment and behavior to consistent and nonconsistent characterizations (Moskowitz, Gollwitzer, Wasel, & Schaal, 1999).

Stereotype activations have strong influences on internalized social practices, as they can lead to negative expectations and dehumanization. For example, activation of the stereotype for Black children demonstrates a need to increase ratings of them as more threatening, mean, and aggressive (Sagar & Schofield, 1980; Ryan, Judd, & Park, 1996), less likely to receive positive considerations (Harris & Fiske, 2006), and to provoke more unsympathetic judicial and social distance response when interacting with others (Goff, Steele, & Davies, 2008). In one of the fastest growing school districts in Texas, African American children constitute 41% of all disciplinary actions, yet they make up 16% of the total student population. In particular, school disciplinary actions reflect disparate outcomes for African American male students' experience of discretionary violations (83%) when compared to White male students (59%) and Hispanic male students (74%) in the state of Texas (Fabelo et al., 2011). This pattern of discretionary school disciplinary actions of dehumanized groups is explained by racial disparities in suspensions and even the disparate use of expulsion by school administrators. For example, when examining discretionary violations, African American students were more likely (31%) to receive a school disciplinary action versus comparable violations by White and Hispanic students who were significantly less likely to be given disciplinary action (Fabelo et al., 2011).

In contexts where individuals are dehumanized, a number of theories of racism suggest that Whites' negative regards for African American males is based on the assumption that African Americans violate White cultural values (Wilson & Williams, 2014). When applied, stereotypes and dehumanization breed injustice, fear, misunderstanding, and distance (Goff, Steele, & Davies, 2008). It has been discovered that when Whites experience stereotype threat, a psychological process of internalizing negative stereotypes may cause them to physically distance themselves from Blacks (Goff, Steele

& Davies, 2008). Goff and colleagues (2008) investigated the role of stereotype threat in the racial distancing behavior of participants of various ethnicities. The researchers hypothesized that Whites who experience the stereotype threat would more likely maintain a greater distance from Black participants. During the study, when the targeted participant was a Black man, White participants physically distanced their proximity farther away; but when the participant was White, their physical proximity was closer. Measurable differences occurred between negative subliminal images and physical distance. The researchers concluded that such distancing may expose internal evaluations of dehumanization effect on African Americans. Furthermore, a link was found between the dehumanization view of the potential Black partners and sanctioned violence (Goff et al., 2008).

Goff, Eberhardt, Williams, and Jackson (2008) examined the relationship between dehumanization and association. Their study reviewed the language used to describe criminal cases of Black convicts versus White convicts in order to highlight dehumanized references of ape-like language. The findings revealed that less non-ape-like language was used when written about White convicts than Blacks. This study found that U.S. citizens' basic cognitive processes implicitly associate Blacks with apes. Specifically, this Black-ape association alters their judgments in criminal justice contexts and it increases endorsement of violence against Blacks. Black children are not spared from these types of evaluations.

A more recent study by Goff, Jackson, Di Leone, Culotta, and DiTomasso (2014) examined whether Black boys are given an equal amount of protections of childhood afforded to other ethnicities. In this study, the researchers wanted to investigate three primary hypotheses: (a) whether participants perceive Black boys or White boys as older, (b) whether participants will associate innocent childhood characteristics more with White boys than with Black boy, and (c) whether participants' perceptions would be influenced when Black boys were implicitly associated with apes. Participants in the study were college students from a large public institution who were shown pictures and given vignettes. It was discovered that Black children were perceived to be older, less innocent, and more culpable than White children of the same age. That is, dehumanization begins early for Black children.

This is demonstrated once again how school discipline reports reveal how White students were three times less likely (9.9%) to be sent home for suspension for initial infractions than African American students (26.2%). Blacks receive fewer (71.5%) in-school suspensions because they are receiving more out of school suspensions when compared to first time discretionary dispositions for White (86.5%) and Hispanic (79.1%) students. This line of research mostly emphasizes interpersonal perceptions and potential interactions between Black males and others. For the African male to be singled out, he is exposed to intense and sadistic persecution; he is psychologically castrated, emasculated, and feminized; and he is constantly told that he is devalued and marginal (Wilson, 1990).

The use of stereotypes signify distinction as well as a curse. They reward the user with speed in perception, inference, and decision-making (stereotype activation) of the Black male (Goff et al., 2014; Goff et al., 2008). Thus, African American males exist in constant conflict with the inaccurate, yet popular images upheld in American society.

Conscious Meaning of Being Well: "Umuntu Ngumuntu Ngabantu"

Nobles (2009) stated, "When the human spirit is well whole and healthy, the human being is characterized by confidence, competence and a sense of full possibility and unlimited potentiality."

According to Ubuntu, an inclusive understanding of well-being involves placing the highest value of life on our interpersonal relationships between other humans (Fernando, 2010; Wilson & Williams, 2013). Ubuntu informs us that well-being is the reciprocal relation of one's existence to others. Being human is determined by maintaining quality, interdependent relationships—"I am because you are" (African philosophy of being). Therefore, wellness for African American males is the self-appraisal of image reflective behaviors, values, norms, failures, and successes (Wilson & Williams, 2013; Wilson, 2012). Ogundiran (2009) states,

> Ubuntu asks us to work towards equity, peace, and harmony as the foundation of building [a healthy person] for each and every one of us. Ubuntu emphasizes partnership, collaboration, and understanding. Ubuntu recognizes the humanity of all, and charges us to rediscover who we are, to rediscover our own human qualities through our interactions with peoples who are different from us. (p. 2)

Wellness of Ubuntu is established by oneness in spirit, and the spirit's quest for harmony with others (Ogundiran, 2009). Since well-being is a subjective evaluation of how the individual connects socially, culturally, and in the historical contexts of his identity, when any of these are violated, our Ubuntu is destroyed; the community and our spiritual essence weakens. In the practice of Ubuntu, another subjective quality is the fulfilling of pure psychological functioning of competence and autonomy (Ryan & Deci, 2000). We should explore and exchange our knowledge, culture, and build one community (Ogundiran, 2009). The cultural essence within Ubuntu suggests that the value of harmonious relationships are meaningful manifestations of wellness (Wilson, 2012).

This Ubuntu, when recognized, can be demonstrated in young Black males. For instance, Jagers, Sydnor, Mouttapa, and Flay (2007) discovered that communal values helped decrease violent behavior in boys. When engaged in affirmative interactions with family, social structures within community, and peer groups, boys were more likely to demonstrate prosocial behaviors. It was suggested that social commitments or contracts were great equalizers for demonstrating being human for boys more than for girls (Jagers et al., 2007). It is essential that the African American male is able to be confident in his capability to negotiate potentially effective and harmonious circumstances. This has implications for direct intervention techniques. Incorporating Ubuntu of wellness in therapeutic settings aimed at African American males should focus on what connections are established, the impact of communal ways of functioning, and authentic development of Black personality. For example, Black personality development should be examined within the context of geographic location—urban or rural life experiences—as well as White environment versus Black environment, which will yield important correlates of the expressions of communalism and other cultural orientations among African American males. The next section examines such contexts and their effect on mental health (connectedness, competency, and consciousness) via the narratives of Black male college students over a 25-plus year period (Kambon, 2014a).

African Narrative

Examining the narratives of African American males based on the varied relationships that contribute to the identification of positive mental health within the context of Black personality is warranted. Kambon examined the narratives of Black male college students at a historically Black university over a 25-plus year period. The narratives were collected from a highly diverse group of young adult Africans in North America and from the Caribbean Islands, particularly through undergraduate courses in African/Black psychology. They had only recently left home, usually for the first time, and were primarily sophomores, juniors, and seniors between 18 and 25 years of age. The bulk of these students grew up between the mid-1960s and mid-1980s. Within that context, they represented the products of contemporary African child-rearing throughout this geographical region of the African diaspora. As indicated, these youngsters came from very diverse socioeconomic backgrounds, ranging from low to relatively high SES levels, with many, perhaps a little over one third, representing the first in their families to attend college.

For about the last 25 years of that period, the students developed original essays representing "autobiographical sketches" (Harley & Reese, 1999;

Jackson, 2004) where they were required to apply the African-centered knowledge base they had acquired in the course to their life experiences. Specifically, they were asked to try to recognize instances where the African worldview (AWV), the European worldview (EWV), or some aspects of both were occurring in their lives from the earliest most significant experience (such as personal events, family, school or neighborhood events, etc.) they could recall up to the present. (pp. 1–2)

This work was examined through a triadic analysis of mental health, which incorporates (a) an African cultural grand narrative analysis (memory and imagination; Nobles, 2015), (b) Black personality theory (Kambon & Bowen-Reid, 2010), and (c) the Ubuntu model of mental health (Wilson & Williams, 2013). Utilizing an African epistemic reflection (Nobles, 2015), major issues and themes were identified from the narratives of African American male college students' biographical sketches of Black personality[1] development (Kambon, 2014a).

Recent analysis (Kambon, 2014a) revealed that Black male college students' experiences centered on family, generational child-rearing practices, and strong peer conformity/pressures for gender specific behaviors (connectedness). The narratives also revealed that the participants' cultural appreciations and apperceptions (Nobles, 2015) commonly focus on the stability of family, intense mother-son interaction, and unsafe communities (connectedness). Throughout the process of Black personality development, Blacks males are required to make sense of events and deep intrinsic beliefs (Nobles, 2015) in coping with absent fathers and positive and negative interactions with their mothers' male friends (competence). The African descriptive and explanative discourse of Black personality requires the capacity to use deception of private behaviors, maneuver racially implicated tension related to dating and sexual activity, and grapple with the status determined by socioeconomic factors (Kambon, 2014a; consciousness).

Black personality also takes into account the African intellectual mindset (Nobles, 2015), providing guidance and structure to issues and themes related to sports over academics (competence), both subtle and overt negative racially toned interactions of disrespect and insensitivity throughout early and later school years with teachers and athletic coaches (connectedness), and using sports as a means of establishing one's sense of self and social importance (consciousness; Kambon, 2014a). This African knowing framework (Nobles, 2015) of Black personality development (Kambon & Bowen-Reid, 2010) demonstrates factors needed for an Ubuntu state of well-being. As Kambon (2014b) states:

> As can be gleaned from these summary contrasts of experiences, it seems clear that several major deficits and psycho-emotional stresses occurred in the lives of many of these young people that echoes the critical need for culturally af-

firmative instruction and role modeling during their early developmental and
school experiences, especially in the roles of parents, guardians and teachers, in order to neutralize some of the intrinsic invisible societal-institutional
forces of Eurocentrism and racism, which can and often attack the sense of
self, self-image, and self-confidence of those Black children so exposed. (p. 6)

How African American males deal with the sociocultural circumstances
that have been described is a critical aspect of healthy mental development.
The model of the Ubuntu state of well-being suggests that African Americans demonstrate distress in somatic fashion in dealing with socially stressful environmental conditions (Jenkins, Kleinman, & Good, 1991). In fact,
African American adults and adolescents who are depressed tend to exhibit
greater somatic complaints than White counterparts (Choi, Meininger, &
Roberts, 2006; Iwata, Turner, & Lloyd, 2002). In addition, African Americans' psycho-behavior modality is to discourage expressing weakness such as
sadness. Moreover, research studies have suggested that African Americans
tend to reject such internal feelings and demonstrate more external expressions of irritability and anger (Baker, 2001; Manning & Hussong, 2006). In
contrast, some scholars suggest that African American adolescents do display
evidence of depressive symptoms (Breland-Noble, Burriss, & Poole, 2010).

A recent study concluded that African American adolescents suffer from
more severe depressive symptoms than European Americans (Jacobs et
al., 2008). However, while African American adolescents did demonstrate
more *observed* depressive symptoms, they reported fewer internal symptoms
including pessimistic cognitive distortions of self, humanity, global expectations, and stable attributions for positive events when compared to European American youth (Jacobs et al., 2008). The study's erroneous conclusion
reveals a lack of cultural understanding due to bias by evaluators assessing
members of a different cultural background. Since clinical assessments are
inevitably conducted through the cultural viewpoint of the assessor, mental
health practitioners require greater cultural awareness in the evaluation of
behaviors of African American youth in a clinical setting (Stein et al., 2010).

A less-biased study by Breland-Noble et al. (2010) explored the assessment of depression in outpatient treatment of African American adolescents, and it uncovered multiple themes. The first theme, adolescent
pluralism, reveals a confused consciousness in adolescents dealing with depression (Breland-Noble et al., (2010). According to the researchers, Black
youth cycle from being alone and feeling isolated, to wanting attention from
peers and significant others, to feeling overwhelmed by not knowing how
to handle such attention when provided. A second theme that emerged
focused on the primary triggers for depression, specifically romantic relationship problems, academic problems, and coping with bereavement and
stress (Breland-Noble et al., 2010). The third theme centered on youths'
unfavorable impressions of mental health treatment. African American

youth described clinicians as lacking in competence due to clinicians' mis-comprehension of their narrative, making futile efforts to establish a genu-ine connection with them, and challenging their sense of consciousness by wanting to prescribe medications instead of explaining why and how medication therapy would be of benefit to the client (Breland-Noble et al., 2010). In a fourth theme—trust and frustration—youth expressed how they struggled with distrust of others and clinicians whom they believed failed to help or in some cases exacerbated their depressive symptoms. Lastly, youth expressed the importance of confidentiality and having "drop in" sessions, meaning when students are confronted with issues that need addressing in the present moment they wish to speak to their counselor or therapist as soon as possible while attending school instead of waiting for a later date for scheduling. Students would be inconspicuously dealt with when attend-ing sessions for depression.

When examining the responses of the youth from the Ubuntu model perspective, clear evidence exists relating to their need for connectedness. Their ability to express the need for humanity, warmth, tolerance, and un-derstanding from others during and after treatment demonstrates a desire for connectedness. Youth's cognitive appraisal of treatment experiences tended to challenge the competency of the treatment provider. Youth did not feel respected, nor did they sense a level of commitment from the pro-vider thus challenging the consumers' social competency. Lastly, within the Ubuntu model, youth expressed feeling a lack of appreciation, compassion, and love. Sometimes these informal impromptu counseling sessions allow for African American students to feel a more optimistic therapeutic pro-cess and enhances their conscious development as young African American youth. Such strategies reflect conscious attempts at engaging more effective models for African American males' mental health.

One innovative strategy for engaging youth who might be ambivalent about seeking treatment is "mind modeling." Mind modeling allows Af-rican American youth to identify African and African American men and women of excellence who have publicly acknowledged bouts with depres-sion and successful treatment by comparing and contrasting celebrity pre-clinical and postclinical behavioral treatment for issues like depression. The next section examines this strategy further as it explores ways to effec-tively impact African American male mental health.

Epistemological Reflection of African American Male Mental Health

In developing African American male mental health functioning, healthy consciousness plays an important role. Synthesis of awareness of deep cultural structures and concrete conditions establishes the foundation for analyzing, interpreting, and transforming both the individual and collective psychocognitive reality (Nobles & Goddard, 1992; Wilson, Moore, & Bland-Munzy, 2008). The process to achieve this objective of African values and consciousness should include the recognition of African values instilled within African American male college students—recognition of their Afri-sense or African self-consciousness (Kambon, 1992, 2014b).

This Ubuntu defined mental health dimension for the Black male recognizes the need to be human, based on critical examinations of identity: (a) how African humanity in males is recognized, (b) how the African male becomes aware of his humanity, and (c) epistemological reflections of how African males make sense of their reality. This African socialization process instills the affinity to be culturally aware of one's social competence (see Table 4.2).

This type of African-centered critical analysis of Black male mental health is important to recognize how culturally self-affirming activities develop psychosocial competency. Fu-Kiau (2003) identifies social competency as an individual's appraisal of his or her capacity to purposively and positively impact others. Psychosocial competency requires formal and informal training experiences developing one's *sense of excellence* and *sense of appropriateness*. How does this translate to practical application for the African American male college student? This requires the understanding of African and American social practices, which set the tone for making proper decisions. For African American males, the need to make appropriate decisions emanates from culturally consistent strategies. Culturally consistent problem solving locates strategies or solutions that lead to the elimination or opposition to any situation that prevents the positive development of self, family and community. Change occurs in a natural, evolutionary cycle from one generation to the next. Another technique, mentioned previously, is that of mind modeling, or

TABLE 4.2 Culture and Mental Health		African Mental Health	European Mental Health
African American Core Value			
Humanness	Warmth, Tolerance, Understanding, Peace, Humanity	Connectedness	Individuation
Caring	Empathy, Sympathy, Helpfulness, Charity, Friendliness, Sharing, Unconditional giving, Re-distribution, Open-handedness	Connectedness	Individuation
Respect	Commitment, dignity, Obedience, Order	Social Competency	Self Competency
Compassion	Love, Cohesion, Informality, forgiveness, Spontaneity	Social Competency	Personal Conciousness

instilling African-centered personality in African American males. The identification of successful African and African American males requires one to incorporate how these great men think and respond in situations that were common to them. For instance, they would incorporate how Marcus Garvey would respond to today's drug, economic, or education problem in the African American community. This allows for youth to evaluate personal situations and bring into account famous great African American men of excellence to demonstrate how young men could infuse the greatness of African people's thoughts, ideas and solving of problems developing competency.

UBUNTU IN THE ASSESSMENT PROCESS

Ubuntu as a model of mental health locates healthy functioning around three essential themes: connectedness, competency, and consciousness (Wilson, 2012). The use of this African philosophical model of wellness may assist in the assessment of mental health for African American males and how they express well-being. A recent report conducted by the California Reducing Disparities Project (CRDP) revealed multilayered issues associated with mental illness in the Black population (Woods, King, Hanna, & Murray, 2012). Coded themes reflected 24% of the subjects' content responses related to a lack of connectedness, 38% reflected challenged competency, and 39% demonstrated content associated with consciousness (Wilson, 2012). This suggests that well-being should be evaluated around these contexts. Themes identified were dehumanizing encounters: "lack of respect," "overt and covert racism," and "being ignored and microaggression by mental health professionals." This reflected their level of consciousness in relation to access to mental health care. Another theme, inadequate or innappropriate treatment, highlights issues of competency. Lastly, levels of connectedness were identified as expressed here by one research participant, who said,

> I get there are three kinds of connections that are ... important. ... you have to have at least one ... to be mentally healthy ... first connection is with family. ... Then you have a community connection and you have spiritual connection. And I think that if a person has any of the three they can be okay. (Woods et al., 2012, p. 162)

AFRICAN VOICE: IMPLICATIONS
FOR THERAPISTS/COUNSELORS

For African men in America, there exist at least two significant psychological experiential sociocultural realities: Africentric and Eurocentric socio-cultural space. This is the bicultural physiological space where Black personality develops and unfolds (Kambon & Bowen-Reid, 2010; Kambon, 1992). Healthy Black personality reflects a sense of connectedness within his environment (Wilson & Williams, 2014; Wilson & Williams, 2013; Wilson et al., 2008). According to the African/Black psychology paradigm (Kambon, 1992), *normal-healthy* Black personality development occurs from collectivist characteristics such as our psychological need to relate to others, collectivistic and kinship orientation, and proximity to family; while individualistic characteristics include independence, antagonism, individuation, and desire-driven motives. Relating to other Blacks or engaging in Africentric social institutions is essential for normal-healthy functioning.

The culturecology model developed by Nobles, Goddard, and Gilbert (2009) helps us organize the location of Black personality development. Allocated into four sections, the vertical axis of the model represents our personhood, how individuals see their innate existence: vertical individualism (VI) versus vertical collectivism (VC; Wilson & Williams, 2014). The horizontal axis consists of the nature of communication of the prevailing culturally driven ethos, episteme, ontology, and cosmology: horizontal individualistic (HI) culture versus horizontal collectivist (HC) culture (Wilson & Williams, 2014; see Figure 4.1). Assessment of how Black males

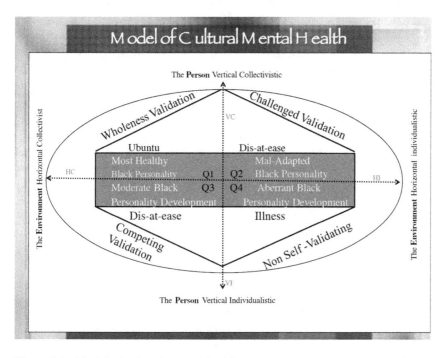

Figure 4.1   Model of cultural mental health.

operate examined within this culturecology model (Nobles et al., 2009) of Ubuntu helps us to locate their Black personality functioning. Therefore, healthy Black personality development occurs when operating in Quadrant 1 where their Ubuntu yields wholeness in validation of the individual within his community. When the individual operates within non-self-validation experience, there will be incongruence between his internal personhood and community, feeling less connected, less competent, and less consciousness. This results in an aberrant personality development and abnormal, unhealthy functioning. This Ubuntu model of analysis may yield greater understanding of mental health functioning for all Black males.

This Ubuntu defined mental health recognizes the humanity of the Black male. Since culture plays a vital role in fashioning our way of thinking, assessment and interventions must be culturally based and part of the contemporary socialization process, that is, by understanding key authentic appropriate and aberrant cultural expressions of the African American male. Those who wish to be professionally committed to working with African American male college students must understand the complexities for developing healthy consciousness. In exploring consciousness, the African male becomes aware of his developing a healthy Black personality. If we are going to work toward developing a Black personality, the purpose of our intervention should be to build an African model of mental health through authentic centering of an African grand narrative. When accurately defined, the Black male ways of knowing, or his epistemological reflection, allows for him to make sense of his reality. The need to understand clearly our responsibility to diagnose and treat the African American male's mental health status requires counselors to operate from the correct cultural orientation. With such recognition, African American males will be able to record, acknowledge, and define their reality through an African narrative. The African American male can only be as healthy as the African community and, ultimately, the African race. Therefore, a culturally centered paradigm increases understanding of the psychological health and social development of African American males. Lastly, African voice allows for the African American male to express his sense of being. The shaping of African grand narratives requires the redirection of African consciousness to benefit in advancing the interest and image of all African and African American people.

SUMMARY

The Afrocentric worldview is a circular view in which all events are intertwined. Cooperation, collective responsibility, and interdependence lead to people working together for a common cause. When applying such culturally consistent assessment principles and practices to African American clients, successful interventions have been demonstrated. To show the successes of effective therapeutic interventions and approaches, there is a need for more research on the factors of connectedness, competency, and consciousness in African American clients, particularly Black males.

Utilization of an African-centered model such as Ubuntu when examining the mental health status of African American male college students is long overdue. Therapists and counselors need to evaluate African American male college students' values, knowledge, and experiences they bring to the classroom. Accordingly, counselors and therapists also need to know about the client's level of involvement in the community. Ultimately, the clinician must understand how to best support African American male students in consistently achieving educational excellence in spite of oppressive educational environments. The Ubuntu model of psychological functioning fosters within African American male college students an understanding and appreciation of their collective human spirit built on connectedness, competency, and consciousness, which are the markers for their greatness.

NOTE

1. Healthy Black personality development as defined by Kambon is consistent with Wilson's Ubuntu model of positive mental health functioning and thus will be used interchangeably within this section of examining the narratives of Black male college students.

REFERENCES

Adeola, F. O., & Perry, J. A. (1997). Global study: Smooth or bumpy ride: Global study is to diversity as internship is to job experience. *The Black Collegian Online, 10*. Retrieved from http://www.black-collegian.com/issues/1997-10/bumpy.shtml

Akbar, N. (1994). *Light from ancient Africa*. Tallahassee, FL: Mind Productions.

Azibo, D. A. (1998). The distinction between African personality personologists and other African personality scholars: Implication and an entreatment for reconceptualization of racial identity issues. In R. Jones (Ed.), *African American identity development*, (pp. 207–215). Hampton, VA: Cobb and Henry.

Baker, F. M. (2001). Diagnosing depression in African Americans. *Community Mental Health Journal, 37*(1), 31–38.

Breland-Noble, A. M., Burriss, A., & Poole, H. K. (2010). Engaging depressed African American adolescents in treatment: Lessons from the AAKOMA project. *Journal of Clinical Psychology, 66*(8), 868–879.

Choi, H., Meininger, J. C., & Roberts, R. E. (2006). Ethnic differences in adolescents' mental distress, social stress, and resources. *Adolescence, 41*(162), 263–283.

Fabelo, T., Thompson, M. D., Plotkin, M., Carmichael, D., Marchbanks, M. P., III, & Booth, E. A. (2011). *Breaking schools' rules: A statewide study of how school discipline relates to students' success and juvenile justice involvement.* New York, NY: Council of State Governments Justice Center.

Feagin, J. R., & Cobas, J. A. (2008). Latinos/as and white racial frame: The procrustean bed of assimilation. *Sociological Inquiry, 78*(1), 39–53.

Fernando, S. (2010). Mental health, race, and culture. New York, NY: Palgrave MacMillan.

Fu-Kiau, K. K. B. (2003). *Self-healing power and therapy: Old teachings from Africa.* Baltimore, MD: Black Classic Press.

Goff, P. A., Eberhardt, J. L., Williams, M. J., & Jackson, M. C. (2008). Not yet human: Implicit knowledge, historical dehumanization, and contemporary consequences. *Journal of Personality and Social Psychology, 94*, 292–306. doi:10.1037/0022-3514.94.2.292

Goff, P. A., Jackson, M. C., Di Leone, B. A. L., Culotta, C. M., & DiTomasso, N. A. (2014). The essence of innocence: Consequences of dehumanizing Black children. *Journal of Personality and Social Psychology, 106*(4), 526–545.

Goff, P. A., Steele, C. M., & Davies, P. G. (2008). The space between us: Stereotype threat and distance in interracial contexts. *Journal of Personality and Social Psychology, 94*(1), 91.

Hammack, P. L. (2008). Narrative and the cultural psychology of identity. *Personality and Social Psychology Review, 12*, 222–247.

Harris, L. T., & Fiske, S. T. (2006). Dehumanizing the lowest of the low neuroimaging responses to extreme out-groups. *Psychological Science, 17*(10), 847–853.

Haslam, N. (2006). Dehumanization: An integrative review. *Personality and Social Psychology Review, 10*, 252–264.

Hobfoll, S. E., Schröder, K. E. E., Well, M., & Malek, M. (2002). Communal versus individualistic construction of sense of mastery in facing life changes. *Journal of Social and Clinical Psychology, 21*(4), 362–399.

Iwata, N., Turner, R. J., & Lloyd, D. A. (2002). Race/ethnicity and depressive symptoms in community–dwelling young adults: A differential item functioning analysis. *Psychiatry Research, 110*(3), 281–289.

Jacobs, R. H., Klein, J. B., Reinecke, M. A., Silva, S. G., Tonev, S., Breland-Noble, A.... March, J. S. (2008). Ethnic differences in attributions and treatment expectancies for adolescent depression. *International Journal of Cognitive Therapy, 1*(2), 163.

Jagers, R. J., Sydnor, K., Mouttapa, M., & Flay, B. R. (2007). Protective factors associated with preadolescent violence: Preliminary work on a cultural model. *American Journal of Community Psychology, 40*(1/2), 138–145.

Jenkins, J. H., Kleinman, A., & Good, B. J. (1991). Cross-cultural aspects of depression. In J. Becker & A. Kleinman (Eds.), *Advances in affective disorders: Theory and research,* (Vol. 1) *psychosocial aspects,* (pp. 67–99). London, England: Erlbaum.

Kambon, K. K. (2014a). *Issues and themes in Black child development from the autobiographical sketches of African American college students: An Africentric analysis.* Unpublished manuscript.

Kambon, K. K. (2014b). *Toward the construction of a model of African self-consciousness development in Black children.* Unpublished manuscript.

Kambon, K. K. (1992). *The African personality in America: An African-centered framework.* Tallahassee, FL: Nubian Nations.

Kambon, K. K. (1998a). An African-centered paradigm for understanding the mental health of Africans in America. In R. Jones (Ed.), *African American mental health: Theory, research and intervention,* (pp. 33–50). Hampton, VA: Cobb and Henry.

Kambon, K. K. (1998b). *African/Black psychology in the America context: An African-centered approach.* Tallahassee, FL: Nubian Nations.

Kambon, K. K., & Bowen-Reid, T. (2010). Theories of African American personality: Classification, basic constructs and empirical predictions/assessment. *The Journal of Pan African Studies, 3*(8), 83–108.

Khatib, S. M., & Murray, C. B. (1998). Competency and legitimacy as organizing dimensions of the Black self-concept. *African American Mental Health,* 187.

Macrae, C. N., & Bodenhausen, G. V. (2000). Social cognition: Thinking categorically about others. *Annual Review of Psychology* (51), 93–120. doi:10.1146/annurev.psych.51.1.93

Manning, J. S., & Hussong, A. M. (2006, March). Ethnic differences in adolescent depressive symptomatology. Poster session presented at the biennial meeting of the *Society for Research on Adolescence.* San Francisco, CA.

Moskowitz, G. B., Gollwitzer, P. M., Wasel, W., & Schaal, B. (1999). Preconscious control of stereotype activation through chronic egalitarian goals. *Journal of Personality and Social Psychology, 77*(1), 167–184.

Myers, L. J., & Haggins, K. L. (1998). Optimal theory and identity development: Beyond the cross model. In R. Jones (Ed.), *African American identity development,* (pp. 255–274). Hampton, VA: Cobb and Henry.

Nobles, W. W. (1985). *Africanity and the Black family.* Oakland, CA: Black Family Institute.

Nobles, W. W. (2006). *Seeking the sakhu: Foundational writings for an African psychology.* Chicago, IL: Third World Press.

Nobles, W. W. (2009). *The African sense of being: Rescuing and reclaiming humanity for us all,* Unpublished manuscript.

Nobles, W. W. (2012). "Culturecology" Model©. In V. D. Woods, N. J. King, S. M. Hanna, & C. Murray (Eds.) *"We ain't crazy! Just coping with a crazy system": Pathways into the Black population for eliminating mental health disparities* (pp. 221–224). San Bernardino, CA: African American Health Institute.

Nobles, W. W. (2015). *The island of memes: Haiti's unfinished revolution.* Baltimore, MD: Black Classic Press.

Nobles, W. W., Goddard L. L., & Gilbert, D. G. (2009). Culturecology, women, and African-centered HIV prevention. *Journal of Black Psychology, 35*(2), 228–246.

Ogundiran, A. (2009, February 8) *Ubuntu: An African philosophical reflection on "one community, one humanity."* Invited address given at the 2009 Unity Day of the city of Newton, NC.

Perlin, M. L. (2001). *The hidden prejudice: Mental disability on trial.* Washington, DC: American Psychological Association.

Ryan, C. S., Judd, C. M., & Park, B. (1996). The effect of stereotypes on judgments of individuals: The moderating role of perceived group variability. *Journal of Experimental Social Psychology, 32,* 71–103.

Ryan, R. M., & Deci, E. L. (2000). Self-determination theory and the facilitation of intrinsic motivation, social development and well-being. *American Psychologist, 55,* 68–78.

Sagar, H. A., & Schofield, J. W. (1980). Racial and behavioral cues in Black and White children's perceptions of ambiguously aggressive acts. *Journal of Personality and Social Psychology, 39*(4), 590.

Stein, G. L., Curry, J. F., Hersh, J., Breland-Noble, A., March, J., Silva, S. G. . . . Jacobs, R. (2010). Ethnic differences among adolescents beginning treatment for depression. *Cultural Diversity and Ethnic Minority Psychology, 16*(2), 152.

Tov, W., & Diener, E. (2007). Culture and subjective well-being. In S. Kitayama & D. Cohen (Eds.), *Handbook of cultural psychology* (pp. 691–713). New York, NY: Guilford Press.

Wilson, A. (1990). *Black on Black violence: The psychodynamics of Black self annihilation in service of White domination.* New York, NY: Afrikan World Infosystems.

Wilson, D. (2012). Competency, connectedness, and consciousness. In V. D. Woods, N. J. King, S. M. Hanna, & C. Murray (Eds.) *"We ain't crazy! Just coping with a crazy system": Pathways into the Black population for eliminating mental health disparities,* (pp. 159–161). San Bernardino, CA: African American Health Institute.

Wilson, D., Boyd, E., & Moore, P. (2008). Psychological disorder in juvenile offenders and the impact of placement. *Journal of Knowledge and Best Practices in Juvenile Justice and Psychology, 2*(1).

Wilson, D., & Williams, V. (2013) Ubuntu: A model of positive mental health for African Americans. *Psychology Journal, 10*(2), 80–100.

Wilson, D., & Williams, V. (2014) Mental illness defined: Sociological perspectives. In A. Scull (Ed.), *Cultural sociology of mental illness: An A-to-Z guide* (pp. 518–521). Thousand Oaks, CA: Sage.

Wilson, D. J., Moore, P. A., & Bland-Munzy, M. (2008). The impact of a culturally enriched extracurricular program on academic and social performance for African American adolescent male students. *Journal of the Alliance of Black School Educators, 7*(1), 58–74.

Wilson, D. J., Moore, P. A., Boyd, E. L., Easley, J., & Russell, A. (2008). The identification of cultural factors that impact well-being among African American college students. *Psychology Journal, 5*(2).

Woods, V. D., King, N. J., Hanna, S. M., & Murray, C. (2012). *"We ain't crazy! Just coping with a crazy system": Pathways into the Black population for eliminating mental health disparities.* San Bernardino, CA: African American Health Institute.

Zittoun, T. (2008). Speaking in tongues: Commentary on Cubero, de la Mata and Cubero. *Culture & Psychology, 14,* 431–441.

CHAPTER 5

HUMANISTIC THEORIES AND AFRICAN AMERICAN MALES IN COUNSELING

Yolanda Hamilton

One shift in wanting to assist African American males in counseling is the notion of multicultural counseling in which all counselors must take Council for Accreditation of Counseling and Related Educational Programs (CACREP) courses. In these courses, counselors are required to take a genuine look at themselves, recognize their prejudices and stereotypes, and begin to help the African American by first abandoning negative labels. CACREP standards call for counselors to expand their knowledge of their different ethnicities and call for introspection of any biases one may hold against persons from different backgrounds.

Protecting one's community and environment and creating culture rests on the responsibility of the Black male. As the assumed leader of his household and community, he has been robbed of resources to do so, and counselors may have to acknowledge and/or keep in their consciousness the impact of current discriminations that prevent him from advancing his community. Put another way, any attempt to counsel Black men cannot be

Counseling African American Males, pages 81–96
Copyright © 2016 by Information Age Publishing

successful unless the counselor (more particularly White counselor) is willing to address the Black male psychogenic history and his worldview of the emotional and mental toll of living with/under past and present discriminatory conditions.

How does one begin to offer empathy and concern toward a race of Black men who have been denigrated for centuries and their families pathologized by society? How can we find within ourselves a bright light to offer them when we believe they have always caused their light to dim? In order for a societal amendment, a cathartic societal shift would have to take place. Even then, would it mean America is ready to extinguish its racist ideologies and its crippling stereotypical mental models that have soaked into the fabric of the United States?

The call to counseling of African American males suggests previous models have not worked for African American male populations. The polarities of Caucasian theories and models versus the worldview of African American theories and models as they pertain to mental health have yet to intersect. Some of the existing gaps and challenges are still the dominant culture thinking applied to African American individuals and communities without understanding their complicities in African Americans' plight. Stereotypes from the dominant culture can interfere with effective treatment of these unique and different populations; henceforth, counselors must address their unconscious, perhaps even their conscious "fears" of counseling African American males. This chapter will offer a pliable look at the lack of Black men in treatment and offer considerations for this population beyond the obvious such as, Black men being vilified by society and not wanting to speak with White counselors for fear of being further depreciated. To that end, the chapter will focus on inferring the sensitivities of African American males due to the trauma of losing their fathers from childhood to adulthood. I will speak on the intimacy of Black men and creating a safe space for them to be sensitive. Another area is the existence of Black men in White society. That is, how do they begin to reach their full potential within the limiting constructs made for them? Lastly, I will examine the African American matriarch and why she has to lead the community when 40% of African American men are incarcerated, another portion are unable to resume the leadership role after being incarcerated, and other stumbling blocks prevent African American male leadership in their communities.

In summation, the call for counseling African American males requires a shift in our thinking. It requires of us to be vulnerable and trusting toward a population once deemed untrustworthy. It requires self-reflection, an empathetic view of the racial identity models, and a precise use of them as well. There is a real opportunity to practice being inclusive of all, regardless of ethnicity, who may need mental health help. And it provides clinicians a chance at personal growth.

THE LOSS OF THEIR FATHERS

This author is in defense of three Black boys, currently being raised father-less, who, when they are older and enter adult relationships, will be referred to as "no good." And this author is in defense of the African American household being predominantly matriarchal because women have to keep our families together with the African American male incarceration rate at least 40% (West & Sabol, 2009). In defense of the first, I have observed two mother-to-son relationships in their natural environment. One mother is raising a 7-year-old, and the other mother is raising two 10-year-old Black boys. I have been in their private space for extended periods of time and observed the boys interact with their mother, and it is not their fault that they will be "no good." Most immediately, the boys will mirror the primary person in their lives (even if they see their fathers "once and a while"). In other words, the boys will be more socialized toward a feminine socializa-tion than a male socialization. Some male traits will be at risk, and these are critical moments for young boys searching for their male identity. This no-tion is distinct from the old adage of mothers "loving their sons and raising their daughters." I am referring to the (male) intimacies that escape a large portion of Black men, which then renders them inept in adult relationships with women, who will eventually leave the relationship feeling like that man is "no good." Let's define no good.

The social learning theory of Bandura (Benton & Bandura, 1953) suggests behavior is acquired. He believed that people acquire behaviors through the observation of others and then imitate what they have observed. Ban-dura has demonstrated this theory in the Booboo-the-doll experiment and through several studies involving television commercials and videos con-taining violent scenes that have supported this theory on modeling (Ban-dura, 1977). According to this theory, boys will most likely model after their mothers. So why does the maturity for intimacy escape them? Universally, we have all undergone a nature versus nurture competition. The internal (genetics) versus the external (environment) and which will outweigh the other? Which set of emotions will the boys take into adulthood and which set of "emotions" will they leave behind? The boys to men will still have a need to overcompensate for the loss of their part-time father figure, and give into displaced anger toward their mothers because the fathers are not around, and a love hate dependency is fostered between mother and son. Perhaps in this development, boys become intimately stunted.

There is a fine line between getting basic needs met and being depen-dent on someone to do things for you. For example, two of the 10-year-old boys that stayed with me for a while had a morning routine of getting up to wash their face and brush their teeth. However, when each was done brush-ing their teeth, they would call to the caregiver to wash their faces. In this scenario, had the father been present, the father would have interrupted that infantile dependency by telling the boys, "Get in there and wash your face and don't come out until it's clean." This answers in-part is why part-time dads are not enough. The father figure is needed to intervene on that dependency to help grow an independent, "good" man. However, the female caregiver easily gets up and washes their faces, unknowingly furthering female dependency within the boys and unconsciously furthering her own need to be needed rather being able to create interdependency, a more healthy relationship for all parties involved.

The caregiver is between rushing to provide for the boys, rushing to send them to bed, rushing to get them off to school, while she rushes off to work and the father only gets to be concerned with getting himself off to work, if he works. Fathers are absent from the aforementioned scenario; they are absent from the emotional exchange of helping the female in the morning, from creating in their sons' heads an image of a positive male-to-female relationship, and from the responsibility of helping to create an intimate male image because fathers are absent from raising their sons to be men. The lack thereof of modeling such behaviors from fathers to sons produces voids, and this is what men will carry into their adult relationships.

The female caregiver taking on all roles by herself is unable to decipher and teach certain things because (a) she has become conditioned to the role of giving and doing for the boys and building a dependency of "no good," and (b) the mother is challenged in shaping within her son how to be a man. Vygotsky (1978) is best known for his work called zone of proximal development (ZPD). Children in this stage need temporary supporters in completing tasks like in the previous scenario of the mother washing the 10-year-old boys' faces. The crux of the concept is helping the child to do it until they can do it on their own; Vygotsky calls this scaffolding. Scaffolding is a support mechanism provided by a more competent individual that helps a learner (10-year-old boy) successfully perform a task within the zone of proximal development. The next two layers are level of potential development-tasks that children can perform with assistance, and actual development-tasks children can perform on their own. These fathers are unaware of how much they are needed.

The fine line between getting basic needs met and being dependent on someone to do for you can be summed up into two questions: when and from whom will the child learn to perform age-appropriate tasks? This fine line of dependency or not requires the relationship of both parents in rearing a more independent boy to man. However, something else is resoundingly clear through my observation of the relationship between sons and their less-than-part-time fathers; their fathers were not around to raise "good" sons. The three boys' fathers unconsciously, as studies have shown, mirrored their own broken relationship pattern between their fathers and themselves. This is a cyclical epidemic that less-than-part-time and/or absentee fathers are unable to offer emotional support to their Black sons that would make them intimately capable in relationships, because their fathers' fathers have felt the effects of those childhood father-to-son relationship disturbances. Consequently, the Black man needs to be affirmed and to what degree do we fully embrace the professional organizations' creed on multidiversity counseling to include Black men (Bieschke, Perez, & DeBord, 2007, p. 206).

INTIMACY OF BLACK MEN

Among many labels, Black men have been depicted as insensitive and demonized; some of this has been internalized by them, forming within them a disassociation from self. Men have been robbed of a platform to indulge in intimacies with their female partner; thus, this erodes any possibilities of boys growing into manhood with a sensitive "side." It has been said many times, "It takes a man to raise a man"; let's define *man*. Scientifically, it is the male sperm that determines the sex of the zygote by adding a (Y) chromosome to the females (X) chromosome. Communally, he is the head of his household; societally, his is the force that helps to propel evolution. The Black man's first intimate relationship is with a female and has been bred in a sense of warmth, attention, sensitivity etc., from his caregiver (providing normal development has occurred). Thus, he grows up in a society that has been constructed for him based on skin color and gender, not his humanness. These constructs are invisible yet penetrable; they are confusing and limiting. But eventually, he understands if he makes it beyond the boundaries set up for him, that as a Black male he has a certain nominal value, and as a Black male he has a certain categorical value "over" the Black female.

These concepts (categorical and nominal values) are American ideological expressions for men and women. However, African American ideologies conceptualize notions such as community and spirituality of men and women. Although in the African American communities, both sexes experienced the same collective unconscious of their history, Black men, like White men, are able to give into the exploitation of women; therefore, emotionally they have placed an American devaluation of them and are able to treat them unequally while building up anger toward them. They are able to become even more insensitive to women, which allows more emotional distance between themselves and them, thus creating their own construct of oppression toward their female counterparts. How do we get these men into counseling?

Relationships of Black men and Black women seem to be explained through a sociopolitical background that is less intimate and more mechanical. When

I refer to intimacy, it is the removal of the world's script for the male and female to create a genuine atmosphere of love that will be externalized. It is removal of the stereotype of Black men are hypersexual and not intimate. Yes, this gets pronounced through the genre of hip-hop music, but if the premise is that all beings need love (in society), then I recognize the surface and superficiality of these pronouncements and so should you.

To delve into a sociosexual background immediately disqualifies the notion of intimacy, although society has found a way to make it political. A sociosexual political model is a cover and contrived, and will only benefit men and their reserve. So, no, my theory will be without such structures and stems from the basic nature of desiring a loving relationship with a partner. Do I believe men want that? Yes, I do. Do I believe they are afraid and have been made afraid to want that? Yes, they have.

Cooper, in *A Voice from the South* (1988), understood there is a feminine and masculine side, not an inferior or superior, and the opposites were to complement each other. The Black male must relearn himself without the internalization of oppression, and by doing so begin to reassociate himself to himself and thereby externalize a confident, productive, intimate person who is able to denounce more easily his former labels.

Generally, men are reared to achieve material gain, and within this lies the seat of their emotions, their ego. Ego here has to take on a different and nonthreatening concept, but one which serves to motivate them and simultaneously protect them. Maslow's hierarchy of needs, Kohlberg's moral development theory, Vitgosky's stepual process to task completion—all unequivocally suggest the Black males basic need of love must be met before addressing the next need. Their maturation of right and wrong and wanting to abide in society must be uninterrupted to their moral development by the stigma(s) of their tanned skin. And they must have a platform that will help them achieve lower level tasks to becoming that productive citizen we criticize most African American men for not being. Let's begin to consider African American men in these terms as a way to employ empathy toward counseling.

BLACK MEN IN WHITE SOCIETY

Sociology is the critical study of community from the macro level to the micro level. It is the study of interrelationships among family, groups, institutions, values and views. We must examine the Black male within these two constructs: the macro level and its imposition of instituting biases, and the micro level system as it is conjoined to the larger system. The macro system feeds in part this lower system and indubitably produces an ill effect or maladaptive subsystem in which the Black man struggles to navigate within his environment. The concept of environment, community, culture, and identity are the epitome of the Black male responsibility. He is expected to conquer his environment, protect his community, expose himself and others to cultures, all while expected to resonate a strong, proud Black identity within the discriminatory constructs he was "born" into. The following is an illustration:

> Cross' model to Black Identity (1978) begins with an observed declaration that "African Americans have absorbed many of the beliefs and values of the dominant White Culture, including the notion that "White is right" and "Black is wrong" (p. 35). Cross' model has been developed and shaped over the years and identified stages people go through as they affirm and come to understand their own Black identity. The four stages are: the Encounter stage, the Immersion-Emersion stage and the final stage Internalization, is marked by self-acceptance . These stages offer a hopeful point of view of overcoming a negative identity to a positive self-identity to gain a positive self-identity in being in black skinned. (Hays & Erford, 2010, p. 35)

Research suggests that because of the historical and current experiences of oppression in the United States, along with other sociopolitical realities of minorities to include different ethnicities, has led to a conscious effort of training counselors in research and practice (Arredondo, 1999; Sue, Arredondo, & McDavis, 1992; USDHHS, 2007). To state it another way, this raised consciousness and penetrable awareness of multicultural counseling (MC) began the process of perhaps extinguishing oppressive constructs and carrying out MC-guided precepts in counselors' practice.

Nevertheless, some White Americans struggle to grasp the concept of "being born into White privilege" versus "being born into oppression." Both are realities and the status quo for each respective race. White privilege is unconscious, invisible, subliminal to the deferment of material things that White people having not worked for, but is given to them based on their white skin color, and therefore, it can help to create the atmosphere of an encapsulated society. In other words, White privilege is the positive ways Whites benefit from racism (Hayes & McLeod, 2010, p. 81). According to Hayes and McLeod:

> White counselors must become aware of their white privilege that is, become knowledgeable about the various ways oppression and social inequities can be manifested at the individual, cultural, and societal levels, along with the various ways such inequities might be experienced by various individuals, groups, organizations and macro systems; and secondly,understanding ones' own white privilege. Multicultural counseling no longer assumes counseling is primarily for white and middle to upper class, heterosexual persons. (Hayes & McLeod, 2010, p. 1)

We must become aware of concepts like cultural encapsulation, which refers to a narrow and rigid view of the world and other cultural groups using one's own cultural group as a reference, as a standard of normality; this is also known as ethnocentrism (Hays & McLeod, 2010, p. 6). All counselors must work to become aware of other worldviews and keep their worldviews, opinions, and judgments to themselves in order to come from a helping position. These are just some tools toward deconstructing discrimination in counseling.

How do we go from ignoring African American persons' history, ignoring them in research and studies to now including them? How do we dismantle the prejudices and discrimination about them that have permeated society and African Americans' microcosms? How will White counselors adjust their own historical "right" thinking? Self-reflection begins that answer by renegotiating personal attitudes held against this race.

Of course, not all African American men fit the above grim description of survival in the United States. Of course, not all of them struggle with their identities, some may accept their complacency, and others want more. Of course, society should not take the entire blame for African American males' struggles; however, reform is a backward admission of having done something wrong. Because of African American values and traditions, it would be remissive to analyze the Black male in whole without discussing his counterpart, the Black female. When it comes to relationships African American male and female unions are examined through a sociopolitical landscape. This relationship is not enveloped in family Adlerian theory, according to Murray Bowen (2013), who postulates that Black males and females are more dependent and reactive to one another than they would like to think. No, its platform is sociopolitical constructs. This relationship is already interrupted by traps set by the Black male being born into oppression and then learning how to sabotage his family, community, and future. The female is the "object" White America dangles in his face as he begins to understand the educational gaps between them, as she was able to navigate through some traps. This is how their relationship is publicized, through dismal statistics of 55% of African American women enrolled in colleges, while the incarceration rate for African American males is 44%. This is the man we are supposed to have empathy for? How? When we attempt to examine the African American male, we use study titles such as, "The Trouble with Black Boys," "Educating and Motivating African American Males to Succeed," "The Disproportionate Placement of African American Males in Special Education Programs," and "The Effect of School Context, Structure and Experience on African American Males in Middle and High School," to name a few of the current existing titles that do not allow for a pliable analysis of the African American male.

THE AFRICAN AMERICAN MATRIARCH

The African American matriarch concept provokes many competing emotions of either denouncing it or embracing it. It has become a more controversial issue among Black scholars than in the greater Black community. However, Black scholars would agree it is a phrase coined by White men purposefully to create more division in the African American household. Why are Black families analyzed through a sociopolitical lens rather than using Adler's theory on birth order or Piaget's model on human development, as with White families? When it comes to empirical research of the Black community, White researchers usually begin by accepting a set of premises based on negative notions and disdained ideologies they are trying to further substantiate rather than by denouncing stereotypes to promote Black women's welfare. Because studies are established with White philosophies, notions, and concepts, it is hard to find empirical research that promotes African Americans' well-being.

I am not under the illusion of historical feminism like Joan of Arc, or concepts of matriarchal prehistoric times, or believe Black women subscribe to a feminist matriarchal spiritual movement. We have a dilemma; that is, we are the most exploited race of Black men and women (Afrocentric) trying to live and adapt to the dominant values that White America upholds (Eurocentric). Black women are scorned for being heads of their households; White women in this same position are seen as caretakers. Black men are scorned as lazy. White men support Black men's inferiority complex of losing their White privileges by building correctional facilities to house them. The history of slavery shows that Black women protected their families and community by laying with their White oppressors. She birthed half Black men and throughout slavery gave of her body to protect the man because the Black man was a formidable threat to the White man. This is our history. So if White America's view of the Black woman is matriarchal and seen as an anomaly, then this is how she arrived. This is where matriarchism began for us, not in some dream-like imagery of Greek or Roman mythology; our matriarchal herstory began with slavery, further exacerbated by discrimination on American soil. Wouldn't it follow, then, that if Black men who pose a threat to White men would be obliterated, their women, impregnated by White men, would need to be caregivers to the biracial children conceived?

Because of its controversy, I must define my use of the word *matriarchy*, which is based on sheer population count in which more women are heads of households because men are not, due to lower or no income, living out of the home, or incarceration. In her article, "Black American Families Are Not 'Matriarchal,'" Hamiltori (2013) cites that White males are threatened by Black matriarchy because it's oppressive to their White privilege, which includes dominancy of political power and most work industries. The article reveals that Euro thinking is too embedded in society and even in African American females' thinking for them to operate in any other capacity. Even for a female head of household, her thinking is still patriarchal, and there does not need to be a male presence for this to be carried out. Patriarchy, on the surface, is White male dominance; on deeper levels, patriarchy customs are absorbed by all and perpetuated by all. So perhaps, once again, African American males have been positioned against their female counterparts.

In *Human Behavior in the Social Environment*, the authors crystallize the notion that an African American woman head of household is an anomaly by stating, "African American mothers are blamed for the violence of young African American men," (Anderson, Carter, & Lowe, 1999, p. 167). That statement begs the questions: Who's blaming the mothers? Where is the theoretical model of the collective psychogenic response of why African American men seem violent? Why haven't the researchers employed an anthropological model of African American women ancestors being raped and its cyclical tragedies still being manifested today? The European construct is built for African Americans to be unable to function, and, as a result, African American men are violent. Of course, these constructs are not solely to blame for African American men's ill behavior, but neither are their mothers solely to blame.

According to Hays and Erford (2010),

> The concept of race was created or constructed to serve a particular social function. Race and the original racial classification system were instituted by English colonists to ensure that the demand for agricultural labor was met as transatlantic entrepreneurial markets emerged. This was accomplished by the establishment of a hierarchical system of oppression that exclusively granted basic human rights, social privileges, and prestige to individuals of European descent. (p. 195)

Robert Staples in his essay on Black sociology, wrote, "If white sociology is the science of oppression, Black sociology must be the science of liberation," (as cited by Karenga, 1993, p. 269).

BROACHING

The entity that has the power to create stigmas and labels and instill racism(s) is the same entity that must begin the eradication thereof. Ethnic sensitive language (ESL) is a subsequent way to offer a softer, empathetic look at counseling African American males. For example, Baird takes note of the tone that is used to depict the author's sensitivity to the student who is hesitant about diversity.

The first worry pertains to the content of what students are learning, particularly as they are required to study the history and ongoing dynamics of oppression. A second fear is of self-revelation, making the students feel "stupid" or "racist" or possibly forcing them to discover aspects of themselves that they had been unaware of and would not be comfortable realizing. (Baird, 2011, p. 87)

Now, let's examine language and tonality used by Hays and Erford (2010) to describe concerns about African American males' guidelines to receiving counseling. "The following suggestions to counselors help to facilitate client investment in the therapeutic process: (a) establish a collaborative working relationship; and (b) provide the client with a brief explanation of the treatment, how it works, and how you generally interact with clients" (p. 210). Let's stop here. Can you hear the difference in tonality? Can the client feel sensitivity? In fact, as you read the rest of the guideline's words, such as facilitate, hypothesize, and reconstruct your thoughts and feelings about the client. The language used in scripting these guidelines is cold, insensitive, matter of fact, and even distant; all making it insurmountable for a Caucasian counselor to connect with an African American male client.

Let's switch scenarios. From Baird's example of "Resistance to Diversity," let's use African American males. For example, the first worry pertains to African American males being misdiagnosed. This is particularly likely if they meet a White counselor and project that the counselor may not have studied history and might remain unconscious to ongoing dynamics of oppression. A second fear African American males may have is mistrust of the counseling profession. The client may feel "stupid" or even offer language conducive to sensitivity, openness, humility rather than the description used for guidelines with working with African American males. One last question: How do these two persons come together for the client to be successful in counseling?

PERSON-CENTERED THERAPY

Among the few theoretical frameworks sophisticated enough to effectively counsel African American males, person-centered therapy leads. This humanistic therapy modality proposes that the therapist can deliver unconditional positive regard/empathy toward a race or a gender in a way it has not been previously regarded. The person-centered counseling of Carl Rogers is grounded in the goal of self-actualization, which is the innate predisposition to develop all of one's capacities for the maintenance and growth of personality (Rogers, 1987). This modality, applied to one born into oppression, garners empathy; along with the client having a predisposition of a "bad" attitude and his abilities to develop are diminished because he does not have the same opportunities for positive growth and maintenance. Not all fit this description, but it should be a consideration when the African American male walks through the door for help. Again, the counselor's worldview takes a back seat, and the client's worldview is present. An empathetic understanding of the African American male's feeling comes through the counselor's genuine experience of his or her own feelings, and since this is grounded in the client/therapist relationship that brings about growth, there is no set technique (Rogers, 1987). Unconditional positive regard is moving into multiculturalism, in which the client's history is noted and his present day situation of current discriminations and prejudices is noted simultaneously with respect for being an African American male individuality, stemming from trust in the client's self-directing capacity for positive regard (Rogers, 1987).

This humanistic modality emphasizes the worth of the African American male and keeps in the forefront his human values. For any African American male going into therapy who understands this premise, his defenses will already be half way down. This technique requires a genuine respect for the client's subjective experience and a trust in the client's capacity to make positive and constructive choices; both are experiential- and relationship-oriented (Rogers, 1987).

The cognitive-behavioral therapy model is another model that can assist the African American male in counseling. If we were to take the stereotypical stance that most Black men are angry and will project that anger on us, then when a Black man walks through the counseling door, we may not be able to offer empathy immediately. However, with cognitive therapy, we must focus on changing dysfunctional cognitions, emotions, and behavior, and displacement of anger (Hutchinson, 2009). Keep in mind that societal views lead some African American males to adopt negative perceptions and stereotypes as normative, thereby shaping emotions and learned behaviors (Owens, Simmons III, Bryant, & Henfield, 2011, p. 166). The primary focus here is to help the client identify his negative or distorted automatic thoughts, which are usually based on faulty logic or errors in reasoning: however, from his experience, he may fall into a deep sense of personalization about the stigmas associated with his skin complexion and, therefore, have a predisposition toward faulty logic or errors in his reasoning. For example, because of the ill-treatment he may experience throughout life because of his skin complexion, he may see coming to therapy as negative and accompanied with feelings that someone else is judging him negatively as well. This is where the first level of work begins, as you can see he has already jumped to many conclusions, and these have to first be dismantled; in doing so, empathy allows the counselor to assist with deconstructing his distortions.

IMPLICATIONS FOR THERAPISTS AND COUNSELORS

The view toward the future involves a collective utilitarian worldview shift. After apposite to CACREP counseling guidelines and diversity counseling training, we must remain as self-critical, social actors and role takers (Tsekeris & Lydaki, 2011) Our experiences guide our thoughts and actions within a narrow scope of self. These experiences then help to explain cause and effect and lead to us expecting certain results. Because of our narrow scope, we are blind to other facts and ideas that challenge or defy our deeply held beliefs (mental model book). To arrive at a society that works to reduce racism and become more inclusive of other ethnicities before interventions, before apologies, before reformations, will require us, also, functioning in roles as change agents. Properties of change is concurrently an outward examination. How can we change institutional biases and an inward examination? How can we change our conscious and unconscious beliefs about certain things and people? The African American male can be substituted for anyone who has experienced undue maltreatment because of differences.

There is no surprise that, in true essence, the effective therapeutic interventions and approaches for African American males in counseling are other attempts or a repetitive silhouette of the structure of micro versus macro conflict. The shared norms and values of society embeds its focus on a particular order and agreement that it expects between groups and organizations in order to be sustained (Perso, 2012). This is so much so that consequences are an inherited proponent of this sustainment. For example, according to the understanding of structural functionalism, the relationship among the parts of society will have conflicts and consequences as it tries to balance (Perso, 2012). Therefore, institutionalized racism seems beneficial to White privileges and its polar opposite is the negative consequences of dysfunctional outbreaks and breakdown of communities. Inherit in this structure is human emotions and human error that perhaps interrupt what could have been an equivalent ground for other ethnicities other than just White privilege to be included in shared norms and values. Tsekeris (2011) calls it *internal conversation,* as a hidden mediatory process that intervenes between agency and structure (Giddens), the lifeworld and the system (Habermas), and the habitus and the field (Bourdieu). This author concurs with the notion of internal conversation, but will go a step further. The individual who has power to label and stigmatize, while having this internal conversation (input) is an emotional being and will react and respond in an emotional way (output). Let's say he is neurotic about maintaining his superior complex and, therefore, projects his anxiety (biased mental models) onto policy and society. The results of his internal emotional conversations become grounded in policy, are carried out by society, and can be another barrier to racial equality.

Multicultural counseling is a large-scale sociopolitical movement in which the field of counseling is working to gain inclusionary and homeostatic representation for African American males and other ethnic and nonaccepted gendered groups. This phenomenon takes into consideration members of all racial, ethnic, and cultural groups and the impact of oppression(s) of each ethnicity and its worldviews. The conceptualization compels implicit guidance toward astuteness, care, and self-criticalization.

Counselors' understanding of clients is often shaped by the theoretical models and diagnostic criteria most commonly taught (Hays & Erford, 2010). Furthermore, the studies conducted on a particular population become the "norm" by which all populations are to "fit" or adhere by, and this is no longer acceptable. Psychometrics is an intermediary sociopolitical system to the counseling field as it affects clients. It is the technical aspect of testing that eventually allows for an amalgamation of the theories to which counselors adhere. The interpretation of such tests would offer a range of behaviors or reactions from White subjects, and deviation from such a "standard" is deemed an anomaly. As psychometrics uses tests to obtain this data, this field is concerned with the objective measurement of skills and knowledge, abilities, attitudes, personality traits, and educational achievement. For example, psychometric research has concerned itself with the construction and validation of assessment instruments such as questionnaires, tests, raters' judgments, and personality tests (Groth-Marnat, 2003). Reliability and validity are the two most critical components in which traditional use of predominantly Caucasians subjects must be expanded. In other words, counselors must know that if they are administering a test or adhering to and applying test results to a different ethnic client, the test was based on more than just Caucasian subjects.

According to Groth-Marnat (2003), reliability refers to a degree of stability, consistency, predictability, and accuracy. Validity assesses whether the test is accurate or not. These two forceful components of psychometrics are the backbone, determining whether or not the test is good enough to be standardized. If we were to administer the test to a similar population, would we get the same results? If so, are we confident that the test measured what we intended it to measure? Test results shape our thinking; we rely on them to make judgment calls and predictions from them. With CACREP invoking a different level of consciousness, standardized tests that are used, what may seem to be against other ethnicities must come under severe scrutiny, as well as its inherent biases. Moving forward, in development of more culturally sensitive tests, or taking into consideration tests that are based on a population other than the ethnicity to which they will be administered, we must take into account the inherent flaws of such. When reliability and validity procedures become more diverse in test construction, it will be easier for all who look to this area for answers to instinctively think to include non-White counterparts, and this, perhaps, can be another method of spreading diversity.

I contend that these psychometrics, the intermediary of the sociopolitical conscientious of counseling, have an added responsibility. We, as enlightened counselors, have an added responsibility, and our clients, too, have an added responsibility, to broaden the approaches effective to counseling techniques to include becoming familiar or "close" to those cultures that have been deemed invisible to help.

CONCLUSION

The sociological idea of learning and implementing effective therapeutic interventions and approaches for this particular target group, African American males, offers both autonomy structures and a sense of empathy toward healing. This chapter outlined a more intimate platform that society rarely considers when viewing or discussing African American males. The approaches must include an understanding of their historic/background, their environment that may or may not support their development, their relationship with themselves and with the Black female, and their vulnerabilities to first engage in counseling. In that sense, it is the discipline of empathy and openness that must be maintained to achieve counseling success with this group.

Conversely, not all African American males will enter counseling with similar constructs; therefore, the client–counselor relationship may be easily gained. However, a counselor should still tread lightly around the relationship, take precautions, and have respect for the ethnicity and culture of the African American male. The implications of CACREP public policies offers counselors and the like an opportunity toward eradicating superior complexes while eradicating inferior complexes in a neutral ground of human respect.

REFERENCES

Anderson, E., Carter, I., & Lowe, G. (1999). *Human behavior in the social environment: A social systems approach* (5th ed.). New York, NY: Aldine de Gruyter.

Arredondo, P. (1999). Multicultural counseling competencies as tools to address oppression and racism. *Journal of Counseling & Development, 77,* 102–108.

Baird, B. N. (2011). *The internship, practicum, and field placement handbook: A guide for the helping professions.* Upper Saddle River, NJ: Prentice Hall.

Bandura, A. J. (1977). *Social learning theory.* New York, NY: General Learning Press.

Benton, A. L., & Bandura, A. (1953). " Primary" and" secondary" suggestibility. The *Journal of Abnormal and Social Psychology, 48*(3), 336.

Bieschke, K. J., Perez, R. M., & DeBord, K. A. (2007). *Handbook of counseling and psychotherapy with lesbian, gay, bisexual, and transgender clients* (2nd ed.). Washington, DC: American Psychological Association.

Bowen, M. (2013). *The origins of family psychotherapy: The NIMH family study project.* Lanham, MD: Jason Aronson.

Cooper, A. J. (1988). *A voice from the south.* New York, NY: Oxford University Press.

Groth-Marnat, G. (2003). *Handbook of psychological assessment* (4th ed.). New York, NY: Wiley.

Hamiltori, T. (2013). *Black American families are not matriarchal.* Retrieved from http://www.gradientlair.com/post/52886656990/black-american-families-are-not-matriarchal

Hays, D. G., & Erford, B. T. (2010). *Developing multicultural counseling competence: A systems approach.* Upper Saddle River, NJ: Prentice Hall.

Hutchinson, L. (2009). *The study guide for the NCE exam.* Winter Park, FL: Licensure Exams.

Karenga, M. (1993). *Introduction to Black studies* (2nd ed.). Los Angeles, CA: The University of Sankore Press.

Owens, D., Simmons, R., III, Bryant, R. M., & Henfield, M. (2011). Urban African American males' perceptions of school counseling services. *Urban Education, 46*(2), 165–177.

Perso, T. F. (2012). *Cultural responsiveness and school education: With particular focus on Australia's first peoples; A review and synthesis of the literature.* Menzies School of Health Research, Centre for Child Development and Education, Darwin Northern Territory.

Rogers, C. R. (1987). Rogers, Kohut, and Erickson: A personal perspective on some similarities and differences. In J. K. Zieg (Ed.), *The evolution of psychotherapy.* New York, NY: Brunner/Mazel.

Sue, D. W., Arredondo, P., & McDavis, R. J. (1992). Multicultural counseling competencies and standards: A call to the profession. *Journal of Counseling & Development, 70*(4), 477–486.

Tsekeris, C., & Lydaki, A. (2011). The micro-macro dilemma in sociology: Perplexities and perspectives. *Sociologija, 53*(1), 67–82.

United States Department of Health and Human Services (USDHHS). (2007). *Health, United States 2007.* Hyattsville, MD: National Center for Health Statistics.

Vygotsky, L. (1978). Interaction between learning and development. *Readings on the Development of Children, 23*(3), 34–41.

West, H. C., & Sabol, W. J. (2009). *Prison inmates at midyear 2008: Statistical tables.* NCJ, 225619.

CHAPTER 6

UTILIZING THE EMPATHY WHEEL TO COUNSEL AFRICAN AMERICAN MALE STUDENTS

David Julius Ford, Jr.

Edward, an African American male and first-generation college student, is a senior in high school and is applying to colleges. He is in the top 2% of his class and has been taking AP courses throughout his time at high school. He is heavily involved in co-curricular activities and has held several leadership positions. He has taken the SAT and scored in the 95th percentile on each section. He has chosen his college choices: Wake Forest (his top choice), Virginia Tech, East Carolina, and Duke. He sought the assistance of his school counselor, who is also African American. Not only did she question his college choices, but she told him he should be applying to other schools: Winston-Salem State, Fayetteville State, UNC Pembroke, and Shaw University. Feeling defeated, Edward decided that that would be his last conversation with her. Edward worked on his own college applications, found other people to write letters of recommendation, and ended getting into his top choice and was offered a full tuition scholarship (Ford, 2014).

Why did the school counselor not assist Edward? Why did she not validate his college choices? What would have been a more appropriate response

Counseling African American Males, pages 97–106
Copyright © 2016 by Information Age Publishing
All rights of reproduction in any form reserved.

to Edward? The purpose of this chapter is to address these questions and provide a framework for working with African American male students, a framework based on empathy. The Empathy Wheel (Ford, 2014) is based on the dissertation research conducted by David Julius Ford, Jr. He investigated the impact that membership in Black Greek-letter organizations had on the overall college experiences of African American males and the role that counselors and college student personnel play in supporting African American male students. According to Ford (2014), showing empathy to African American male students positively impacts their academic and psychosocial outcomes.

This chapter begins by explaining empathy and how it enhances the counseling relationship. Next, the Empathy Wheel is explained. Then, strategies based on the Empathy Wheel will be proposed. These strategies include a sense of belonging and inclusion. Then, implications for counselors working with African American males will be discussed. Finally, Edward's story will be revisited based on the strategies of the Empathy Wheel. The information in this chapter can be used by counselors in various settings to improve the persistence and academic success of African American male students.

Empathy is one of nine essential characteristics of an effective counselor and involves a deep understanding of the client (Neukrug, 2011, 2012). Rogers (1961) describes it as entering the client's phenomenal world and experiencing it as if it were your own without losing the "as if" quality. To be empathic, an effective counselor perceives the cultural frame of reference of the client, including the client's perceptual and cognitive process (Weinrach, 1987). Empathic understanding builds rapport, elicits information, and helps the client feel accepted (Egan, 2010; Neukrug & Schwitzer, 2006). Empathy allows the counselor to enter the private world of the client and become thoroughly at home in it (Rogers, 1980). The counselor becomes sensitive to the feelings the client experiences. Empathy also means living in the client's life and moving through it without judging the client. It also involves sensing feelings below the client's level of awareness, frequently checking the accuracy of those sensings, and being guided by the client's responses (Rogers, 1980). Empathy opens the door for further discussion at a deeper level and empowers the client (Seligman & Reichenberg, 2013). Empathic responding involves active listening. Listening of the special and active kind is one of the most powerful agents of change (Rogers, 1989). Rogers (1959) viewed sensitive, accurate, and active listening, which is deeply grasping the client's subjective world and transmitting understanding of that world to enhance the client's self-awareness, in this way. By listening, the counselor accurately perceives the client's internal frame of reference with the client's emotional components and meanings as if he or she were the client, but maintaining the "as if" condition (Rogers, 1957). A good listener does not give advice, which removes the client's autonomy (Neukrug, 2012). Instead, the counselor encourages and supports the client and validates the client's story. Empathic responding makes the client feel heard and listened to. When a client feels heard and listened to, he or she feels valued. Counselors who are empathic value the stories of their clients, value them as persons, and value their clients' choices. Counselors seek clarification regarding the needs of their clients and help create an inclusive environment for their clients; thus, they create a sense of belonging for their clients. Empathy allows counselors to develop a deep level of understanding of their clients and shows that they care for their clients.

African American males experience invisibility at varying levels on a daily basis and empathy helps to alleviate those feelings of invisibility (Dowden, Gunby, Warren, & Boston, 2014). According to Warren (2014), empathy improves student-teacher relationships between teachers who are White females and male students who are African American. Warren also posited that empathy helped these teachers improve the academic outcomes of African American male students. Empathy produces higher academic expectations and success and instructional programs that affirm students' cultural and racial identities. Empathy is the tool that allows teachers to be sensitive to the needs of individual students in a homogenous cultural group (Warren, 2014). According to Dowden et al. (2014), in order to effectively counsel African American males, empathic understanding must be a key component of the therapeutic approach. The Empathy Wheel (Ford, 2014), which is based on this concept and diagrams how this concept impacts the counseling relationship, is discussed in the next section. The Empathy Wheel (Ford, 2014) is based upon David Julius Ford, Jr.'s dissertation work. Ford (2014) investigated what factors impact the academic and psychosocial outcomes of African American male students. The dissertation explored the impact that membership in Black Greek-letter organizations (BGLOs) had on the academic and psychosocial outcomes of African American male students and the perceived role of counselors and college student personnel have in supporting African American male students. One recommendation for improving these outcomes is counselors and college student personnel showing a deeper level of empathy toward African American male students. Empathic responding involves getting to know the African American male and discovering their norms, their needs, and what motivates them (Ford, 2014).

THE EMPATHY WHEEL

According to Ford (2014), empathy begins with being warm and welcoming to African American male students. Empathy also involves professionals showing that they genuinely care for African American male students;

they have to take some honest and authentic steps in showing that they truly want to understand these students and want to cultivate a culture of belonging. Counselors can be empathic by showing they value the presence of African American male students and they genuinely care about these students' plight. Empathy allows school counselors to assist African American males to prepare for college. This preparation includes getting to know these students and their history, their story, their needs, and their goals and aspirations. It also includes knowing what barriers African American males face when pursuing their education. The counselor's role is to support African American male students so they can be successful.

Ford (2014) found four themes, each with subcategories, that center around empathy; thus, counselors and college student personnel showing empathy can be a positive influence on the academic and psychosocial outcomes of these students (see Figure 6.1). The four themes include: sense of belonging (collaborative relationships and familial relationships), inclusion (accountability and achievement), diversity (identity and image), and resources (giving back). The focus of this chapter will center upon two of the four main themes: sense of belonging and inclusion (Ford, 2014).

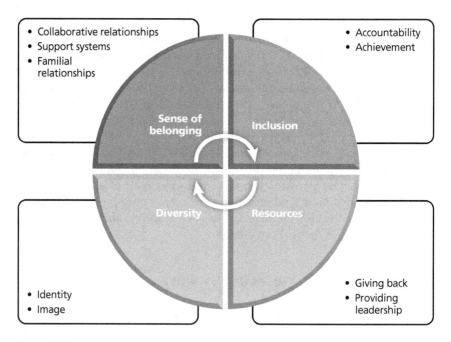

Figure 6.1

SENSE OF BELONGING

African American male students need to feel as though they belong, and counselors in various settings can create this sense of belonging in the counseling relationship (Ford, 2014). In order to create a sense of belonging, counselors must be warm and welcoming to African American male students. Counselors present themselves as nonjudgmental and exude caring and understanding when working with African American males. Counselors must listen to these students and provide encouragement in their decision-making processes. They take interest in the students' stories and experiences. They learn the history of African American males, their barriers to pursuing education, and what motivates them. Counselors also learn and validate their goals and aspirations and help equip them with the tools to achieve those goals and aspirations. Counselors can take interest in what African American male students' needs are and help them find the resources to fulfill those needs. With creating a sense of belonging, counselors can be inclusive of African American male students (Ford, 2014).

SENSE OF INCLUSION

Showing empathy also creates a sense of inclusion for African American male students (Ford, 2014). The sense of inclusion extends the sense of belonging. In order to create a sense of inclusion, counselors come from a place of wanting their offices and their schools to be an inclusive environment. College campuses, especially those that are predominantly White institutions (PWIs), have to be intentional about the engagement of African American male students. One strategy is showcasing African American male students. African American males can be included in university publications such as brochures and the university website. Another strategy is allowing for and supporting student organizations geared toward students of color, especially Black Greek-letter organizations (BGLOs). These organizations can also be showcased on university publications and during welcome week activities. They can also be showcased during campus visits, admissions activities, and homecoming activities. Counselors can get involved with these organizations by serving as advisers and/or cosponsoring programs with these organizations.

Counselors can also serve as mentors for African American male students and partner with BGLOs (Ford, 2014). Counselors in various settings can seek out members of male BGLOs to serve as mentors for African American male students. Mentoring African American males is a primary purpose of Black Greek fraternities and members of these organizations are well-equipped to provide guidance. On college campuses, Black Greek fraternities have been found to improve the academic and psychosocial outcomes of African American male students. They have a positive effect on the students' GPA, improve study habits, and provide an academic support structure for students. The members of the fraternity hold each other accountable for keeping their grades up and improving any academic deficits. These fraternities also help create that sense of belonging, that sense of inclusion, and provide familial relationships for the members. They also provide a means by which African American males can give back to their community by mentoring and supporting other African American males on campus and in the community. By partnering with Black Greek fraternities, college counselors can help demystify the counseling process and improve counseling utilization rates for African American male students. Being introduced to counselors who show they are supportive can improve the motivation to seek out counseling services to work through mental health concerns (Ford, 2014).

In middle schools, mentoring by members of Black Greek fraternities has been shown to curb misbehavior and disciplinary referrals in young African American males (Moore & Ratchford, 2007). School counselors can partner with members of Black Greek fraternities to mentor young African American males (Ford, 2014). Members of graduate and undergraduate chapters are well equipped and have a strong desire to give back and mentor young African American males. Seeing positive images of African American males can allay any alienation that these students feel, thus creating an inclusive environment. Seeing these images can also improve the students' self-efficacy and they can begin to see college as an option.

Another strategy school counselors at all levels (i.e., elementary, middle, and high school) can employ is allowing students to form step teams, utilizing the BGLOs to help establish these teams. Membership is predicated upon exemplary performance, and being a part of the team gives the students something to work toward. While being a part of the team, the students can learn discipline and respect for self and others, improve physical well-being, improve self-efficacy, and improve leadership skills. Membership on the team can also unify the students and teach them cooperation and collaboration.

IMPLICATIONS FOR COUNSELORS WORKING WITH AFRICAN AMERICAN MALES

Empathy is one of the core conditions of an effective counselor. It is putting yourself in another person's shoes and experiencing their world as they do, but keeping yourself intact. It is understanding their inner world and walking through it as though you were that person. Being empathic involves active listening, validating the client's thoughts, feelings, and meanings, and providing encouragement. Ford (2014) posited that when working with African American male students, being empathic allows counselors in various settings to hear these students' stories, validate them, validate their stories, and help create a sense of belonging and inclusion. Empathic listening allows an effective counselor to learn about the history of African American males, understand what motivates them, and find the resources they need. Once counselors learn what resources these students need, they can help the students fulfill those needs (Ford, 2014).

Empathic understanding is a key component in effectively teaching and counseling African American males (Dowden et al., 2014; Warren, 2014). Empathy improves academic outcomes of African American male students, improves student-teacher relationships, and improves cultural responsiveness of teachers (Warren, 2014). Dowden et al. (2014) posited that African American male students desire visibility and want their experiences validated, both achieved by empathic understanding. African American males need counselors to express empathy. Counselors must broaden their empathy and understanding by listening to African American males, being open to their experiences, and moving beyond book information regarding African American males. In other words, counselors must truly get to know African American males and seek contact with them. Counselors must create a sense of belonging and create an inclusive environment for African American males (Dowden et al., 2014; Ford, 2014).

CONCLUSION

Empathy is one of Rogers's nine essential characteristics of an effective counselor. Empathy allows the client to enter the client's world and experiencing it as if he or she were the client, while maintaining his or her own boundaries. Empathy involves active listening, showing interest in the client's experiences, validating their experiences, and understanding their perspective. When working with African American males in an educational setting, empathy improves their academic and psychosocial outcomes. In a counseling setting, empathy allows counselors to move beyond what is in the textbook and truly get to know the African American male. When a counselor shows empathy, African American males no longer feel invisible and are more apt to return to counseling. The Empathy Wheel takes this concept further and explains that African American males desire a sense of belonging and a sense of inclusion. Teachers and school counselors at all levels would benefit by being empathic regarding African American male students. Teachers and counselors learn what motivates African American

males, what their needs are, validate them and their experiences, and assist
them in fulfilling their needs.

EDWARD REVISITED

Let's revisit Edward. Edward, an African American male, has made up his
mind about his college choices and goes to his school counselor, an African
American female, for assistance in applying to college. Instead of listening
to him, supporting him, validating his choices, and helping him with the
resources to apply to these schools, she questioned his choices and tells
him to apply to other schools instead of the schools he wanted. Feeling
defeated and unsupported, Edward decides that he will no longer seek out
her assistance and that was the last conversation he had with her. He seeks
out other persons to assist him. Because of the school counselor's lack of
empathy, Edward did not get the support he needed from the person who
was supposed to support him.

Let's change the scenario and replace this school counselor with one
(named Ms. Stone) who empathically responds to Edward. The dialogue
could ensue as follows:

> **Edward:** Hello Ms. Stone, I need your assistance with applying to
> college.
> **Ms. Stone:** Edward, I would be more than willing to assist you. Where
> are you applying?
> **Edward:** My top choice is Wake Forest, but I am also applying to
> Duke University, Virginia Tech, and East Carolina.
> **Ms. Stone:** Okay, those are some good schools. Tell me what draws
> you to those schools.
> **Edward:** Well, I love science and each of those schools has a strong
> science program. Also, they all have good financial support.
> I will have a chance to get away from home, but be close
> enough to come home if I need to. I want to study abroad
> and I checked into their international programs.
> **Ms. Stone:** Edward, I see that you are committed to getting into
> college and you have done your research. You have made
> some good college choices. I have some suggestions for you.
> I know of some resources to assist you with the application
> fees. Also, let's plan some visits to each of these universi-
> ties. Let's look up some other African American males who
> are alumni or are currently attending these universities to
> speak to you. I know that you are a member of our step team
> and you may be interested in connecting with the Black

Greek-letter organizations. All of them have Black Greek-letter organizations and these students would be more than happy to speak with you about their universities. I also have friends in these organizations who are alumni of these schools. I know they would love to speak with you, also. How does that sound?

Edward: Ms. Stone, that sounds great. I've wanted to speak with the guys who work with the step team. I would love to talk to them or other students about fraternities. I appreciate the assistance.

Ms. Stone: Great! We need to get your parents involved so they'll know what's going on and we can get their approval.

Edward: Okay, Ms. Stone. We can call them now and set that up.

In this dialogue, the school counselor exudes the empathy needed to work with Edward and assist him in the application process. She listens to him and validates his college choices. She provides encouragement and creates an environment of inclusion that helps foster a sense of belonging. She shows interest in how he chose those schools and reflects feelings to show that she is listening. She also offers some suggestions to help him navigate the application process and make an informed decision about his college choice. She uses her connections to help him get the resources needed for the application process. Edward was able to apply to college, was awarded admission into all of his schools, and decided to attend his top choice. He was awarded the Gates Millennium Scholarship, which paid his tuition. He also had a student mentor who was a member of a Black Greek-letter organization.

REFERENCES

Dowden, A. R., Gunby, J. D., Warren, J. M., & Boston, Q. (2014). A phenomenological analysis of invisibility among African American males: Implications for clinical practice and client retention. *The Professional Counselor, 4*(1), 58–70.

Egan, G. (2010). *The skilled helper: A problem management and opportunity-development approach to helping* (9th ed.). Belmont, CA: Brooks/Cole

Ford, D. J., Jr. (2014). *A grounded theory of the college experiences of African American males in Black Greek-letter organizations.* (Doctoral dissertation). Old Dominion University, Norfolk, VA. Retrieved from ProQuest Dissertations & Theses (3580583).

Moore, E., & Ratchford, V. F. (2007). Decreasing discipline referrals for African American males in middle school. *AASA Journal of Scholarship and Practice, 4*(2), 20–24.

Neukrug, E. (2011). *Counseling theory and practice.* Belmont, CA: Brooks/Cole.

Neukrug, E. (2012). *The world of the counselor: An introduction to the counseling profession* (4th ed.). Belmont, CA: Brooks/Cole.

Neukrug, E., & Schwitzer, A. M. (2006). *Skills and tools for today's counselors and psychotherapists: From natural helping to professional counseling.* Pacific Grove, CA: Brooks/Cole.

Rogers, C. R. (1957). The necessary and sufficient conditions of therapeutic personality change. *Journal of Consulting Psychology, 21*(2), 95–103. doi:10.1037/h0045357.

Rogers, C. R. (1959). A theory or therapy, personality and interpersonal relationships as developed in the client-centered framework. In S. Koch (Ed.). *Psychology: A study of science, formulations of the person and the social context* (Vol. 3, pp. 184–256). New York, NY: McGraw-Hill.

Rogers, C. R. (1961). *On becoming a person.* Boston, MA: Houghton Mifflin.

Rogers, C. R. (1980). *A way of being.* Boston, MA: Houghton Mifflin.

Rogers, C. R. (1989). A client-centered/person-centered approach to therapy. In H. Kirshenbaum (Ed.), *The Carl Rogers reader* (pp. 135–152). Boston, MA: Houghton Mifflin

Seligman, L., & Reichenberg, L. W. (2013). *Theories of counseling and psychotherapy: Systems, strategies, and skills* (4th ed.). Upper Saddle River, NJ: Pearson.

Warren, C. A. (2014). Towards a pedagogy for the application of empathy in culturally diverse classrooms. *Urban Review: Issues and Ideas in Public Education, 46*(3), 395–419.

Weinrach, S. G. (1987). Microcounseling and beyond: A dialogue with Allen Ivey. *Journal of Counseling & Development, 65*(10), 532–537.

CHAPTER 7

SOCIOPOLITICAL RAP MUSIC AS A THERAPEUTIC INTERVENTION TO WORK WITH AFRICAN AMERICAN MALES

Ahmad R. Washington

On August 5, 2014, John Crawford stood in an aisle at a Walmart store near Dayton, Ohio. As Crawford perused various items on the store's shelves, he held an air rifle, without packaging, that he retrieved from the sporting goods department. Unbeknownst to Crawford, another store patron called 911 saying Crawford could be seen waving what was believed to be a real rifle loaded with live ammunition at other customers. Just minutes after receiving the call, members of the local police descended on the store cornering John Crawford in pet supplies. Startled by the swarming authorities with guns drawn, Crawford retreated still clutching the toy weapon; the police approached and within seconds shot Crawford twice. John Crawford died shortly thereafter in possession of an artificial weapon, in a state where

Counseling African American Males, pages 107–125
Copyright © 2016 by Information Age Publishing

residents regularly open carry weapons of every conceivable caliber to affirm their Second Amendment rights (Butler, 2014; Izadi, 2014). July 17, 2014, Staten Island New York. Eric Garner, son, cousin, husband, father, and grandfather, stands outside a beauty supply establishment. Garner, who is reported to have been selling untaxed single cigarettes, diffuses a fight between two individuals in the immediate vicinity. Police, who have arrived on the scene to respond to the altercation before it escalates, see Garner and demand that he refrain from selling the cigarettes illegally. Garner expresses his frustration to the officers and insists that the harassment he has been receiving from the officers regarding his sales was going to end today. While standing in front of one officer, Garner is grabbed from behind by another officer and eventually wrestled to the ground. As the primary restraining officer refuses to relinquish his clasp of Garner's neck, Garner repeatedly pleads to be released because, as he stated, "I can't breathe." The officer refuses. Within minutes, Garner's lifeless and handcuffed body lay on the sidewalk. Minutes pass before the EMS arrive and attempt to revive Eric Garner. Their attempts fail. Eric Garner is dead and the footage of his demise is captured on a civilian's cell phone (Baker, Goodman, & Mueller, 2015). On August 9, 2014, Mike Brown and his friend were returning to their apartment complex after an excursion to a nearby store. Contradictory reports exist as to what transpired at that store; some contend Mike Brown robbed the convenience store, while others argue the cigars, which were removed from the store, were purchased before Mike and his friend exited. As they were en route to their destination, Mike and his friend were approached by Office Darren Wilson's police vehicle. Wilson stated that Brown and his friend were walking in the street, possibly obstructing traffic, a claim that Brown's friend vehemently denies. According to Brown's friend, the officer was verbally abusive and yelling profanities while demanding that they move onto the sidewalk. Words were exchanged between the office and the young men. While complete clarity about what actually transpired after the verbal exchange has not been achieved, several eyewitnesses recount that Officer Wilson was the instigator antagonizing the two pedestrians. Several of these witnesses went on to say that Officer Wilson initiated contact with Mike Brown by pulling him into the vehicle, and that Brown acted in self-defense to free himself from Wilson's clutches. During this skirmish, Wilson unholsters his weapon and fires a round. Brown, now fleeing, is pleading for Wilson to stop shooting. Brown eventually surrenders, apparently with his hands up to illustrate that he did not possess a weapon. Officer Wilson disregards Brown's submissive posture and pleas before firing several rounds into Brown's body. Mike Brown died that warm summer afternoon; his body lay in spectacle in the street for at least four hours visible for all to see. On November 24, 2014, Robert McCulloch, the attorney for St. Louis, Missouri, announced that a grand jury deliberated and determined that

Officer Wilson would not face charges for Brown's murder (McLaughlin, 2014; Milbank, 2014).

Public discourse surrounding each of these killings is illuminating about the status of African American males in this country. A critical dissecting of how these incidents unfolded and were subsequently framed within the media produces startling revelations about the ways in which Black maleness and masculinity are characterized and represented. These characterizations and representations were very reminiscent of stereotypical tropes of Black males in the early- to mid-1800s that, overwhelmingly, portrayed Black males as lawless and inherently violent brutes who ran afoul of the law, incessantly terrorizing law-abiding White civilians. From that historical period to the contemporary moment, these depictions have functioned "as a universal story to make sense of all African American males. These narratives exist in the news media, popular culture, police reports, educational conferences, special education meetings, parent–teacher conferences, and everyday language" (Brown, 2011, p. 2049).

Support for Brown's assertion is reflected in much of the news coverage and commentary of Mike Brown and Eric Garner's deaths, which included repeated references to their physical stature (Brown was 6'4" tall, 295 lbs.; Garner was 6'3" tall, 350 lbs.). The opinion held by some was that Brown and Garner were menacing and imposing figures, whose literal "beingness" legitimized the violent responses from law enforcement that contributed to their deaths. For example, Ben Stein said, contrary to reports, Mike Brown was, indeed, armed because his body constituted a weapon, which meant Officer Wilson was well within his rights to defend himself (Garcia, 2014). Stein's comments about Brown are perfectly aligned with the aforementioned stereotypical Black brute trope and harken back to a time when similar propaganda was used to justify the wanton lynching and mutilation of Black male bodies across the country (Jackson, 2006). In the case of John Crawford, he was not afforded the presumption of innocence as other open carry residents of the state; thus, although his physical dimensions did not generate public hysteria, he was assumed to be carrying a live firearm, one he might conceivably use on innocent civilian Walmart shoppers. In addition to these egregious examples of criminalization and debasement of adolescent and adult African American males, quantitative and qualitative research has shown that racist perceptions are even ascribed to prepubescent African American boys.

Resistance to these examples of state sanctioned forms of police brutality has been swift and persistent. Marching with their hands aloft while wearing shirts emblazoned with "I can't breathe," actions in remembrance of Michael Brown and Eric Garner, human rights demonstrators have demanded, with righteous indignation, an end to the hyper-surveillance, hyper-criminalization and extrajudicial murder of unarmed Black and

Brown people. Organizing and mobilizing in ways often unlike the nonviolent civil rights avant-garde, the contemporary incarnation of social justice protest often reflects and embodies, rhetorically and visually, a hip-hop aesthetic (Jackson, 2014). For instance, rap music has repeatedly functioned as the literal and symbolic soundtrack in Ferguson, Missouri, Baltimore, Maryland, and Chicago, Illinois for protestors confronting militarized police forces to demand transformative changes in the ways law enforcement engages communities of color (Love, 2016). Rap artists like Sa-Roc, Narubi Selah, Tef Poe, Talib Kweli, and Kendrick Lamar have all engaged issues of criminalization, police brutality, mass incarceration and the prison industrial complex in their lyrics. In the current moment Kendrick Lamar's song Alright typifies how rap music serves as a vehicle for critically interrogating systemic and institutional oppression that adversely impact communities of color, Black communities, in particular (King, 2016). Because so many rap music artists, historically and contemporarily, have generated compellingly incisive musical criticisms of various forms of racialized social injustice, many have suggested sociopolitical rap music can be used to broach liberatory discussions with racially marginalized youth about forms of oppression they constantly confront (Akom, 2009; Love, 2016, 2013; Washington, 2016, 2015). This premise, that sociopolitical rap music can serve a unique therapeutic function with regards to marginalized youth, is the primary impetus for this chapter.

In this chapter, the author intends to support this position by addressing the following points. First, the author will discuss the myriad ways African American males are criminalized, such that criminal behavior and African American males have become virtually synonymous. This will include a discussion of how this happens in school settings. Second, this manuscript will highlight the genre of sociopolitical rap music. Focus will center on the social conditions that helped birth hip-hop culture and illustrate how many of these conditions remain intact for many African American males around the country. Third, the author will connect the work of particular sociopolitical rap artists (e.g., Common, Shad) to the idea of empowerment and how it is applied to African American males within the professional school counseling nomenclature. Finally, the author will provide actual strategies on how he has integrated sociopolitical rap lyrics in his work in various secondary education settings.

THE CRIMINALIZATION OF AFRICAN AMERICAN MALES

When the *ation* suffix is applied to a word, it denotes action. When *ation* is attached to a noun, *ation* activates the noun or suggests the noun is being acted upon by outside influences. When the word criminal becomes criminalization,

ation conveys that a confluence of factors contribute to whether an individual is perceived as a criminal, and under what circumstances this ascribing of criminality occurs. Additionally, if we attempt to understand criminalization from a sociohistorical perspective, criminalization suggests these external factors are pervasive and operate constantly in the lives of these individuals, and the general public, to such a degree that these criminalized individuals are overwhelmingly presumed guilty by virtue of their very existence (Alexander, 2012; Muhammad, 2010). If and when the process of criminalization continues unabated, the public can internalize and come to rely on these common-sense notions about groups of individuals believed to be prone to criminal behavior. In other words, there is often a historical legacy of criminalization to which vulnerable populations are subjected.

The stereotypical image of African American males as criminal is old, and has undergone a long, meticulous, and strategic developmental process (Burrell, 2010; Jackson, 2006). The stubbornness of the criminal African American male narrative and image, and its purported legitimacy, is borne of a complete devaluation of African American life in general. A precursor to the criminal Black male trope was the pervasive depiction of non-Whites, especially African Americans, as odd, peculiar, barbaric, lazy, shiftless, and intellectually underdeveloped (Fredrickson, 1971). From this, a subsequent typology of disparaging and stereotypical images of African American males evolved, which included, most notably, the Coon, the Uncle Tom, the Sambo, and the Buck (Jackson, 2006). The fundamental characteristics of these figures were an aversion to work, a lack of ingenuity and resourcefulness. Again, relying on the presumption Blacks were devoid of virtually any intrinsic motivation or the capacity for self-sufficiency, it was easy to portray African American males as incapable of making any modicum of contribution to American society. Harkening back to the pre-Antebellum period, the criminalization of Black masculinity in this country was executed through a number of mediums. Some of this country's most influential academics and politicians regularly utilized the print media and scientific publications to circulate the belief that African American males were intellectual infants when compared to Whites and were predisposed to criminality (Guthrie, 2004; Jackson, 2006). Hierarchies of intelligence were presented to the public and, not surprisingly, African Americans were positioned on these hierarchies of intelligence firmly at the bottom. Once the print and visual media had effectively conditioned White Americans to accept the belief African Americans were intellectual inferiority and that this inferiority was attributable to genetic deficiencies, the criminalization of African American males was a logical consequence. Popular culture was also instrumental in fabricating and disseminating myths of African American male criminal proclivities. For instance, D. W. Griffith's *The Birth of a Nation* (1915) is, perhaps, the quintessential example of how the movie screen became a powerful conduit for circulating messages about the purported intrinsic deviance of Black males to White audiences at the turn of the 20th century. Additionally, the minstrel shows of the late 19th century, which preceded Griffifth's work by approximately 85 years, also showed Blacks monolithically as "infantile and pathological," which "affirmed the notion that Black men were unfit for the responsibilities of democracy" (Ogbar, 2007, p. 13). Promoting the narrative of African American male criminality served the important function of justifying the system of White domination and Black subjugation. Moreover, the conviction that African American males were inherently criminal engendered sweeping endorsements from White Americans that the social agency and mobility of African American males needed to be restricted at all costs.

THE CRIMINALIZATION
OF AFRICAN AMERICAN MALES IN SCHOOLS

The author agrees with Welch's (2007) observation that "In American society a prevalent representation of crime is that it is overwhelmingly committed by young Black men" (p. 276). Seemingly robbed of their innocence well before they reach puberty, African American males are often seen as disposable and undeserving of second chances. Goff, Jackson, Di Leone, Culotta, and DiTomasso's (2014) study produced data that suggests the dehumanization of Black children is correlated with police officers' utilization of force against Blacks. Additionally, this dehumanization was related to college students' likelihood of assessing Black boys as being nearly five years older than their actual age and less innocent than White boys.

Schools are tremendously potent socializing institutions that operate as microcosms of the larger society; this means that many of society's common sense notions, including those about race, exist and are reproduced within schools (Isom, 2009; Ladson-Billings, 2011). Perhaps what is most disheartening is the fact that myths about the deviance and criminality of African American males begin so early in the educational pipeline (Ferguson, 2001; Ladson-Billings, 2011). In her seminal ethnography on the construction of Black masculinity in educational settings, Ferguson (2001) offers the following chilling and unsettling anecdote about the educational settings African American males must attend and navigate. Here, Ferguson details how the assumptions about African American males' propensity to commit crimes led an elementary school to habitually label its African American male students as deviant:

> In the course of my study, it became clear that school labeling practices and the exercise of rules operated as part of a hidden curriculum to marginalize

and isolate Black male youth in disciplinary spaces and brand them as criminally inclined. (p. 2)

Ladson-Billings paints a demoralizing picture of how this process of criminalization happens as African Americans transition out of childhood and into early adolescence when she writes, "Before long they [Black boys] are moved to a category that resembles criminals. Their childhood evaporates before they are eight or nine-years old when teachers and other school officials begin to think of them as 'men'" (p. 10). Ladson-Billings words resonate greatly, particularly when placed alongside qualitative and quantitative research that indicates this happens to Black males quite frequently (Ferguson, 2001; Goff, Jackson, Di Leone, Culotta, & DiTomasso, 2014).

Tagged as criminals who are uninterested in learning, it is not surprising, then, that jargon like "at risk, endangered, remedial, in crisis, uneducable, extinct, and left behind" are used frequently when discussing African American males' social and educational status (Howard, 2013, p. 57). Habitually labeled as academically at-risk in schools, many African American males are seen as a detriment to the academic mission of the schools they attend. Envisaged as chronic academic underachievers, these students are routinely ushered into vocational education tracks, exposed to lowered teacher expectations and beliefs about their incapability to achieve academic success in more rigorous academic courses, and referred to special education while also being virtually absent from talented and gifted (TAG) programs (Ford & Moore, 2013; Henfield, 2013; Jenkins, 2006). Moreover, in the current educational milieu, where zero-tolerance disciplinary policies are commonplace, African American males are suspended and expelled more frequently for longer periods of time and at earlier ages than any other student groups (Baldridge, Hill, & Davis, 2011; Monroe, 2009). Feeling emotionally and psychologically alienating, numerous African American males find themselves pushed out of schools, which statistically increases the likelihood of their being engulfed by the school-to-prison pipeline (Kunjufu, 2002, 2005; Nocella & Socha, 2013). To rectify this situation, conceptual frameworks and tangible resources that contextualize African American males' life experiences are desperately needed. In the following section, the conversation will shift to sociopolitical rap music and how this art form can assist in this endeavor.

SOCIOPOLITICAL RAP MUSIC

Sociopolitical rap music is operationalized here to describe a body of rap music, past and present, that has been produced for the specific purpose of heightening the social and political awareness of the listener about historical and contemporary events that profoundly impact people belonging to different racial and socioeconomic categories and possessing disparate degrees of power (Travis & Deepak, 2011). For members of those groups possessing less power, this power imbalance means that those possessing more power dictate their access to vital resources. Not surprisingly, those possessing greater degrees of power often act in their own self-interest and restrict the availability to resources for less powerful groups.

Historically, for African Americans, this type of power arrangement is best exemplified in the fact they were forcefully brought to this country as chattel and later subjected to wholesale marginalization and disempowerment. A more contemporary example of this marginalization and disempowerment are the discriminatory housing policies (e.g., redlining) that literally relegated innumerable qualified African American families to the least desirable urban communities in the north and midwest beginning in the 1930s, while at the same time allowing White families unfettered access to low-interest loans to build homes in America's developing and sprawling suburbs (Massey & Denton, 1993; Wilson, 2009). More than relics of a chapter of America's distant history some would like to forget, these policies are vitally important in understanding the evolution of contemporary educational and wealth disparities in this country, and how those disparities manifest in the lives of countless African American males today.

Although a prevailing opinion might be that rap music is utterly incapable of doing anything other than arresting the consciousness and cognitive functioning of the listener (McWhorter, 2000), I propose that sociopolitical rap music is ideal for facilitating meaningful conversation about an array of subjects including racism, classism, and other forms of social injustice. Sociopolitical rap music can serve as a catalyst in engendering solidarity and promoting resistance against systemic forms of injustice that act as barriers to African American males' life opportunities. This premise rests firmly on the fact that sociopolitical rap is, first and foremost, highly political in its nature and orientation. Unlike the more accessible and ubiquitous forms of rap music, which often carelessly recycle old narratives about violence and drug trafficking being endemic to Black ghettos (Ogbar, 2007; Rose, 2008), sociopolitical rap is conceptualized as an empowering genre of rap music that is concerned with the plight of oppressed groups, especially poor and working-class inner-city residents of color. Ascribing criminal deviance to African American male students epitomizes educational malpractice, educational inequality, and oppression (Hipolito-Delgado & Lee, 2007). This branding dehumanizes African American males and depicts them is such a way that makes empathizing with their plight practically impossible. Indeed, this branding can "marginalize, demonize, and rob" African American males of educational opportunities that other students enjoy (Potts, 2003).

Because this is the reality for innumerable African American males, educational leaders and social change agents like professional school counselors must seriously consider the role they can play in confronting these educational barriers. The social justice school counseling approach relates perfectly to this topic because it deals specifically with the ways disenfranchised African American males can move from the margins to the center of the educational, social, and political conversation to combat the devastating ways power and oppression operate to their detriment (Dahir & Stone, 2009; Dixon, Tucker, & Clark, 2010; Goodman & West-Olatunji, 2010; Kiselica & Robinson, 2001; Ratts, DeKruyf, & Chen-Hayes, 2007).

Twenty-first century professional school counselors working with African American males must imagine strategies and approaches that facilitate the interruption of the aforementioned systemic forces that brand African American males as criminal. To this end, professional school counselors are expected to operate as agents of educational social change and social justice, particularly in those instances where institutional and systemic barriers impede the development of students, like African American males, who have been historically marginalized (ASCA, 2012). Therefore, not only is the social justice paradigm an applicable and pervasive part of the contemporary school counseling landscape (Dahir & Stone, 2009; Hipolito-Delgado & Lee, 2007; Ratts, DeKruyf, & Chen-Hayes, 2007) it is germane to the unique ways oppression has and continues to operate in the lives of so many African American males (Dale & Daniel, 2013; Toporek, 2013). As Shin and his colleagues (2010) suggest, the social justice counseling orientation is a transformative conceptual lens because it empowers school counselors to engender conversation about the unique sociopolitical forces (e.g., reduction in the funding of public education, zero tolerance school disciplinary policies, presence of resource officers in schools, redlining/educational gerrymandering, stereotypical messages within the media, etc.) that constrain educational and social opportunities for students of color (Caton, 2012; O'Connor, Hill, & Robinson, 2009; Whiting, 2009). Social justice oriented school counselors who work to equip students of color with this critical concept support these students in self-advocating and seeking the removal of unjust barriers and practices that impinge on their educational and social success (Akom, 2009; Prier & Beachum, 2008).

SOCIOPOLITICAL RAP MUSIC
AND AFRICAN AMERICAN MALE EMPOWERMENT

Despite a substantial body of literature on social justice school counseling and how it can be applied to the experiences of African American males, a glaring omission remains. It is the author's belief that sociopolitical rap music—because of its focus on sociopolitical power, power differentials, and cultivating the sociopolitical consciousness of marginalized and disenfranchised groups—is tremendously salient and relevant to the oppression that besieges African American males. Recognizing how social and political disempowerment reverberates in the lives of those who are racially and economically marginalized, sociopolitical rap music seeks, as Public Enemy defiantly shouted, to "Fight the powers that be!" Due to the fact that for many African American males hip-hop culture exists as "their main site of cultural politics to negotiate their identities, and make meaning of their social world" (Prier & Beachum, 2008, p. 519), professional school counselors working with African American males should seriously consider, if they have not already, how speaking the language of sociopolitical rap music with African American males about the oppression they face can be beneficial to their transition from adolescence to adulthood (de Leon, 2004; Lee, 1987).

It is the author's contention that sociopolitical rap music can be applied to a plethora of African American males' life experiences where negative myths about them are present. Here, though, the focus will be on narrow and stereotypical portrayals of Blackness and how they manifest in the various contexts in which adolescent African American males have to maneuver. Priority is given to these stereotypical portrayals for two reasons. First, these images permeate every conceivable facet of our society, which means they have the potential to frame African American males as threatening (Burrell, 2010; Entman & Rojecki, 2000). Moreover, if African American males internalize these images, it could contribute to them developing adverse self-evaluations (Love, 2013). Second, by helping African American males critique these sensationalized images of African American males as hypercriminals, professional school counselors help nurture these students' healthy personal/social development, which falls under the purview of responsibilities school counselors should ideally assume (ASCA, 2012). According to Fredrickson (1971), White Americans have maintained a historical fascination with the African American image. Moreover, through the control and manipulation of the news media, White Americans have been able to shape and alter, whenever it is convenient and necessary, the image of African Americans. As previously stated, one of the most enduring representations of African American males has been that of a savage brute incapable of adhering to prescribed standards of moral behavior and social decency. In present times, the proliferation of social media sites like Facebook make the dissemination and circulation of images and video footage unbelievably simple and startlingly fast. With access to Facebook and other social media sites, it is not difficult to encounter images and video footage of African Americans engaging in what may be described as abhorrent and maladaptive behaviors. Coupled with the expansive reach of popular culture of which rap artists are a prominent part, one can literally be saturated with images that may confirm preconceived notions about the depravity of African American males, particularly those African American males narrowly defined as the urban poor. In his song *Brother (Watching)* on the album *The Old Prince* (2007), Canadian hip-hop artist Shad discusses how predominant sordid images of Blackness can impede the optimum racial and ethnic identity development of young Black people. On *Brother*, Shad composes a gripping and heartfelt synopsis of how young Black people have to construct their racial and ethnic identities in a social context where one-sided notions of Blackness are so prevalent:

> I opted not to bring that to the booth
> But after a while, it sort of starts naggin' at you
> The crazed infatuation with blackness
> That trash that gets viewed
> And the fact that the tube only showed blacks
> Actin the fool and I was watching...
>
> (saturated with negative images and a limited range of
> Possibilities is strange...)
>
> And it's sad cause that naturally do
> Sort of condition your mind and over time
> That's what's attractive to you
> So young blacks don't see themselves in
> Scholastic pursuits
> Or the more practical routes
> It's makin' tracks or it's hoops
> Or God-forbid movin' packs for the loot
> Even with this music we so limited—it's rap or produce
> And that narrow conception of what's black isn't true
> Of course, still we feel forced to adapt to this view
> Like there's something that you"re havin' to prove...

Shad seriously engages the issue of overly simplistic and reductionist representations of Blackness he describes as "limited" and "narrow" because they monolithically portray Blacks "actin the fool." He expounds by suggesting continual exposure to stereotypical messages works to "condition" the minds of young Blacks so efficiently that these disparaging images appear "attractive." As a consequence of this type of conditioning, Shad argues "young blacks don't see themselves in scholastic pursuits." Shad provides a poignant analysis that reflects the work of researchers and historians who have studied the formation of racial stereotypes and how these stereotypes have been mobilized historically to justify the mass incarceration and literal destruction of Black bodies (Fredrickson, 1971; Jackson, 2006; McInyre, 1993). South Side Chicagoan Common provides his own examination of how skewed images and common sense notions of Blackness reverberate in the lives of Black people. On his track *Real People* on the critically acclaimed album *Be* ((Lynn, West, & Frazier, 2005)), Common invokes the names of his ancestors as he contemplates how members of local law enforcement harass Black residents because they are presumed guilty:

> I wonder if the spirits of Bob Marley and Haile Selassie
> Watch me as the cops be tryna pop and lock me.
> They cocky, plus they mentality is Nazi
> The way they treat blacks, I wanna snap like paparazzi

Here, Common connects the practice of hyperpolicing inner city Black neighborhoods to tactics employed by the Nazis, in particular the undergirding ideology of White Aryan supremacy. Common contends that it is this mentality that provokes cops to go to extraordinary lengths to apprehend and incarcerate Black inner city residents. Interestingly, this thesis, that the hyperincarceration of inner city Black male residents is precipitated by racially motivated hyperpolicing of Black communities, is buttressed by research (e.g., Goff, Jackson, Di Leone, Culotta, & DiTomasso, 2014) and held by other prominent thinkers (e.g., Alexander, 2012; Muhammad, 2010).

SUGGESTIONS FOR PROFESSIONAL SCHOOL COUNSELORS

On several occasions, as a doctoral student and faculty member, the author has been invited by elementary and secondary schools to speak with African American male students. As a hip-hopper himself, the author routinely integrates themes from sociopolitical rap lyrics to stimulate discussion about how stereotypical narratives about Black masculinity inform public policy and shape the way people in their immediate environments perceive them. Due to the fact the author has received positive verbal feedback from African American male students, professional school counselors, and school administrators about this approach, the following list of suggestions reflects strategies he has previously employed.

Compose a Sound Rationale for Using Rap Music

Although hip hop and rap music are seen as legitimate forms of cultural expression and academic areas of inquiry, narrow and uninformed conceptions of hip hop and rap music persist. This means that even though professional school counselors may be absolutely convinced that many of the African American males they serve hold hip-hop and rap music in high regard, it cannot be assumed that teachers, parents, and members of the administration feel the same (Henfield, Washington, & Owens, 2010). Additionally, although it is widely accepted that hip-hop is meaningful in how African American males perceive themselves and their environment (Love, 2013; Prier & Beachum, 2008), research to support this belief within the school counseling literature is sparse, at best. Therefore, professional school counselors who are contemplating utilizing sociopolitical rap music should compose a sound rationale for why they are intending to use rap music and how this music will be used therapeutically. Since sociopolitical rap music frequently addresses the intersection of race, racism, oppression, and power, professional school counselors can connect this lyrical content to ASCA's (2012) emphasis on social advocacy and social justice as well as The Education Trust's (1996) Transforming School Counseling Initiative. ASCA and the Transforming School Counseling Initiative both emphasize the importance of school counselors advocating on behalf of racial and ethnic minority students, particularly in those situations where prevalent social injustices obstruct students' paths to immediate and long-term educational success.

Develop a Catalogue of Sociopolitical Rap Music

As professional school counselors prepare to utilize rap music with African American male students, it is important that they first create a prospective playlist of music. There are a number of hip-hop artists who have a noteworthy catalogue and track record of producing critical, intellectually stimulating music. Some of the author's favorite artists include Dead Prez, Narubi Selah, Jasiri X, Skipp Coon, Common, Talib Kweli, and Yasiin Bey, aka Mos Def. Many of these artists have not achieved the recognition and notoriety of other better-known artists; this will require more diligence from professional school counselors as they attempt to compile the work these artists have to offer.

Integrate the Music Into Individual and Group Counseling

Utilizing the comprehensive school counseling model as a framework (ASCA, 2012), professional school counselors can integrate the socially conscious rap music they select into the counseling modalities they implement with African American male students. Due to overwhelming counselor to student ratios, group counseling will most likely be the modality of choice, as it is much more time efficient. In relation to the topic of the criminalization of African American males, for instance, professional school counselors can broach the subject by connecting criminalization to the school to prison pipeline. For instance, here on Masta Killa's song *School* (Turner & Diggs, 2004), the RZA rhymes:

> Sat in the back of the class with my hand up
> Two wild security guards, grabbed my man up
> Threw him in detention for 5 days suspension
> Cuz he said, the teacher was lyin' about the Indians

In these lyrics, the RZA captures how schools often take excessive measures, including employing resource officers, to alleviate student-teacher disagreements. In this scenario, The RZA describes an insistent and inquisitive African American male student who demands that his teacher explain what he considers the romanticization of Euro-American accomplishments. As a result of his persistent questioning, he is forcefully removed from the class and placed in suspension.

IMPLICATION FOR THERAPISTS

Based on available data, which clearly illustrates that a substantial number of African American males identify as participants in hip-hop culture and consume rap music on a daily basis (Cohen, Celesine-Michener, Holmes, Merseth, & Ralph, 2007; Rideout, Roberts, & Foehr, 2005), school counselors and other clinicians must seriously consider how, and under what circumstances, they can utilize hip-hop and rap music with African American male students and clients. Fundamentally, this challenges school counselors and other therapists to seriously dissect their perceptions of hip-hop and rap music, and be willing to unpack any presumptions about how detrimental this content is to the optimal holistic development of school-aged African American males.

This process does not come without legitimate challenges. The primary challenge is the realization that conversations about hip-hop and rap music are not, yet, a consistent part of the school counseling discourse. For instance, although a robust body of scholarship about the intersection of hip-hop, rap, and the lived realities of African American males exists within sociology, critical and cultural studies, teacher education, and social work (Boyd, 2003; Chang, 2005; Dyson, 2007; Forman, 2002; Hill, 2009; Kitwana, 2005, 2002; Ogbar, 2007; Rose, 2008; Travis & Deepak, 2011; Tyson, 2006), an analogous repository of conceptual papers and empirical research within the school counselor education profession hardly exists. Unless these issues are explored during some form of professional development (e.g., Hip Hop Literacies Conference held annually at Ohio State University), school counselors are usually not afforded the necessary time and space, especially during their coursework, to reflect alternatives to traditional counseling modalities, namely hip-hop culture and rap music, for engaging African American male youth. Therefore, sufficient learning opportunities for school counselors and scholarship by school counselor educators about the relevance of hip-hop and rap to African American males in the 21st century would address an obvious dearth in school counselor education and school counseling literature respectively.

CONCLUSION

To suggest that African American males are subjected to a cascade of racial stereotypes and disparaging presuppositions would be stating the obvious. These stereotypes are ominous and influence how members of this society regularly perceive young Black males (Goff, Jackson, Di Leone, Culotta, & DiTomasso, 2014). The author contends professional school counselors can contribute to African American male students' attempts to liberate themselves from the stereotypes they encounter by using empowering messages couched within sociopolitical rap music. Due to the fact that criminalization has been associated with the hyperincarceration of African American males, disrupting the process through which this criminalization occurs is an urgent matter (Love, 2013). Using the principles of social justice as a guide and mandate for practice (Hipolito-Delgado & Lee, 2007), professional school counselors are advised to consider innovative strategies for promoting the liberation of historically marginalized students. Therefore, it seems prudent for professional school counselors to seriously consider how they might integrate sociopolitical rap music responsibly during their clinical interactions with adolescent African American males.

REFERENCES

Akom, A. A. (2009). Critical hip hop pedagogy as a form of liberatory praxis. *Equity & Excellence in Education, 42,* 52–66.

Alexander, M. (2012). *The new Jim Crow: Mass incarceration in the age of colorblindness.* New York, NY: The New Press.

American School Counselor Association. (2012). *ASCA national standards for students.* Alexandria, VA: Author.

Baker, A., Goodman, J. D., & Mueller, B. (2015). *Beyond the chokehold: The path to Eric Garner's death.* Retrieved from http://www.nytimes.com/2015/06/14/nyregion/eric-garner-police-chokehold-staten-island.html?_r=0

Baldridge, B. J., Hill, M. A., & Davis, J. E. (2011). New possibilities: (Re)engaging Black male youth within community-based educational spaces. *Race, Ethnicity and Education, 14,* 121–136.

Boyd, T. (2003). *The new H.N.I.C.: The death of civil rights and the reign of hip hop.* New York, NY: New York University Press.

Brown, A. L. (2011). "Same old stories": The Black male in social science and educational literature, 1930s to the present. *Teachers College Record, 113,* 2047–2079.

Burrell, T. (2010). *Brainwashed: Challenging the myth of Black inferiority.* New York, NY: SmileyBooks.

Butler, A. L. (2014). *Open carry for Whites and open season on Blacks.* Retrieved from http://www.theroot.com/articles/politics/2014/08/john_crawford_shooting _open_carry_for_whites_open_season_on_blacks.html

Caton, M. T. (2012). Black male perspectives on their educational experiences in high school. *Urban Education, 47,* 1055–1085.

Chang, J. (2005). *Can't stop, won't stop: A history of the hip hop generation.* New York, NY: St. Martin's Press.

Cohen, C. J., Celesine-Michener, J., Holmes, C., Merseth, J. L., & Ralph, L. (2007). *The attitudes and behavior of young Black Americans: Research summary.* The Black Youth Project. Retrieved from: http://www.blackyouthproject.com/wp-content/uploads/BYP-Research-Summary.pdf

Dahir, C. A., & Stone, C. B. (2009). School counselor accountability: The path to social justice and systemic change. *Journal of Counseling & Development, 87,* 12–20.

Dale, S. K., & Daniel, J. H. (2013). Talking about the Trayvon Martin case in psychology and counseling training and psychotherapy. *Journal for Social Action in Counseling and Psychology, 5,* 37–49.

De Leon, A. (2004). Hip hop curriculum: A valuable elements for today's after-school programs. Retrieved from http://www.hiphoparchive.org/files/aahiphop_0.pdf

Dixon, A. L., Tucker, C., & Clark, M. A. (2010). Integrating social justice advocacy with national standards of practice: Implications for school counselor education. *Counselor Education & Supervision, 50,* 103–115.

Dyson, M. E. (2007). *Know what I mean: Reflections on hip hop.* New York, NY: Basic-Civitas Books.

Education Trust. (1996). *National center for transforming school counseling.* Retrieved from www.edtrust.org

Entman, R. M., & Rojecki, A. (2000). *The Black image in the White mind: Media and race in America.* Chicago, IL: University of Chicago Press.

Ferguson, A. A. (2001). *Bad boys: Public schools in the making of Black masculinity.* Ann Arbor, MI: University of Michigan Press.

Ford, D. Y., & Moore, J. L. (2013). Understanding and reversing underachievement, low achievement, and achievement gaps among high-ability African American males in urban school contexts. *Urban Review, 45,* 399–415.

Fredrickson, G. M. (1971). *The Black image in the White mind: The debate on Afro-American character and destiny, 1817–1914.* Middleton, CT: Wesleyan University Press.

Forman, M. (2002). *The 'hood comes first: Race, space, and place in rap and hip hop.* Middletown, CT: Wesleyan University Press.

Garcia, A. (2014). Ben Stein: Michael Brown was 'armed with his incredibly strong, scary self.' *Talking Points Memo.* Retrieved from http://talkingpointsmemo.com/livewire/ben-stein-michael-brown-unarmed

Goff, P. A., Jackson, M. C., Di Leone, B. A. L., Culotta, C. M., & DiTomasso, N. A. (2014). The essence of innocence: Consequences of dehumanizing Black children. *Journal of Personality and Social Psychology, 106,* 526–545.

Goodman, R. D., & West-Olatunji, C. A. (2010). Educational hegemony, traumatic stress, and African American and Latino American students. *Journal of Multicultural Counseling and Development, 38,* 176–186.

Griffith, D. W., & Aitken, H. (Producers), & Griffith, D. W. (Director). (1915). *The birth of a nation* [Motion picture]. United States: Epoch Producing Co.

Guthrie, R. V. (2004). *Even the rat was white: A historical view of psychology.* Boston, MA: Pearson Education.

Henfield, M. S. (2013). Special issue: Meeting the needs of gifted and high-achieving Black males in urban schools. *Urban Review, 45,* 395–398.

Henfield, M. S., Washington, A. R., & Owens, D. (2010). To be or not to be gifted: The choice of a new generation. *Gifted Child Today, 32,* 17–25.

Hill, M. L. (2009). *Beats, rhymes, and classroom life: Hip hop pedagogy and the politics of identity.* New York, NY: Teachers College Press.

Hipolito-Delgado, C. P., & Lee, C. C. (2007). Empowerment theory for the professional school counselor: A manifesto for what really matters. *Professional School Counseling, 10,* 327–332.

Howard, T. C. (2013). How does it feel to be a problem? Black male students, schools, and learning in enhancing the knowledge base to disrupt deficit frameworks. *Review of Research in Education, 37,* 54–86.

Isom, D. (2009). Performance, resistance, caring: Racialized gender identity in African American boys. *The Urban Review, 39,* 405–423.

Izadi, E. (2014). Ohio Wal-Mart surveillance video shows police shooting and killing John Crawford III. *The Washington Post.* Retrieved from https://www.washingtonpost.com/news/post-nation/wp/2014/09/25/ohio-wal-mart-surveillance-video-shows-police-shooting-and-killing-john-crawford-iii/

Jackson, K. (2014). Ferguson rapper Tef Poe: Barack Obama has forsaken us, but we will not stop fighting injustice. *Time.* Retrieved from http://time.com/3330800/tef-poe-ferguson-missouri-police-militarization-civil-rights/

Jackson, R. L. (2006). *Scripting the Black masculine body: Identity, discourse, and racial politics in popular media.* New York, NY: State University of New York Press.

Jenkins, T. S. (2006). Mr. nigger: The challenges of educating Black males within American society. *Journal of Black Studies, 37,* 127–155.

Kabango, S. (2007). Brother (Watching). On *The old prince* [CD]. Mississauga, ON: Black Box Recordings.

King, J. (2016). The improbable story of how Kendrick Lamar's "Alright" became a protest anthem. *Identities.Mic.* Retrieved from http://mic.com/articles/134764/the-improbable-story-of-how-kendrick-lamar-s-alright-became-a-protest-anthem#.5IJVnV2jl

Kiselica, M. S., & Robinson, M. (2001). Bringing advocacy counseling to life: The history, issues, and human dramas of social justice work in counseling. *Journal of Counseling & Development, 79,* 387–397.

Kitwana, B. (2002). *The hip hop generation: Young Blacks and the crisis in African American culture.* New York, NY: BasicCivitas Books.

Kitwana, B. (2005). *Why White kids love hip hop: Wankstas, wiggers, wannabes, and the new reality of race in America.* New York, NY: BasicCivitas Books.

Kunjufu, J. (2002). *Black students: Middle class teachers.* Chicago, IL: African American Images.

Kunjufu, J. (2005). *Counseling the conspiracy to destroy Black boys.* Chicago, IL: African American Images.

Ladson-Billings, G. (2011). Boyz to men? Teaching to restore Black boys' childhood. *Race, Ethnicity and Education, 14,* 7–15.

Lee, C. C. (1987). Black manhood training: Group counseling for male Blacks in grades 7–12. *Journal for Specialists in Group Work, 12,* 18–25.

Love, B. (2013). "Oh, they're sending a bad message": Black males resisting and challenging Eurocentric notions of Blackness within hip hop & the mass media through critical pedagogy. *International Journal of Critical Pedagogy, 4,* 24–39.

Love, B. L. (2016). Good kids, mad cities: Kendrick Lamar and finding inner resistance in response to FergusonUSA. *Cultural Studies ↔ Critical Methodologies, 16,* 320–323.

Lynn, L., West, K., Frazier, C. (2005). Real people. On *Be* [CD]. New York, NY: GOOD, Geffen.

Massey, D. S., & Denton, N. A. (1993). *American apartheid: Segregation and the making of the underclass.* Cambridge, MA: Harvard University Press.

McIntyre, C. C. L. (1993). *Criminalizing a race: Free Blacks during slavery.* Queens, NY: Kayode.

McLaughlin, E. C. (2014). *What we know about Michael Brown's shooting.* Retrieved from http://www.cnn.com/2014/08/11/us/missouri-ferguson-michael-brown-what-we-know/

McWhorter, J. (2000). *Losing the race: Self-sabotage in Black America.* New York, NY: Perennial.

Milbank, D. (2014). *Bob McCulloch's pathetic prosecution of Darren Wilson.* Retrieved from https://www.washingtonpost.com/opinions/dana-milbank-bob-mccullochs-pathetic-prosecution-of-darren-wilson/2014/11/25/a8459e16-74d5-11e4-a755-e32227229e7b_story.html

Monroe, C. R. (2009). Teachers closing the discipline gap in an urban middle school. *Urban Education, 44,* 322–347.

Muhammad, K. G. (2010). *The condemnation of Blackness: Race, crime, and the making of modern urban America.* Cambridge, MA: Harvard University Press.

Nocella, A., & Socha, K. (2013). Old school, new school, no school: Hip hop's dismantling of school and the prison industrial complex. *International Journal of Critical Pedagogy, 4,* 40–54.

O'Connor, C., Hill, L. D., & Robinson, S. R. (2009). Who's at risk in school and what's race got to do with it? *Review of Research in Education, 33,* 1–34.

Ogbar, J. O. G. (2007). *Hip-hop revolution: The culture and politics of rap.* Lawrence, KS: The University Press of Kansas.

Potts, R. G. (2003). Emancipatory education versus school-based prevention in African American communities. *American Journal of Community Psychology, 31,* 173–183.

Prier, D., & Beachum, F. (2008). Conceptualizing a critical discourse around hip-hop culture and Black male youth in educational scholarship and research. *International Journal of Qualitative Studies in Education, 21,* 519–535.

Ratts, M. J., DeKruyf, L., & Chen-Hayes, S. F. (2007). The ACA advocacy competencies: A social justice advocacy framework for professional school counselors. *Professional School Counseling, 11,* 90–97.

Rideout, V., Roberts, D. F., & Foehr, U. G. (2005). *Generation M: Media in the lives of 8-to18-year-olds report.* Program for the study of entertainment media and health, KFF publication no. 7251. Menlo Park, CA: Kaiser Family Foundation.

Rose, T. (2008). *The hip hop wars: What we talk about when we talk about hip hop-and why it matters.* New York, NY: Basic Books.

Shin, R. Q., Rogers, J., Stanciu, A., Silas, M., Brown-Smythe, C., & Austin, B. (2010). Advancing social justice in urban schools through the implementation of transformative groups for youth of color. *The Journal for Specialists in Group Work, 35,* 230–235.

Toporek, R. L. (2013, Special issue). Violence against individuals and communities: Reflecting on the Trayvon Martin case. *Journal for Social Action in Counseling and Psychology, 5,* 1–10.

Travis, R., & Deepak, A. (2011). Empowerment in context: Lessons from hip-hop culture for social work practice. *Journal of Ethnic and Cultural Diversity in Social Work, 20,* 203–222.

Turner, E., & Diggs, R. F. (2004). School. On *No Said Date* [CD]. New York, NY: Nature Sounds.

Tyson, E. H. (2006). Rap-music attitude and perception scale: A validation study. *Research on Social Work Practice, 16,* 211–223.

Washington, A. R. (2015). Addressing social injustice with urban African American young men through hip-hop: Suggestions for school counselors. *Journal of Social Action in Counseling and Psychotherapy, 7,* 101–121.

Washington, A. R. (2016). School counseling for the hip-hop generation: Meeting African American male students where they are. In M. S. Henfield and A. R. Washington (Eds.) *School counseling for Black male student success in 21st-Century urban schools* (pp. 155–172). Charlotte, NC: Information Age.

Welch, K. (2007). Black criminal stereotypes and racial profiling. *Journal of Contemporary Criminal Justice, 23,* 276–288.

Whiting, G. W. (2009). Gifted black males: Understanding and decreasing barriers to achievement and identity. *Roeper Review, 31,* 224–233.

Wilson, W. J. (2009). *More than just race: Being Black and poor in the inner city.* New York, NY: W.W. Norton.

CHAPTER 8

AFRICAN AMERICAN MALE SUICIDE

An Eco-System Framework to Understand, Assess, and Intervene

Darron Garner

Suicide remains the third leading cause of death for youth ages 15 to 24 (CDC, 2010). Among African American males aged 15 to 44, suicide is the third, fifth, and sixth leading cause of death, respectively, when categorizing the age groups as follows: 15–24, 25–34, and 35–44 (CDC, 2010). While it is true that suicide was not a leading cause of death for African Americans 40 years ago, this recent decade has shown an increase in the rate of suicide completion and nonfatal suicidal behavior among adolescent and young adult African American males between the ages of 15 and 24 (Garlow, Purselle, & Heninger, 2005). Traditionally, suicide was viewed as a phenomenon that primarily affected young White men; however, suicidality has emerged as a significant health issue for young African American men (Goldsmith, Pellmar, Kleinman, & Bunney, 2002).

Suicidality is not a topic that is discussed often in the African American community. The focus tends to be on dealing with homicides or

Counseling African American Males, pages 127–144
Copyright © 2016 by Information Age Publishing
127

health-related fatalities. And cultural stereotypes, stigma, and assumptions suggest that suicidality is a "White thing." Consequently, community leaders and mental health professionals have not been trained to see suicidality as an important issue in young African American men. Why only young African American men and not young African American females? Because studies indicate that the suicide rate is lowest among African American females (Joe, Baser, Neighbors, Caldwell, & Jackson, 2009). Plus, young African American males disproportionately carry the burden in terms of higher incidences of different sorts of health conditions and illness, and higher rates of joblessness, criminal victimization, school suspension and failure to graduate, and incarceration. So, it is beneficial for mental health professionals and community leaders to start learning about the patterns of young African American male suicidality and be prepared to provide potentially life-saving interventions.

Topics for this chapter include: (a) defining the problem of suicidality; (b) discussing the prevalence and incidence of suicidality for young African American men; (c) exploring the ecosystem framework to outline contextual and interpersonal influences on young African American men suicidality; and (d) suggestions for prevention, assessment, and intervention.

DEFINING SUICIDALITY

There is wide variation in how suicide is defined. Most scholars classify suicidality as suicide, attempted suicide, and suicidal ideation. The definition of suicide, death from self-inflicted injury where there is evidence that the decedent intended to kill himself or herself (King, 1997, p. 63), and suicidal ideations (thoughts of committing suicide and written plans to commit suicide) are straightforward. However, the definition of attempted suicide becomes confusing when meshed up in establishing suicidal intent. For example, "when causal suggestive comments are made to others of suicidal intent, followed by an 'accidental' self-harmful and perhaps lethal event, related to reckless driving or drug overdose, was the incident a suicidal one?" (King, 1997, p. 63). Intent is difficult to assess in completed suicides. Self-destructive behavior also can be viewed as suicide if it appears intentional, but could be considered as an accident. Intent may be particularly difficult to determine in suicides involving young African Americans males, among whom the expression of suicidal intent is generally taboo, and where suicidal communication is often expressed as self-destructive behavior within that community (Poussaint & Alexander, 2001).

Furthermore, defining self-destructive behavior in terms of suicidality for young African American men serves two major purposes. First, it takes into account the historical effects on young African American men's feelings of isolation, inferiority, and rejection embedded in their psyche in understanding the lasting psychological repercussions. The deterioration of the African male image has had a profound effect on the socialization of young African American men as evidenced by the speaking of life-threatening behaviors and placing little value on their life. Second, defining self-destructive behavior starts the process of de-stigmatizing suicidality conversation for the African American community and for young African American men.

PREVALENCE AND INCIDENCES OF SUICIDALITY

The CDC (2010) reported that in 2009 there were approximately 36,900 completed suicides in the United States, an average of 101 a day. Among 15- to 24-year-olds, suicide completions account for approximately 20% of all deaths annually and currently rank as the third leading cause of death, third only to unintentional injury and homicides (CDC, 2010). Studies suggest significant changes in the rates of completed suicide and nonfatal suicidal behaviors among young African American men (CDC, 2002; Garlow, Purselle, & Heninger, 2005; Joe & Marcus, 2003). The gap in the rates of suicide between African American and Caucasian youth significantly narrowed from 1980 to 1995. During this period, the differences in suicide rates between African American and Caucasian males aged 15 to 24 decreased from a ratio of 1.83 in 1981 to 1.45 in 2004 (Joe et al., 2009; Kaslow, Ivey, Berry-Mitchell, Franklin, & Bethea, 2009).

This significant spike in African American adolescent suicide was largely due to a 233% increase in suicides among African American males between the ages of 10 and 19 (CDC, 2010). This increase was more than any other ethnic minority group during this time period (Walker, Lester, Joe, 2006) and has largely been contributed to suicide by firearms (Kubrin & Wadsworth, 2009). Between 1979 and 1997, there was a 133% increase in the rate of firearm-related suicides among African American males aged 15 to 19 (Joe & Kaplan, 2001). In 2009, the CDC reported that suicide still remained the third leading cause of death for African Americans adolescents aged 15 to 24 (CDC, 2010). In 2009, African American adolescents as a whole reported higher rates of suicide attempts than Caucasian adolescents (CDC, 2010). And African Americans male adolescents' suicide rates exceeded female suicide rates by a factor of six, whereas nationally men complete suicide four times more than women (Kochanek, Murphy, Anderson, & Scott, 2004).

African American men are dying at alarming rates to self-destructive behaviors. Nationally published reports on death rates for substance use (drug and alcohol related), risky sexual behaviors (HIV/AIDS), and violence (homicide) among young African American men are astounding.

Drug-related deaths are relatively higher among African Americans than Whites and Hispanics, and homicide is the fourth leading cause of death for men aged 18 to 64 and the leading cause of death for African American men between the ages of 18 and 34 (National Vital Statistics Report, 2007). The death rate for HIV/AIDS is 25.9 per 100,000 among the male population (National Vital Statistics Report, 2007). In 2005, the United States Department of Health and Human Services reported that although African Americans made up only 13% of the total U.S. population, they accounted for 50% of HIV/AIDS cases and were more than nine times as likely to die from HIV/AIDS as non-Hispanic White men. There has to be underlying causes for the high death rates among young African American men! The following section will examine an ecosystem framework on the suicidality context of young African American men in America.

THE ECOSYSTEM FRAMEWORK AND YOUNG AFRICAN AMERICAN MALE SUICIDALITY

The ecosystem framework is a triadic model that helps in conceptualizing the multiple levels of interactional factors that place young African American men at risk for suicidality and other social ills (Bronfenbrenner, 1979). The framework addresses the historical implications that impact Black male identity, the environmental and structural factors that aid and sometimes hinder progress for young African American men, the cultural stereotypes that are often projected toward young African American men, the influences and adaptation of family structures, and the biopsychosocial (biological, psychological, and social) characteristics mental health practitioners face in counseling this population. It is essential that suicidality and solutions be focused on the individual client as well as take into account the very dynamic relationships among individuals, family, culture, environment, and historical implications.

Historical Level

History helps to document the struggles, adversities, and success of both young African American men within a larger society. Young African American men were subjugated by Whites, bought and sold as property, subjected to the harsh fields of Southern plantations, and victims of the brutality suffered through the civil unrest of the 1960s. The psychological impact of these injustices are interwoven into the young African American male psyche and continue to create irreparable damage for a number of young African American men. Slavery set the stage for what Karenga (2002) calls the emasculation, dehumanization, and/or inferiorization process that occurs today. A number of young African American men maintain feelings of inferiority and emasculation in their everyday activities and appear to accept the view of the African American male that has been embedded into their psyche (Billingsley, 1968).

Young African American men have been ego-centrically defined (in an attempt by Whites to maintain feelings of superiority and control) as lazy and worthless, and this has been consistently reiterated into the young African American male socialization process. Without intervention, young African American men fall victim to believing these stereotypes about themselves, which solidify feelings of inferiority and is detrimental to their mental health. According to Karenga (2002), the crisis of the African male in America began with the landing of the first slave ship in 1619, nearly four hundred years ago. The inhumane abuse that African descendants have endured has been destructive to the psychological health of the population and continues to deteriorate the quality of life for young African American men. It is important to examine these factors to conceptualize the true estimate of the damage that has been inflicted upon young African American men and how these psychological ramifications lead to self-injurious behaviors.

Environmental-Structural Level

The least studied influence on young African American men suicidality is broad environmental-societal conditions. These conditions are extremely important for the development of self-esteem and self-worth in young African American men. African American children are not socialized (as in the past) to understand the structural inequities, unfairness, and injustice in America that affects them as adolescents. If young African American men are not prepared with the necessary coping skills to adapt to life experiences that are inevitably the root of many stressors for them, it is not surprising that these same individuals present with mental health issues related to depression, PTSD, hopelessness, low self-esteem, and suicidality (Joe et al., 2009).

Racism Discrimination and Injustice

It is important to examine the impact that racism has on young African American men. Williams and Williams-Morris (2000) purport that young African Americans men are the victims of both institutional and internalized racism, but there is very little research that emphasizes depression, anxiety, self-esteem, and the lasting ramifications of racism. Utsey and Payne (2001) conducted a study to examine the differential impacts of racism on the psychological well-being of a clinical versus "normal" subsample of young African American men. The results indicated that the clinical subsample had significantly higher depression and anxiety scores than the "normal" sample. More research is needed in this area to understand the ramifications of racism on young African American men in general, as well as its causality to suicidality.

Erosion of Cultural Distinctiveness

Culture factors highlight the strengths within the traditional African American community and the problems associated with assimilating into the larger culture of European occupational, residential, political, and educational integration (Shaffer, Gould, & Hicks, 1994). Before integration and few years thereafter, many young African American men received their cultural conditioning or culture distinctiveness from social settings that included "street corners" and other local hangouts. In the socialization process, the "streets" or "hood" emphasis was in the role and function of conventional socialization institutions (e.g., the family, church, educational system, community-based organizations, and mass media) in shaping identity and behavior (Wilson, 1987). The "streets" as a ghetto institution was an American social structure (Wilson, 1987) that assisted with cultural adaptations to intergenerational structural challenges confronting young African American males (Feagin & Vera, 1995; Wilson, 1987).

Today, many young African American men are exposed to the streets as a second family, but without an emphasis on the role and function of conventional socialization institutions. The "streets" or "hood" remain as an institution that exists primarily to meet the psychological and social needs of socially and economically marginalized Black males (Kitwana, 2002). However, the hip-hop culture has emerged and played a significant role in this process for young African American men over the last three decades. Hip-hop culture, particularly "gangsta rap" music and videos of the early 1990s, have been influential in the evolution and transmission of contemporary street culture socialization and the social construction of gender identity among young African American men (Kitwana, 2002). To a larger degree, hip-hop culture has had a huge impact on the way that young African American men perceive their environment and their status in society. The consistent images of wealth, expensive clothes, flashy cars, jewelry, and beautiful women all represent a reality that is not available to most of this population and therefore creates a desire to obtain these material possessions and status. The desire to obtain these materials can lead to drug dealing and criminal activities that seek to obtain economic security and social status. Young people who listen to hip-hop and rap may be more likely to engage in self-destructive behaviors than those who listen to other types of music (Chen, Miller, Grube, & Waiters, 2006).

For prior generations of young African American men, music expressed views about the conditions, experiences, and aspirations of young African

Americans men living in urban ghettos (Dyson, 1993); but musical genre over the past two decades has glamorized America's obsession with achieving status through material acquisition and the manner through which material and social success is sometimes alternatively pursued and ritualized. These fundamental beliefs by young African American men that status and material items represent one's worth can be distorted and result in a continued and magnified belief that they are worthless and inferior without these possessions. This creates issues with self-esteem and self-worth that can manifest into depression, mental health problems, and suicidality among this population.

Ease of Access to Lethal Means/Handguns

Availability of lethal means, particularly handguns, is one of the best documented risk factors for suicide among young African Americans men, and Americans in general (Campbell & Muncer, 2008). Scholars suggest that large numbers of guns were diffused throughout the African American community during the crack cocaine epidemic (Blumstein, Rivara, & Rosenfeld, 2000) and at the height of "gangsta rap." Given this easy access to guns along with mountains of frustration, an increased risk of suicide might be expected (Kubrin & Wadsworth, 2009).

Family Level

The family has perhaps been the most studied institution in the African American community, and the dynamics of the African American family have often been compared to a traditional White family model. This comparison can post numerous problems, as traditional American social and family's values hardly "fit" with traditional African American social and family values. Family and the extended members of one's collective circle of blood relatives and nonrelatives may be particularly important to young African American men because they have historically played a major role in their survival and acted as a cohesive force (Fitzpatrick, Bettina, & Elizabeth, 2008). The flexibility of family boundaries and social roles promotes each family member's ability to adapt to difficult situations (Boyd-Franklin, 1989). In addition, the kinship network of African American families fosters cohesiveness through the mutual interdependence of its members, and the loss of such support can result in character depreciation, identity confusion, and suicidal ideation.

Empirical studies have identified family problems, parent-child conflict, and separation from a parental figure as risk factors for suicide attempts among young African American men (Joe et al., 2009; Kaslow, Ivey, Berry-Mitchell, Franklin, & Bethea, 2009). Fitzpatrick, Bettina, and Elizabeth (2008) have also linked young African American men's happiness and mental well-being to the perception of family cohesion. Higher level of depression in young African American men has been associated with lower levels of family cohesion (Neblett, White, Ford, Philip, Nguyen, & Sellers, 2008). Low family organization and high degrees of family conflict have been correlated with depressive symptoms and suicidal behavior among young African American men (Neblett et al., 2008). Suicidal young African American men also tend to view their families as less cohesive (Scottham, Sellers, & Nguyen, 2008). In fact, several previous studies have documented the relationship between lower levels of family cohesion and higher levels of suicide ideation (Field, 2009) and depression (Neblett et al., 2008). Other studies have linked lack of family support with suicide attempts (Scottham, Sellers, & Nguyen, 2008) and depression (Sullivan, Helms, Kliewer, & Goodman, 2010).

Individual Level

The most commonly examined risk factors are individual factors. This section describes individual characteristics that may perpetuate young African American men suicidality.

Black Masculinity Identity

Black masculine identity is a product of American history; and it has been socially constructed from a narrowly defined understanding of White maleness. However, young African American men are subject to a very different set of socializing influences than young Caucasian men; and they live in a different social reality and have a different masculinity. White masculinity as "gender ideal" provides a double bind for some young African American men who, due to poverty and the opportunity structure, are blocked from achieving certain aspects of the mainstream culture's masculine ideal (Wester, Vogel, Wei, & McClain, 2006).

The relationship between suicidal behaviors and masculinity may be identified in the historical foundation of Black masculine identity and describe the feelings of inadequacy that men often face trying to live by White cultural norms in a society that does not provide them with the necessary supports. If these fundamental desires of young African American men are denied due to societal circumstances preventing them from performing the tasks that encompass their masculinity, it is not difficult to imagine the psychological damage that will result, which can manifest itself as depression, anxiety, low self-esteem, and anger (Daniel, Goldston, Erkanli,, Franklin & Mayfield 2009). Such feelings can then result in behaviors such as violence against self and others, sexual risk behaviors, and substance use, which ultimately lead to death (Wester, Vogel, Wei, & McClain, 2006).

Substance Use and Illicit Drug Use

Substance use is more closely associated with suicide and suicide attempts for young African Americans men than among young Caucasian men for two reasons. First, young African Americans men are less likely to have access to appropriate mental health services that may prevent or ameliorate substance use, and prescription medications cannot be as easily obtained (Poussaint & Alexander, 2001). Second, young African American men are less likely to use mental health care or medications due to distrust of mental health professionals. Consequently, many young African American men choose other chemical means to relieve severe stress or mental disorders. Substances found to be associated with suicide among African American men are heroin (Burrow-Sanchez, Jenson, & Clark, 2009), alcohol (Chassin, Dmitrieva, Modecki, Steinberg, Cauffman, Piquero, & Losoya, 2010), cocaine (Connell, Gilreath, Aklin, & Brex, 2010), marijuana (Burrow-Sanchez et al., 2009), and PCP. Given the negative view of suicide and the strong mores condemning it in the African American community, young African American men may be using "mental lubricant" to help clear any social, cultural, or personal psychological hardships that make acts like suicide seem "easier."

Mental Disorders

Research suggests that almost 90% of all persons who commit suicide are afflicted with a mental disorder including substance use/dependence. All types, including anxiety disorder (Knopf, Park, & Mulye, 2008), conduct disorders (Feldman & Wilson, 1997), personality disorders (Greenberg & Schneider, 1994), schizophrenia (Horwath, Johnson, Horning, & Weissman, 1993), panic disorders (Horwath et al., 1993), posttraumatic stress disorders (Kaslow et al., 2009), and severe types of depression (Knopf et al., 2008) have been associated with young African American men suicidality, as they have in the general population. Mental disorders may have a more "hazy" association with young African American men suicidality because of cultural differences in symptom presentation complicating DSM classifications. The mental illness most closely associated with suicide is depression, but recent research has suggested that depression is "masked" when standard diagnostic tools are used for young African American men and other ethnic groups (Kaslow et al., 2009). Researchers have theorized that instead of turning feelings of anomie, depression, and hopelessness into both interpersonal and self-directed violence, young African Americans men externalize these feelings as interpersonal violence (Kaslow et al., 2009).

Scholars suggest that depression is underdiagnosed and conduct disorder is overdiagnosed among young African American men (Stevenson, Cameron, Herrero-Taylor, & Davis, 2002). At the core of the misdiagnosis of depression in young African American men is the universal assumption that depression is linked to more internalizing symptoms rather than externalizing symptoms. Stevenson et al. (2002) suggested that American society's troubled fear and overreaction to the culturally styled emotional expressions of young African American men contribute to misdiagnoses and youth underfunctioning. Although depression may be underlying suicidal behavior among young African American men, it may be important to consider anger as a presenting symptom of depression (Daniel et al., 2009).

Avoidance of Mental Health Professionals and Underutilization of Mental Health Services

Young African Americans men are less likely to use and have access to mental health services due to residential location, distrust of medical professionals, poor service quality, or lack of insurance coverage (DeNavas-Walt, Proctor, & Smith, 2009). Furthermore, egocentrism, or the belief that obstacles can be overcome by hard work and determination, and that asking for help or assistance as a sign of weakness, perpetuates avoidance of mental health services. Research suggests that avoidance of mental health services also presents a risk of suicidality for young African American men (DeNavas-Walt et al., 2009). Due to limited access and less willingness to seek proper mental health care, psychotropic and talk therapy is used less among young African American men who are at risk for suicidality.

Protective Factors

The majority of research has considered risk factors, with few investigations looking for factors that promote mental wellness among young African American men. Studies have not reached an overall consensus on why some youth commit suicide and others do not. There are plenty of young African American men with risk influences who do not commit suicide, but the research is scarce about the factors that make young African American men resilient and protect them from suicidality. Much is speculative about factors that protect against suicidality, but most protective factors coalesce around young African American men belief system and the lens through which they view the world. Crucial to the process of molding these young men belief structure are families, communities, religiosity, etc. (Ross, Handal, Clark, & Vander Wal, 2009).

ASSESSMENT FOR SUICIDALITY IN AFRICAN AMERICAN MALE YOUTH

Instrumentation should not be the sole basis for determining suicidality in young African American men. Crosscultural epidemiology has frequently used standardized diagnostic interviews based on egocentric conceptions and philosophies of psychopathology. Instruments should form part of a comprehensive assessment derived from multiple sources and methods, including a face-to-face meeting. A finalized assessment should include a plan of action for the young men, family, peers, and service provider (Rudder, Freedenthal, & Osman, 2008).

Furthermore, being cultural proficient as a mental health practitioner helps with structuring clinical reality. Suicidality is far more complex in its origins and structure than what most of us have previously imagined. Taking a focused approach to assessment, diagnosis, and treatment is inappropriate and limits the therapeutic relationship. Individuals have thoughts, feelings, emotions, social relationships, and, most important, they have culture; culture schemas structure their individual and collectively experienced realities.

A variety of assessment methods are available. The most rigorous approach is to use structured clinical interviews whereby the clinician can assess for the presence of clues for suicidality as well as personality characteristics and risk factors. Three instruments that have been well-reviewed (Padilla & Borsato, 2008) are (a) the Diagnostic Interview Schedule for Children and Adolescents (DICA; Reich, 2000), (b) the Interview Schedule for Children and Adolescents (ISCA; Sherrill & Kovacs, 2000), and (c) the Beck Scale for Suicide Ideation (BSI; Beck & Steer, 1991). To avoid false negatives, instruments should also assess personality characteristics and decision-making associated with suicidality (Rudder, Freedenthal, & Osman, 2008). Three scales in particular are (a) The Interpersonal Needs Questionnaire (Van Orden, Witte, Gordon, Bender, & Joiner, 2008), which assesses the critical interpersonal issues of burdensomeness to others and lack of belongingness; (b) the Painful and Provocative Events Scale (Bender, Gordon, Bresin, & Joiner, 2011), which is a self-report of how much the client engages in impulsive, dangerous, pathological, and risk-taking activities; and (c) the Reasons for Living Scale (Linehan, Goodstein, Nielsen, & Chiles, 1983), which queries a person's reasons for staying alive by asking why people would not kill themselves.

CLINICAL INTERVIEW

During the clinical interview, science and art commingle and the interview and diagnostic skill of the practitioner must come into play. Clinicians should conduct clinical interviews to examine suicide plans and clues when attempting to gauge the possibility of suicide attempts. The clues may be verbal, behavioral, situational, or syndromic. All of these clues may be considered as cries for help, no matter how subtle or camouflaged they are.

Therefore, the clinical interview and how it is structured and handled are critical in making on-target assessments of suicidality.

Culturally Appropriate Measures

There are no known instruments developed specifically for young African American men who have been tested. The National Organization of People of Color is beginning to pull together different literature around depression or different psychiatric disorders and how to begin to work with young African American men. Clinicians have to think broadly about the symptoms and the indicators that might suggest that these young men might be in trouble.

IMPLICATIONS FOR PREVENTION, INTERVENTION, AND TREATMENT

A range of responses from prevention to treatment must be adopted to address the myriad of factors related to young African American men suicidality. Macgowan (2004) describes a model for interrupting risk processes, and provide some general guidelines for practice. Broad strategies are needed that not only focus on suicidality but also include "a large-scale ecological, environmental, system oriented approach" addressing social problems such as unemployment, school failure, delinquency, mental health stigma, health, and welfare. Two commonly used prevention methods that have had some success include gatekeeper training and culturally relevant programing.

Prevention

Gatekeeper training program teaches community's members (not limited to paraprofessionals, clergy, teachers, police, barbers, and workers from community agencies) appropriate referral strategies and how to identify suicide risk factors, ideation, and behaviors. Reviews suggest that gatekeeper training is effective in improving knowledge about the risk factors and intentions to intervene and refer potentially suicidal individuals (Maris, Berman, & Silverman, 2000). More studies are needed to determine the efficacy (reduction in suicidality) and unintended negative effects (for instance, normalizing suicide as an option to problems) among some youth. Gatekeeper training programs in the African American community can avoid making suicidality a normalized behavior by focusing more on self-destructive behavior. This helps to destigmatize the conversation about suicidality in a community in which suicidality is taboo and highly stigmatized.

More culturally relevant prevention programs include the Afrocentric approach (Asante, 1988) and rites of passage programs. Afrocentricity focuses on initiation into rituals that reinforce ethnic identity and allow for a healthy transition from adolescent to adulthood. Instilling ethnic pride is an important theme in prevention and intervention. Afrocentricity appears to be promising for a variety of self-destructive behavior of young African American. More research should be conducted on Afrocentric approach in the prevention of suicidality.

Intervention and Treatment

An infused approach of cognitive behavioral therapy and culturally relevant experiences is beneficial for young African American men at high risk for suicidality (Corey, 2012). Hays (2008) recommends group work be closed to six to eight members who meet weekly during 50-minute sessions over a 12-week period. Culturally relevant experiences, includes the engagement of positive African American men from the community to introduce themselves to the group and answer members' questions about how they persevered and succeeded in life as well as to share their talents (Sue & Sue, 2008). Behaviors familiar to the youth, such as physical posturing, spontaneous participation during group session (rather than each person taking a turn), using cultural language, and wearing attire of their choice, are allowed or encouraged. Corey (2012) considers these practices important to the young African American men's expression and identity formation. Group work should target positive changes, mood management, as well as healthy Black male masculinity. Healthy Black male masculinity encourages acknowledging vulnerabilities, seeking help, and finding places to discuss thoughts and emotions in a way that is going to be appropriate (it takes much more strength to talk about your problems than to conceal your problems).

Family-based behavioral interventions have the potential to address self-destructive behavior and suicidality in young African American men. Family-based behavioral programs should attempt to address family risk factors that are correlated with social problems (family conflict, family disengagement, etc.) and enhance the protective factors of African American families such as, spirituality, mutual support, and resiliency even in the face of adversity (Chao, 2012). Family-based behavioral interventions have been shown to be more effective than both group and individual treatment in retaining clients, increasing family functioning, and decreasing various problems, including aggression, hopelessness, and family hassles (Sullivan, Helms, Kliewer, & Goodman, 2010).

Individual cognitive behavioral therapy shows promise in reducing suicidality of young African American men (Maimon & Kuhl, 2008). Attitude and behavioral change should be target interventions, especially attitudes and behaviors of concern in the spectrum of self-destructive behaviors. Once the therapeutic relationship has been developed, clinicians can address other targets, such as having faith, perspective taking, problem solving, etc. Furthermore, the universality of struggles and hardships must be discussed, in addition to how things can get better if they don't self-destruct. Young African American men must learn that emotional pain will not be constantly intense and interminable, and that they can have faith that things are going to get better, contrary to the abundance of evidence to suggest that things are never going to get better. It's therapeutic for clinicians to talk about faith, not just hope because hope takes a long time to build, and faith is the fuel for hope.

IMPLICATIONS FOR COUNSELOR

Although several investigators have studied the factors associated with young African American male suicidality, there is a paucity of research regarding this population. The literature revealed that young African American males are underserved in society for a variety of reasons. Therefore, experienced counseling professionals should place more emphasis on training other counseling professionals to assess suicidality ideation and behaviors in young African American males. Counseling professionals should be competent in research skills and more culturally sensitive to the needs of this diverse youth population in America. In particular, counseling professionals who are working with young African American males should understand their needs and aspirations within an ecosystems framework to effectively intervene with strategic programs to address the needs of young African American males who are receiving or who are reluctant to receive mental health treatment services. More importantly, intervention efforts should be proactive and use a multisystems strategy and approach to address African American male youth suicidality in society.

CONCLUSION

Researchers are beginning to make some much needed progress in understanding young African American male suicidality. Scholars know more about what factors put young African American men at risk and protective influences that may moderate risk. More research is needed to develop interventions and services for young African American men. For example, what services are available to help families who are grieving with a suicide? What's the postvention protocol? That sort of information is scarce, so scholars and clinicians must work together to develop that information.

REFERENCES

Asante. (1988). *Afrocentricity.* Philadelphia, PA: African World Press.

Beck, A., & Steer, J. (1991). *Manual for the Beck scale for suicidal ideation.* San Antonio, TX: Psychological Corporation.

Bender, T. G., Gordon, K. H., Bresin, K., & Joiner, T. E. Jr. (2011). Impulsivity and suicidality: The mediating role of painful experience. *Journal of Affective Disorders, 129*(1/3), 301–307.

Billingsley, A. (1968). *Black families in White America.* Englewood Cliff, NJ: Prentice Hall.

Blumstein, A., Rivara, F., & Rosenfeld, R. (2000). The rise and decline of homicide—and why. *Annual Review of Public Health, 21,* 505–541.

Boyd-Franklin, N. (1989). *Black families in therapy: A multisystems approach.* New York, NY: Guilford Press.

Bronfenbrenner, U. (1979). *The ecology of human development: Experiments by nature and design.* Cambridge, MA: Harvard University Press.

Burrow-Sanchez, J. J., Jenson, W. R., & Clark, E. (2009). School-based interventions for students with substance abuse. *Psychology in the Schools, 46*(3), 238–245.

Campbell, A., & Muncer, S. (2008). Intent to harm or injure? Gender and the expression of anger. *Aggressive Behavior, 34,* 282–293.

Center for Disease Control and Prevention. (2002). *Web-based injury statistics query and reporting systems (WISQARS).* National Center for Injury Prevention and Control, Centers for Disease Control and Prevention. Retrieved from: http://webapp.cdc.gov/sasweb/ncipc/mortrate.html

Center for Disease Control and Prevention. (2010). *Suicide facts at a glance.* National Center for Injury Prevention and Control. Retrieved from www.cdc.gov/violenceprevention/pdf/Suicide_DataSheet-a.pdf

Chao, R. (2012). Racial/ethnic identity, gender role attitudes, and multicultural counseling competence: The role of multicultural counseling training. *Journal of Counseling & Development, 90*(1), 35–44.

Chassin, L., Dmitrieva, J., Modecki, K., Steinberg, L., Cauffman, E., Piquero, A. R., & Losoya, S. H. (2010). Does adolescent alcohol and marijuana use predict suppressed growth in psychosocial maturity among male juvenile offenders? *Psychology of Addictive Behaviors, 24*(1), 48–60.

Chen, M., Miller, B., Grube, J., & Waiters, E. (2006). Music, substance use, and aggression. *Journal of Studies on Alcohol, 67*(3), 373–381.

Connell, C. M., Gilreath, T. D., Aklin, W. M., & Brex, R. A. (2010). Social-ecological influences on patterns of substance use among non-metropolitan high school students. *American Journal of Community Psychology, 45*(1–2), 36–48.

Corey, G. (2012). *Theory and practice of group counseling* (8th ed.). Belmont, CA: Brooks/Cole-Thomas Learning.

Daniel, S. S., Goldston, D. B., Erkanli, A., Franklin, J. C., & Mayfield, A. M. (2009). Trait anger, anger expression, and suicide attempts among adolescents and young adults: A prospective study. *Journal of Clinical Child and Adolescent Psychology, 38*(5), 661–671.

DeNavas-Walt, C., Proctor, B. D., & Smith, J. C. (2009). *Income, poverty, and health insurance coverage in the United States: 2008* (U. S. Census Bureau, Current

Population Reports No. P60-236). Washington, DC: U.S. Government Printing Office. Retrieved from http://www.census.gov/prod/2009pubs/p60-236.pdf

Dyson, M. (1993). *Reflecting Black.* Minneapolis, MN: University of Minnesota Press.

Feagin, J. R., &. Vera, H. (1995). *White racism: The basics.* Mishawaka, IN: Routledge.

Feldman, M. & Wilson, A. (1997). Adolescent suicidality in urban minorities and its relationship to conduct disorder, depression, and separation anxiety. *Journal of the American Academy of Child and Adolescent Psychiatry, 36*(1), 75–84.

Field, J. (2009). *Wellbeing and happiness, Inquiry into the future of lifelong learning thematic paper 4.* Leicester, England: NIACE.

Fitzpatrick, K. M., Bettina, P. F., & Elizabeth, M. (2008). Suicide ideation and attempts among low-income African Americans adolescents. *Suicide and Life Threatening Behavior, 38*(5), 552–563.

Garlow, S. J., Purselle, D., & Heninger, M. (2005). Ethnic differences in patterns of suicide across the life cycle. *American Journal of Psychiatry, 162,* 319–323.

Goldsmith, S. K., Pellmar, T. C., Kleinman, A. M., & Bunney, W. E. (2002). *Reducing suicide: A national imperative.* Washington, DC: Institute of Medicine, National Academies Press.

Greenberg, M., & D. Schneider (1994) Young black males is the answer, but what was the question? *Social Science Medicine, 39*(2) 112–119.

Hays, P. (2008). *Addressing cultural complexities in practice: Assessment, diagnosis, and therapy.* (2nd ed.). Washington, DC: American Psychological Association.

Horwath, E., Johnson, J., Hornig, C. D., & Weissman, M. M. (1993). Agoraphobia without panic: Clinical reappraisal of an epidemiologic finding. *American Journal of Psychiatry, 150,* 1496–1501.

Joe, S., Baser, R.., Neighbors, S., Caldwell, H., & Jackson, C. (2009), 12-month and lifetime prevalence of suicide attempts among Black adolescents. *Journal of the American Academy of Child and Adolescent Psychiatry 48*(3), 271–282.

Joe, S., & Kaplan, M. (2001). Suicide among African American men. *Suicide and Life Threatening Behavior, 31,* 106–121.

Joe, S., & Marcus, S. (2003). Datapoints: Trends by race and gender in suicide attempts among U.S. adolescents, 1991–2001. *Psychiatric Services, 54,* 454–461.

Karenga, M. (2002). *Introduction to Black studies.* (3rd ed.). Los Angeles, CA: University of Sankore Press.

Kaslow, D., Ivey, P., Berry-Mitchell, T., Franklin, F., & Bethea, M. (2009) Suicide among racial and ethnic groups: Implications for research and practice. In G. Frederick & T. L. Leong (Eds.), *Handbook of multicultural mental health* (2nd ed.; pp. 282–310). Boston, MA: Allyn & Bacon.

King, C. (1997). Suicidal behavior in adolescence. In M. S. R. Maris (Ed.), *Review of Suicidology* (pp. 61–95). New York, NY: Guilford Press.

Kitwana, B. (2002). *The hip hop generation: Young Blacks and the crisis in African American culture.* Cleveland, OH: Basic Books.

Knopf, D., Park, M. J., & Mulye, T. P. (2008). *The mental health of adolescents: A national profile, 2008.* San Francisco, CA: National Adolescent Health Information Center. Retrieved from http://www.dmh.cahwnet.gov/prop_63/MHSA/Prevention_and_Early_Intervention/docs/MentalHealthBrief.pdf

Kochanek, K. D., Murphy, S. L., Anderson, R. N., & Scott, C. (2004). Deaths: Final data for 2002. *National Vital Statistics Reports, 53,* 1–116.

Kubrin, C. E., & Wadsworth, T. (2009). Explaining suicide among Blacks and Whites: How socioeconomic factors and gun availability affect race-specific suicide rates. *Southwestern Social Science Journal, 10,* 1540–1561.

Linehan, M. G., Goodstein, J. L., Nielsen, S. L., & Chiles, J. A. (1983). Reasons for staying alive when you are thinking of killing yourself: The reason for living inventory. *Journal of Consulting and Clinical Psychology 51*(2), 276–286.

Macgowan, M. (2004). Prevention and intervention in youth suicide. In P. Allen-Mears & M. W. Fraser (Eds.), *Intervention with children and adolescents: An interdisciplinary perspective* (pp. 282–310). Boston, MA: Allyn & Bacon.

Maimon, D., & Kuhl, D. C. (2008). Social control and youth suicidality: Situating Durkheim's ideas in a multilevel framework. *American Sociological Review, 73*(6), 921–943.

Maris, R., Berman, A., & Silverman, M. M. (2000). *Comprehensive textbook of suicidology.* New York, NY: Guilford Press.

National Vital Statistics Report. (2007). *United States Department of Health and Human Services.* Washington, DC.

Neblett, E. W., Jr., White, R. L., Ford, K. R., Philip, C. L., Nguyên, H. X., & Sellers, R. M. (2008). Patterns of racial socialization and psychological adjustment: Can parental communications about race reduce the impact of racial discrimination? *Journal of Research on Adolescence, 18,* 477–515.

Padilla, A. M., & Borsato, G. N. (2008). Issues in culturally appropriate psychoeducational assessment. In L. A. Suzuki & J. G. Ponterotto (Eds.), *Handbook of multicultural assessment: Clinical, psychological, and educational applications* (pp. 5–28). San Francisco, CA: Jossey-Bass.

Poussaint, A. P., & Alexander, A. (2001). *Lay my burden down: Unraveling suicide and the mental health crisis among African Americans.* Boston, MA: Beacon Press.

Reich, W. (2000). Diagnostic interview for children and adolescents (DICA). *Journal of the American Academy of Child and Adolescent Psychiatry, 39,* 59–66.

Ross, K., Handal, P. J., Clark, E. M., & Vander Wal, J. S. (2009). The relationship between religion and religious coping as a moderator between religion and adjustment. *Journal of Religion and Health, 48*(4), 454–467.

Rudder, P. A., Freedenthal, S., & Osman, A. (2008). Assessing protection from suicide risk: Psychometric properties of the suicide resilience inventory. *Death Studies, 32*(2), 142–153.

Scottham, K. M., Sellers, R. M., & Nguyen, H. X. (2008). A measure of racial identity in African American adolescents: The development of the multidimensional inventory of Black identity—teen. *Cultural Diversity and Ethnic Minority Psychology, 14,* 297–306.

Shaffer, D., Gould, M., & Hicks, R. C. (1994). Worsening suicide rate in Black teenagers. *American Journal of Psychiatry, 151*(12), 1810–1812.

Sherrill, J. & Kovacs, M. (2000). The interview schedule for children and adolescents (ICSA). *Journal of the American Academy of Child and Adolescent Psychiatry, 39,* 67–75.

Stevenson, H. C., Cameron, R., Herrero-Taylor, T., & Davis, G. Y. (2002). Development of the teenage experience of racial socialization scale: Correlates of race-related socialization from the perspective of Black youth. *Journal of Black Psychology, 28,* 84–106.

Sue, D. W., & Sue, D. (2008). *Counseling the culturally diverse: Theory and practice.* (5th ed.). Hoboken, NJ: John Wiley.

Sullivan, T. N., Helms, S. W., Kliewer, W., & Goodman, K. L. (2010). Associations between sadness and anger regulation coping, emotional expression, and physical and relational aggression among urban adolescents. *Social Development, 19,* 30–51.

Utsey, S., &. Payne, Y. (2001). Race-related stress, quality of life indicators, and life satisfaction among elderly African Americans. *Cultural Diversity & Ethnic Minority Psychology, 8*(3), 224–233.

Van Orden, K. W., Witte, T. K., Gordon, K. H., Bender, T. W., & Joiner, T. E., Jr. (2008). Suicidal desire and the capability for suicide: Tests of the interpersonal psychology theory of suicidal behavior among adults. *Journal of Consulting and Clinical Psychology, 76,* 72–83.

Walker, R. L., Lester, D., & Joe, S. (2006). Lay theories of suicide: An examination of culturally relevant suicide beliefs and attributions. *Journal of Black Psychology, 32,* 320–334.

Wester, S. R., Vogel, D. L., Wei, M., & McLain, R. (2006). African American men, gender role conflict, and psychological distress: The role of racial identity. *Journal of Counseling & Development, 84*(4), 419–429.

Williams, D. R., & Williams-Morris, R. (2000). Racism and mental health: The African American experience. *Ethnicity and Health 5*(3/4), 243–268.

Wilson, W. J. (1987). *The truly disadvantaged.* Chicago, IL: University of Chicago Press.

CHAPTER 9

RESILIENCE THEORY AND THE HEALTH BELIEF MODEL AS INTERVENTIONS FOR AFRICAN AMERICAN MALES WITH DEPRESSION

Mallory Struggs and Sandra Harris

BACKGROUND

Depression is a mental health condition that affects approximately 10% of adults in the United States in any given year (Conner et al., 2010a). Green et al. (2014) predicted that by 2030 depression will be the leading cause of disability worldwide. When left untreated, depression can be costly both to society and to the individual. Research has linked depression to decreased worker productivity (Wang et al., 2004) as well as high inpatient and outpatient healthcare costs (Green, et al., 2014). Bazargan-Hejazi, Ani, Gaines, Ahmadi, & Bazargan (2010) provided financial estimates showing that depression costs the United States over $50 billion a year in treatment expenses. Depression also has adverse effects on the individual in areas such as interpersonal relationships, impaired social functioning, and overall poor

Counseling African American Males, pages 145–163
Copyright © 2016 by Information Age Publishing
All rights of reproduction in any form reserved.

quality of life (Green et al., 2014). Other research has linked depression to two thirds of the suicides committed in the United States each year (Jackson, Knight, & Rafferty, 2010).

Even though depression is well documented in the United States, research has shown that depression affects certain groups differently. For instance, results from epidemiological studies have consistently found that African Americans in the United States have a lower lifetime prevalence of depressive episodes than Whites; however, depression tends to be more persistent in African Americans (Gibbs et al., 2013). In addition, a study by Bailey, Blackmon, & Stevens (2009) revealed that 56.6% of African Americans, compared to 38.6% of Caucasians, reported their depression as being disabling. Snowden, Hastings, & Alvidrez (2009) revealed that African Americans, especially males, were overrepresented in the inpatient psychiatric setting for mental illnesses such as depression.

PROBLEM STATEMENT

Mangino (2009) argued that racialized disadvantage in the United States is especially relevant for African American males. The plight of the African American male begins at an early age, typically around the third grade, and continues into the higher education setting. According to the U.S. Department of Education (2009), the dropout rate for African Americans between the ages of 16 and 24 is 12%. Several studies have shown that African American males further experience a significant number of social, cultural, and environmental stressors that predispose them to depression (Conner, Copeland, Grote, & Koeske, 2010b; Holden, McGregor, Blanks, & Mahaffey, 2012).

Social stressors for African American males include high unemployment rates (Carter, 2009; Holden et al., 2012), high incarceration rates (Harper, Terry, & Twiggs, 2009), and racial discrimination (Green et al., 2014). Past research has shown that African American males are two times more likely to be unemployed than European American males; when employed, African American males earn only 75% as much per year as their Caucasian counterparts (Harper et al., 2009). African American males in the United States experience more frequent encounters with law enforcement when compared to other racial groups. The encounters result in higher rates of adverse outcomes in the criminal justice system such as of false criminal accusations, arrests, false imprisonment, and unfair sentencing (Joseph, 2010; Lewis, 2010). Harper, Terry, & Twiggs, (2009) determined that African American males were nearly seven times more likely to be incarcerated, and the average jail sentences were 10 months longer than those of Caucasian males even for the same offense.

Tucker (2009) has argued that years of psychological abuse and deterioration of the image of the African American male has had a profound, negative effect on their psyche. African American males, unlike their predecessors in Africa who were prepared for their roles as fathers, providers, head of families, protectors, and decision makers, African American males in the North American culture have been rendered unable to protect their families, and they often feel powerless to make decisions in their communities (Harris, 2010; Reverby, 2008). It should not be surprising that this group would experience depression. However, despite the numerous social, psychological, and environmental stressors imposed upon them, depression is one of the most undetected diseases among African American men (Holden, McGregor, Blanks, & Mahaffey, 2012; Mallory, 2005). Depression is often overlooked in African American males for several reasons. First, there are cultural differences in how depression is experienced and manifested by members of various groups. Results from one study showed that African Americans may cope with daily life stressors by engaging in unhealthy behaviors (such as bad eating habits, substance use, and smoking), which leads to poorer overall physical health (Aranda et al., 2012). At least one epidemiological study revealed that African Americans showed a higher prevalence of somatic symptoms (15%) than Caucasians (9%) (Bailey et al., 2009). That same study revealed that African Americans experienced more severe sleep disturbance, appetite and weight loss, and hypochondriasis than their Caucasian counterparts.

In addition to the social and environmental variables associated with depression, researchers have documented statistically significant relationships between depression and a number of demographic variables such as age, education, and income. Edwards, Green, Wellington, & Muhammad, (2009) noted that even though depression can begin at any age, the average age of onset is in the mid-20s. Researchers in one study revealed a statistically significant negative relationship between low educational attainment and depression (Bjelland et al., 2008). Findings from another study showed significant relationships between depression, income, and employment (Hudson, Neighbors, Geronimus, & Jackson, 2012). The prevalence of depression has been found to be higher in individuals of low incomes and individuals who were unemployed (Green et al., 2014).

Past research has shown that even when diagnosed with mental illnesses such as depression, African Americans are less likely to seek professional help than other racial groups (Bryant, Greer-Williams, Willis, & Hartwig, 2013; Conner et al., 2010a). One study showed that less than half of the African American adults (45.0%) in the study who met the diagnostic criteria for depression received professional treatment (Aranda et al., 2012). African Americans, particularly, males may be less likely to seek professional help for several reasons. First African Americans are 1.5 times more likely to be uninsured, or receive public insurance, than Caucasians (Bailey et al., 2009). Second, African Americans mistrust the health care system and required more specialized and innovative services (Watkins & Jefferson, 2012). Third, stigmas associated with depression have had a profound impact on the African American culture for years (Bryant, Greer-Williams, Willis, & Hartwig, 2013; Holden et al., 2012). According to Conner et al. (2010b), the stigmas associated with having a mental illness may prevent African Americans from seeking mental health treatment. Fourth, research has shown that in general, African American men prefer to solve their problems on their own or with the help of a friend or family member rather than through the use of professional therapists (Watkins & Jefferson, 2012; Woodward, Taylor, & Chatters, 2011). Finally, mental health professionals are more likely to be found in urban areas (Bailey et al., 2009). Subsequently, African Americans living in rural areas have less access to mental health services. Regardless of the reason, the lack of help seeking among African American males needs to be recognized, acknowledged, and addressed by the professional community in order to develop effective therapeutic interventions for this group.

THEORETICAL FOUNDATION

There are several theoretical approaches that may be instrumental for explaining the lack of help seeking for depression in African American males. These approaches could be utilized by healthcare professionals to develop culturally sensitive therapeutic interventions that ensure the proper treatment of minority clients, especially African American males. Two such models are the health belief model and the resilience theory.

Health Belief Model

The health belief model (HBM) describes how individual perceptions regarding life situations affect a person's willingness to take actions to address those situations (Rosenstock, 1974). The principles of HBM posit that individual perceptions of the following five conditions affect a person's decision to take action: (a) susceptibility, the person's thoughts regarding his or her personal vulnerability to a condition; (b) severity, individual thoughts concerning the seriousness of the condition; (c) benefits, the degree to which an individual believes a specified action will lead to a favorable outcome; (d) barriers, presence of real or imagined obstacles to achieving positive outcomes; and (e) self-efficacy, personal beliefs of personal capacities to take actions.

Principles of the HBM have been effectively applied to address a range of health seeking behaviors such as child influenza vaccinations (Chen, et al., 2011), weight management in African American women (James, Pobee, Oxidine, Brown, & Joshi, 2012), and the knowledge of HIV/AIDS transmission in African American male college students (Ifegwu, 2013). Middleton (2009) asserted that the HBM can be useful for understanding African Americans' health seeking behaviors, especially males. Counselors must also be aware of how demographic variables may be related to individual experiences of life events and how principles of the HBM may be used to build resilience in African American males.

Resilience Theory

Resilience theory (RT) addresses how individuals adapt to and rebound from life stressors (Hendrick & Young, 2013). Some researchers (Hendrick & Young, 2013; Rutter, 2006) have suggested that resilience should be viewed as a process through which individuals develop strategies for coping with adversity. The resilience model can be utilized by therapists and healthcare professionals to assist African American males with developing strategies to help them bounce back from depression (Lowdermilk & Brunache, 2013). In spite of the multiple environmental stressors experienced by African Americans, the lower prevalence of diagnosed depression in this racial group may be attributable to their utilization of resources that promote resilience, such as religion and family support, that protect individuals against the deleterious effects of those stressors (Aranda et al., 2012). The support systems offered by friends and family may enhance one's chances of surviving and bouncing back from depression to become a productive member of society, especially from the perspective of the African American male. Principles of resiliency theory could be used to develop culturally sensitive therapeutic techniques to mitigate the psychological distress that is associated with depression. Counselors could utilize principles of resilience theory to assist African American male in seeking and utilizing resources that can be used to build their resiliency and help them better cope with depression. In order to build resiliency in clients, counselors must be aware of the demographic variables that are related to depression in various populations of individuals. Through this knowledge, counselors can then utilize principles from the HBM and RT to build effective therapeutic alliances.

PURPOSE STATEMENT

Much of the research that has addressed depression in the African American community has stemmed from epidemiological studies conducted at the national level. Such studies may not accurately reflect the occurrence of depression in specific African Americans communities (Green et al., 2014). Thus, there are few studies that have directly addressed depression in rural populations, and there is a paucity of studies that have addressed depression in African American males living in rural areas (Green et al., 2014; Holden et al., 2012). Therefore, the purpose of this article is to present research that investigated the relationships between demographic variables and depression in African American males living in rural Alabama. This article also addresses the implications of those findings for developing effective therapeutic interventions for this group of individuals.

METHODOLOGY

This quantitative, nonexperimental, correlational study gathered data from a sample of African American males between the ages of 18 and 54 who had been diagnosed with depression. We used a purposeful sampling to recruit participants for the study. The sample was drawn from individuals who obtained services for depression from two rural mental health agencies located near Montgomery, Alabama. The inclusion criteria required that participants had to be: (a) African American, (b) males between the ages of 18 and 54, (c) have a diagnosis of depression, and (d) be receiving treatment at one of the facilities in Montgomery, Alabama.

Procedures

Data utilized for this article was collected to fulfill requirements for obtaining a doctoral degree requirement at a major university. The research therefore received institutional review board approval before data were collected. The director from each agency granted permission to recruit participants and to conduct the research. Letters that described the research were distributed to possible participants as clients left each facility. The letters contained contact information whereby interested individuals were instructed to contact the researcher directly for possible inclusion in the study. During the initial contact, the researcher provided a brief overview of the study. The researcher also explained the length of time it would take to complete the study. The researcher also scheduled a time and place for a follow-up meeting for administration of the assessment. The follow-up meeting took place in a local rural mental health outpatient clinic to ensure privacy and confidentiality for the participants.

During the data collection meeting, the researcher explained the consent form, emphasized the voluntary nature of participation in the study, and informed participants that they could withdraw from the study at any time. The researcher assured participants that their privacy and confidentiality would be protected at all times. Participants were also informed that their responses would remain anonymous. No individually identifying data was presented in any form, and all participant responses have been reported in aggregated form.

Data Collection and Instrumentation

Data were collected from the agency records and through the administration of the Beck Depression Inventory-II (BDI-II; Beck et al., 1996). The agency records were used to gather demographic information such as age, age when diagnosed with depression, education, yearly income, and length of time in treatment. The BDI-II is a 21-item self-report inventory that assesses depressive symptoms in individuals aged 13 years and older. The BDI-II was selected for this study because it has been the most widely utilized assessment in diagnosing the severity of depressive symptoms over 35 years (Beck, Steer, & Brown, 1996).

Participants were asked to use the 21 items on the DBI-II to describe themselves for the "past two weeks, including today." Each item was rated on a 4-point scale that ranged from 0 to 3. Scoring of the BDI was completed by summing the ratings for each of the 21 items. Total scores could range from 0 to 63. Beck et al. (1996) used total scores from the BDI-II to classify the level of severity of depressive symptoms according the following rating system: (a) total scores ranging from 0 to 13 represent "minimal" depression, (b) total scores ranging from 14 to 19 represent "mild" depression, (c) total scores from 20 to 28 represent "moderate" depression, and (d) total scores from 29 to 63 represent "severe" depression.

Beck et al. (1996) provided evidence that the BDI-II possesses adequate reliability and validity. The BDI-II yielded a coefficient alpha of .92 for the outpatient population ($n = 500$) and .93 for college students ($n = 120$) reported in the test manual. The 1-week test–retest reliability was ($r = .93$, $p < .001$) for 26 outpatients who completed the BDI-II. Convergent validity has also been established for the BDI-II as it has achieved positive correlations with other measures of depression such as the Beck Hopelessness Scale ($r = .68$, $n = 158$), the Hamilton Psychiatric Rating Scale for Depression ($r = .71$, $n = 87$), and the Hamilton Rating Scale for Anxiety ($r = .47$, $n = 87$) (Smith & Erford, 2001).

Data Analysis

Multiple regression analysis was conducted to test the null hypothesis for the research question. The independent variables were: (a) age (in years), (b) age when first diagnosed with depression (in years), (c) education (number of years of schooling), (d) yearly income, (e) level of functioning (measured by GAF scores), and (f) how long in current treatment (in months). The dependent variable was depression scores on the BDI-II (Beck et al., 1996).

RESULTS

Demographic Data

Table 9.1 presents a summary of the descriptive statistics for the demographic data. Results revealed that average age of the participants was 42-years-old. On average, the attained educational level of the participants was 11th grade. The average yearly income was $11,791. Data further revealed that on average, participants were almost 40-years-old when they were diagnosed with depression. Results indicated that participants had been in treatment for an average of 20 months.

Prescreening Data

Data were prescreened to determine the accuracy and validity of the data before statistical procedures were conducted to test the null hypothesis (Mertler & Vanatta, 2005). Prescreening data allows researchers to assess the degree to which analytical errors may be present and it allows them to interpret findings within and appropriate context (Onwuegbuzie & Daniel, 2003). The following were considered during the prescreening phase of the data analysis: accuracy of data collection, adequacy of sample size, missing data, reliability of data collected using the BDI-II instrument, outliers, skewness, and degree to which assumptions were met for multiple regression. All results indicated the data were suitable for subjecting to regression analysis.

TABLE 9.1 Summary Descriptive Statistics of Participant Demographic Information

	N	Range	Minimum	Maximum	Mean	sd
Current age in years	65	36	18	54	41.88	10.77
Years of education	65	8	6	14	11.31	2.07
Yearly income in dollars	65	43,512	4,200	47,712	11,791.49	7851.00
Age at diagnosis in years	65	36	17	53	39.98	10.68
Level of functioning	65	8	50	78	66.32	8.028
Months in treatment	65	71	1	72	20.95	17.26

Reliability of BDI-II for Current Sample

A major requirement of survey research is that researchers report information about the psychometric properties of the survey for the sample of participants included in the study (Trochim & Donnelly, 2007). Reliability is a key psychometric property that must be reported because reliability is a function of scores obtained by an instrument, and scores on an instrument can vary from sample to sample (Harris, 2013). Cronbach's coefficient alpha (α) was used to measure the internal consistency of the scales included in the survey (Trochim & Donnelly, 2007). The significance of the obtained alpha was tested against the value of $\alpha = .70$, because research has indicated that values of .70 or greater indicates a reliable scale (Kaplan & Sacuzzo, 2009; Mertler & Vanatta, 2005). Results from the reliability analysis generated a Cronbach's $\alpha = .893$, 95% CI (.851–.927). The obtained alpha was significantly different (F [64, 1280] = .000, $M = 18.92$, $sd = 8.91$, $n = 21$) from the test value of $\alpha = .70$. The BDI-II was deemed to have collected reliable data for the participants in the study.

Correlations Among Variables

A major step in regression analysis pertains to addressing the degree of correlations among the variables of interest (Mertler & Vanatta, 2005). This step enables researchers to examine results for possible multicollinearity among the variables of interest and take steps to address multicollinearity when present. Results revealed several statistically significant correlations and possible multicollinearity among some variables. Table 9.2 presents a summary of results from the correlation analysis. The data revealed a significant positive correlation ($r = .99$, $p = .00$) between current age and age when diagnosed. Results also showed a statistically significant correlation ($r = .94$, $p \leq .001$) between level of functioning and level of depression. The high correlations between current age and age when diagnosed as well as the high correlations between level of functioning and level of depression indicated multicollinearity between the two sets of variables. To minimize possible suppressor effects among those variables, current age and clinical diagnosis were excluded from the regression analysis.

Results further showed that education was significantly and negatively correlated with clinical diagnosis ($r = -.32$, $p \leq .01$) and with level of depression ($r = -.31$, $p \leq .01$). However, education was significantly and positively correlated with level of functioning ($r = .35$, $p \leq .01$). Clinical diagnosis was negatively correlated with level of functioning ($r = -.38$, $p \leq .01$) and positively correlated with level of depression ($r = .92$, $p \leq .001$). Level of depression was

TABLE 9.2 Pearson Correlation Matrix for the Dependent and Independent Variables

Variable	Education	Income	Age when diagnosed	Clinical diagnosis	Level of functioning	Length of time in treatment	Level of depression
Current age	-.04	.01	.99**	.12	.19	.18	.14
Education		-.01	-.04	-.32**	.35**	.02	-.31*
Income			.02	-.03	-.02	-.03	.02
Age when diagnosed				.12	.16	.07	.14
Clinical diagnosis					-.38**	.00	.94**
Level of functioning						.30*	-.39**
Months in treatment							.00

Note: $n = 65$ for all correlations.
* Correlation is significant at the 0.05 level (2-tailed); ** Correlation is significant at the 0.01 level (2-tailed).

negatively correlated with level of functioning ($r = -.39$, $p \leq .01$) and positively correlated with length of time in treatment ($r = .30$, $p \leq .05$).

Research Question and Data Analysis

The research question that guided this study was: To what extent do the demographic variables (income, education, age when diagnosed with depression), depression diagnosis, level of functioning, and length of time in current treatment predict total scores on the BDI-II among African American males in rural areas diagnosed with depression? Multiple regression analysis was used to test the null hypothesis. The independent variables were: (a) age (in years), (b) age when first diagnosed, (c) diagnosis (as given by physician), (d) education (number of years of schooling), (e) yearly income, (f) level of functioning [measured by Global Assessment of Functioning (GAF) scores], and (g) length of current treatment measured in months. The dependent variable was depression scores on the BDI-II. Results as presented in Table 9.3 show that SPSS generated five statistically significant regression models. Further analysis of data shows that Model 4, $R^2 = .256$, $R^2\text{adj} = .206$, $F(4, 64) = 5.153$, $MSE = 324.466$, $p < .001$, accounted for the largest proportion of variance (21%) in scores on the BDI-II.

Review of the beta coefficients for Model 4 revealed that education ($t = -1.083$, $p = .039$, 95% CI [-2.112, $-.054$]), age when diagnosed ($t = 2.241$, $p = .029$, 95% CI [$.023$, $.401$]), and level of functioning ($t = -2.502$, $p = .015$, 95% CI [$-.604$, $-.067$]) were statistically significant predictors of BDI-II scores. Education and level of functioning were negatively related to BDI-II scores, which indicated that low scores on those variables were associated with high scores on the BDI-II. Age when diagnosed was positively correlated with BDI-II scores. The obtained power for the change in F ($F\Delta$) associated with Model 4 was 90.3, which indicated there was a 90.3% of correctly rejecting the null hypothesis. The regression equation using the unstandardized regression coefficients is summarized as follows:

TABLE 9.3   Regression Model Summary Statistics

Model	R	R^2	Adjusted R^2	Std. Error of the Estimate	ΔR^2	$F\Delta$	df1	df2	Sig. $F\Delta$
					Change Statistics				
1	.367	.134	.121	8.35068	.134	9.784	1	63	.003
2	.371	.137	.110	8.40294	.003	.219	1	62	.642
3	.422	.178	.138	8.26973	.041	3.014	1	61	.088
4	.506	.256	.206	7.93481	.078	6.258	1	60	.015
5	.511	.261	.199	7.97115	.006	.454	1	59	.503

Total score on BDI-II = 45.796 + (–1.083 * education) + (–7.149E-5 * income) + (.212 * age when diagnosed) + (–.336 * level of functioning)

DISCUSSION

Our goal in this research was to determine how well certain demographic variables predicted depression in African American males living in rural areas. Results from the correlation analysis yielded some interesting results. Edwards et al. (2009) reported that the average age for a diagnosis of depression was the mid-20s. Results from this study showed that the average age of diagnosis for depression in this sample of participants was almost 40. Past studies have shown that depression tends to persist in African Americans for longer periods of time (Gibbs et al., 2013), and that African Americans experience higher rates of somatic complaints (Bailey et al., 2009). It may be that the participants in this study experienced symptoms of depression at an earlier age, yet delayed seeking treatment until their coping mechanisms were no longer effective and the depression had become disabling, which would be consistent with findings from other studies (Snowden et al., 2009).

Past research has also demonstrated links between demographic variables such as income and employment (Hudson et al., 2012). The average annual income of participants in this study was $11,791, which placed them below the $11,888 poverty threshold as indicated by U.S. Census Bureau (2013) guidelines. The data showed that 60% of participants were below the poverty level, and 83% earned less than $15,000 yearly. However income was not a statistically significant predictor of depression scores in this sample. This finding may be related to the fact that most participants in the study were unemployed and receiving disability payment. Consequently, the restricted range of income may have suppressed the predictive relationship between income and depression.

The negative correlations between education and clinical diagnosis as well as between education and level of depression were similar to findings from previous research (Bjelland et al., 2008; Green et al., 2014). Results from this study support the reality that individuals with lower educational attainment are more likely to experience depression. Data from this study also revealed that level of functioning was negatively related to clinical diagnosis and level of depression. We did not find any studies that addressed relationships between level of functioning, clinical diagnosis, and level of depression. However, these findings confirm results from other research. Snowden et al. (2009) found that many individuals delayed seeking treatment for depression until the disorder became disabling, which implied that their overall functioning had declined. Consequently, one would expect that as the level of depression increases, a person's level of functioning would decrease.

The bivariate correlations showed relationships between pairs of variables, and multiple regression showed how the variables combined to predict depression scores. We did not locate any studies that addressed the predictive relationships between education, income, age when diagnosed with depression, level of functioning, and depression scores in African American males living in rural areas. These findings make a unique contribution to the literature, and they offer implications for practice.

PRACTICAL IMPLICATIONS OF FINDINGS

Findings from this study have practical implications for therapists working with African American males living in rural areas who have been diagnosed with depression. A major implication is related to the need for counselors to become advocates for culturally sensitive mental health services. Depression has been linked to socioeconomic factors such as poverty, lower educational attainment, and limited resources (CDC, 2011). There is also a high cost associated with treatment from depression (Bazargan-Hejazi, et al., 2010). Counselors must become advocates and educate political leaders on the importance of providing mental health treatment for economically disadvantaged populations such as African American males. Tucker (2009) further posited that when developing therapeutic interventions, therapists must develop a broader worldview for understanding the variables that affect their psychological functioning and well-being. This worldview should include an understanding of how demographic variables are related to depression in African American males and how principles from theoretical models can be used to address their help-seeking behaviors for depression.

Health Belief Model

Middleton (2009) asserted that the health belief model (HBM) can be utilized to develop effective therapeutic alliances with African American males. To do so, counselors must be aware of how the five individual perceptions presented in the HBM affect mental-help-seeking behaviors in the African American community. First, counselors must address individual perceptions about the susceptibility of African American males to depression. This could be accomplished by developing and promoting awareness programs that address the relationships between race, ethnicity, and the mental status of adults in the United States (Gibbs et al., 2013). Awareness programs could also discuss the connections between environmental stressors such as racism, discrimination, and depression (Aranda et al., 2012). Second, counselors must address individual perceptions regarding the severity of depression as well as how it affects individuals and society. The information should highlight how depression impacts individuals in terms of their professional work behavior (Wang et al., 2004) and their interpersonal lives (Green et al., 2014). The counselor should also provide information about the economic costs of depression and how those costs affect individuals and the nation (Bazargan-Hejaki et al., 2010). Individuals should also be informed of the link between depression and suicide (Jackson et al., 2010).

Additional actions must be taken to address individual perceptions related to the barriers, either real or imagined, that serve as obstacles, preventing African American males from seeking treatment for depression. The first step in addressing those barriers is for counselors to be aware of the internal and external factors that prevent help-seeking behaviors among African American males. Previous research has identified internal, personal barriers such as the desire to maintain privacy, denial of depression, having the mindset that depression is a part of life, and masking symptoms of depression (Bryant et al., 2013). Research has further identified external factors such as spiritual beliefs, lack of resources, lack of education, and stigma as factors that pose barriers to seeking help for mental illness in African Americans (Bryant et al., 2013). Counselors can become aware of how various perceptions affect the willingness of African American males to seek therapeutic interventions for depression by becoming knowledgeable of literature that addresses the barriers to seeking treatment. Counselors must also become abreast of literature that presents evidence-based practices that adapt strategies for mitigating the effect of those barriers. Once the individual perceptions related to depression have been adequately addressed, therapists can then use principles from resilience theory to develop strategies for increasing the self-efficacy beliefs in African American males regarding their ability to take positive actions to effectively address depression.

Resilience Theory

Principles of resilience theory can be utilized by therapists and healthcare professionals to build effective therapeutic alliances to help African American males bounce back from depression. According to William, Roberta, Karina, Heidi, & Richard, (2009), "counselors must be aware of the characteristics of clients and should develop and provide intervention strategies to maximize protective factors for enhancing a client's chance of fulfillment" (p. 151). Consequently, the first step to promoting resilience is to recognize that although African American males are exposed to a significant number of environmental stressors that are linked to depression

(Carter, 2009; Conner et al., 2010a; Harper et al., 2009), and they typically do not seek treatment until the disorder becomes disabling (Snowden et al., 2009). Data from this study provided evidence to support Snowden et al.'s (2009) research regarding the delayed seeking of treatment for depression among African Americans. Findings from the study showed participants were, on average, much older (40-years-old) than what previous research indicated to be the average age of onset for depression, which was the mid-20s (Edwards et al., 2009). It is possible that participants had experienced symptoms of depression for years before seeking treatment. Consequently, instead of waiting for African American males to go to the counseling professional's office, practicing professionals should go to where this population is located (Shallcross, 2010). Past research has shown that church-based health promotion programs have been effective outlets for addressing the health needs of African Americans (Hankerson & Weisman, 2012). Effective therapeutic interventions must, therefore, consider establishing collaborative partnerships with churches and other community-based organizations in order to reach out to African American males living in rural areas who may be experiencing depression. To promote resilience in African American males, counselors must also be aware of the traditional methods that this population adopts to cope with distress. Research has shown that African American men prefer to solve their problems on their own or with the help of a friend or family member rather than through the use of professional therapists (Watkins & Jefferson, 2012; Woodward, Taylor, & Chatters, 2011). Therefore, effective therapeutic interventions must incorporate strategies that empower or involve African American males in developing solutions for their problems. Those interventions should promote an awareness of how suppression and denial of emotions have been linked to increased psychological distress (Mclaughlin, Hatzenbuehler, & Keyes, 2010). Therapeutic interventions must therefore provide forums whereby African American males can openly discuss their experiences with and reactions to environmental stressors such as discrimination. Past research has shown that individuals who do not accept discrimination and those who actively seek ways to discuss their depression had lower rates of psychological distress than African Americans who accepted discrimination and silently endured their experiences (McLaughlin et al., 2010). Counselors must also understand the role that family, religion, and other community support networks have in promoting the resilience of African American males (Gibbs et al., 2013). Effective therapeutic interventions must include intentional efforts to involve family and extended family members in the treatment of depression for African American males (Sanders, Bantum, Owen, Thornton, & Stanton, 2010).

LIMITATIONS

There are several limitations associated with this study. The first limitation pertains to the small sample size. Although the obtained sample size (*N*=65) was larger than the minimum sample size calculated in the a priori power analysis (*N*=65), a larger, more diverse sample of African American males from different geographic regions may produce different results. The findings from this study may reflect similarities in the participants due to the similarities in the communities and cultural norms of the communities in which they reside. Additional studies should be conducted using larger samples of African American males residing in different rural areas around the United States. The second limitation is related to the nuances of collecting self-report data. Participants may not give an accurate ratings of their beliefs, feelings, or attitudes regarding their behaviors in the two weeks prior to completing the BDI-II. Participants may have been influenced by the social desirability phenomenon, and they may have answered according to what they believed was the correct response. These limitations limit the generalizability of the results to other samples.

CONCLUSION

Results from this study provided information about how demographic variables predict depression in African American males living in rural areas of the southeastern United States. Professionals in the mental health field must be educated on the factors that impact depression in the African American male population. Counselors must develop culturally-sensitive therapeutic interventions that address the health beliefs and factors that promote resiliency in this population.

REFERENCES

Aranda, M. P., Chae, D. H., Lincoln. K. D., Taylor, R. J., Woodward, T. T., & Chatters, L. M. (2012). Demographic correlates of *DSM-IV* major depressive disorder among older African Americans, Black Caribbeans, and non-Hispanic Caucasians: Results from the National Survey of American Life. *International Journal of Geriatric Psychiatry, 27*(9), 940–947. doi:10.1002/gps.2805

Bailey, R. F., Blackmon, H. L., & Stevens, F. L. (2009). Major depressive disorder in the African American population: Meeting the challenges of stigma, misdiagnosis, and treatment disparities. *Journal of the National Medical Association, 101*(11), 1084–1088.

Bazargan-Hejazi, S., Ani, C., Gaines, T., Ahmadi, A., & Bazargan, M. (2010). Alcohol misuse and depression symptoms among males and females. *Archives of Iranian Medicine, 13*(4), 324–333. doi:010134/AIM.0013

Beck, A. T., Steer, R. A., & Brown, G. K. (1996). *Manual for the Beck Depression Inventory-II.* San Antonio, TX: Psychological Corporation.

Bjelland, I., Krokstad, S., Mykletun, A., Dahl, A. A., Tell, G. S., & Tambs, K. (2008). Does a higher educational level protect against anxiety and depression? The HUNT study. *Social Science Medicine, 66*(6), 1334–1345. doi:10.1016/j.socscimed.2007.12.019.

Bryant, K., Greer-Williams, N., Willis, N., & Hartwig, M. (2013). Barriers to diagnosis and treatment of depression: Voices from a rural African American faith community. *Journal of National Black Nurses' Association, 24*(1), 31–38.

Carter, M. (2009). Unequal crime decline: Theorizing race, urban inequality, and criminal violence. *Western Journal of Black Studies, 33*(4), 293–295.

Chen, M., Wang, R., Schneider, J. K., Tsai, C., Jiang, D. D., Hung, M., & Lin, L. (2011). Using the health belief model to understand caregiver factors influencing childhood influenza vaccinations. *Journal of Community Health Nursing, 28*(1), 29–40. doi:10.1080/07370016.2011.539087

Conner, K. O., Copeland, V. C., Grote, N. K., & Koeske, G. (2010b). Mental health treatment seeking among older adults with depression: The impact of stigma and race. *The American Journal of Geriatric Psychiatry, 18*(6), 531–544.

Conner, K. O., Lee, B., Mauers, V., Robinson, D., Reynolds, C. F., Albert, S., & Brown, C. (2010a). Attitudes and beliefs about mental health among African American older adults suffering from depression. *Journal of Aging Studies, 24*(4), 266–277. doi:10.1016/j.jaging.2010.05.007

Edwards, C. L., Green, M., Wellington, C. C., & Muhammad, M. (2009). Depression, suicidal ideation, and attempts in Black patients with sickle cell disease. *Journal of the National Medical Association, 101*(11), 1090–1096.

Gibbs, T. A., Okuda, M., Oquendo, M. A., Lawson, W. B., Wang, S., Thomas, Y. F., & Blanco, C. (2013). Mental health of African Americans and Caribbean African Americans in the United States: Results from the National Epidemiological Survey on Alcohol and Related Conditions. *American Journal of Public Health, 103*(2), 330–338. doi:10.2105/AJPH.2012.300891

Green, K. M., Fothergill, K. E., Robertson, J. A., Zebrak, K. A., Banda, D. R., & Ensminger, M. E. (2013). Early life predictors of adult depression in a community cohort of urban African Americans. *Journal of Urban Health, 90*(1), 101–115. doi:10.1007/s11524-012-9707-5

Hankerson, S. H., & Weissman, M. M. (2012). Church-based health programs for mental disorders among African American males: A review. *Psychiatric Services, 63*(3), 243–249. doi: 10.1176/appi.ps.201100216.

Harper, F. D., Terry, L. M., & Twiggs, R. (2009). Counseling strategies with Black boys and Black men: Implications for policy. *The Journal of Negro Education, 78*(3), 216–235.

Harris, G. (2010). Cultural competence: Its promise for reducing healthcare disparities. *Journal of Health and Human Services Administration, 33*(1), 2–53.

Harris, S. M. (2013). Development of the perceptions of mentoring relationships survey: A mixed methods approach. *International Journal of Multiple Research Approaches, 7*(1), 83–95.

Hendrick, A. S., & Young, S. (2013). Working the 'spaces' between policy and practice: The contributions offered by resilience theory and action research. *Child and Family Social Work, 18,* 179–188. doi:10.1111/j.1365-2206.2011.00819.x

Holden, K. B., McGregor, B. S., Blanks, S. H., & Mahaffey, C. (2012). Psychosocial, socio-cultural, and environmental influences on mental health help-seeking among African American men. *Journal of Men's Health, 9*(2), 63–69. doi:10.1016/j.jomh.2012.03.002

Hudson, D. L., Neighbors, H. W., Geronimus, J. S., & Jackson, J. S. (2012). The relationship between socioeconomic position and depression among a U.S. nationally representative sample of African Americans. *Social Psychiatry and Psychiatric Epidemiology, 47*(3), 373–381. doi:10.1007/s00127-011-0348-x

Ifegwu, O. O. (2013). HIV/AIDS *Knowledge, attitudes, and behaviors of southern African American male college students.* (Doctoral dissertation). Retrieved from: http://search.proquest.com/docview/1341304556

Jackson, J. S., Knight, K. M., & Rafferty, J. A. (2010). Race and unhealthy behaviors: Chronic stress, the HPA axis, and physical and mental health disparities over the life course. *American Journal of Public Health, 100*(5), 933–940.

James, D. C. S., Pobee, J. W., Oxidine, D., Brown, L., & Joshi, G. (2012). Using the health belief model to develop culturally appropriate weight-management materials for African-American women. *Journal of the Academy of Nutrition and Dietetics, 112*(5), 664–670. doi:10.1016/j.jand.2012.02.003

Joseph, M. L. (2010). Understanding the economic costs of incarceration for African American males. In W. E. Johnson (Ed.), *Social work with African American males* (pp. 311–325). New York, NY: Oxford University Press.

Kaplan, R. M., & Saccuzzo, D. P. (2009). *Psychological testing: Principles, applications, and issues.* Belmont, CA: Thomson-Wadsworth.

Lewis, C. E. (2010). Incarceration and family formation. In W. E. Johnson (Ed.), *Social work with African American males* (pp. 293–310). New York, NY: Oxford University Press.

Lowdermilk, E., & Brunache, J. (2013). Experiencing unexpected pathways: A grounded theory study of the surprising transformation of inner-city youth. *Social Work and Christianity, 40*(3), 322–351.

Mallory, K. (2005). Black men have straight talk about health. *Afro-American Red Star,* p. A9. Retrieved March 5, 2009, from Ethnic News Watch (ENW).

Mangino, W. (2009). Neighborhoods, racial discrimination. The downside of social closure: Brokerage, parental influence, and delinquency among African American boys. *Sociology of Education, 82*(2), 147–173.

McLaughlin, K. A., Hatzenbuehler, M. L., & Keyes, K. M. (2010). Responses to discrimination and psychiatric disorders among Black, Hispanic, female, and lesbian, gay, and bisexual individuals. *American Journal of Public Health, 100*(8), 1477–1484. doi:10.2105/AJPH.2009.181586

Mertler, C. A., & Vanatta, R. A. (2005). *Advanced and multivariate statistical methods* (3rd ed.). Glendale, CA: Pyrczak.

Middleton, J. (2009). A proposed new model of hypertensive treatment behavior in African Americans. *Journal of the National Medical Association, 101*(1), 12–18.

Onwuegbuzie, O. J., & Daniel. L. J. (2003). Typology of analytical and interpretational errors in quantitative and qualitative educational research. *Current Issues in Education 6*(2). Retrieved from http://cie.ed.asu.edu/volume6/number2/

Reverby, S. (2008). Inclusion and exclusion: The politics of history, difference, and medical research. *Journal of the History of Medicine and Allied Sciences, 63*(1), 103–114.

Rosenstock, I. (1974). Historical origins of the health belief model. *Health Education and Behavior, 2*(4), 328–335. doi:10.1177/109019817400200403

Rutter, M. (2006) Implications of resilience concepts for scientific understanding. *Annals of the New York Academy of Sciences, 1094*(1), 1–12.

Sanders, S. L., Bantum, E. O., Owen, J. E., Thornton, A. A., & Stanton, A. L. (2010). Supportive care needs in patients with lung cancer. *Psycho-Oncology, 19,* 480–489. doi:10.1002/pon.1577

Shallcross, L. (2010, August). Men welcome here. *Counseling Today, 53,* 25–31.

Smith, T., & Erford, B. T. (2001). *Test review: Beck Depression Inventory-II.* Association for Assessment in Counseling. Retrieved from http://aac.ncat.edu/

Snowden, L. R., Hastings, J. F., & Alvidrez, J. (2009). Overrepresentation of Black Americans in psychiatric inpatient care. *Psychiatric Services, 60*(6), 779–785.

Trochim, W. M. K., & Donnelly, J. P. (2007). *Research methods knowledge base* (3rd ed.). Macon, OH: Thomson.

Tucker, T. M. (2009). *Examining the impact of historical/developmental, sociodemographic, and psychological factors on passive suicide among African American men.* (Unpublished doctoral dissertation). Howard University, Washington, DC.

U.S. Census Bureau (2013). *How the Census Bureau measures poverty.* Retrieved from http://www.census.gov/hhes/www/poverty/about/overview/measure.html

U.S. Department of Education (2009). *The condition of education 2009: Indicator 20 status dropout rates.* Retrieved from http://nces.ed.gov.gov/programs/coe/2009pdf/20_2009.pdf

U.S. Department of Health and Human Services. (2011). Centers for Disease Control and Prevention. National Center for Health Statistics. *Health, United States, 2011: With special feature on socioeconomic status and health.* Retrieved from http://www.cdc.gov/nchs/data/hus/hus11.pdf

Wang, P. S., Beck, A. L., Berglund, P., McKenas, D. K., Pronk, N. P., Simon, G. E., & Kessler, R. C. (2004). Effects of major depression on moment-in-time work performance. *American Journal of Psychiatry, 161,* 1885–1891. doi:10.1176/appi.ajp.161.10.1885

Watkins, D. C., & Jefferson, S. O. (2012). Recommendations for the use of online social support for African American men. *Psychological Services,10*(3), 323–332. doi:10.1037/a0027904

William, P., Roberta, E., Karina, R., Heidi, M., & Richard, C. (2009). Academic resilience among undocumented Latino students. *Hispanic Journal of Behavioral Sciences, 31,* 149–181. doi:10.1177/0739986309333020

Woodward, A. T., Taylor R. J., & Chatters L. M. (2011). Use of professional and informal support by Black men with mental disorders. *Research on Social Work Practice, 21,* 328–336. doi:10.1177/1049731510388668

CHAPTER 10

AFRICAN AMERICAN GRADUATE AND UNDERGRADUATE MALE STUDENTS' ATTITUDES REGARDING COUNSELING

A Comparative Analysis

Candy H. Ratliff, Joyce P. Finch, and Jessica D. Davis

There has been a preponderance of literature indicating that African American males are reluctant to utilize the counseling center at their university or college even though they have expressed a need to seek help for their vocational, environmental, and emotional concerns (Duncan & Johnson, 2007). To understand the reluctance of Black males underutilizing counseling services, one must focus on Black male students' attitudes toward counseling in relationship to their racial consciousness (Duncan & Johnson, 2007). In this chapter, African American/Black and graduate/postbaccalaureate are used interchangeably. In this exploratory research, the authors will present a comparative analysis of the attitudes of African American graduate and

Counseling African American Males, pages 165–176
Copyright © 2016 by Information Age Publishing

undergraduate male students regarding counseling services in order to gain further insight concerning the differences between students 18 to 24 years old and students over age 25. The purpose of this study is to examine the relationship between selected demographic factors, counseling factors, and factors that contribute to the underutilization of counseling services. Recommendations to make counseling more comfortable and available to African American males on college campuses will be presented.

Aud, Fox, & KewalRamani (2010) reported that approximately 32% of Black 18- to 24-year-olds were enrolled in a college or university, with a rise to 42% in 2011 (U.S. Department of Education, 2013). Additionally, U.S. Department of Education (2013) data suggest that between 2001 and 2011, the number of full-time male postbaccalaureate students increased by 36%; among part-time postbaccalaureate students, the number of males increased by 14%. For decades, African American men over the age of 25 who earn a college degree have risen from 11.1% in 1990, to 13.2% in 2000, and 15.8% in 2010 (Ruffins, 2013). With this increase, colleges and universities have found that African American males are utilizing informal sources of support and underutilizing counseling services (Chiang, Hunter, & Yeh, 2004; Duncan & Johnson, 2007; Evans, 2013). Evans (2013) suggested there is a disparity in the number of Black males seeking counseling, and this may be attributed to education, ethnicity, cultural and socioeconomic stigmas, and racial factors. Furthermore, Evans (2013) points out that Black males come in contact with the mental health system because they are more likely to be referred by the social and legal systems.

PERSONAL AND SOCIAL FACTORS THAT CONTRIBUTE TO UNDERUTILIZATION OF COUNSELING SERVICES

Personal and social factors that contribute to underutilization of counseling services include previous counseling experiences (Williams & Justice, 2010), socialization (Masuda, Anderson, & Edmonds, 2012; Watkins, Walker, & Griffith, 2010), and Black males' degree of mistrust toward Whites stretching from special education classes to the prison industrial complex (Duncan & Johnson, 2007; Ruffins, 2013). White supremacy and oppression created a belief of inferiority, blatant racism, and the denial of educational opportunities to African Americans (Ruffins, 2013). Because of this, researchers have proposed that these high levels of cultural mistrust are negatively associated with attitudes toward counseling, especially if the counseling center staff is predominately White (Duncan & Johnson, 2007). Fyffe (2000) posited that African American college students perceived Black counselors as more cross culturally competent than White counselors. "Black help-seeking behavior and counselor preference have been found to be influenced by commitment to one's group ethnicity, gender, socioeconomic status, and level of cultural mistrust" (Duncan & Johnson, 2007, p. 698). Williams and Justice (2010) mentioned that African American males have been the most publicized group in the United States, and, unfortunately, they are remembered in a negative connotation. This "memory" may heavily impact the interaction between counselor and client. What's more, cultural mistrust (Chandler, 2010; Harvey & Afful, 2011; Suite, Bril, Primm, Harrison-Ross, 2007; Whaley, 2001a) may possibly drive the fears of African American male college students toward not seeking counseling. Specific fears regarding mental health services include being misdiagnosed and being admitted into a hospital for treatment (Williams & Justice, 2010). African American men view counseling as a sign of weakness and are concerned that others would see them as unmanly (Williams & Justice, 2010; Evans, 2013). It is a challenge creating mental health interventions with the Black male because of his unique psychological and social pressures and because he associates obtaining professional help with guilt and shame (Chiang et al., 2004; Williams & Justice, 2010).

Socialization

When an African American male shows up for therapy, his physical attributes are presented before his presenting problems. Messages learned during childhood about gender and race have been internalized by him and the therapist, whether the therapist is male or female or of the same race. These messages contribute to perceptions, which in turn, influence stereotypes that will impact the therapeutic relationship. Pauker, Ambady, and Apfelbaum (2010) investigated the emergence and antecedents of racial stereotyping in a sample of 3- to 10-year-olds. Children's knowledge and application of positive and negative in-group and out-group stereotypes were measured. They found that children start to apply stereotypes to the out-group starting around age 6. This knowledge, acquired through socialization, is applied throughout the life span. Mosher and Tomkins (1988) point out that through socialization, cultural expectations are transmitted by family, peer, education, and the media. According to Brown (2005), "Slavery had the unintended side effect of forming and strengthening a separate Black community with its own beliefs, values, and practices" (p. 2). Delpit (as cited in Brown, 2005) noted, "The ills that plague Black males . . . are a responsibility of society as a whole" (p. 3). Males learn during childhood that to be a "man" one must be aggressive, assertive, competitive, and independent (Choi, 2004); however, slavery profoundly impacted how this message was or is being transmitted to African American boys (Boykin & Toms, 1985; Clarke, 2004; Hill, 2002; Mutisya & Ross,

2005; Peters, 1985; Wallace, 2007). When compared to the Euro-American male, the African American male was viewed as irrational, unintelligent, and animalistic (Wallace, 2007). The goal of African American parents is to "raise children with positive self-esteem in a society in which being African American is perceived negatively (Peters, as cited in Ratliff, 2014, p. 23). "Black masculinity is portrayed as a 'hyper' version of everything negative representing hegemonic white masculinity, casting it as frightening and ominous" (Pass, Benoit, & Dunlap, 2014, p. 170). According to Ratliff (2014), "Stereotypes created by whites during slavery pervade contemporary society and continue to influence societal perceptions of African Americans, especially males" (p. 23.) Furthermore, Adams (2007) points out that defining Black masculinity as pathological has been preserved by a system of oppression and exclusion.

Mistrust

For years, researchers (Brazziel, 1958; Himes, 1948; Hypps, 1959; Tolson, 1972; Waters, 1953; Williams, 1949) have been concerned with the provision of adequate counseling services for African Americans. Some recommend culturally sensitive interventions (Harvey & Afful, 2011, Resnicow et al, 2005; Resnicow, Soler, Ahlwalia, Buttir, & Braithwaite, 2000), modification to experiential aspects of counselor preparation programs (Smith, as cited in Jackson, 1977), and "synthesis of the emerging Black perspective in counseling" (Jackson, 1977). Researchers (Duncan 2003; Jarrett, Bellamy, & Adeyemi, 2007; Terrell & Terrell, 1981) show underutilization of counseling services by African Americans. Moreover, researchers pinpoint cultural mistrust, lack of access, poverty, transportation, mental health stigma, and self-concealment (Diala et al., 2000; Keating & Robertson, 2004; Masuda, Anderson & Edmonds, 2012; Whaley, 2001b) as possible reasons for underutilization.

African Americans experienced inhumane and unethical treatment (Suite et al., 2007) from the medical and mental health communities. For examples refer to "Mississippi Appendectomy" (Roberts, 2000) and the Tuskegee Syphilis experiments (Gamble, 1997; Crenner, 2012). Blacks fleeing captivity were considered to have "drapetomania" described as "Uncontrollable urge to escape slavery, destroy property on the plantation, be disobedient, talk back, fight with their masters, and refuse to work" (Suite et al., 2007, p. 881). What's more, Suite et al. (2007) said, "It is not difficult to imagine how those experiences, communicated to families and children, fostered mistrust in medical practices" (p. 880).

Attitudes Regarding Counseling

Counseling is a cultural barrier for African Americans. The consensus of African Americans seeking counseling is associated with weakness and diminished pride, especially when it involves the African American male who is seeking counseling (Chiang, Hunter, & Yeh, 2004). The Black male who seeks counseling is also seen as unmanly (Williams & Justice, 2010). One support network for African Americans is the family because of the importance Blacks place on the family in regards to support and coping (Williams & Justice, 2010; Owens, Lacey, Rawls, & Holbert-Quince, 2010). African Americans have strong religious convictions, and they address their problems with their minister and/or prayer. Another informal network is seeking help from their trusted friends. The African American male has also sought help "at social activity centers such a barbershops, bars or taverns, and social/fraternal organizations" (Williams & Justice, 2010, p. 160). Williams and Justice (2010) conducted a study of 212 African American undergraduate males who were 18 years or older and their attitudes toward counseling at four Texas universities. Two universities were predominately White and two were historically Black universities (HBCUs). They administered the Attitudes Toward Seeking Professional Psychological Help (ATSPPH) scale survey in order to understand their perceptions regarding counseling. The researchers concluded that African American males' attitudes were negative even at HBCUs and were unwilling to participate in counseling sessions (Williams & Justice, 2010).

THIS STUDY

In this exploratory study, researchers examined the relationship between selected demographic factors, counseling factors, and attitudes toward seeking professional counseling. They hypothesized that participants who scored high on the ATSPPH scale will be open to seeking professional counseling.

METHOD

Participants and Procedure

This exploratory study was conducted at a historically Black college and university in the South. Fifty African American males from one graduate and one undergraduate class were invited to participate. Participants were informed that participation was voluntary and they could withdraw from the study at any time. Participants were not compensated.

Researchers were able to analyze data from 70% of the instruments since incomplete surveys were not used. The final sample consisted of 35 African American males ranging from 18- to 44-years-old. There were 57% graduate students and 43% undergraduates; single participants made up 86% of the sample, while 14% reported they were married; 57% were age 24 or younger, and 43% were above age 25; 83% reported never receiving professional counseling services, and 17% reported they did receive counseling.

This study was reviewed and approved by the internal review board at the university. Help-seeking attitudes were measured using the 29-item Attitudes Toward Seeking Professional Psychological Help (ATSPPH) scale (Fisher & Turner, 1970). Reliability ranged from .83 to .86. Items are scored using a 4-point scale ranging from 0 (disagreement) to 3 (agreement). No modifications were made to the original scale. Participants also completed a demographic form created for this study. Participants provided data anonymously.

Results

Four regression models were computed to determine the predictability of selected factors on the attitude of African American males seeking professional counseling. Professional counseling attitude for this investigation was measured by the following four indicators: trust, cultural stigma, socialization, and open to counseling shown in Table 10.1, when the four factors of age, classification, marital status, and prior counseling were entered with the trust component, a statistically significant relationship was not found between the four predictors and the trust component of seeking professional counseling ($F = -260$, df = 4/30, $p > .05$). These variables only accounted for 3.4% of the variance in the trust component. None of the factors was found to be an independent predictor of trust in seeking professional counseling.

TABLE 10.1 Regression Results Regarding the Four Factors and the Trust Component

	B	Std. Error	Beta	t	Sig.
(Constant)	7.814	1.418		5.510	.000
Age	.743	1.060	.151	.701	.489
Classification	−.007	1.060	−.001	−.007	.995
Marital Status	.326	1.333	.047	.245	.808
Counseling Services Received	−.356	1.165	−.055	−.305	.762

$R = .183$, $R^2 = .034$, F = .260, df = 4/30, $p > .05$

TABLE 10.2   Regression Results Regarding the Four Factors and the Cultural Stigma Component

	B	Std. Error	Beta	t	Sig.
(Constant)	12.601	1.884		6.687	.000
Age	−.437	1.408	−.066	−.311	.758
Classification	−.437	1.408	−.066	−.311	.758
Marital Status	−.093	1.771	−.010	−.052	.959
Counseling Services Received	−1.856	1.548	−.214	−1.199	.240

$R = .236$, $R^2 = .056$, F = .441, df = 4/30, $p > .05$

Shown in Table 10.2 were the regression results pertaining to the relationship between the four predictors' age, marital status, classification, prior counseling, and the cultural stigma component of seeking counseling. A statistically significant relationship did not exist between the four predictors and the cultural stigma component (F = .441, df = 4/30, $p > .05$). These factors collectively explained 5.6% of the variance of the cultural stigma component of seeking professional counseling. None of the four predictors was found to be an independent predictor of the cultural stigma component of seeking professional counseling.

Reported in Table 10.3 were the regression findings regarding the predictive power of the variables age, classification, marital status, and prior counseling on the socialization component of seeking professional counseling. A statistically significant relationship was not found between the four predictors and the socialization component of seeking professional counseling (F = .388, df = 4/30, $p > .05$). The four predictors combined only accounted for 4.9% of the variance in the socialization component. None of the predictors was found to contribute significantly to the socialization component of seeking professional counseling.

Presented in Table 10.4 were the regression analyses concerning the predictability of the factors age, marital status, classification, and prior

TABLE 10.3   Regression Results Regarding the Four Factors and the Socialization Component

	B	Std. Error	Beta	t	Sig
(Constant)	24.491	3.065		7.990	.000
Age	−1.229	2.290	−.115	−.536	.596
Classification	−1.229	2.290	−.115	−.536	.596
Marital Status	2.337	2.880	.155	.811	.424
Counseling Services Received	.834	2.518	.059	.331	.743

$R = .222$, $R^2 = .049$, F = .388, df = 4/30, $p > .05$

TABLE 10.4 Regression Results Regarding the Four Factors and the Open to Counseling Component

	B	Std. Error	Beta	t	Sig
(Constant)	31.416	3.492		8.997	.000
Age	−.679	2.609	−.057	−.260	.796
Classification	−.679	2.609	−.057	−.260	.796
Marital Status	−.684	3.281	−.040	−.208	.836
Counseling Services Received	.162	2.868	.010	.057	.955

$R = .121$, $R^2 = .015$, F = .111, df = 4/30, $p > .05$

counseling on open to counseling component of seeking professional counseling. A statistically significant relationships was not found between the four predictors and the open to counseling component of seeking professional counseling (F = .111, df 4/30, $p > .05$). The four predictors together accounted for 1.5% of the variance in open to counseling component. None of the four predictors was independent related to the criterion variable.

DISCUSSION

African American underutilization of counseling services has been well-documented (Masuda, Anderson, & Edmonds, 2012; Townes, D. L., Chavez-Korell, & Cunningham, 2009; Phelps, Taylor, & Gerard, 2001). Preliminary findings show that African American graduate and undergraduate males do not seek professional help. This is supported by Williams and Justice (2010) who found that African American male students attending HBCUs were unwilling to participate in counseling sessions. The African American male places a high regard on the family for coping and support, which suggests a strong cultural emphasis on interdependence (Chiang et al., 2004). It is more appropriate for African American males to seek the advice of close family friends, trusted friends, ministers, or someone in a local Black church (Chiang, 2004; Williams & Justice, 2010). They have also sought help "at social activity centers such as barbershops, bars or taverns, and social or fraternal organizations" (Williams & Justice, 2010, p. 160).

IMPLICATIONS FOR COLLEGE COUNSELORS

Owens et al. (2010) wrote an article that provided strategies for counselors on college campuses to help first generation African American male college students so they could have higher completion rates. They stated that counselors must be aware of the challenges facing first generation African

American male college students, such as inadequate educational preparation and conflict between college environment and the cultures where they
were raised (Owens et al., 2010). Some of their suggestions to college counselors were to understand the worldviews of the African American men, to
enable them to choose a satisfying career, to establish a strong mentoring
program, and to involve faculty members.

To assist African American male graduate and undergraduate students,
the authors recommend the following:

- Counselors must be comfortable in working with African American
  male students by exploring their interests, goals, and abilities as they
  relate to their worldviews.
- Counselors can provide strategies and resources on campus that will
  enable African American students to become successful.
- Counselors can institute a mentoring program to assist in academic
  needs as well as adjusting to college life.
- Counselors should set up a table in the student center to inform
  students about the counseling center on campus and pass out a bro-
  chure that states its purpose, the issues they may be facing or may
  face in the future, and the location of the counseling center.
- Counselors should attend the general meeting the campus conducts
  for all the organizations on campus and talk about the counseling
  center.
- Counselors should post signs about the counseling center in all the
  buildings on campus.
- Counselors can implement outreach programs, such as offering
  workshops in residence halls.
- Counselors can create electronic newsletters and send them to all
  students.
- At freshmen orientation, counselors can speak about the counseling
  center and its purpose.
- Electronic fliers should be sent to faculty and staff announcing special events the counseling center is hosting so they can announce it
  to their students and display it on their bulletin boards.

CONCLUSION

African American males are a unique group because of environmental
and cultural factors that have influenced them, such as racism, disenfranchisement, and low achievement (Owens, Lacey, Rawls, & Holbert-Quince,
2010). The Black male is disadvantaged because of high unemployment,
low high school graduation rates, low college attendance rates, inadequate

educational preparation, and high incarceration rates (Owens et al., 2010). Counselors working with African American males should be aware of the challenges they are facing and develop a firm knowledge and understanding of Black males' worldview, culture, and environment.

REFERENCES

Adams, C. J. (2007). Respect and reputation: The construction of masculinity in poor African American men. *Journal of African American Studies, 11,* 157–172. doi:10.1007/s12111-007-9021-6.

Aud, S., Fox, M., & KewalRamani, A. (2010). *Status and trends in the education of racial and ethnic groups* (NCES 2010-015). U.S. Department of Education, National Center for Education Statistics. Washington, DC: U.S. Government Printing Office.

Boykin, A. W., & Toms, F. D. (1985). Black child socialization: A conceptual framework. In H. P. McAdoo & J. L. McAdoo (Eds.), *Black children: Social, educational, and parental environments* (pp. 33–51). Thousand Oaks, CA: Sage.

Brazziel, W. F. (1958). Meeting the psychosocial crisis of Negro youth through a coordinated guidance service. *Journal of Negro Education, 27,* 79–83.

Brown, L. (2005). America's Black male: Disadvantaged from birth to death. *Penn GSE Perspectives on Urban Education, 3*(2), 1–16.

Chandler, D. (2010). The underutilization of health services in the Black community: An examination of causes and effects. *Journal of Black Studies, 40*(5), 915–931. doi:10.1177/0021934708320723.

Chiang, L., Hunter, C. D., & Yeh, C. J. (2004). Coping attitudes, sources, and practices among Black and Latino college students. *Adolescence, 39*(156), 739–815.

Choi, N. (2004). Sex role differences in specific, academic, and general self efficacy. *The Journal of Psychology, 138*(2), 149–159.

Clarke, L. (2004). There is but little ... scruple about separating families. In S. Mintz (Ed.), *African American voices: The life cycle of slavery,* (3rd ed.; pp. 123–124). St. James, NY: Brandywine Press.

Crenner, C. (2012). The Tuskegee Syphilis Study and the scientific concept of racial nervous resistance. *Journal of the History of Medicine & Allied Sciences, 67*(2), 244–280. doi:10.1093/jhmas/jrr003

Diala, C., Muntaner, C., Walrath, C., Nickerson, K. J., LaViest, T. A., & Leaf, P. J. (2000). Racial differences in attitudes toward professional mental health care and in the use of services. *American Journal of Orthopsychiatry, 70*(4), 455–464. doi:10.1037/h0087736

Duncan, L. E. (2003). Black male college students' attitudes toward seeking psychological help. *The Journal of Black Psychology, 29*(1), 68–86.

Duncan, L. E., & Johnson, D. (2007). Black undergraduate students' attitude toward counseling and counselor preference. *College Student Journal, 41*(3), 696–719.

Evans, M. P. (2013). Men in counseling: A content analysis of the Journal of Counseling & Development and Counselor Education and Supervision

1981–2011. *Journal of Counseling & Development, 91*(4), 467–474. doi:10.1002/p1556-6676.2013.00119.x

Fisher, E. H., & Turner, J. L. (1970). Orientations to seeking professional help: Development and research utility of an attitude scale. *Journal of Consulting and Clinical Psychology, 35*(1), 79–90. doi:10.1037/h0029636.

Fyffe, C. D. (2000). *Effects of trust, cultural mistrust, counselor's race and race-sensitive orientation on perceived trustworthiness in Black college women.* (Unpublished doctoral dissertation). Hofstra University, Hempstead, NY.

Gamble, V. (1997). Under the shadow of Tuskegee: African Americans and health care. *American Journal of Public Health, 87*(11), 1773–1778.

Harvey, R. D., & Afful, S. E. (2011). Racial typicality, racial identity, and health behaviors: A case for culturally sensitive health interventions. *Journal of Black Psychology, 37*(2), 164–184. doi:10.1177/0095798410376244

Hill, S. A. (2002). Teaching and doing gender in African American families. *Sex Roles, 47*(11), 493–506.

Himes, J. S. (1948). Guidance in Negro secondary schools in the southeastern region. *Journal of Negro Education, 17,* 106–113.

Hypps, I. C. (1959). The role of the school in juvenile delinquency prevention (With special reference to pupil personnel services). *Journal of Negro Education, 28,* 318–328.

Jackson, G. G. (1977). The emergence of a Black perspective in counseling. *Journal of Negro Education, 46*(3), 230–253.

Jarrett, N. C., Bellamy, C. D., & Adeyemi, S. A. (2007). Men's health help-seeking and implications for practice. *American Journal of Health Studies, 22*(2), 88–95.

Keating, F., & Robertson, D. (2004). Fear, Black people and mental illness: A vicious circle? *Health & Social Care in the Community, 12*(5), 439–447.

Masuda, A., Anderson, P. L., & Edmonds, J. (2012). Help-seeking attitudes, mental health stigma, and self-concealment among African American College Students. *Journal of Black Studies, 43*(7), 773–786. doi:10.1177/0021934712445806

Mosher, D. L., & Tomkins, S. S. (1988). Scripting the macho man: Hypermasculine socialization and enculturation. *The Journal of Sex Research, 25*(1), 60–84.

Mutisya, P. M., & Ross, L. E. (2005). Afrocentricity and racial socialization among African American college students. *Journal of Black Studies, 38*(3), 235–247.

Owens, D., Lacey, K., Rawls, G., & Holbert-Quince, J. (2010). First-generation African American male college students: Implications for career counselors. *The Career Development Quarterly, 58*(4), 291–300.

Pass, M., Benoit, E., & Dunlap, E. (2014). "I just be myself": Contradicting hypermasculine and hypersexual stereotypes among low-income Black men in New York City. In B. C. Slatton & K. Spates (Eds.), *Hypersexual, hypermasculine? Gender, race and sexuality in the identities of contemporary Black men* (pp. 19–31). Burlington, VT: Ashgate.

Pauker, K., Ambady, N., & Apfelbaum, E. P. (2010). Race salience and essentialist thinking in racial stereotype development. *Child Development, 81*(6), 1799–1813.

Peters, M. F. (1985). Racial socialization of Black children. In H. P. McAdoo & J. L. McAdoo (Eds.), *Black children: Social, educational, and parental environments* (pp. 234–247). Newberry Park, CA: Sage.

Phelps, R. E., Taylor, J. D., & Gerard, P. A. (2001). Cultural mistrust, ethnic identity, and self-esteem among ethnically diverse Black university students. *Journal of Counseling and Development, 79*(2), 209–216.

Ratliff, C. (2014). Growing up male: A re-examination of African American male socialization. In B. C. Slatton & K. Spates (Eds.), *Hypersexual, hypermasculine? Gender, race and sexuality in the identities of contemporary Black men* (pp. 19–31). Burlington, VT: Ashgate.

Resnicow, K., Jackson, A., Blissett, D., Wang, T., McCarty, F., Rahotep, S., & Periasamy, S. (2005). Results of the healthy body healthy spirit trial. *Health Psychology, 24,* 339–348.

Resnicow, K., Soler, R., Ahlwalia, J., Buttlr, J., & Braithwaite, R. (2000). Cultural sensitivity in substance use program. *Journal of Community Psychology, 28,* 271–290.

Roberts, D. (2000). Forum: Black women and the pill. *Family Planning Perspectives, 32*(2), 92–93.

Ruffins, P. (2013). Challenging stereotypes. *Issues in Higher Education, 29*(26), 10–11.

Suite, D. H., Bril, R. L., Primm, A., & Harrison-Ross, P. (2007). Beyond misdiagnosis, misunderstanding and mistrust: Relevance of the historical perspective in the medical and mental health treatment of people of color. *Journal of the National Medical Association, 99*(8), 879–885.

Terrell, F., & Terrell, S. L. (1981). An inventory to measure cultural mistrust among blacks. *Western Journal of Black Studies, 3,* 180–185.

Tolson, N. (1972). Counseling the "disadvantaged." *Personnel and Guidance Journal 50,* 735–738.

Townes, D. L., Chavez-Korell, S., & Cunningham, N. (2009). Reexamining the relationships between racial identity, cultural mistrust, help-seeking attitudes, and preference for a Black counselor. *Journal of Counseling Psychology 56*(2), 330–336. doi:10.1037/a0015449

U.S. Department of Education, National Center for Education Statistics. (2013). *Digest of Education Statistics, 2012* (NCES 2014–015, Ch. 3). Retrieved from http://nces.ed.gov/fastfacts/display.asp?id=98

Wallace, D. M. (2007). It's a m-a-n-thang: Black male gender role socialization and the performance of masculinity in love relationships. *The Journal of Pan African Studies, 1*(7), 11–22.

Waters E.W. (1953). Problems of rural Negro high school seniors on the eastern shore of Maryland: A consideration for guidance. *Journal of Negro Education, 22,* 115–125.

Watkins, D. C., Walker, R. L., & Griffith, D. M. (2010). A meta-study of Black male mental health and well-being. *Journal of Black Psychology, 36*(3), 303–330. doi:10.1177/0095798409353756

Whaley, A. L. (2001a). Cultural mistrust and mental health services for African Americans: A review and meta-analysis. *The Counseling Psychologist 29*(4), 513–531.

Whaley, A. L. (2001b). Cultural mistrust: An important psychological constructs for diagnosis and treatment of African Americans. *Professional Psychology, Research & Practice, 32*(6), 555–562.

Williams A., & Justice, M. (2010). Attitudes of African American males regarding counseling in four Texas universities. *Education, 131*(1), 158–168.

Williams, C. T. (1949). Special consideration in counseling. *Journal of Educational Sociology 22,* 608–613.

CHAPTER 11

THEORIES OF REHABILITATION AND PRINCIPLES OF EFFECTIVE INTERVENTION FOR AFRICAN AMERICAN MALE OFFENDERS

Karla Sapp

According to the Sentencing Project Report in 1990, African American males accounted for 23% of the population between the ages of 20 and 29, who were currently under the supervision of a criminal justice system to include parole, probation, prison, and/or jail (Mauer & Huling, 1995). It has also been reported that more than one third of African American males not enrolled in college were incarcerated by the early 2000s, and that nearly twice of those younger than 40 years of age had a bachelor's degree. Western and Wildeman (2009) noted that men of African American descent were "eight times more likely to be incarcerated than Whites" (p. 228) and that there were significant disparities among various age groups and different

Counseling African American Males, pages 177–189
Copyright © 2016 by Information Age Publishing
177

education levels. According to Horton (2013), African American males currently account for 40.1% of the criminal justice incarcerated population. Drug use and crime among the African American male offender population tend to go hand in hand. At a young age, African American males are likely to become involved with criminal activity, more specifically drugs and gangs, as a result of several environmental factors. Marlowe (2003) noted that the use of drugs suggestively increased the probability that an individual would participate in criminal activities. In recent years, strict drug policies have been a contributing factor in the increase of incarcerated offenders. Mauer and Huling (1995) noted that the arrest rates for violent crimes among African Americans were disproportionate to the number of African American males who used drugs nationally. Research has shown that the majority of the offender population was under the influence of mood-altering substances during the commission of their crime. Therefore, it has been established that offenders who abuse mood-altering substances are "responsible for a disproportionate amount of crime and violence" (Marlowe, 2003, p. 5). According to Jing-ying (2012) there are suspicions as to "what is going on in offender counseling and how offender counseling could help inmate change" (p. 1028). The offender population has long been considered the most difficult to engage in psychotherapy. A marginalized group, offenders are a unique, culturally diverse population who tend to find themselves in a cycle of judicial merry-go-round consisting of arrests, convictions, incarcerations, and releases. Although the recidivism rate of offenders continues to be at an all-time high, the number of mental health professionals specializing in assessment and treatment with this population continues to be at an all-time low. The lack of knowledge and engagement by mental health professionals makes it difficult for the culturally oppressed to utilize available resources and disclose pertinent information that would assist in their lifestyle change and decrease the recidivism rates among offenders. It is vital that the mental health profession begin to seek to understand how history, society, the unhealed, and worldviews of offenders, more specifically African American male offenders, has limited our ability to speak their language and provide treatment that is appropriate. In order to effectively treat the male offender who is African American, mental health professionals must develop an understanding of the individual unique issues, which will allow the clinician to tailor treatment interventions specifically to the offender. This chapter will explore the use of Adler's theory of individual psychology as a way to conceptualize and understand the lifestyle of a criminal offender, examine rehabilitation theories as a foundation for best practices, as well as identify treatment modalities and interventions that will assist mental health professionals in helping African American male offenders become aware of their faulty beliefs and behaviors, in order to effect a positive lifestyle change.

CRIMINAL BEHAVIOR: AN INDIVIDUAL PSYCHOLOGY PERSPECTIVE

Individual psychology was founded by Alfred Adler as a comprehensive theory, holistic in nature, with a focus on the individual psychological and cognitive style within a social setting. Comprehensive in its approach to assess and treatment the issues experienced by individuals, individual psychology has been known to address criminal behavior, although not until recently has it begun to be applied to the criminal justice offender population. According to Adler (1930/1976), "crime is a coward's imitation of heroism. Criminals are striving for a fictitious goal of personal superiority, and they like to believe that they are heroes but this is again a mistaken scheme of apperception, a failure of common sense" (p. 134). Individual psychology addresses the behaviors of offenders, utilizing concepts from Adler's theory, to include: development of lifestyle, striving for superiority, and social interest deficit.

Development of Lifestyle

Adler held the belief that it is during one's childhood that he or she begins to formulate their thoughts, which help them develop their concept of the world (Ozpolat & Akbaba, 2012). Adler hypothesized that individuals develop their style of life by the age of 6. According to Day (2008), an individual style of life is influenced by their societal and family construct, and consists of the following features: social, psychological, and biological, which ultimately lead to the development of personality features. According to Ozpolat & Akbaba (2012), self-concept, self-ideal, view of the world, and ethics are four principles used to conceptualized lifestyle. Concept of self, a part of the lifestyle, is inclusive of the individual's perceptions of self. How one defines oneself, such as, "I am nice," "I am always helping people," or "I am lazy," are examples. There is, however, a difference between the concept and ideal of oneself. The ideal self is defined as a guideline for superiority striving, to include hopes, dreams, and aspirations. Within the context of the ideal self, one may hold the belief that, "In order to have respect of others and feel like somebody, I must earn six figures and own nice things." An individual worldview is not focused on the self, but rather focused on others, the world, and institutions. Lastly, the idea and beliefs about what is right and what is wrong are ethical beliefs that are essentially learned throughout one's childhood. Criminal behavior, according to Adler (1930/1976) is not the result of an individual environment, nor is it heredity, but rather a choice that one makes as a result of their faulty cognitions, as postulated by Glenn Walters in his theory of lifestyle criminality.

According to Walters (1990), an individual is responsible for the choices he or she makes within their societal context, as a result of their individual personality traits and environmental factors. As a result of Walters's (1990) theory, offenders are characterized by their behavioral patterns, to include blatant disregard for societal rules and norm, irresponsibility, self-indulgence, and interpersonal intrusiveness, which are demonstrated through the following concepts: conditions, cognitions, and choices. Although an offender's lifestyle is reflective of their choices, those choices are considered to be a result of the individual's environmental and biological conditions, both during childhood and adulthood as well as the thought process regarding such conditions, also called cognitive style. Ultimately, it was Walters's position that until an offender pattern of thinking changes, their behavior will remain the same, which is in accordance to Adler's belief that "individuals are masters of their own actions" (Clark, 2011, p. 566). The lifestyle concept in relation to an individual's level of criminality has proven to be a valuable conceptual tool that bridges the gap between the classical and positivist orientation among criminology (Clark, 2011).

Striving for Superiority

According to Day (2008), adults tend to react to uncomfortable situations and problems by utilizing patterns learned during their childhood. Such reactions are considered a result of experiencing feelings of inferiority and weakness; when faced with these feelings, attempts to compensate are referred to as a process of striving for superiority. An individual's striving for superiority can be both positive and negative. Striving for superiority in a positive way is one's way of achieving a positive goal; for example, striving to obtain employment as a teacher and, eventually, after attending school, becoming one. However, engaging in the lifestyle that is criminal in nature in order to obtain material possessions is a striving for superiority in a negative manner. In his research, Adler (1930/1976) found that criminal offenders typically strived to achieve a level of superiority over family, peer associates, and other individuals within their environment. Having a sense of courage, offenders, when faced with issues that to individuals not engaging in the criminal lifestyle would be frustrating, are likely to take the easy way out, acting irresponsibly, asserting their power, and being deceptive. Clark (2011) mentioned that although Walters (1990) was aware that individuals act in irresponsible manners, the criminal offender irresponsibility is characterized by a pattern of behaviors with the following aspects of their lives: family, work, relationships, leisure, and community. African American males characteristically have encountered the several psychosocial factors such as "adverse childhood experiences" (Klinteberg, Almquist, Beiher,

& Rydelius, 2011, p. 2), which according to Dutton and Hart (1992) "can have serious and long-lasting psychosocial sequeale" (p. 129). Other psychosocial factors that are encountered include: socioeconomic deprivation; negative peer associations; lack of parental support and/or absent parents as a result of substance use, births outside of wedlock, and incarcerations; rejection by peers; history of family substance use and conflicts; incarceration; mental illnesses; and poor academic matriculation (Horton, 2013), all of which contribute to their irrational cognitive thinking, development of a lifestyle that is criminal, and are all characteristics of an individual etiology that are a result of an inferiority complex.

Social Interest Deficit

Thinking of one's self and violating the rights and space of others are two other ways offenders strive to achieve superiority and make others feel inferior, but are also characteristics of an offender's lack of social interest. Walters (1990) defines these behaviors as self-indulgent acts and interpersonal intrusiveness and contends that an individual is not born to be selfish or intrude on the feelings and rights of others (Clark, 2011), but that such behaviors are also learned. Social interest is an individual's attentiveness to their community and their attitudes toward dealing with the societal world. Social interest is expressed through a respect that is mutual and concern for the welfare of others. Offenders tend to have minimal empathy, lack in remorse, and utilize manipulation tactics, to include persistent lying. These behaviors reinforce the offender's indifferent attitudes toward others and a continued decrease in social interest. It is evident that as a result of lifestyle development that is criminal and a superiority complex, an offender began to lack a connection with others, leading him or her to feel dissatisfied with life and themselves and act in a reckless manner.

Offender Rehabilitation Theories: Foundation for Best Practices

Theories of rehabilitation are differentiated from treatment theories (e.g., person-centered, solution focused, cognitive-behavioral, and psychodynamic), which are considered to be more specific and involve the application of interventions that will affect change in cognitions, feelings, and behaviors of individuals. Rehabilitation theories are considered "integrative practice frameworks that contain a combination of ethical, theoretical, scientific, and practice elements" (Ward, Yates, & Willis, 2012, p. 95). The purpose of correctional rehabilitation treatment is to decrease the rate of recidivism through the implementation and utilization of interventions that are effective with the offender population. An evidenced-based approach and rehabilitation theory that has been found to be effective is the Principle of Effective Intervention (Spiropoulos, Salisbury, & Van Voorhis, 2014). Considered to provide a theoretical framework for correctional rehabilitation treatment, according to Andrews and Bonta, (2007), Andrews, Bonta, and Hoge, (1990), and Gendreau (1996), the Principle of Effective Intervention is comprised of "a series of empirically and professionally supported treatment techniques to reduce recidivism (Spiropoulos, Salisbury, & Van Voorhis, 2014, p. 836). Three general principles were identified, to include risk, need, and responsivity, which have led to the development of the Risk-Need-Responsivity (RNR) approach to offender assessment and treatment. The central concepts of these principles are described to aid in the development of effective treatment interventions for the offender population.

The Risk-Need-Responsivity (RNR) Approach

An assessment and prevention model, utilized within the correctional environment for offender rehabilitation, the Risk-Need-Responsivity (RNR) approach was developed in the 1990s by Andrews, Bonta, and Hoge. According to their model, the identified three principles are targeted for the purpose of decreasing the likelihood that the offender would continue to engage in behaviors that are criminal. The first principle in the RNR approach is risk assessment that focuses on the offenders overall treatment progress and recidivism probability that will assist the therapist with appropriate intervention. Varghese (2013) identified eight categories of risk factors for offenders to include "friendship with criminal peers (antisocial/criminal associates), substance use, employment and education problems, criminal history (record), antisocial (criminal) attitudes, antisocial personality, poor family relationships, and lack of prosocial recreational activities" (p. 1017). Of these factors, there are four that are crucial to an offender recidivism risk, to include antisocial attitudes, personality, and associates, along with criminal history (Varghese, 2013). Upon assessing the offenders' recidivism risk, an assessment of needs should follow. A subset of the offender's level of risk and dynamic in nature, criminogenic needs are defined as "deficits that directly drive offenders into criminal behavior" (Jolley & Kerbs, 2010, p. 284). Criminogenic needs, in relation to an offender's decision to return to the criminal lifestyle, are influential and have the ability to be changed with the utilization of effective interventions. Of the eight risk factor categories, Jolley and Kerbs (2010), identified the following as criminogenic needs: antisocial personality, associates, and attitudes; academic/vocational/occupational poor performance and satisfaction; family and marriage problems; use of alcohol and/or drugs; and decreased involvement in leisure activities that are not criminal. It is noted that an offender's criminal history, static in nature, cannot be changed and therefore is not as vital to the needs assessment (Varghese, 2013). Having identified the offender's risk and needs, it is vital to determine the severity for each area. Assigning severity of risk and needs is an effective way of determining treatment programming needs and individualizing treatment. In other words, although offenders may have similarities in their severity level, their experiences are unique and will likely differ. Among the offender population, a low-risk rating would be indicative of a mild difficulty with identified needs, whereas a moderate risk rating would be suggestive of noticeable impairment or functioning, while a rating of high would be of immediate concern. An offender with a risk severity of high is likely to experience severe difficulty, present with a high likelihood of reoffending, and would warrant a higher intensity of interventions to provide the offender support and decrease the likelihood of recidivism. According to the Principles of Effective Interventions, by assessing both risk and criminogenic needs, treatment can then be tailored to the individual's needs. Considered to be the hardest principle to support, responsivity is categorized in two types: general and specific. General responsivity focuses on the incorporation and efficacy of various treatment modalities among the offender population treatment. On the other hand, specific responsivity takes into consideration the characteristics of the offender, to include "demographics, learning styles, motivations, personalities, and strengths" (Jolley & Kerbs, 2010, p. 284), as well as the characteristics of the clinician to ensure that the interventions chosen are tailored specifically toward the offender and not a one-size-fits-all approach, utilizing interventions that have been found to be effective with other populations. Ultimately, according to Varghese (2013), responsivity is consistent with the ideals of counseling psychology as it places an emphasis on developing a collaborative therapeutic relationship with the offender, identifying strengths, and working to eliminating barriers that would hinder their ability to achieve a positive lifestyle change.

Integrative Approach to Offender Lifestyle Change

Utilizing an integrative approach allows for clinicians to recognize that offenders have several different things going on beyond their criminality, which has both individual and compounding effects on their ability to develop prosocial lifestyle habits and not reoffend. An integrative approach to offender rehabilitative treatment is an objective way of not only assessing the offender risk, needs, and treatment progression, but also their treatment strengths and resources, taking into consideration various areas of the offender's life and the impact their criminal behaviors have had on them. Although there are several traits that are common among offenders, each offender should be conceptualized as a unique case. One of the main benefits of incorporating an integrative approach when working with the

African American male offender population is that it allows for the clinician to assist the offender in identifying and setting treatment priorities during the assessment, which lead to the development of collaborative and comprehensive treatment plans and interventions.

Case Conceptualization

Saunders (1993), as noted in Horton (2013), developed the Iceberg Model of treatment for African American males. According to Horton (2013), Saunders suggested that presenting problems of African American males are usually the tip of the iceberg; however, it was the issues that are buried underneath the presenting problems "in the symptoms associated with substance use is some combination of [their] core issues: many loses, self-hate, bottled up emotions, and pain caused by racism" (p. 1). During the conceptualization phase of treatment, it is imperative that the mental health professional comprehend the offender's unique style of life. According to Clark (2011), exploring the lifestyle of habitual offenders provides insight into the development of an offender's criminal career and assists in the identification of an intervention that will affect a positive change.

There are various interview methods, both subjective and objective, that can be utilized to develop an understanding of the offender's experiences and examine the offender's lifestyle by connecting the past, present, and future, along with identifying and assessing the criminogenic needs of the offender. The psychosocial interview, generally a collection of data among specific areas of the offender life (to include social background, criminality, substance use, mental illness, and personal goals) is obtained during the clinical assessment and aids the clinician in conceptualizing the offender. Furthermore, utilizing elements of the Adlerian lifestyle questionnaire, ascertaining information concerning the offender's family constellation, and climate, dreams, and childhood memories (Jones & Butman, 1991), are important as it has been noted that an individual lifestyle is not only affected by their experiences, but by an individual's "family, friends, and teachers. Besides these environmental effects, neighbors and cultures are the factors that affect lifestyles" (Ozpolat & Akbaba, 2012, p. 2). Ultimately, by exploring the lifestyle of an offender, one is able to understand the development of behavior and thoughts that are criminal, assess their relationship with the individual's criminogenic needs, and identify treatment interventions that are focused on decreasing the likelihood of reoffending or engaging in criminal behaviors. Having the knowledge of the Principles of Effective Interventions, and integrated with the Transtheoretical Model of Behavior Change, motivational interviewing, and cognitive behavioral therapy will assist in the determining how to the approach the information provided by the offender.

Transtheoretical Model of Behavior Change and Motivation for Change

Although there has been a lot of research focused on behavioral change, the most integrated approach has been the Transtheoretical Model of Behavior Change. Incorporating several behavior theories, to include motivational interviewing (Zalmanowitz, Babins-Wagner, Rodger, Corbett, & Leschled, 2012) and cognitive behavioral therapy (Usher & Stewart, 2012), the Transtheoretical Model of Behavior change can be utilize to assess and recognize offenders within the stages. According to DiClemente, Schlundt, & Gemmell (2004), the Transtheoretical Model of Behavior Change, is a "multidimensional process of intentional behavior change" (p. 104). The five stages of change are precontemplation, contemplation, preparation, action, and maintenance (D'Sylva, Graffam, Hardcastle, & Shinkfield, 2010). Within the spectrum, the offender's level of readiness to change can range from not wanting to make changes to actively working and maintaining behavioral change. Offenders can be in different stages of change for a variety of issues or problematic behaviors; Zalmanowitz et al. (2013) noted that "individuals do not progress through such stages in a linear fashion, but rather move forward and backward between stages through the course of their treatment" (p. 958). Motivation, according to DiClemente, Schlundt, & Gemmell (2004), is a central component of the Transtheoretical Model of Change. Often characterized by offender uncertainty, there is a distinct difference among therapeutic motivation, internally and externally (Zalmanowitz et al., 2013), and is considered multidimensional. Motivation is also influenced by social factors, which can be both a hindrance as well as support. An offender's motivational level can be assessed at different times during the change process and can be highly affected by the mental health professional approach, which can ultimately influence the treatment outcomes. Furthermore, motivation can be elicited and enhanced through collaboration. If the approach that is collaborative and encouraging is utilized, the offender can become empowered to begin making positive changes. Motivation is best understood in three main components: readiness, willingness, and ability. Readiness encompasses the offender's willingness and/or openness to begin engaging in the process. Elicited through motivational interviewing, readiness is characterized by two aspects, which are change readiness and treatment readiness (DiClemente et al., 2004). Change readiness differs from treatment readiness, change readiness is a combination of the offender's perception of their issues and their assurance in their ability to make changes; whereas, treatment readiness focuses on the offenders motivation to entertain help and their level of preparedness for treatment engagement. Motivational readiness, an aspect of change readiness, is utilized to identify and implement intervention strategies using the Transtheoretical Model of Behavior Change stages. Motivational interviewing is a counseling intervention developed by Miller and Rollnick (1991) to increase treatment and change readiness (Zalmanowitz et al., 2013). According to Taft, Murphy, Elliot, and Morrel (2001), utilizing motivational interviewing during the conceptualization phase of treatment can lead to an improvement in "retention and lower recidivism rates among men" (Zalmanowitz et al., 2013). Key components of motivational interviewing include: argument avoidance, the use of resistance as well as empathy, and self-efficacy support, which leads to a reduction in blaming, increased level of acceptance, improvement in behaviors that are help-seeking, treatment participation, and completion of therapeutic activities (Zalmonowitz et al., 2013).

Cognitive Behavioral Therapy

Criminal thinking, as theorized by Yochelson and Samenow (1976), posits that the thinking among the offender and nonoffender populations differs and "developed an early theoretical framework for conceptualizing criminals' thought processes" (Mandraccia & Morgan, 2011, p. 442). According to their theory, the offender thinking process, this is demonstrated through their continuous pattern of behaviors that are criminal and problematic, has been present throughout their existence, and thus a change in behaviors that are antisocial, must require a change in erroneous thinking (Mandraccia & Morgan, 2011). Upon developing an understanding of the offender thought process development, "assessments can best direct how to apply criminal thinking conceptualizations into practice" (Mandraccia & Morgan, 2011, p. 443). There is support for the utilization of correctional interventions that are evidenced based among the offender population who is considered the ethnically minority, more specifically offender rehabilitative treatment that adheres to principles of effective interventions (RNR) and elements of cognitive behavioral therapy appear to be effective with a broad range of ethnicities (Usher & Stewart, 2012). Cognitive behavioral therapy is, according to Usher and Stewart (2012), "a model of intervention in which programming aims to address maladaptive cognitions and behaviors, while emphasizing training on skills for prosocial living" (p. 210). Furthermore, cognitive behavioral therapy is designed and has been proven to address the criminogenic needs of offenders. Examining the functioning of offenders in the following areas—thoughts, feelings, and behavior—cognitive behavioral therapy explores how those areas are interrelated, and focuses more specifically on how an individual's feelings and actions are influenced by their thoughts. Founded by Aaron Beck, cognitive behavioral therapy has evolved throughout the years and now encompasses many theories, to include rational emotive behavior therapy and rational behavior therapy.

IMPLICATION FOR MENTAL HEALTH PROFESSIONALS

There is a need for mental health professionals to develop an understanding of the unique characteristics of African American male offenders and begin to apply them to theory so that interventions specific to this population can be developed. Although recidivism outcomes are important, it is vital that mental health professionals understand the lifestyle and attitudes of the offender as they are the mediating factor between selected interventions and the overall desired outcome. An ongoing assessment of offender risk, needs, and treatment progress can be supported by the knowledge of the Principles of Effective Interventions, more specifically the Risk-Needs-Responsivity Model. Collaboratively identifying with the offender their current criminogenic needs needing to be addressed can provide an idea of which life areas need the most attention and the severity of risk. Staying focused on the targeted needs area can help the offender become an active participant in the behavior change process, instead of passive receipts of services. Having an understanding of an offender's faulty cognitive style will provide knowledge of other problems areas, to include strained relationships, mental illnesses, behaviors that are self-injurious, as well as be predictive of recidivism. Varghese (2012) has noted that in order to increase positive outcomes among criminal offenders, mental health professionals must utilize approaches that will target the attitudes of behaviors of the offender, changing their criminal characteristics. According to Nee, Ellis, Morris and Wilson (2012), the principle of responsivity takes into consideration "the offender's individual characteristics, such as ability to learn, motivation, and personality traits" (p. 1349) when implementing treatment programming and interventions, which would increase the likelihood of change. According to DiClemente et al. (2004), conceptualizing an offender's motivation utilizing the Transtheoretical Model of Behavior Change is theoretically appealing and is widely used among clinicians. Ultimately, by integrated concepts of individual psychology with the RNR approach, motivational interviewing, the Transtheoretical Model of Behavior Change, and cognitive behavioral therapy, the conceptualization and identification of interventions for the African American male offending population targeting their unique needs will assist them in overcoming barriers, developing, and maintaining a positive lifestyle change.

REFERENCES

Adler.A. (1930/1976). Individual psychology and crime. *Journal of Individual Psychology* 32(2), 131–144.

Andrews, D. A., Bonta, J., & Wormith, J. S. (2011). The risk-need-responsivity (RNR) model: Does adding the Good Lives model contribute to effective crime prevention? *Criminal Justice and Behavior, 38*(7), 735–755.

Andrews, D. A., Zinger, I., Hoge, R. D., Bonta, J., Gendreau, P., & Cullen, F. T. (1990). Does correctional treatment work? A clinically relevant and psychologically informed meta-analysis. *Criminology, 28*(3), 369–404.

Bonta, J., & Andrews, D. A. (2007). Risk-need-responsivity model for offender assessment and rehabilitation. *Rehabilitation, 6*, 1–22.

Clark, M. (2011). Exploring the criminal lifestyle: A grounded theory study of Maltese male habitual offenders. *International Journal of Criminology and Sociological Theory, 4*(1), 563–583.

D'Sylva, F., Graffam, J., Hardcastle, L., & Shinkfield, A. J. (2012). Analysis of the stages of change model of drug and alcohol treatment readiness among prisoners. *International Journal of Offender Therapy and Comparative Criminology, 56*(2), 265–280.

Day, S. X. (2008). *Theory and design in counseling and psychotherapy* (2nd ed.). Boston, MA: Houghton Mifflin.

DiClemente, C. C., Schlundt, D., & Gemmell, L. (2004). Readiness and stages of change in addiction treatment. *The American Journal on Addiction, 13*, 103–119.

Dutton, D. G., & Hart, S. D. (1992). Evidence for long-term, specific effects of childhood abuse neglect on criminal behavior in men. *International Journal of Offender Therapy and Comparative Criminology, 36*(2), 129–137.

Gendreau, P., Little, T., & Goggin, C. (1996). A meta-analysis of the predictors of adult offender recidivism: What works! *Criminology, 34*(4), 575–608.

Holliday, S. B., King, C., & Heilbrun, K. (2013). Offenders' perceptions of risk factors for self and others theoretical importance and some empirical data. *Criminal Justice and Behavior, 40*(9), 1044–1061.

Horton, A. (2013). African American male drug use and gambling and criminal behavior the need for more effective treatment. *Journal of Alcoholism and Drug Dependence, 1*(6), 1–3.

Jing-ying, G. (2012). For the sake of whom: Conversation analysis of advice giving in offender counseling. *International Journal of Offender Therapy and Comparative Criminology, 57*(8), 1027–1045.

Jolley, J. M., & Kerbs, J. J. (2010). Risk, needs, and responsivity: Unrealized potential for the international delivery of substance abuse treatment in prison. *International Criminal Justice Review, 20*(3), 280–301.

Jones, S. L., & Butman, R. E. (1991). *Modern psychotherapies: A comprehensive Christian appraisal.* Downers Grove, IL: InterVarsity Press.

Klinteberg, B., Almquist, Y., Beiger, U., & Rydelius, P. (2011). Family psychosocial characteristics influencing criminal behavior and mortality—possible mediating factors: A longitudinal study of male and female subjects in the Stockholm Birth Cohort. *BMC Public Health, 11*(176), 1–14.

Mandracchia, J. T., & Morgan, R. D. (2011). Understanding criminals' thinking: Further examination of the measures of offender thinking styles-revised. *Assessment, 18*(4), 442–452.

Marlowe, D. B. (2003). Integrating substance abuse treatment and criminal justice supervision. *Science & Practice Perspectives, 2*(1), 4–14.

Mauer, M., & Huling, T. (1995). *Young Black Americans and the criminal justice system: Five years later.* Washington, DC: The Sentencing Project.

Miller, W. R., & Rollnick, S. (1991). *Motivational interviewing: Preparing people to change addictive behavior.* New York, NY: Guilford.

Nee, C., Ellis, T., Morris, P., & Wilson, A. (2012). Addressing criminality in childhood: Is responsivity the central issue. *International Journal of Offender Therapy and Comparative Criminology, 57*(11), 1347–1373.

Ozpolat, A. R., & Akbaba, S. (2012). Lifestyles scale and its language adaptation, reliability and validity studies. *Turkish International Journal of Special Education and Guidance & Counseling, 1*(1), 1–10.

Sanders, M. (1993). *Treating the African American male substance abuser.* Chicago, IL: Winds of Change.

Spiropoulos, G. V., Salisbury, E. J., & Van Voorhis, P. (2014). Moderators of correctional treatment success: An exploratory study of racial differences. *International Journal of Offender Therapy and Comparative Criminology, 58*(7), 835–860.

Taft, C. T., Murphy, C. M., Elliott, J. D., & Morrel, T. M. (2001). Attendance-enhancing procedures in group counseling for domestic abusers. *Journal of Counseling Psychology, 48*(1), 51.

Usher, A. M., & Stewart, L. A. (2012). Effectiveness of correctional programs with ethnically diverse offenders: A meta-analytic study. *International Journal of Offender Therapy and Comparative Criminology, 58*(2), 209–230.

Varghese, F. M. (2013). Vocational interventions with offenders: Interdisciplinary research, theory, and integration. *The Counseling Psychologist, 41*(7), 1011–1039.

Walters, G. (1990). *The criminal lifestyle: Patterns of serious criminal conduct.* London, England: Sage.

Ward, T., Yates, P. M., & Willis, G. M. (2012). The good lives model and the risk need responsivity model: A critical response to Andrews, Bonta, and Wormith. *Criminal Justice and Behavior, 39*(1), 94–110.

Western, B., & Wildeman, C. (2009). The Black family and mass incarceration. *The Annals of the American Academy of Political and Social Science, 621,* 221–242.

Yochelson, S., & Samenow, S. E. (1976). *The criminal personality* (Vol. 1): *A profile for change.* Northvale, NJ: Jason Aronson.

Zalmanowitz, S. J., Babins-Wagner, R., Rodger, S., Corbett, B. A., & Leschled, A. (2013). The association of readiness to change and motivational interviewing with treatment outcomes in males involved in domestic violence group therapy. *Journal of Interpersonal Violence, 28*(5), 956–974.

CHAPTER 12

STRATEGIES AND INTERVENTIONS FOR WHITE SCHOOL COUNSELORS WORKING WITH AFRICAN AMERICAN MALE STUDENTS

Lauren Moss, Christy Land, and Matthew Rozzi

Many whites who concede that Negros should have equal access to public facilities and the untrammeled right to vote cannot understand that we do not intend to remain in the basement of the economic structure, they cannot understand why a porter or a housemaid would dare dream of the a day when his work will be more useful, more remunerative and a pathway to rising opportunity. This incomprehension is a heavy burden in our efforts to win white allies for the long struggle.
—Martin Luther King (1986)

In the above quote, Dr. King acknowledges the good intentions of White individuals who believe in "equal access to public facilities" yet do not extend themselves intellectually or empathically by taking action toward manifesting equitable dispositions. Accordingly, many White professional school counselors have wonderfully altruistic ideals regarding their work with African American male students. However, effective school counseling

Counseling African American Males, pages 191–214
Copyright © 2016 by Information Age Publishing
All rights of reproduction in any form reserved.

requires substance behind intent, it requires competency, and most importantly it requires action. By taking intentional action steps toward social justice, White school counselors can emerge as racial justice allies with their African American male students. However, this process requires increased social awareness, self awareness, and counselor competence to help navigate the complex obstacles faced by African American male students.

African American male students may encounter multiple barriers to education, including: negative academic experiences, feelings of isolation, power differences, increased discipline referrals, low retention rates, and decreased graduation rates (Holcomb-McCoy, 2007; Losen, 2011). Current scholarship addresses the school counselor's role regarding inequities that exist in schools (Bailey, Getch, & Chen-Hayes, 2003; Cox & Lee, 2007; Holcomb-McCoy, 2007). However, this chapter aims to isolate specific skills, strategies, and behaviors for White school counselors striving to become allies with African American male students as they navigate tumultuous academic settings (Taylor, Gillborn, & Ladson-Billings, 2009). Specifically, this chapter highlights: (a) the effects of school counselor identities on the student–counselor relationship, (b) culturally responsive school counseling interventions, (c) assessing school counselors' multicultural competence, (d) a social justice approach to school counseling, (e) the influence of race and culture on intervention planning, and (f) the student–counselor relationship and theoretically sound practices.

EFFECTS OF SCHOOL COUNSELOR IDENTITIES ON THE STUDENT–COUNSELOR RELATIONSHIP

The educational gap between Whites and African American students is well documented. White students graduate at higher rates from high school (87% as compared to 84%), and significantly higher rates (30% versus 19% bachelor's degree completion) from postsecondary institutions (Sue & Sue, 2013). The educational environment is often negative and sometimes hostile to African American male students. They are between two and five times more likely to be suspended from school and receive more severe punishments than their White counterparts for similar school offenses (Sue & Sue 2013). When considering a systemic context for a rationale to explain the disparate demographic data, Sue and Sue (2013) indicated, "School personnel often hold stereotypes of African American parents as being neglectful or incompetent, and blame children's problems on lack of parental support for schooling."

Given the current sociocultural climate of American public schools, school counselors must become culturally competent in order to emerge as effective practitioners. This is especially important for school counselors who hold dominant, majority identities (i.e., male, White, Christian, able-bodied, heterosexual). Although the American School Counselor Association does not report on the demographics of school counselors as a specific cohort of educators, research indicates that the racial and ethnic demographics of the (approximately) 90,000 school counselors (who provide services for 47 million students in the United States) are similar to those of teachers and school psychologists, suggesting the school counselor population is largely (85% to 95%) dominated by White professionals (Curtis, Grier, Abshier, Sutton, & Hunley, 2002; National Center for Educational Statistics, 2002). In contrast, it is estimated that by 2050 almost 60% of all school-age children in the United States will be students of color (Yeh & Arora, 2003). These demographic statistics further highlight the need for White school counselor multicultural competence. Accordingly, this chapter reviews developmental models created to explore White and African American ethnic identity formation and how culture influences problem identification, child behavior and development, childrearing practices, roles of the extended family, school history, insight, judgment, and coping skills.

THE SIGNIFICANCE OF RACIAL IDENTITY DEVELOPMENT

White school counselors are exposed to countless invisible social conditioning factors, including chronic exposure to ethnocentric monoculturalism—the belief in the superiority of one group's culture, imposed misinformation, and the omnipresent "invisible veil" of White culture (Sue & Sue, 2013). Yet, in order for White school counselors to become effectively multiculturally competent, they must detach from the cultural conditioning by developing a nonracist White identity (Sue & Sue, 2013). To address such movement, multiple developmental models have been proposed to illuminate White racial development.

Janet Helms, one of the most influential White identity developmental theorists, proposed six identity statuses: contact status, disintegration status, reintegration status, pseudoindependence status, immersion/emersion status, and autonomy status (Helms, 1990). In contact status, White individuals are unaware of racism and naively adopt the belief that everyone has equal chances for success (Helms, 1990). Accordingly, in Helms's disintegration status, White individuals become conflicted because of irresolvable racial dilemmas, followed by the reintegration status, in which the White individual shifts back to the comforting belief in White superiority (Helms, 1990). In pseudoindependence status, White individuals intellectually acknowledge racism in America and make purposeful decisions to interact with minority group members; however, in this stage, a White person may unintentionally perpetuate racism by assisting African Americans to conform to White standards/values (Helms, 1990). In the immersion/emersion status, White individuals continue their individual exploration as racial beings and seek the personal benefits of White privilege (Helms, 1990). Someone at this stage begins to explore racism on both an intellectual and affective level (Helms, 1990). Finally, in the autonomy stage, White people continue increasing their awareness of personal Whiteness, accepting negative feelings of White guilt, and are no longer fearful or intimidated by race (Helms, 1990).

Helms's model poses a drastic contrast to the implication of race on the identities of people of color who often find race quite salient to their identity. On the contrary, as seen in Helms's model, White individuals often do not consider race important to their identity (Sue & Sue 2013). Paradoxically, the most precise assessment of bias may not come from those who hold the biases, but from those who are disempowered by them (Sue & Sue 2013). Thus, White school counselors must interact and collaborate with African American counselors, educators, students, and families not only to increase their competence in working with African Americans, but also to increase their understanding of themselves in context and, subsequently, attempt to locate and reduce unconscious biases. The goal of bringing cultural biases to a conscious level is for those who do so to become decreasingly prone to inequitable action due to the misinterpretation of behaviors of students who are culturally different from themselves (Weinstein, Curran, & Tomlinson-Clarke 2003). Therefore, White school counselors who identify overt or covert racist thoughts need further exposure, training, reflection, and counseling to obtain cultural competency.

Racial identity development is a critical aspect of multicultural counseling competence, particularly for White counselors and counselor trainees who may be unaware of the complexities their racial identity holds, and specifically with respect to how it mitigates the counseling process (Leuwerke, 2005). Holcomb-McCoy (2007) stressed the importance of school counselors' and counselor trainees' understanding of the impact of racial identity development in the lives of their students. Similarly, scholars stress the significance of counselor and counselor educator use of racial identity models to identify the developmental stages of their racial identity to successfully prepare for multicultural competence (Pack & Brown, 1999; Sue and Sue, 2008). Only after White school counselors are able to acknowledge their own racial identity and recognize its impact on the counseling relationship can they begin to grow in their development as an ally to the African American male students and families with whom they work.

ALLY IDENTITY DEVELOPMENT

Holding an ally identity is imperative for White school counselors who seek to increase their competence when working with African American students. However, developing an ally identity is more complex than adopting a set of counseling skills and practices. A counselor's thoughts, beliefs, attitudes, experience, education, skills, and strengths must be inventoried to consider how they all contribute to the counselor's overall identity and, thus, subidentity as an ally for social justice. Ultimately, the most meaningful assignment of allies comes from members of the oppressed population (Edwards, 2006). From this paradigm, African American male students are the experts in identifying White school counselors who function as their allies.

Edwards (2006) indicated that the complexity of becoming an ally is created, in part, due to each ally relationship having its unique risks, parameters, responsibilities, and benefits. What all effective allies have in common, however, is that they bring attention to privilege, power, and prejudice that typically remains unaddressed (Reason & Davis, 2005). Broido (2000) explored factors associated with social justice ally development and found three common developmental markers of social justice allies: (a) they possessed knowledge around issues of social justice and diversity to increase their ally competence, (b) they yearn to discuss the information they amass in order to make meaning of it, and (c) they use acquired knowledge to propel them toward action in pursuit of social justice.

Edwards (2006) proposed a model for conceptualizing Aspiring Ally Identity Development. Edwards included three stages to delineate ally behaviors: (a) aspiring ally for self-interest, (b) aspiring ally for altruism, and (c) ally for social justice. Aspiring allies for self-interest are generally inspired to become an ally in order to protect those they care about and, therefore, often forge alliances with individuals with whom they have a preexisting personal connection (Edwards, 2006). Aspiring allies for altruism attempt to use ally relationships as a way to cope with guilt and emotional responses to their awareness of their privileges (Edwards, 2006). Finally, allies for social justice seek to create alliances with those from the oppressed group in order to collaboratively end systems of oppression.

This third and final stage of Edward's model explains that effective allies share certain beliefs, traits, motivations, foci of work, and assumptive worldview (Edwards, 2006). Specifically, Edwards (2006) explained that effective allies are motivated by a blend of selfish (based on the understanding that inequality is harmful for everyone) and altruistic reasons. Ultimately, effective allies view the victims of oppression as not simply the minority population traditionally affected by inequality, but as the entire population in which oppression is present. Subsequently, effective allies beyond individuals to a broader mission of "escaping, impeding, amending, redefining, and destroying" (Edwards 2006) the status quo and creating a more equitable system in its wake.

ACTION STEPS FOR WHITE SCHOOL COUNSELORS

By attending to their racial identity, utilizing a model such as Helms's (1990) White Identity Development Model, and considering their ally identity development by using a model such as Edwards's (2006) Ally Identity

Development Model, White school counselors increase their awareness of Whiteness as a construct and gain a clearer understanding of implications race holds for their students and their work as a professional school counselor. This collaborative and systemic aspect of how allies operate are congruent with the American Counseling Association's (ASCA) vision for comprehensive school counseling and ACA Advocacy Competencies, and calls for culturally responsive school counseling practices (American Counseling Association, 2012; Lewis, Arnold, House, & Toporek, 2002).

CULTURALLY RESPONSIVE SCHOOL COUNSELING INTERVENTIONS

When analyzing how to intervene in response to gaps in academic, social, or emotional performance, the school counselor must remain mindful of culturally responsive and social justice counseling practices. Accordingly, African American male students may benefit from individual or small group interventions to effectively combat elements of oppression (McAuliffe, 2008; American Counseling Association, 2012). When planning for such interventions, there exists a very real danger to students at every stage in their educational journey if educators and school counselors are not culturally competent (Holcomb-McCoy, 2007).

Given that students of color are more likely than their White counterparts to be taught by teachers with less experience, educated in schools with fewer resources, and come from homes with less income, African American students are hit with multiple barriers to educational success (Holcomb-McCoy, 2007). The role of the White school counselor is to assist African American students and schools with addressing these barriers and not to make them worse, Thus, when considering culturally responsive counseling interventions with African American males, White school counselors should first consider the dictate, "above all, do no harm" or, as it is worded in the American Counseling Association Code of Ethics, the concept of nonmaleficence (American School Counselor Association, 2012).

Do no harm or nonmaleficence is one of the five moral principles viewed as the ethical guidelines of the counseling profession (Forester-Miller & Davis, 1995). As Edwards (2006) indicated, some aspiring social justice allies ultimately perpetuate systems of oppression they seek to change. Subsequently, many White school counselors working with African American male students need to ask themselves how they can take preventative action to halt the cycle of oppression they are seeking to change.

The concept of willingness to challenge authority and battle the status quo is one seen often in school counseling literature. Griffin and Steen (2011) argue that taking a social justice approach requires counselors to "question authority, challenge the injustices they see in the schools, and work collaboratively with one another." Accordingly, effective White school counselors are ideally positioned as a "squeaky wheel" with respect to championing social justice. However, this presents a challenge for White school counselors, as they are themselves positioned as part of the machinery of the status quo.

PLANNING CULTURALLY RESPONSIVE INTERVENTIONS

As discussed in the previous section, establishing related identity and awareness provides a first step in generating culturally responsive counseling interventions. Once awareness and an understanding of White ethnic identity in relation to African Americans has been established, White school counselors must use their knowledge and insight to become models of social justice in the school. White school counselors apply this insight to become effective models, educators, and mediators within the school context. Most importantly, they partner with their African American students and their families in order to support their navigation though academic and related contexts. Griffin and Steen (2011) offer action strategies for school counselors working with students of color beginning with developing cultural competencies, including:

- Use data to support work
- Acquire allies
- Speak up (advocate) for and on behalf of students' needs
- Educate parents and families
- Engage politically
- Be bold in efforts to promote the culture of students
- Remain persistent
- Conduct research that will help to expand understanding of cultural competence

Additionally, Griffin and Steen (2011) notably suggested the importance of school counselors working at multiple levels of advocacy, including individual, family, institutional, and societal levels, as seen in the ACA Advocacy Competencies (see Figure 12.2). White school counselors hold an obligation to address concerns at these multiple levels, and to no longer maintain the status quo by implicitly and explicitly agreeing to maintain the traditional and externally defined school counselor's role (Bemak & Chung, 2005). White school counselors can approximate this by attending closely to the social, political, and economic realities of the students and families with whom they work while concurrently addressing these elements as a critical part of the school counselor's role (Bemak & Chung, 2005).

In the instance of African American males, school counselors benefit from considering the cultural context and support that surrounds them, and the

African American students with whom they work, in order to make decisions regarding how to deliver support. Some specific strength-based interventions for African American male students include the use of metaphors and traditional African storytelling (Sue & Sue, 2013). Also, counselors may encourage students to utilize quotes of famous African Americans or music lyrics that address presenting issues (Sue & Sue, 2013). Furthermore, counselors can review family phrases, sayings, and values to explore how students internalize these values and how they may clash with dominant culture values.

White school counselors may find their students a part of the traditionally strong extended family networks within the African American culture. This support system may serve as a strong source of strength for African American males who are coping with oppression through racial socialization (Sue & Sue, 2013). Accordingly, gaining support from family, especially extended family, is an integral part of effective counseling with African American students (McAuliffe, 2008). Therefore, viewing students within their cultural environment helps professional school counselors to determine when social justice advocacy is appropriate.

ASSESSING SCHOOL COUNSELORS' MULTICULTURAL COMPETENCE

Holcomb-McCoy (2007) posited that one of the most profound challenges confronting the social justice movement is acquiring multicultural counseling competence (Erford, 2007). Ponterotto and Casas (1987) believed that multicultural competence is achieved when a counselor has the skillset to effectively meet the needs of clients from various cultural backgrounds. Over the past three decades, scholarly literature focused on multicultural competence highlights three dimensions: awareness, knowledge, and skills (Erford, 2007; Holcomb-McCoy, 2007; American Counseling Association, 2012). Therefore, a counselor with high multicultural competence possesses the awareness, knowledge, and skills to recognize cultural differences and similarities as significant to the counseling process. While a counselor with low multicultural competence provides counseling interventions with little or no regard for cultural considerations (Erford, 2007; Holcomb-McCoy, 2007; American Counseling Association, 2012).

MULTICULTURAL COMPETENCY AND THE ASCA NATIONAL MODEL

Professional school counselors are charged to implement comprehensive school counseling programs that enhance the academic, career, and personal-social developmental needs of all students (American Counseling Association, 2012; Erford, 2007). Further, utilizing data to drive decision-making, school counselors implement interventions that help to close attainment, achievement, opportunity, and funding gaps among groups of students in the school setting. In order to effectively support students of historically oppressed backgrounds, such as African American males, school counselors must provide interventions that create and foster environments for all students that support multicultural competence and social justice (Erford, 2007).

Culturally responsive counseling interventions assist White professional school counselors in becoming culturally competent when working with African American students. Professional school counseling literature offers a conceptualization of what a culturally competent White school counselor thinks, feels, says, and most importantly *does*. Similarly, culturally alert counseling can be defined as "a consistent readiness to identify the cultural dimensions of clients' lives and a subsequent integration of cultural into counseling work" (McAuliffe, 2008, p. 5). Further, culturally responsive counseling involves a student-centered approach in which an individual's unique cultural strengths are identified and nurtured in order to promote student achievement and a sense of social/emotional well-being about the students' cultural, connection to the school, and society at large (Richards, Brown, & Forde, 2004). Moreover, culturally alert counseling consists of counselor culturally competence in regards to the impact of culture on their students accompanied by a set of culturally alert practices. In response to this need, numerous existing counseling practices and theories can be utilized if done in a culturally sensitive and intentional way (McAulifee, 2008; American Counseling Association, 2012).

When White school counselors consider how to engage in counseling with African American males, they must contemplate how they, and the counseling process, may be perceived. Williams and Justice (2010) concluded that African American male students generally hold negative views on counseling, resulting from their belief in negative stigmas, concern of showing signs of weaknesses, fear of embarrassment and misdiagnosis, and concern of hospitalization and treatment. However, Williams and Justice (2010) suggest that African American male students' perceptions of counseling may be based on inaccurate information.

Given the concerns identified by Williams and Justice (2010), it is important for school counselors to consider how they can work to break down barriers to counseling for African American male students. For instance, if White school counselors ensure students receive accurate information regarding counseling services and how it may benefit them, they may become more open to engaging counseling services. Furthermore, if school counselors ensure that African American male students are "exposed to the positive nature of counseling through preparation programs, retention programs, and mentorships," they may begin to see the benefits of counseling and become more likely to seek counseling (Williams & Justice, 2010).

A STRENGTHS-BASED APPROACH

Also, a strengths-based approach that focuses on individual resiliencies, talents, supports, skills, and gifts offers an approach to shifting the negative beliefs brought in by African American students as well as changing the system that may have perpetuated institutional oppression leading to the students' negative beliefs. In an article about strengths-based school counseling, Galassi, Griffin, and Akos (2008) wrote,

> We suspect that most school counselors have been called upon to counsel (also known as "fix") students who have been referred for behavior problems. Often the relationship and interaction stays focused on the problem or deficit within the student who caused the problem. This type of deficit-focused approach "may also unwittingly generate a negative relationship" (Ahmed & Boisvert, 2006, p. 334), and perhaps reinforce noncompliance and a lack of connection. (Galassi, Griffin, & Akos, 2008)

In this pattern of focusing on the student and the student's deficits, the school counselor becomes stuck in a situation that alienates the student and does not resolve the problem. Worse, this norm perpetuates a system that leads to students being less inclined to seek assistance. Although there is no single formula for a culture-specific intervention list, McAuliffe (2008) recommend several guidelines for school counselors to consider when working with African American male students:

- Be genuine in nonverbal and verbal communications.
- Actively engage in advocacy efforts.
- Utilize nonpsychological methods such as spirituality.
- Embrace language flexibility.
- Judiciously apply assessment methods.
- Proactively acknowledge societal bias.
- Practice culturally informed consent.

By adopting McAuliffe's (2008) and William and Justice's (2010) action-oriented recommendations, White school counselors will further increase their awareness of injustices their African American male students face and begin to take form as an ally. Subsequently, the importance of taking an overarching socially just approach to school counseling will begin to take shape.

A SOCIAL JUSTICE APPROACH TO SCHOOL COUNSELING

Social justice reflects a fundamental valuing of equity and fairness in resources, rights, and treatment of marginalized populations who do not share equal power in society (Constantine, Hage, Kindaichi, & Bryant, 2007). The social justice movement has emerged in the field of school counseling as a powerful approach to meeting the diverse needs of students (Lee, 2007; Ratts, D'Andrea & Arrendo, 2004). Specifically, this movement promotes social justice as a fundamental principle of counseling by systemically eliminating various forms of oppression and social injustice (Smith, Reynolds, & Rovnak, 2009). In order to address issues of social justice, school counselors must integrate a professional commitment to global and societal change. Such a commitment is pivotal to understanding the interdependence of microsystems and macrosystems, particularly in the lives of individuals from marginalized groups (Constantine, Hage, Kindaichi, & Bryant, 2007).

SOCIAL JUSTICE AND THE AMERICAN SCHOOL COUNSELOR ASSOCIATION

The American School Counselor Association (2012) maintains that professional school counselors work toward socially just outcomes by acting on the following ASCA national model themes of: (a) leadership, (b) advocacy, (c) collaboration, and (d) systemic change. Therefore, school counseling programs with a social justice orientation include advocacy for equity and access for all students as well as special considerations for students who may benefit from additional support. The statistics outlined in the previous section of this chapter clearly point to African American male students as a group of students requiring the attention and specific skillset of professional school counselors.

PRACTICAL ACTION FOR WHITE SCHOOL COUNSELORS

Professional school counselors are charged to address and advocate for systemic change to meet the needs of all the students they service (American School Counselor Association, 2012; Griffin & Steen, 2010; Lewis, Ratts, Paladino, & Toporek, 2010; Singh, Urbano, Haston, & McMahon, 2010). Specifically, Constantine, Hage, Kindaichi & Bryant (2007) identified nine specific social justice competencies that they believe are important for practitioners to consider as they work to meet the increasingly diverse needs of their populations. These competencies are as follows:

- Become knowledgeable about the various ways that oppression and social inequalities can manifest at the individual, societal, and cultural levels.
- Participate in ongoing critical reflection on issues of race, ethnicity, oppression, power, and privilege in their own life.
- Maintain an ongoing awareness of how their own positions of power or privilege might inadvertently replicate experiences of oppression and injustice.
- Question and challenge therapeutic interventions that appear inappropriate.
- Possess knowledge about indigenous models of health and healing and actively collaborate with such entities when necessary.
- Cultivate an ongoing awareness of the various types of social injustices that occur within international contexts.
- Conceptualize, implement, and evaluate comprehensive preventive and remedial mental health interventions that are aimed at addressing the needs of marginalized populations.
- Collaborate with community organizations in democratic partnerships to promote trust and minimize power differentials.
- Develop system intervention and advocacy skills to promote social change processes within institutional, neighborhood, and community settings.

Furthermore, Singh et al. (2010) implemented a study to explore strategies that school counselors who self-identified as social justice agents used to advocate for systemic change within their school communities. The purpose of this study was to analyze how school counselors manifest advocacy practice. Findings included seven overarching themes:

- Use political savvy to navigate power structures.
- Engage consciousness-raising exercises with students and the community.
- Initiate difficult dialogues.
- Build intentional relationships.
- Teach students self-advocacy skills.
- Use data for marketing.
- Educate others about the school counselor role of advocate.

By implementing the recommendations of Constantine, Hage, Kindaichi, and Bryant (2007) and Singh et al. (2010), school counselors will become increasingly responsive to the needs of African American male students. Additionally, utilizing the strategies presented helps school counselors create a social justice framework that will better serve the African American male students and families for whom they work. Operating from this structure will naturally position professional school counselors in a place of leadership within the school. However, it is important for professional school counselors to acknowledge and own their leadership positionality in order to remain effective in their efforts to support groups of diverse students.

SCHOOL COUNSELOR LEADERSHIP

As the role of the professional school counselor continues to evolve, the importance of effective leadership skills continues to emerge (Briggs, Kielty, Staton, Gilligan, & Davis 2009). Davis (2004) defines leadership as "the process of influencing others to create a shared commitment to a common purpose" (p. 216). This definition includes the following tenets: (a) commitment to the cause, (b) shared responsibility, (c) being driven to the mission, and (d) promoting core values. Similarly, Chen-Hayes, Ockerman, and Mason (2014) maintain that "leadership is an ethical educational imperative for educators if the educational system is to gain traction on issues of access and equity found in the achievement and opportunity gaps that plague K-12 schools" (p. 1). School counselors, as leaders, play an essential role as change agents for equity to ensure that all students reach their full potential academically, personally, and in the area of career and college readiness (American School Counselor Association, 2012; Chen-Hayes, Ockerman, & Mason, 2014). School counselors must embrace the unique power that they hold enabling them to either foster or dampen the aspirations of the students they serve (Holcomb-McCoy, 2007). Chen-Hayes, Ockerman, & Mason utilize the change agent for equity (CAFE model) to demonstrate that school counselors' professional identity as leaders and advocates come first, ultimately generating equity based school-counseling programs (see Figure 12.1).

ADVOCATING FOR CULTURALLY RESPONSIVE
PRACTICES IN SCHOOLS

As ASCA states, "There should be no stronger student advocate than school counselors. They must be the heart and soul of the school and lead the charge in creating a school culture that promotes an equitable education for every student" (American School Counselor Association, 2012, p. 18). ASCA maintains that school counselors are advocates for social-justice-oriented outcomes when they address inequitable policies and procedures that may impede the academic achievement or personal/social development of students. Crethar, Rivera, and Nash (2008, p. 6) define *advocacy* as, "proactive efforts carried out by counseling professionals in response

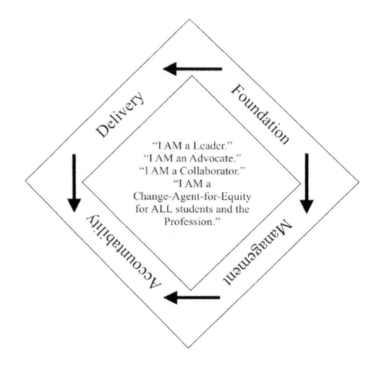

Figure 12.1 Change Agent for Equity (CAFE) School Counselor Model (Chen-Hayes, Ockerman, & Masonn, 2014)

to institutional, systemic, and cultural impediments to their clients' well-being." Additionally, White school counselors who maintain a client advocacy disposition conceptualize problem remediation beyond individual students' lives by allocating time and energy to "implement preventative helping interventions and services that are intentionally aimed at promoting a greater level of social justice by fostering systemic changes in clients' environmental context" (Crethar, Rivera, & Nash, 2008, p. 6).

While the mindset toward advocacy and social justice is clearly appropriate and necessary for White school counselors to attend to, it is not without barriers. For instance, many people enter the profession of counseling driven by a desire to work one-on-one with individual clients, never considering that they would be charged with making a systemic impact on forces of broader systems of oppression (Ratts, Toporek & Lewis, 2010). However, the primary role of the school counselor who serves as an advocate for all students is to create opportunities for all students to define, nurture, and accomplish high expectations with a focus on removing institutionalized barriers to success (Akos & Galassi, 2004; American School Counselor Association, 2012; Field & Baker, 2004).

The American Counselor Association (ACA) advocacy competencies provide an additional framework for school counselors working to transition social justice and advocacy tenets into practice (Figure 12.2). Toporek, Lewis, and Crethar (2009) define advocacy competence as "the ability, understanding, and knowledge to carry out advocacy ethically and effectively" (p. 262). The development of the advocacy competencies acknowledges that oppression and systemic barriers interfere with an individual's health and well-being and may even cause distress (Toporek, Lewis, & Crethar, 2009). Advocacy extends the impact that counselors can have on their clients and students by working to remove systemic barriers to success, therefore causing less stress and harm to individuals (Toporek, Lewis, & Crethar, 2009). The advocacy competencies play an instrumental role in school counselors' growth toward holding an ally and advocate identity.

Although school counselors may find leadership and advocacy out of their comfort zone, leadership and advocacy roles and responsibilities lie in the hands of professional school counselors. By leaning on professional organizations such as ASCA and ACA, professional school counselors can operate within a clear, supported role to best advocate with and on behalf of African American male students and their families. In this light, school counselors can emerge as effective leaders, steering their school stakeholders toward more socially just policies, procedures, and interventions.

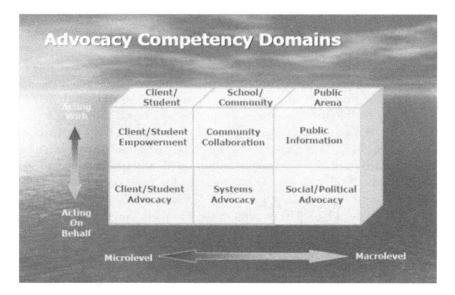

Figure 12.2 American Counseling Association Advocacy Domains (Ratts, Toporek, & Lewis, 2010)

THE INFLUENCE OF RACE AND CULTURE
ON INTERVENTION PLANNING

Even with the best intentions, the identification of problems for African American male students may be hindered or occluded by cultural differences. African American males may not come to counseling willingly; thus, creating a strong therapeutic alliance may be particularly important as well as exploring the reasons for resistance both personal and societal (Sue & Sue, 2013). Race and culture influence intervention planning for White professional school counselors working with African American students in three ways: (a) race and culture influence the client's (student's) perspective on and reception to treatment, (b) race and culture influence the professional counselor's perspective and treatment delivery, and (c) the race and the culture of the client and the counselor coming together form a therapeutic alliance that is unique given the mixture of cultural influences brought into the alliance from client and counselor (Sue & Sue, 2013). While White school counselors need to be acutely aware of their own ethnic identity, it is of paramount importance for White school counselors to possess competence in understanding the identity of African American male students. Additionally, White school counselors need to be aware that race salience (how important race is to the identity of individuals) varies greatly from individual to individual.

A MODEL FOR AFRICAN AMERICAN RACIAL IDENTITY

Perhaps the most widely cited and well-documented developmental model of racial identity for African American individuals is the Cross model of psychological nigrescence (the process of becoming Black) (1978). Created during the Civil Rights Movement, it explores how Black individuals in the United States move from a White perspective to a positive Black perspective (Sue & Sue 2013). There are five stages in the Cross model: (a) pre-encounter, (b) encounter, (c) immersion-emersion, (d) internalization, and (e) internalization-commitment. The pre-encounter stage is characterized by African Americans devaluing their own Blackness and valuing White values and ways (Cross, 1978). The encounter stage involves the African American encountering a problem that challenges the White values held, causing a reinterpretation of worldviews (Cross, 1978). In the immersion-emersion stage, the Black individual removes himself or herself from the White culture and becomes immersed in Black culture. The fourth stage, internalization, involves the Black person obtaining security and resolution between previously held White values/identity and Black values/identity (Cross,

1978). In the final stage, internalization-commitment, the Black individual commits to social change, social justice, and civil rights (Cross, 1978).

School counselors have a specific obligation at each stage of an African American male's cultural development. In the pre-encounter stage, counselors can educate and assist the student in sorting out conflicts related to racial/cultural identity (Sue & Sue, 2013). The immersion-emersion stage may create the most difficult stage for White school counselors to navigate, as African American males may view the White school counselor with suspicion and/or hostility during this stage, and typically view the counselor as a symbol of an oppressive society (Sue & Sue 2013). However, White school counselors must resist becoming defensive or personalizing the attacks as this will cause the White school counselor to lose effectiveness in working with the client (Sue & Sue, 2013). Furthermore, Sue and Sue (2013) indicated the importance of remaining unintimidated or afraid of the anger that is likely to be expressed, as it is legitimate and not personal (Sue & Sue, 2013).

CONSIDERATIONS FOR PLANNING SPECIFIC INTERVENTIONS

Both White school counselors and African American male youths are in danger of being victims of ethnocentric monoculturalism (Sue & Sue, 2013). It is important for the professional school counselor to not perpetrate this concept (Sue & Sue, 2013). Instead, the White school counselor must provide space and support for African American male students to be where they are is in regards to ethnic identity and foster the development of a unique cultural identity for each student (Sue & Sue, 2013). Through these means, the White school counselor places the African American male student at the center of counseling, rather than on the fringe of the sociopolitical structure in which he exists. African American males come from families who are more likely to be composed of extended nontraditional families, homes run by single mothers, flexible family roles, and families with strong community support. It is important to note that different does not mean worse; differences are not deficits. For example, while African American males are more likely to experience harsh punishment from their family members, this type of discipline is often culturally perceived by children as an indication of care or concern (Sue & Sue, 2013). The African American family structure has a number of strengths including the strong kinship bonds, flexible family roles, strong work and achievement ethic, and strong religious orientation (Sue & Sue, 2013). African Americans value assertiveness, and African American males who manifest this value in the classroom may be perceived as having a behavioral problem.

THE STUDENT–COUNSELOR RELATIONSHIP
AND THEORETICALLY SOUND PRACTICES

Current literature indicates the importance of school counselors in addressing inequities that exist in schools (Bailey, Getch, & Chen-Hayes, 2003; Cox & Lee, 2007; Holcomb-McCoy, 2007; Singh, Urbano, Haston, & McMahan, 2010). Additionally, scholarship increasingly maintains the ideology that the field of school counseling requires a shift from traditional methods of counseling (focused on interpersonal or intrapersonal concerns) to social justice counseling (Goodman et al., 2004), which is addressed throughout this chapter. However, by leaning on a broader theoretical framework, which specifically addresses relational (relational cultural theory) and racial (critical race theory) components, White school counselors may more explicitly anchor the theoretical framework from which they work and artfully craft sound practices accordingly.

THEORETICAL TENETS AROUND RACE
AND POWER STRUCTURES

When "personality traits" are ascribed to a subordinate group (i.e., racial minority groups) and pathologized, traditional psychological theories often assist in justifying and conserving the culture's existing power distribution (Jordan, 2010). However, critical race theory (CRT) and relational cultural theory (RCT) offer alternatives to traditional theoretical counseling models and ways of conceptualizing the work of school counselors (Figure 12.3). From a critical race perspective, we see an important distinction between the viewpoints of White individuals and people of color: White people do not see their perspective as one way of experiencing the world, but as the sole reality (Taylor, Gilborn, & Ladson-Billings, 2009). Similarly, Miller (2002) discussed this concept from a relational-cultural perspective as controlling images. Miller indicated that dominant groups create controlling images about themselves and subordinate groups. Essentially, controlling images create a fear for those in power and those who are oppressed around losing status if one does not behave as the controlling image indicates (Miller, 2002). For instance, those in power may risk association with others not in power and even groups who lack sociocultural power risk affiliation with even lesser desirability (Miller, 2002).

In order to work toward an increased common understanding of reality, relational cultural theory places a strong emphasis on how power is distributed relationally in both intimate interactions and on a broader, societal scale (Figure 12.3). Likewise, critical race theory specifically addresses how the political, legal, and educational systems in the United States are

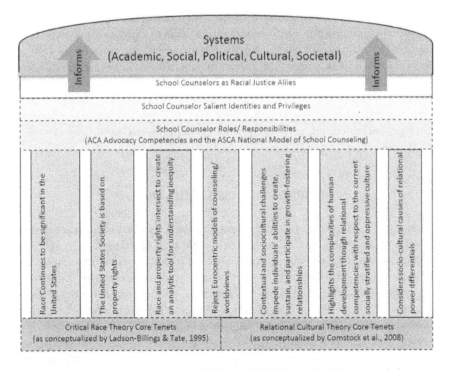

Figure 12.3 Visual Illustration of a RCT and CRT Theoretical Framework for White school counselors.

built upon the inequitable platform of Whites having rights to property and capital which were provided to them by force in the form of land (by native people) and labor (in the form of slave and immigrant labor) (Taylor et al., 2009, p. 7). Jonathan Kozol (1991), a social activist and education critic, described the way these inequities are manifested in the current American education system as "savage inequities" when speaking to the clear imbalances that exist between the academic experiences of White middle-class students and those of poor African American and Latino students. Ladson-Billings and Tate (1995) further explored these inequities in their article, "Toward a Critical Race Theory of Education" and explained that, "these inequalities are a logical and predictable result of a racialized society in which discussion of race and racism continue to be muted and marginalized" (p. 47).

Relational cultural theory maintains that the counselor undoubtedly holds a level of expert power in the therapeutic relationship and should attend to this by leveling power between the therapist and client through a variety of growth-fostering techniques. Both relational cultural theory and critical race theory maintain that growth through connection lives far beyond the confines of therapy. In fact, sociocultural context is of the utmost importance when considering implications of power structures (Jordan, 2010; Taylor et al., 2009). By placing culture at the theoretical epicenter, this framework shifts the power, illuminating the complex systems of connection—countering the idea of separation (Miller & Stiver, 1997). In this way, critical race theory and relational cultural theory provide a theoretical framework from which practitioners can begin to challenge the cycle of oppression through relational connection and movement toward a common understanding of reality (Figure 12.3).

OPPOSING THE STATUS QUO

There are healthy and unhealthy ways for relationally minded practitioners to effectively oppose the status quo of a workplace (Jordan, 2010). Scholars agree that while healthy opposition can lead to constructive movement and change, unhealthy opposition often results in pernicious disconnection, alienation, isolation, and harm to clinicians, clients, and the workplace as a whole (Miller, 1976). Specifically, Miller (1976) proposed that healthy opposition can be defined as "waging good conflict," meaning that it is "respectful and empathic to those with whom we disagree, resisting the temptation to separate ourselves by degrading, dismissing, or objectifying them as human beings" (Hartling & Sparks, in Jordan, 2010. p. 167). This "good conflict" allows relationally minded clinicians to keep the ideal relational goal at the forefront of their work while creating conditions in which relational shifts, albeit micromovements, can begin to occur at the organizational level.

Many school counselors may note institutional barriers, or unhealthy opposition, as blocking the achievement of students of color. School counselors who operate from the relational cultural and critical race blended theoretical framework presented for this work would likely look to several avenues when analyzing their efforts. First, school counselors operating from this framework understand the connection between race, law, and education. Specifically, they understand how movements such as desegregation and civil rights have affected the current curriculum, instruction assessment, and funding of schools (Taylor et al., 2009, pp. 28–33). Furthermore, while school counselors operating from this theoretical perspective aim to help the students with whom they work, they also expect their own personal growth and development as an outgrowth from their interactions with their student-clients. For instance, they may see the world differently from hearing about the lived experiences of their students of color. Additionally, White school counselors who utilize a blended critical race-relational cultural theoretical framework must also consider how professional relationships in the school and greater community contexts may act as conduits to consciousness raising around sociopolitical realities or as elements that perpetuate the current, oppressive status quo.

SUMMARY

Despite the shift toward social justice and advocacy counseling, many African American males remain marginalized, subsequently leading to vastly different educational experiences than their peers who identify as part of the dominant group (Sue & Sue, 2008). Accordingly, key tenets of the ASCA National Model include the beliefs that effective school counselors' advocacy efforts are aimed at a comprehensive, outcome-based service model for all students, which accounts for fluctuating needs and abilities, elements that align it with the ACA Advocacy Competencies (Crethar, 2010). Although the ASCA National Model aims for a comprehensive approach to school counseling and integrates multicultural competence, a void remains around White school counselors exploring their racial privilege and how they can leverage it on behalf of students of color (Edwards, 2006; Cross, 1978).

As the ACA Advocacy Competencies (Lewis, Arnold, House & Toporek, 2002) indicate, advocacy efforts of White school counselors who identify as racial justice allies to African American students occurs in domains that often involve their direct contact and collaboration with African American students and their families. The relational element of these efforts requires White school counselors to consider how power differentials and growth fostering relationships affect this work, which is addressed by relational cultural theory (Jordan, 2010). It is also imperative for White school counselors to remain mindful of how the sociopolitical and educational policies and practices of the past inform the current context in which they work, which is the foundation of critical race theory (Ladson-Billings & Tate, 1995).

Despite the need for counselors to consider ACA Advocacy Competencies and operate from a social justice advocacy paradigm, White school counselors still often struggle with how to put skills into practice to improve oppressive social, political, and economic conditions to impact poor academic achievement for students of color in K–12 schools (Holcomb-McCoy, 2007). In contrast, social justice counseling supports professional school counselors' work to challenge the status quo as a means of empowering clients while also confronting inequities (Holcomb-McCoy, 2007). This chapter suggests practical strategies as adopted from current scholarship (i.e., Constantine et al., 2007; Chen-Hays et al., 2014; Griffin & Steen, 2011; McAuliffe, 2008; Williams & Justice, 2010; Singh et al., 2010) to guide White school counselors' practice in a culturally responsive manner. This will support their racial justice ally development so that they can better support the African American males with whom they work.

REFERENCES

Ahmed, M., & Boisvert, C. M. (2006). Using positive psychology with special mental health populations. *American Psychologist, 61*(4), 333–335. doi:10.1037/0003-066X.61.4.333

Akos, P., & Galassi, J. P. (2004). Training school counselors as developmental advocates. *Counselor Education & Supervision, 43,* 192–208.

American Counseling Association. (2012). *Code of ethics.* Retrieved from http://www.counseling.org/Resources/CodeOfEthics/TP/Home/CT2.aspx

American School Counselor Association. (2012). *The ASCA national model: A framework for school counseling programs.* Alexandria, VA: Author. doi:10.1037/e504812012-001

Bailey, D. F., Getch, Y. Q., & Chen-Hays, S. (2003). Professional school counselors as social and academic advocates. In B. T. Erford (Ed.), *Transforming the school counseling profession* (pp. 411–435). Upper Saddle River, NJ: Merrill Prentice Hall.

Bemak, F., & Chung, R. (2005). Advocacy as a critical role for urban school counselors: Working toward equity and social justice. *Professional School Counseling, 8*(3), 196–202.

Briggs, M., Kielty, M., Staton, A., Gilligan, R., & Davis, T. (2009). The girls' leadership experience camp: A parallel process of leadership skills development for school counselors in training. *Professional School Counseling, 13*(2), 125–133.

Broido, E. M. (2000). The development of social justice allies during college: A phenomenological investigation. *Journal of College Student Development, 41,* 3–18. doi:10.1002/ss.162

Chen-Hayes, S. F., Ockerman, M.S., & Mason, E. C. M. (2014). *101 solutions for school counselors and leaders in challenging times.* Thousand Oaks, CA: Sage.

Constantine, M. G., Hage, S. M., Kindaichi, M. M., & Bryant, R. M. (2007). Social justice and multicultural issues: Implication for practice and training of counselors and counseling psychologists. *Journal of Counseling & Development, 85,* 24–29.

Cox, A. A., & Lee, C. C. (2007). Challenging educational inequities: School counselors as agents of social justice. In C. C. Lee (Ed.), *Counseling for social justice* (2nd ed., pp. 3–14). Alexandria, VA: American Counseling Association.

Crethar, H. C. (2010). ACA advocacy competencies in school counseling. In M. J. Ratts, R.L. Toporek, & J. A. Lewis (Eds.), *ACA advocacy competencies: A social justice framework* (pp. 107–117). Alexandria, VA: American Counseling Association.

Crethar, H. C., Rivera, E. T., & Nash, S. (2008). In search of common threads: Linking multicultural, feminist, and social justice counseling paradigms. *Journal of Counseling & Development, 86,* 269–278.

Cross, W. E. (1978). The Thomas and Cross models of psychological nigrescence: A review. *Journal of Black Psychology, 5*(13), 13–30. doi:10.1177/009579847800500102

Curtis, M. J., Grier, J. E. C., Abshier, D. W., Sutton, N. T., & Hunley, S. (2002). School psychology: Turning the corner into the twenty-first century. *Communique, 30* (8), 1, 5–6.

Davis, T. (2004). *Exploring school counseling: Professional practices and perspectives.* Boston, MA: Houghton Mifflin.

Edwards, K. E. (2006). Aspiring social justice ally identity development: A conceptual model. *NASPA Journal, 43*(4), 39–60.

Erford, B. (2007). *Transforming the school counseling profession.* Upper Saddle River, NJ: Pearson.

Field, J. E., & Baker, S. (2004). Defining and examining school counselor advocacy. *Professional School Counseling, 8*(1), 56–63.

Forester-Miller, H., & Davis, T. (1995). *A practitioner's guide to ethical decision making.* Retrieved from http://www.counseling.org/docs/ethics/practitioners_guide.pdf?sfvrsn=2

Galassi, J. P., Griffin, D., & Akos, P. (2008). Strengths-based school counseling and the ASCA national model. *Professional School Counseling, 12*(2), 176–181.

Goodman, L., Liang, B., Helms, J., Latta, R., Sparks, E., & Weintraub, S. R. (2004). Training counseling psychologists as social justice agents: Feminist and multicultural principles in action. *The Counseling Psychologist, 6*, 793–837.

Griffin, D., & Steen, S. (2010). A social justice approach to school counseling. *Journal for Social Action in Counseling and Psychology, 3*(1), 74–87.

Hartling, L., & Sparks, E. (2010). Relational-cultural practice: Working in a nonrelational world. In J. Jordan (Ed.), *The power of connection* (pp. 159–181). New York, NY: NY, Routledge.

Helms, J. B. (1990). *Black and White racial identity: Theory, research, and practice.* New York, NY: Greenwood.

Holcomb-McCoy, C. (2007). *School counseling to close the achievement gap: A social justice framework for success.* Thousand Oaks, CA: Sage.

Jordan, J. V. (2010) *The power of connection: Recent developments in Relational-cultural theory.* New York, NY: Routledge. doi:10.4324/9781315875286

King, M. L. (1986). *A testament of hope.* New York, NY: HarperCollins.

Kozol, J. (1991). *Savage inequalities: Children in America's schools.* New York, NY: Crown.

Ladson-Billings, G., and Tate, W. (1995). Toward a critical race theory of education. *Teachers College Record, 97*(1), 47–64.

Lee, C. C. (2007). *Social justice: A moral imperative for counselors* (ACAPCD-07). Alexandria, VA: American Counseling Association.

Leuwerke, W. (2005). Fostering the development of multicultural counselling competencies: Training, growth and development for White counselors. *Guidance & Counseling, 21*(1), 21–29.

Lewis, J. A., Arnold, M. S., House, R., & Toporek, R. L. (2002). *ACA advocacy competencies.* Retrieved March 20, 2013, from http:www.counseling.org/Publications/

Lewis, J. A., Ratts, M. J., Paladino, D. A., & Toporek, R. L. (2010). Social justice counseling and advocacy. *Journal for Social Action in Counseling and Psychology, 3*(1), 5–18.

Losen, D. J. (2011). *Discipline policies, successful schools, and racial justice.* Boulder, CO: National Education Policy Center. Retrieved March 30, 2013, from http://nepc.colorado.edu/publication/dicipline-policies

McAuliffe, G. (2008). *Culturally alert counseling: A comprehensive introduction.* Thousand Oaks, CA: Sage.

Miller, J. B. (1976). *Toward a new psychology of women.* Boston, MA: Beacon Press.

Miller, J. B. (2002). *How change happens: Controlling images, mutuality, and power* (Work in progress, no. 96). Wellesley, MA: Stone Center Working Paper Series.

Miller, J. B., & Stiver, I. P. (1997). *The healing connection.* Boston, MA: Beacon Press.

National Center for Educational Statistics. (2002). *Public school student, staff, and graduate counts by state: School year 2000–2001.* Retrieved March 30, 2013, from http://nces.ed.gov/pubs2002/snf_report/

Pack-Brown, S. P. (1999). Racism and White counselor training: Influence of White racial identity theory and research. *Journal of Counseling & Development, 77*(1), 87–92.

Ponterotto, J. G., & Casas, J. M. (1987). In search of multicultural competence within counselor education programs. *Journal of Counseling & Development, 65,* 430–434. doi:10.1002/j.1556-6676.1987.tb00749.x

Ratts, M. J., D'Andrea, M., & Arrendondo, P. (2004). Social justice counseling: Fifth force in counseling in field. *Counseling Today, 47*(1), 28–30.

Ratts, M. J., Toporek, R. L., & Lewis, J. A. (2010). *ACA advocacy competencies: A social justice framework for counselors.* Alexandria, VA: American Counseling Association.

Reason, R. D., & Davis, T. L. (2005). Antecedents, precursors, and concurrent concepts in the development of social justice attitudes and actions. In R. D. Reason, E. M. Briodo, T. L. Davis, & N. J. Evans (Eds.), *Developing social justice allies* (110 ed., pp. 5–116).

Richards, H., Brown, A., & Forde, T. (2004). *Addressing diversity in schools: Culturally responsive pedagogy.* Denver, CO: National Center for Culturally Responsive Educational Systems.

Singh, A. A., Urbano, A., Haston, M., & McMahon, E. (2010). School counselors' strategies for social justice change: A grounded theory of what works in the real world. *Professional School Counseling, 13,* 135–145.

Smith, S. D., Reynolds, C. A., & Rovnak, A. (2009). A critical analysis of the social advocacy movement in counseling. *Journal of Counseling & Development, 85,* 483–491. San Francisco, CA: Jossey-Bass.

Sue, D. W. & Sue, D. (2008). *Counseling the culturally diverse: Theory and practice* (5th ed.). New York, NY: Wiley.

Taylor, E., Gillborn, D., & Ladson-Billings, G. (2009). *Foundations for critical race theory in education.* New York, NY: Routledge.

Toporek, R. L., Lewis, J., & Crethar, H. C. (2009). Promoting systemic change through the advocacy competencies: Special section on ACA advocacy competencies. *Journal of Counseling & Development, 87,* 260–268.

Weinstein, C., Curran, M., Tomlinson-Clarke, S. (2003). Culturally responsive classroom management: Awareness into action. *Theory Into Practice, 42*(4) 269–276.

Williams, A., & Justice, M. (2010). Attitudes of African American males regarding counseling in four Texas universities. *Education, 131*(1), 158–168.

Yeh, C. J., & Arora, A. K. (2003). Multicultural training and interdependent and independent self-construal as predictors of universal-diverse orientation among school counselors. *Journal of Counseling & Development, 81,* 78–83.

CHAPTER 13

SOCIAL LEARNING THEORY AND STRENGTH-BASED APPROACHES TO COUNSELING ADOLESCENT AFRICAN AMERICAN MALES

Donald E. Grant, Jr.

The factors that influence self-identity through the lifespan are innumerable. Messages abound telling young and old who they are, who they were, who they should be, and, even worse, who they can or can't be. Defining oneself while immersed in a toxic environment can be a challenging feat wrought with obstacles, many of which hold disastrous consequences.

When one looks at the ecologies where children grow and develop, it becomes important to assess the risk factors related to the development of a healthy and sustainable sense of self. In doing so, one must also evaluate how this ecology is situated to either enhance or diminish optimal development of the child's opportunities for success. Both these factors hold variables that influence a variety of outcomes. Although each variable is critical, some are more salient than others.

Counseling African American Males, pages 215–235
Copyright © 2016 by Information Age Publishing
All rights of reproduction in any form reserved.

According to Harvard professor and historian Dr. Henry Louis Gates, Jr. (2011), the first documented man of African descent, Juan Garrido, arrived on this land as a free man in 1513, over a century before the first documented African slaves. Africans held a documented presence in significant numbers in Mexico and California prior to European colonization. These Africans played a pivotal role in the Olmec culture and those that developed as a result (Restall, 2000). Legrand Clegg (2003) reported that art historian Alexander Von Wuthenault held a noteworthy collection of figurines depicting the prominent existence of people of African descent in pre-Columbian America playing significant roles as clergy, government leaders, chiefs, and musicians. Some academics credit Africans for introducing calendars, writing, pyramids and tomb construction, mummification, certain political systems, and religious traditions to the Native Americans (Clegg, 2003; Sertima, 1976).

It would appear, however, based on historic and contemporary literature, government documentation, and modern media that the Black man's first role in this country, or this world for that matter, was that of a slave, a man who is forcibly bound to the land and recognized as simple chattel or property. When other young men look to history to provide a reference point for self-identity, they can often attach to an image of freedom and pride or innovation at the very least.

Men of European descent are lauded as the founders of the "New World," while men of Latin descent are often embraced by the rich and heroic histories of their countries of origin. Men of Asian descent reflect on their ancestral influence in the development of the world's most sought after nonreligious spiritual disciplines and alternative medical practices. Unlike these men, most Black men, specifically African American men, never gain awareness or insight into even their countries of origin much less the great achievements of those lands. For this reason, and several others, the initial historical self-reference point for Black boys is more often than not a subservient, enslaved, shackled, and emasculated heathen, whose worth is measured by his brawn.

The world, including Black men and boys, is fed consistent images of Black male failure and delinquency in the absence of much noticeable balance. There is no doubt that these images wreck havoc on the availability of a safe, secure, and nurturing environment for appropriate self-development in Black boys. It is easy to see the wide and prevalent disproportionality with which Black men and boys meet across a variety of domains. Incarceration, adjudication, education, occupation, and compensation are but a few of the domains Black men find themselves meeting with dismal inequities.

Disproportionality occurs when a group exists in a condition at a rate that far exceeds their presence in the general population. In 2010, Black men represented a little over 6% of the entire U.S. population, but had a

13% unemployment rate (U.S. Department of Labor, 2014), and made up 40% of all people incarcerated (U.S. Department of Justice, 2010). During the 2009–2010 academic year the national 4-year college graduation rate for Black males was 52%, while non-Hispanic White males boasted a 78% graduation rate (Schott Foundation, 2012).

There are a variety of factors that negatively impact the trajectories of African American males throughout the life span. Understanding some of their details can support culturally competent engagement and culture-centered ecological enhancement with and for Black males in the United States. Clinical, academic, and social service professionals across a myriad of domains would be able to enhance service quality and outcome strength using a more client-centered, multisystemic, ecological approach from assessment/orientation through graduation or termination of services.

STEREOTYPE THREAT, STEREOTYPE BOOST, AND STEREOTYPE LIFT

The nature of stereotypes makes it such that no group or individual in the group is immune to their effects. Even when a stereotype is considered positive, as a result of the broad-brush stroke with which they are painted, it usually results in a negative outcome. For instance, Asian Americans are subject to the "model minority stereotype," a portion of which is related to high degrees of academic achievement and success. Many believe that this works in favor of Asian American students; it is, after all, a great attribution to have. Research by Treichel (2014) and anecdotal evidence on this matter shows that it is a misleading stereotype that disguises uniqueness while masking actual concerns. A true recognition of the dangers of stereotypes is evidenced by this example, as even the "positive stereotypes" can have negative consequences.

Stereotypes are dangerous just by virtue of what they are: widely held beliefs and images that represent an over-simplistic and rigid view of a particular out-group. They have been found to exert powerful effects on cognition and behavior, impacting people's perceptions of themselves and others (Shih, Ambady, Richeson, Fujita, & Gray [2002]).

Stereotypes about Black men are prevalently endorsed across most all modalities of media. It is easy to find images of Black men in modern media fighting, going to prison, selling drugs, or walking away from their children. It, however, remains challenging to find images of these same men as doctors, responsible fathers, and successful businessmen. The more frequently people are exposed to these negative images, the more easily their brain relies on them when making choices about behaviors, attitudes and world views. Research shows that racial cues are perceived more quickly than others and can activate stereotypes that impact decision-making.

Stereotypes create attitudes, and attitudes influence behavior. As more and more dangerous stereotypes of Black men are disproportionately projected onto the consciousness of America, the dangers for Black men and boys grow exponentially. Entman and Gross (2008) found that Black men are overrepresented in news broadcast as perpetrators of violent crimes when compared to actual arrest records, are more likely to be shown in roles on television and movie "perp walks," and are more likely, than other groups, to occupy television mug shots. This disproportionality has dire consequences, one of which was demonstrated by data sets collected from First Person Shooter tests (Markman, 2012). In these computer simulated experiments, as a result of stereotype activation, respondents were more likely to shoot unarmed Black men than White ones and spent more time deliberating before shooting armed White men than armed Black men. These stereotypic cues often make race an inappropriately significant factor in the decision for police officers and civilians to fire their weapon upon men of color, specifically Black men (Markman, 2012).

Stereotypes have sinister consequences, many of which have significant empirical support; these consequences are just as dangerous as the tangible environmental dangers that we fight so diligently to remediate. Constructs like stereotype threat, stereotype boost, and stereotype lift, in the context of their impact on the overall sociocultural wellness of Black males, their interactions with the dynamics of academia, and their potential influence on sociocultural performance factors, must be unpacked and addressed with the same deliberateness dedicated to gang violence, drug abuse, and police brutality.

STEREOTYPE THREAT

Stereotype threat, originally studied by Steele and Aronson (1995), occurs when a group of people are confronted with a situation where fulfilling a negative stereotype of themselves is eminent. As of November 2014, Steele and Aronson's article had been cited more than 4,300 times according to Google scholar. Since the original experiments, the effects of stereotype threat have gained widely accepted empirical support regarding their negative impact on most people who hold at least one social identity to which a negative stereotype is directed. Studies exploring stereotype threat have unequivocally demonstrated its impact on a wide array of the citizenry, including but not limited to women, people of color, White men, poor people, gay men, and the elderly (Bosson, Haymovitz, & Pinel, 2004; Chasteen, Bhattacharyya, Horhota, Tam, & Hasher, 2005). There are a multitude of negative stereotypes that exist about Black men and boys, and research indicates that this can exponentially increase their experiences with stereotype threat. Consistent exposure to stereotype threat can lead to diminished confidence, poor performance, and loss of interest in the relevant area of achievement. (Gilovich, Dacher, & Nisbett, 2005)

STEREOTYPE BOOST

Stereotype boost occurs when the performance of an individual is enhanced by exposure to "positive" stereotypes of themselves. Stereotypes are often spoken of in a context that conveys negative beliefs about a group. These same stereotypes, as a corollary convey positive messages about another group, positive messages that can have positive effects. When compared to young people, the elderly are often devalued across several domains, but there also exists stereotypes that activate positive imagery of this group. Hess, Hinson, and Statham, (2004) discovered that the memory ability of elderly participants was enhanced when positive stereotypes related to wisdom and experience were cued compared to demonstrations of memory deficits in those elderly participants cued by negative stereotypes of senility and dementia. This was further demonstrated by Cheryan and Bodenhausen (2000) when Asian American women performed better on math tests when stereotypes about their ethnic heritage were activated compared to worse performance when gender based stereotypes were activated.

STEREOTYPE LIFT

Stereotype lift occurs when the performance of an individual is increased and/or enhanced as a result of exposure to negative stereotypes about other groups. Groups that engage in downward comparisons with stereotyped out-groups often do so automatically and benefit from performance enhancements at the expense and denigration of the other group. A meta-analysis of research on stereotype threat discovered that the same stereotype activation that diminished performance for the out-group, enhanced performance for the in-group (Smith & Johnson, 2006). By comparing oneself to a socially undervalued group, one may experience a promotion of self-efficacy or sense of personal value that can enhance performance factors (Walton & Cohen, 2003). Awareness of inferior stereotyped out-groups have the capacity to enhance feelings of efficacy and worth that maintain motivation and confidence while changing perceptions of reception from suspicion to respect (Walton & Cohen, 2003).

Of course, there are negative stereotypes about dominant groups including White men and wealthy people. The effects of stereotype threat have even been demonstrated on tests of White men and innate athletic ability, resulting in compromised performance as a result of stereotype activation. These groups however tend to confront fewer stereotypes (negative or positive) that reflect on their intellectual abilities.

Stereotype threat, stereotype boost, and stereotype lift all occur simultaneously, to different groups. While the nondominant group only experiences the negative performance burdens of stereotype threat, the dominant group experiences both a boost, as positive stereotypes about their domain-specific self are affirmed and a lift as the inferior stereotypes about an out-group are highlighted. This interaction of forces is a strong contributor to large and expanding gaps in academic achievement between groups with negative stereotypes about their academic performance, groups with positive stereotypes about their academic performance, and groups with no stereotypes about their academic performance.

Early research indicated that the primary mechanism supporting the effects of stereotype threat was anxiety. They contended that the anxiety evoked when confronted with the possibility of meeting the negative stereotype was directly and solely (in some cases) responsible for compromises in performance. (Shapiro, Williams, & Hambarchyan, 2013). More recent research speaks to variations in the type of stereotype threat experienced and the resultant responses.

The multithreat framework (Shapiro et al., 2013) differentiates between two types of threat: group-as-target stereotype threat (GTST) and self-as-target stereotype threat (STST). STST is experienced when one believes that a stereotype-relevant performance might reflect poorly on the ability or perception of the entire group. For example: Kamal, the only Black student in his class at an Ivy League college, experiences GTST as he prepares for his organic chemistry exam. Kamal's professor posts the scores of all midterm exams so everyone in the class will see his test score. Fear provoked by the thought of getting a poor grade and confirming a lack of cognitive ability about Blacks in general monopolizes cognitive energies that would normally be dedicated to test-taking strategies and memory retrieval. Kamal may also experience additional pressures, as he believes that once this threat is fulfilled, it may also signify the low enrollment rates of Blacks at his school or questions about Black matriculation on a whole.

Self-as-target stereotype threat (STST) is experienced when one believes that a stereotype-relevant performance will reflect poorly on their personal abilities or the perceptions that people have of them as an individual (Shapiro et al., 2013). Using the same example above, Kamal's test performance may also be compromised as a result of the fear that a poor grade will reflect on his cognitive abilities as an individual and potentially create questions about his appropriateness for the program of study. The multithreat framework indicates that each of these stereotype threat types utilize different resources, respond to different interventions, and create concerns in different domains (Shapiro et al., 2013). Understanding these differences informs treatment, engagement, and ecological restructuring.

DISIDENTIFICATION AND DISENGAGEMENT

Identification with any particular life domain implies that the domain plays a part in the individual's global sense of self. An array of domains exists in which identification occurs; in each of them, the strength of the identification is positively correlated with domain specific success (Osborne, 1997). There is significant evidence indicating that the "development of domain identification is arrested in response to stereotype threat" (Woodcock, Hernandez, Estrada, & Schultz, 2012, p. 2). "The experience of chronic stereotype threat is hypothesized to lead to domain disidentification and eventual domain abandonment" (Woodcock et al., 2012, p. 1). The consequences of this disidentification and abandonment are critical and might explain a portion of documented outcomes in a variety of areas for Black boys and men. As a result of the many stereotypes that exist about Black men, there are multiple domains where both implicit and explicit threat might exist, negatively impacting one's ability to navigate the nexus between the existential environment and intrinsic personality.

Academic attrition, fatherlessness, joblessness, and criminality are all domains where Black men and boys exist at a statistically disproportionate rate. The world sees these factors in different ways, but clinicians must look at these conditions and behaviors, in some part, as one component of a larger continuum of responses to mental health experiences and wellness outcomes. Each of these responses may all be domain-specific conditions strongly connected to disidentification and abandonments capacity to incite depression, anxiety, and cognitive fatigue, ultimately resulting in negative outcomes for the men and boys in addition to many people who love and support them.

Disengagement and disidentification can be viewed as opposite ending points on a larger continuum of "self-protective, ego withdrawal from a domain and its standards" (Woodcock et al., 2012, p. 2). Withdrawal is one of many defense mechanisms that the ego employs to increase safety and reduce opportunities for psychic injury. We use a variety of defense mechanisms, often unconscious, that allow us to avoid some painful realities created by our worlds. Disengagement and disidentification are both serious results of this ego withdrawal.

Disengagement is an immediate response to one's experience with stereotype threat by which individuals, in order to protect themselves, literally halt engagement in a particular domain. Schmader, Major, and Gramzow (2001) state that, "Psychological disengagement is a defensive detachment of self-esteem from one's outcomes in a domain such that self esteem is not contingent upon one's success or failure in the domain" (p. 94). When domain specific issues denote a level of subordination informed by racial stereotypes of inferiority, the individual can elude injury by employing (consciously or not) disengagement.

Individuals might experience disidentification across a variety of domains. Each of which is interconnected with outcomes that have huge consequences, particularly for marginalized communities. Academic disidentification, for instance, has been described as "an emotional and physical withdrawal from school, leading to a host of negative behaviors, including poor academic performance, complete withdrawal or 'dropping out' of school, or even potential delinquency" (Williamson, 2011, p. 8). Steele and Aronson (1995) defined disidentification as an absence of affiliation between academic self-esteem and global self-esteem. Disidentification occurs when the individual has no ego dependence on the domain in question. They may even reject encouragement to developing a salient connection to this domain (Steele & Aronson, 1995).

Once a young man is impacted by these factors, it becomes virtually impossible for them to further navigate success in academia without deliberately robust interventions. There are a variety of behavioral concerns associated with disidentification that compound the consequences, resulting in increased risk factors for delinquency, school attrition, misdiagnosis, and a variety of other factors (Steele & Aronson, 1995). Academic disidentification is described as a holistic disengagement from academia (Steele & Aronson, 1995; Woodcock et al., 2012). Research consistently shows that African American male students demonstrate worse academic outcomes than most other groups of U.S. students. These outcomes include but are not limited to lower grades, lower standardized test scores, higher dropout rates, and lower college attendance rates (U.S. Department of Labor, 2014; U.S. Department of Justice, 2010; Schott Foundation, 2012).

Disidentification, however also exists outside of the domain of academia. What happens when stereotypes about the inept and absent Black dad abound in an experience that lacked a positive paternal role model? How is one's performance and assessment impacted when the messages about the lazy, shiftless, and dispensable Black employee weighs more heavily than any evidence from the actual workplace? How does one resolve the dissonance of prosocial behavior in the face of the potential social capital accumulated by behaviors disproportionately identified as antisocial? Clinicians must be adept at assessing how the ecological influences of stereotype threat inform disidentification and work together to impact the mental wellness of these boys and men.

THE SYNERGISTIC EFFECT: WHEN STEREOTYPE THREAT MEETS DISIDENTIFICATION

There is a level of danger that extends well beyond coincidence and conjecture when discussing the combined impact of stereotype threat and disidentification. Each of them, as described earlier in this chapter, independently has the capacity to generate irreversible damage to the sociocultural development of any youth. These already dangerous agents have identifiable outcomes independent of any other factors: outcomes that are exacerbated in the presence of the compounding risk factors faced by African American males.

We know that mere membership in a cultural out-group comes along with some very salient risk factors (Aronson & Aronson, 2011). Privilege occurs when individuals, simply as a result of group membership, gain unearned access to goods that others don't (Wise, 2005). These goods may come in the form of tangible items and resources, but might also be psychosocial freedoms that allow some to subsist oblivious to the varied layers of marginalization in the existential realities of others (Case, 2013; Wise, 2005). A major concern with privilege as it relates to the experiences of African American men and boys is the invisibility that it creates regarding the risky environments in which all Black boys grow, independent of socioeconomic status, culture, or U.S. geographical location. Privilege affords the dominant culture the luxury of ignorance maintenance to generate realities that minimize the daily perils embedded in the ecology of Black men and boys.

Black men and boys, like other polymarginalized groups are often forced to navigate multiple sets of risk factors. Diamond (2009) describes the neuroconstructivist approach where "genes, brain, cognition and environment dynamically interact, multidirectionally influencing one another in multiple ways" (Diamond, 2009, p. 3) This bidirectional pattern of engagement often results in a feedback loop, facilitating the exponential growth of overlapping risk factors and maladaptive outcomes. These factors and outcomes would not likely result in the same level of damage had they occurred independent of one another (Diamond, 2009; Westermann et al., 2007).

For instance, "Black males are incarcerated at a rate that is seven times the rate for White males and are more likely than any other race group to be a victim of a violent crime, including homicide" (Toldson & Lewis, 2012). Each of these factors poses significant independent threats. High incarceration rates and school-to-prison pipelines have a huge impact on African American men and boys. Exposure to violent crimes, particularly homicide, increases individual exposure to trauma stimuli across the life span. Now combine both these factors and we see just one of the countless synergistic dyads and triads in the ecologies of Black men.

The synergistic effect occurs when the coexistence of two or more conditions result in an effect size that is greater than the sum of each individual part. Very few things exist in pure isolation, unconnected to the other events and conditions in its shared chronosystem. In some cases, synergy results in consequences that enhance environments and one's exposure to ecological protective factors. In other cases, the synergy results in consequences that enhance ecological risk factors that deteriorate the most redeemable qualities the overall ecology has to offer. One salient example of this synergy might be illustrated in the early death tax associated with a lack of academic attainment.

In 2005, "remaining life expectancy at age 25" (Humer & Hernandez, 2013), a critical factor of adult health and well-being, illustrated significant disparities between those who completed college and those who never earned a high school diploma. When compared, there was more than a 10-year difference in remaining years of life for both men and women. In 2005, men without high school diplomas had a life expectancy of 69 while those with graduate degrees lived on average until age 85 (Humer & Hernandez, 2013). This 16-year difference expands when the data is disambiguated by ethnicity, culture, and socioeconomic status.

There are many factors that contribute to early deaths in any community. Black men experience higher levels of mortality, disparate morbidity rates, and a "high prevalence of severe functional limitation secondary to chronic illness" (Geronimus, 1998, p. 4) than most other groups. Substance use, homicide, gang involvement, and community violence are but a few factors that hold responsibility in premature deaths for Black men and boys. Coincidentally, each of these factors tends to have strong correlations to academic attrition, remediation, and discipline (U.S. Department of Justice, 2008; U.S. Department of Health and Human Services, 2013). The prevalence of these factors magnifies the impact of early mortality rates for families negatively impacted by undereducation, particularly families that have intergenerational experiences with academic disenfranchisement and accumulated disadvantage in disinvested communities.

There are identifiable benefits associated with communities that experience longevity. The influence of multiple generations on family systems has proven to be beneficial to the development of sustainable protective factors. Community elders have the capacity to continue the oral tradition and instill ancestral value system assets often lost over time. According to the U.S. Department of Health and Human Services Division, Substance Abuse and Mental Health Services Administration (SAMHSA, 2013), elders, grandparents specifically, have the capacity to maximize community protective factors by providing leadership, a sense of family continuity and history, childcare support, and opportunities for growth and development, all while having a vested interest in the well-being and healthy development of their grandchildren and other community youth (U.S. Department of Health and Human Services, 2013).

LOOKING FORWARD TO SOLUTIONS

Although 45% of Black males over 25 years of age have attempted college, only 16% have a 4-year degree, which is half that of White males who have a 4-year degree (Toldson & Lewis, 2012). Although there are countless examples of Black males who have reached a level of academic success, these successes exist both in spite of and as a result of their given circumstances. Many of these men were fortunate enough to have protective factors more profound than the risks, regardless of the quantity on either side. This aforementioned 16% have navigated many of the same roads traveled by those before, but they appear to have access to resources conducive to positive outcomes. These resources may be found in their families, communities, schools, or as intrinsic qualities of the self.

Clinical and academic professionals who work with Black youth have long fought an uphill battle. Black children are readily impacted by the intergenerational patterns and paradigms that decrease the likelihood of their engagement in formal mental wellness activities. Ecological messages regarding dominant cultures proprietary rights to academic excellence and psychosocial well-being have a history of informing outcomes for our children and communities. Believing that academic achievement is a "White thing" is one of the major ramifications of this phenomenon. Academic achievement is closely correlated to a variety of outcomes that can actually translate into life or death situations.

In order to take control of this problem, professionals, researchers, and service providers must begin to make deliberate connections between psychosocial outcomes and academic underachievement, disengagement, and disidentification. When we fail to attack the concerns that contribute to both the disengagement and disidentification of young Black boys in academia, we passively damage the entire ecology for Black boys, and the synergy described earlier becomes an even more salient problem.

In order to effect positive change, communities must employ a variety of techniques and interventions to manage such an insidious interaction. Issues like the school to prison pipeline, fatherlessness, factors in the first five years of life, preschool enrollment, special education disparities, and diverse learning styles of Black boys have all been well documented in illustrating their effects on self-esteem and academic achievement for this group. The remainder of this chapter will discuss several other noteworthy factors, in no particular order, to help address the dangers identified.

Social Learning Theory and Modeling

Modeling, also known as observational learning, is considered by behaviorists as one of the most important ways in which people, particularly children, learn. Social learning theory purports that theories on extrinsic reward and punishment fail to adequately explain all learning. (Hart & Kritsonis, 2006) When children live in a family and community where the value placed on academia is held high, children get examples and models of academics and individuals who value this domain. It is critical that Black boys see Black men as classroom teachers, college professors, doctors, lawyers, and business owners. It is clear that most Black boys don't gain access to adequate examples of Black men in academia to create an effective shift in this paradigm.

As long as adults continue to fail in the academic arena, children will have fewer and fewer models of academic achievers to emulate, increasing the challenges associated with overcoming stereotype threat and potential experiences with disengagement and disidentification. These youth are subsequently bombarded by models that provide motivation against academic achievement and success, and people begin to celebrate the antiacademic and the thug. The athlete, the hustler, and the entertainer become the monolithic roles to model. When older cousins and siblings are seen matriculating and adults have their shingles on display, it provides a very visceral lesson for observers. When youth are exposed to appropriate models who are valued in their family or community, they attend to those models. Attendance breeds retention of information and increases the capacity to reproduce the modeled behaviors when proper motivation is available.

Addressing and Reframing Black Masculinity.

Harper (2004) stated "a healthy, conflict free masculine identity leads to a strong self-concept and positive outcomes in a wide array of areas, including academics." Boys work to define manhood in a space where the influence of their peers plays a critical role, so much so that validation and approval are often required before paradigms can be adopted (Harper, 2004). For instance, athleticism is often an easily peer endorsed exhibition of manhood where alternative ones like doing well in school and nonathletic activities are not.

The influence of American racism, social inequities, and disproportionality has the capacity to create feelings of powerlessness, guilt, and shame for some Black men that can be tied to their masculinity (Harper, 2004; Harris, 1995). Harris (1995) suggests that some African American males, as a result "have redefined masculinity to emphasize sexual promiscuity, toughness, thrill seeking, and the use of violence in interpersonal interactions."

Harper (2004) demonstrated in his study that high-achieving African American male college students expressed a different evaluation on the "perceived nexus between masculinity, materialism and achievement" when compared to stereotypic attributions and endorsements of "acceptable" Black masculinity. This study found that many of these men ascribed to roles consistent with dominant culture definitions of masculinity, with one striking difference: the motive. The men in this study reported that school leadership roles and other activities were critical to the "advancement of African Americans on their campuses." When these same men discussed career aspirations, many indicated the importance of obtaining positions that strategically placed them in roles to provide opportunities for other Blacks (Harper, 2004).

Retraining Attitudes and Stereotypes

We must work to help Black men and boys change the script they get regarding stereotypes. Forbes and Schmader (2010) used a retraining paradigm to test the effects of attitudes and stereotypes on individuals' motivation and cognitive capacity in stereotype-threatening situations. Results suggest that positive attitudes have the capacity to motivate stigmatized individuals to engage with threatening domains and maximize the cognitive capacity critical for success (Forbes & Schmader, 2010). Retraining attitudes and stereotypes in Black men and boys is a very involved task, as it necessitates the capacity to counter the multitude of terrible stereotypes that afflict Black men across the diaspora.

Part of this goal might be achieved by increasing historical and scientific texts that incorporate more positive contributions of African Americans. Utilizing learning materials that aid to minimize the impact of the world's stereotypes and close cultural gaps in classroom curriculum that often exclude people of color is critical to the development of identity and minimization of privilege. These tools will open the eyes of youth to the strength and resilience of their peoplehood, inspiring self-esteem, positive cultural identity development, and a better understanding of diversity.

Black boys' introduction to their historical personhood comes in the form of bondage, disenfranchisement, forced servitude, and barbarianism. How would the foundations of identity development be shifted if Black boys exposure to their personhood began before slavery? Understanding that great African empires thrived prior to the transatlantic slave trade in places like Ghana, Nubia, Egypt, Mali, and Kush could provide any child with the psychic strength to counter the ego injuries associated with academia.

Learning that all across Africa lived mighty kings and queens, scientists, and inventors, all where temples, pyramids, grand libraries, and palaces were erected prior to many other civilizations. In Nubia, African people created Napta Playa one of the world's first tools of astronomy, even older than Stonehenge. The Egyptians wrote in hieroglyphics and created important theories of math and science. The Axum people of Ethiopia created majestic international trading posts along the Red Sea. The people of Ghana were very rich, using gold and iron to make tools and weapons for trade. The Songhai kings used their strong military to create and maintain a thousand miles of empires along the Niger River (Bauval & Brophy, 2011; James, 2009; McKay et al., 2011).

These powerful images, if appropriately and seamlessly integrated into the classroom curriculum where they belong, could provide Black children with additional resources to fight this uphill battle. These stories might be able to promote a paradigm of efficacy and inclusion in domains beyond the stereotypic ones in academia used to promote White privilege and the general oppression of people of color and women as a result of the exclusion of their contributions.

IMPLICATIONS FOR COUNSELORS

Self-Affirmations and Handicapping Behaviors

Evidence clearly demonstrates that these factors all connect to potential self-image instability across significant life domains. A clinician doesn't have the capacity to be an effective helper without knowledge of how the proverbial "whole person" is impacted by their experiences. Attending to these factors provides a cohesive lens to see these men and boys through, and to appropriately conceptualize their lives, experiences, and underlying needs. Research demonstrates a very close correlation between self-esteem and a variety of mental wellness indicators.

Self-esteem and depression have a uniquely reciprocal relationship in that they both have the capacity to negatively impact one another. Self-image instability is a "risk factor for depression, especially for people who experience life stress." (Crocker, Karpinski, Quinn & Chase, 2003, p. 508), while low self-esteem is further eroded by one's experience with depression (Sowislo & Orth, 2013). Recent events have demonstrated clearly that Black men and boys experience ecological stressors not experienced by the majority of their counterparts. These stressors include, but are not limited to increasing preschool suspensions of Black boys, disproportionate expulsions for offenses other students were suspended for, threats and evidence of police violence, under-resourced educational settings and unstable employment opportunities. These life stressors increase the likelihood that one's self-image may be rendered unstable, which, in turn, magnifies the impact of environmental risk factors.

The synergy between these explored issues connects directly to levels of perceived self-esteem, and there are several things clinicians can do to address these concerns with Black men and boys.

Look for signs of self-handicapping in Black men and boys that "involves creating or claiming obstacles to success in order to protect self-esteem in the event of failure" (McCrea & Hirt, 2011 p. 1). Self-handicapping is highly correlated to both stress and anxiety and is implicated in long-term decreases in self-esteem and intrinsic motivation and increases in negative mood and drug use. (McCrea & Hirt, 2011). Self-affirmations in domains different than the one being threatened have the capacity to challenge self-handicapping behaviors and their associated negative impacts. These are most effective when the self-affirmations use intrinsic nonrelated sentence stems for completion (McCrea & Hirt, 2011). Self-affirmation theory demonstrates that affirming valued sources of self-worth can reduce both the psychological and physiological impacts of environmental stressors. This particular approach has even been found to "attenuate cortisol responses" in varied assessments (Sherman, Bunyan, Creswell, & Jaremka, 2009). Finally, the value affirmations have been shown to reliably decrease the negative impact of "social-evaluative stress and boost the psychological and behavioral adjustment of individuals who frequently experience social-evaluative stress, such as members of stigmatized groups" (Thomaes, Bushman, de Castro, & Reijntjes, 2012, p. 1). These affirmations create improvements in prosocial feelings like love, connectedness, and empathy, and can have lasting effects on young adolescents (Thomaes, Bushman, de Castro, & Reuntes, 2012). Clinicians using cognitive behavioral therapy might use self-affirmation sentence prompts as homework, as a part of journaling exercises or even as an intervention within the actual therapeutic sessions.

The Pygmalion Effect

Clinicians must ensure that they are attending to the ecologies preconceived notions of Black boys. These notions will likely negatively impact many of the ways in which these boys are engaged across a litany of domains, even within the therapeutic relationship. Institutionalized racism and classism has created inferior perceptions and expectations for Black men and boys. The Pygmalion effect is a well-documented sociopsychological theory first studied in the 1960s by researcher Robert Rosenthal. The Pygmalion effect proves how expectations impact performance and success across many domains. Studies on the Pygmalion effect included the impact of the expectations classroom teachers have on their students and how that might influence outcomes. In one particular study, researchers randomly assigning 10 students to be identified as "potential academic bloomers" through the school year. After a full school year of instruction under this guise, the students identified as "potential academic bloomers" demonstrated qualities of academic giftedness (Aronson & Aronson, 2011). Rosenthal and Jacobson (1968) stated: "When teachers expected that certain children would show greater intellectual development, those children did show greater intellectual development" (Rosenthal & Jacobson, 1968, p. 85).

Clinicians must see how the treatment from the environment and its players truly impacts these individuals' levels of functioning. When a child is getting poor grades, it is necessary to see if the academic environment is truly enriching before blaming internal characteristics for the child's lack of academic success. Many Black boys are perceived as having a lower cognitive aptitude and may very well be less challenged in an academic setting. Are counselors providing a similar level of robustness in their interventions for these clients, or are they employing a lens that demonstrates a lower expectation, leading to poorer outcomes?

Clinicians, parents, coaches, tutors, and educators at all levels must be trained to identify the personal and professional factors that impact expectations and provide coaching on mindfulness practices, privilege, and the dangers of low expectations. This can only occur through coursework and activities that force professionals to address their own biases, activities that immerse them in cultures of difference, and the provision of opportunities for structured goal-based problem-solving experiences with different groups predicated on principles of the contact hypothesis. Walker and Crogan (1998) described the contact hypothesis as follows:

> The contact hypothesis claims that "Prejudice ... may be reduced by equal status contact between majority and minority groups in the pursuit of common goals ... sanctioned by institutional supports ... provided it is of a sort that leads to the perception of common interests and common humanity between members of the two groups." (Walker & Crogan, 1998, p. 1)

SOCIAL BELONGING AND THE CYCLE OF MISTRUST

Social belonging and connectedness is a human motivation with the capacity to predict favorable outcomes. They both impact school attrition rates, classroom grades, capacity to develop trusting relationships, and the ability to take advantage of critical feedback. These factors are also thought to serve as buffers to both mental and physical wellness. (Walton & Cohen, 2007). As a result of Black boys' existence in an extremely socially stigmatized group, the uncertainty of their social bonds is likely more pronounced and they may be more sensitive to issues of social belonging. Uncertainty can impact intellectual performance and be exacerbated by the consequences of marginalization. Existence in such environments must be noted and addressed. Without attention, "attributional ambiguity—a mistrust of the motives behind others people's treatment of them" (Walton & Cohen, 2007. p. 83) becomes a significant concern.

A clinician's awareness of these concerns can have wide-reaching consequences to the livelihood of Black boys and their progeny. Advocating for opportunities where Black boys experience social belonging and connectedness is critical to the tangential work that happens in the therapeutic space. Ensuring that these boys and young men have access to mentors, tutors, sports teams, travel opportunities, social clubs, and school extracurricular activities is critical to overall well-being and the potential success of these youth. Ignoring the correlations of these factors to therapeutic efficacy and global success is a critical oversight.

To combat mistrust, clinicians must work to create trusting relationships with these youth. Joining clients where they are, being deliberate about informed consent and its limits, keeping your word, being reliable, and identifying strengths are all critical behaviors for clinicians when working with Black boys and adolescents. These clinical practices produce opportunities for corrective emotional experiences by which boys and young men gain evidence to trust that the motives of others may, in fact, be authentic and absent any malice.

Strength-Based Youth Centered Approaches

More often than not, people conceptualize interactions and services through a deficits-based lens. Across disciplines, many have been trained to identify the insufficiencies associated with an individual's diagnosis, condition, or even their prognosis. When working with marginalized populations, it becomes very easy to detect and categorize deficits across several domains. Operating within structures where a system's culture, documentation standards, and billing practices reinforce this deficits-based lens, few mental health professionals ever gain the skillset of strength-based assessment.

Barajas (2011), in his critical review of academic achievement from children in single-parent households, illustrated the importance of identifying and utilizing strengths that might be demonstrated as a result of the condition experienced. It is an inarguable fact that salient risk factors associated with single-parent households exist across socioeconomic statuses. It is this fact that enables us to readily ignore the strengths created by adversity. In addition to the high degrees of resiliency amongst this group, research has identified a myriad of strengths born from this ecology. "Strong parent-child communication, a network of community support, and high levels of adolescent autonomy" were all determined as strengths of single-parent homes (Barajas, 2011). Simply recognizing these strengths in this particular group will inform the entire approach to teaching, counseling, or supporting them in any capacity. Developing a strength-based lens to foster programming, enhance support structures and systems, influence policy, and direct research is a critical skillset when working with any group but of particular importance when the group experiences an intricate web of risk factors that can and have led to death.

If we choose to ignore these staggering statistics and these strategic steps, we choose to defer the dreams of millions of Black boys across America. We choose to increase fatherlessness and incarceration. We choose to allow murder and drugs to steal the souls of our brothers, sons, grandsons, and nephews. Now that you know, what will you do?

REFERENCES

Aronson, E., & Aronson, J. (2011). *The social animal* (11th ed.). New York, NY: Worth Publishers.

Barajas, M. S. (2011) Academic achievement of children in single parent homes: A critical review. *The Hilltop Review, 5*(1).

Bauval, R., & Brophy, T. (2011). *Black genesis: The prehistoric origins of ancient Egypt.* Rochester, VT: Bear.

Bosson, J., Haymovitz, E., & Pinel, E. (2004). When saying and doing diverge: The effects of stereotype threat on self-reported versus non-verbal anxiety. *Journal of Experimental Social Psychology, 40,* 247–255.

Case, K. (2013). *Pedagogy of the privileged.* New York, NY: Routledge.

Chasteen, A., Bhattacharyya, S., Horhota, M., Tam, R., & Hasher, L. (2005). How feelings of stereotype threat influence older adults' memory performance. *Journal of Experimental Aging Research, 31*(3), 235–260.

Cheryan, S., & Bodenhausen, G. V. (2000). When positive stereotypes threaten intellectual performance: The psychological hazards of "model minority" status. *American Psychological Society Status, 11*(5), 399–402.

Clegg, L. (2003). *Before Columbus: Black explorers of the New World.* Retrieved from http://www.rense.com/general43/before.htm

Crocker, J., Karpinski, A., Quinn, D., & Chase, S. (2003). When grades determine self-worth: Consequences of contingent self-worth for male and female engineering and psychology majors. *Journal of Personality and Social Psychology, 85*(3), 507–516.

Diamond, A. (2009). The interplay of biology and the environment broadly defined. *Journal of Developmental Psychology, 45*(1), 1–8.

Entman, R. M., & Gross K. A. (2008). Race to judgment: Stereotyping media and criminal defendants. *Law and Contemporary Problems, 71,* 93–133.

Forbes, C., & Schmader, T. (2010). Retraining attitudes and stereotypes to affect motivation and cognitive capacity under stereotype threat. *Journal of Personality and Social Psychology, 99*(5), 740–754.

Gates Jr., H. L. (2011). *Life upon these shores: Looking at African American history, 1513–2008,* New York, NY: Alfred Knopf.

Geronimus, A. T. (1998). *The health of urban African American men: Excess mortality and causes of death.* Department of Health Behavior and Health Education, University of Michigan School of Health. [Doctoral dissertation]. Retrieved from: https://www.aspeninstitute.org/sites/default/files/content/upload/19Geronimus.pdf

Gilovich, T., Dacher, K., & Nisbett, R. (2005). *Social psychology.* New York, NY: Norton.

Harper, S. R. (2004). The measure of a man: Conceptualizations of masculinity among high-achieving African American male college students. *Berkeley Journal of Sociology, 48*(1), 89–107.

Harris, S. M. (1995). Psychosocial development and Black male masculinity: Implications for counseling economically disadvantaged African American male adolescents. *Journal of Counseling and Development, 73,* 279–283.

Hart, K. E., & Kritsonis, W. A. (2006). Critical analysis of an original writing on social learning theory: Imitation of film-mediated aggressive models by Albert Bandura, Dorothea Ross, and Sheila A. Ross (1963). *National Forum of Applied Educational Research Journal, 19*(3).

Hess, T. M., Hinson, J. T., & Statham, J. A. (2004). Explicit and implicit stereotype activation effects on memory: Do age and awareness moderate the impact of priming? *Psychology and Aging, American Psychological Association, 19*(3), 495–505.

Humer, R., & Hernandez, E. (2013). The effect of educational attainment on adult mortality in the United States. *Population Reference Bureau, 68*(1).

James, G. M. (2009). Stolen legacy: Greek philosophy is stolen Egyptian. *The Journal of Pan African Studies EBook.* Retrieved from http://www.thehouseofsankofa.com/books/eBook%20Stolen%20Legacy.pdf

Markman, A. (2012). Shooter bias and stereotypes. *Psychology Today.* Retrieved from http://www.psychologytoday.com/blog/ulterior-motives/201210/shooter-bias-and-stereotypes

McCrea, S., & Hirt, E. (2011) Limitations on the substitutability of self-protective processes. *Social Psychology, 42*(1), 9–18.

McKay, A., Hill, B. D., Buckler, J., Beck, R. B., Crowston, C. H., Ebrey, P. E., & Wiesner-Hanks, M. E. (2011). *History of world societies since 1450.* Boston MA: Bedford/St. Martins.

Osborne, J. (1997). Race and academic disidentification. *Journal of Educational Psychology, 89*(4), 728–735.

Restall, M. (2000) Black conquistadors: Armed Africans in early Spanish America; the Americas. *Academy of Americas Franciscan History, 57*(2), 171–205. Retrieved from http://www.jstor.org/stable/1008202?seq=1#page_scan_tab_contents

Rosenthal, R., & Jacobson, L. (1968). Pygmalion in the classroom. *The Urban Review.* Retrieved from: https://www.uni-muenster.de/imperia/md/content/psyifp/aeechterhoff/sommersemester2012/schluesselstudiendersozialpsychologiea/rosenthal_jacobson_pygmalionclassroom_urbrev1968.pdf

Schmader, T., Maor, B., & Gramzow, R. (2010). Coping with negative stereotypes in the academic domain: Perceived injustice and psychological disengagement. *Journal of Social Issues, 57*(1), 93–111.

Schott Foundation for Public Education. (2012). *The Schott 50 state report on public education and Black males.* Retrieved from http://blackboysreport.org/bbreport2012.pdf

Sertima, I. (1976). *They came before Columbus: The African presence in ancient America.* New York, NY: Random House.

Shapiro, J., Williams, A. M., & Hambarchyan, M. (2013). Are all interventions created equal? A multi-threat approach to tailoring stereotype threat interventions. *Journal of Personality and Social Psychology American Psychological Association, 104*(2), 277–288.

Sherman, D., Bunyan, D., Creswell, J. D., & Jarmeka, L. (2009). Psychological vulnerability and stress: The effects of self-affirmation on sympathetic nervous system responses to naturalistic stressors. *Health Psychology, 28*(5), 554–562.

Shih, M., Ambady, N., Richeson, J., Fujita, K., & Gray, H. (2002). Stereotype performance boost: The impact of self-relevance and the manner of stereotype activation. *Journal of Personality and Social Psychology, 83*(3), 638–647.

Smith, J. L., & Johnson, C. S. (2006). A stereotype boost or choking under pressure? Positive gender stereotypes and men who are low in domain identification. *Journal of Basic and Applied Social Psychology, 28*(1), 51–63.

Sowislo, J. F., & Orth, U. (2013). Does low self-esteem predict depression and anxiety? A meta-analysis of longitudinal studies. *Psychological Bulletin, 139*(1) 213–240.

Steele, C., & Aronson, J. (1995). Stereotype threat and the intellectual test performance of African American males. *Journal of Personality and Social Science, 69*(5).

Thomaes, S., Bushman, B., de Castro, B. O., & Reuntes, A. (2012). Arousing "gentle passions" in young adolescents: Sustained experimental effects of value affirmations on prosocial feelings and behaviors. *Developmental Psychology, 48*(1) 103–110.

Toldson, I. A., & Lewis, C. W. (2012). *Challenge the status quo: Academic success among school-age African American males.* Washington, DC: Congressional Black Caucus Foundation.

Triechel, T. (2014). *Asian American youth with special needs struggle to gain more recognition & aid.* Retrieved from: http://www.asianfortunenews.com/2014/09/asian-american-youth-with-special-needs-struggle-to-gain-more-recognition-aid/

U.S. Department of Health and Human Services Division, Substance Abuse and Mental Health Services Administration. (2013). *Time with your kids a special family bond—grandparents.* Retrieved from: http://www.bblocks.samhsa.gov/family/Time/grandparents.aspx

U.S. Department of Justice: Bureau of Justice Statistics. (2010, June). *Prison inmates at midyear 2009: Statistical tables.* Retrieved from http://www.bjs.gov/content/pub/pdf/pim09st.pdf

U.S. Department of Justice Office of Justice Programs, U.S. Department of Health and Human Services Centers for Disease Control and Prevention. (2008).

Changing the course: Preventing gang membership. Retrieved from https://www.ncjrs.gov/pdffiles1/nij/239234.pdf

U.S. Department of Labor, Bureau of Labor Statistics. (2014). *Employment status of the civilian population by race, sex, and age.* Retrieved from: http://www.bls.gov/news.release/empsit.t02.htm

Walker, I., & Crogan, M. (1998). Academic performance, prejudice, and the jigsaw classroom: New pieces to the puzzle. *Journal of Community and Applied Social Psychology, 8,* 381–393.

Walton, G., & Cohen, G. (2003). Stereotype lift. *Journal of Experimental Social Psychology, 39,* 456–467.

Walton, G., & Cohen, G. (2007). A question of belonging: Race, social fit, and achievement. *Journal of Personality and Social Psychology, 92*(1), 82–96.

Westermann, G., Mareschal, D., Johnson, M. H., Sirois, S., Spratling, M. W., & Thomas, M. S. (2007). Neuroconstructivism. *Journal of Developmental Science, 10*(1), 75–83.

Williamson, E. W., III (2011). *How and why three potential causes of academic disidentification may affect interests in academic work at the secondary level among inner-city Black males.* [Doctoral dissertation]. Seton Hall University Dissertations and Theses (ETDs). Paper 452, South Orange, NJ.

Wise, T. (2005). *White like me: Reflections on race from a privileged son.* Brooklyn, NY: Soft Skull Press.

Woodcock, A., Hernandez, P., Estrada, M., & Schultz, P. W. (2012). The consequences of chronic stereotype threat: Domain disidentification and abandonment. *Journal of Personality and Social Psychology, 103*(4), 635–646.

CHAPTER 14

A TRAUMA-INFORMED APPROACH TO PLAY THERAPY INTERVENTIONS WITH AFRICAN AMERICAN MALE CHILDREN

Josephine Olson

PHYSICAL DEVELOPMENT

A published report by the American Academy of Pediatrics examined the impact of play upon the emergent child. Play was determined to enhance physical growth and foster agility throughout the child's development (Ginsburg, 2007). When children engage in play, fine and gross motor skills are positively altered (Frost, 2010). Play is fundamental for children and crucial for the optimal physical development of the child (Roopnarine & Johnson, 2012). Children who are provided ample and adequate play opportunities have better overall health and are less likely to be obese. They are also less likely to experience chronic health problems over the course of their lifetime (Lauer, 2011).

Counseling African American Males, pages 237–251
Copyright © 2016 by Information Age Publishing
All rights of reproduction in any form reserved.

COGNITIVE DEVELOPMENT

Sensory experiences associated with play initiate the forming of the brain's circuits and inhibit the loss of the brain's neurons (Perry 1997). Panksepp also contends that play enhances the brain's development as neural pathways are created and stimulated (2005). Children who are exposed to ample and adequate play experiences are less likely to encounter cognitive developmental delays and difficulty performing academically. The ability to think reflectively and to acquire executive functioning skills is contingent upon ample play opportunities (Brown, 2009). Play in essential for children to develop cognitive skills and the ability to process the world around them (Frost, 2010). Language acquisition, literacy, the ability to focus, and comprehension of new concepts are enhanced through play (Lauer, 2011). While engaged in play, children are able to practice problem-solving skills and are better equipped to resolve conflicts and, therefore, more likely to be resilient when adverse experiences occur.

EMOTIONAL AND SOCIAL DEVELOPMENT

Children who are provided ample play experiences are also better able to express and regulate emotions. Play experiences allow children the opportunity to "to try on" a variety of differing feelings. As children engage in play, they acquire an increased awareness of self and the world around them. Through play, children develop emotional intelligence that serves them well in the future. According to Daniel Goleman's theory of emotional intelligence, there are five elements of emotional intelligence: self-awareness, self-regulation, motivation, empathy, and social skills ("Daniel Goleman's Emotional," 2013).

Through play, children gain self-awareness, therefore, becoming more cognizant of their individual strengths and potential growth areas. These children emerge with a healthy self-concept and are better able to determine where they fit in their environment (Frost, 2010).

As children engage in play, the second element of emotional intelligence, self-regulation is enhanced ("Daniel Goleman's Emotional," 2013). Children who are provided ample and adequate play experiences are able to communicate emotions effectively. Through interaction with their environment and peers, children learn appropriate ways to manage emotions. Children are able to better to adjust to transitions, cope with adverse experiences, and are more resilient in the face of traumatic events (Ray, 2011). As children are engaged in play, they can temporarily distance themselves from their current situation. Play also assists children in processing trauma. As a result, children gain a sense of power over their circumstances (Frost 2010).

The third element of emotional intelligence is motivation (Akers & Porter, 2015). Through play, children are motivated to explore the world around them. As children are afforded ample and adequate play experiences, the world in which they live becomes a safer place. It is this perspective that nurtures internal motivation. While immersed in play, children interact with their environment in a manner that is mutually beneficial to both them and their environment. Play allows children to better navigate life's challenges and cultivates an internal desire to be successful while doing so.

A crucial element of emotional intelligence, the fourth element, is empathy (Akers & Porter, 2015). Play contributes to the development of empathy in children (Lauer, 2011). As children engage in play, they are able to comprehend the perspectives and feelings of others. Children who are provided ample and adequate play experiences will have a better understanding of constructs like equity and acceptance of diversity (Frost, 2010). These children are subsequently more empathetic, compassionate, and are able to better relate to peers.

The fifth and final element of emotional intelligence is social skills (Akers & Porter, 2015). Social skills are enriched as children engage in play. As children play, they are able to adopt new roles, engage in expressive activities, and act out different social scenarios. As children engage in free play, they are given a venue for expressing their individual experiences. When ample and adequate play experiences are provided for a child, the social drive is motivated and the child is better able to communicate feelings and ideas (Ray, 2011). Children gain an understanding of their environment and are able to best navigate said environment. Through play, children learn prosocial behaviors. As children engage in play, they learn how to cooperate in groups, how to take turns during games, and how to share toys and resources. Children who are provided ample and adequate play experiences are better able to control impulses, resolve conflicts, and are often recognized for leadership abilities (Lauer, 2011).

DISCUSSION

Play Deprivation

Play deprivation is the notion that play is essential to the optimal development of children and, in the absence of play experiences, physical, cognitive, emotional, and social deficits and difficulties result. In fact, children who are deprived of ample and adequate experiences are at-risk for long-term difficulties that include, but are not limited to: depression, anxiety, substance-abuse, lack of impulse control, self-harm, and antisocial behaviors (Prescott, 1996).

Play Deprivation: Children at Risk

Play deprivation is especially problematic among children who are materially disadvantaged, abused, or neglected. Children who are provided inadequate, unsafe open-air space or cramped indoor space to play are at risk for being play deprived (Lauer, 2011). Children who reside in unsafe neighborhoods are unable to play freely, as they are often surrounded by crime, drugs, and gang activity (Frost, 2010). Unfortunately, many African American male youth, particularly those who reside in low-income neighborhoods are subjected to play deprivation and experience many physical, cognitive, emotional, and social implications as a result.

Play Deprivation Impacts Overall Health

Children who are play deprived often experience difficulties with gross motor skills and agility (Frost, 2010). With the decline of play among the materially disadvantaged, particularly among African American males, there is a greater risk for chronic health problems. These long-term issues include, but are not limited to: obesity, poor overall fitness, and heart disease (Lauer, 2011).

Play Therapy and Cognition

During the first seven years of childhood, the brain is the most plastic and the most malleable as the child interacts with his or her environment (Perry, 1997). In the absence of consistent stimulation of the brain via early play experiences, the developmental processes of the brain are significantly delayed (Prescott, 1996). Panksepp contends that play enhances the brain's development as neural pathways are created and then stimulated (2005). In the absence of play, brain development becomes disrupted and the child then becomes at risk for academic challenges, difficulties with reflective processing, reasoning skills, problem solving, and executive functioning (Gray, 2011). Children who are denied ample and adequate play experiences often have difficulty focusing and find even simple tasks challenging. Play-deprived children may have little imagination and experience difficulty with creativity (Lauer, 2011). African American males who experience the academic challenges indicative of play deprivation may be inclined to not complete their education, thus continuing the cycle of poverty to subsequent generations.

Emotional Issues as a Result of Play Deprivation

When children lack sensory stimulation and emotional interaction in the form of developmentally appropriate play, serious emotional implications may result (Ray, 2011). Children who suffer from play deprivation are at a significantly higher risk for mood disorders, drug and alcohol addiction, impulse control issues, self-sabotaging behaviors, and antisocial behaviors (Prescott, 1996). As African American male youth are deprived of ample and adequate play experiences, they have difficulty managing emotions and are subsequently privy to explosive anger, and they may be destructive of property and aggressive toward peers.

Social Deficits and Play Deprivation

Children who are play deprived are more narcissistic and are unable to empathize with their peers (Gray, 2011). If this lack of empathy is not addressed, it could result in antisocial behaviors (Brown, 2009). Children who lack significant play experiences are also at risk for social isolation (Prescott, 1996). These children have difficulty forming friendships, reading social cues, and are unable to relate to peers and adults. They have difficulty cooperating in a group setting and are often overlooked during structured playtimes (Brown, 2009). As a result of play deprivation, African American male youth may have difficulty forming and maintaining relationships. These destructive relational patterns can continue into adulthood and have serious long-term implications.

Play Deprivation and Implication for Violence Among Juveniles

Play deprivation is associated with increased aggression among juveniles. In Stuart Brown's early work, he conducted interviews with highly violent murderers, he discovered a consistent theme of play deprivation dating back to early childhood in the participants (as cited in Brown, 2009). The lack of ample and adequate play experiences among African American male youth may contribute to difficulty resolving conflicts peacefully and their resorting to violent behaviors among the population. According to Frost, children who are play deprived act out to gain a sense of control over their environment (2010).

TRAUMA-INFORMED PLAY THERAPY: IMPLICATIONS FOR THERAPISTS

Play Deprivation: Childhood Trauma

According to the Substance Abuse Mental Health Services Administration (SAMHSA), Individual trauma results from an event, series of events, set of circumstances that is experienced by an individual as physically or emotionally harmful or threatening and that has lasting adverse effects on the individual's functioning and physical, social, emotional, or spiritual well-being. (SAMHSA, 2014)

Play deprivation or a lack of significant play experience is indeed harmful to the child's optimal development and can have adverse effects on physical, cognitive, emotional, and social health. In an effort to combat play deprivation among African American male youth, the author has created a model of trauma-informed care. The author will also explore evidenced-based play therapy interventions as a solution to play deprivation.

Trauma-Informed Care Defined

Many well-meaning mental health professionals often inadvertently re-traumatize individuals who are in their care. In an effort to prevent retraumatization, the Substance Abuse Mental Health Services Administration set these guidelines for trauma-informed care:

A trauma-informed approach refers to how a program, agency, organization, or community thinks about and responds to those who have experienced or may be at risk for experiencing trauma; it refers to a change in the organizational culture. In this approach, all components of the organization incorporate a thorough understanding of the prevalence and impact of trauma and the role that trauma plays. (SAMHSA, 2014)

Therapeutic Factors of Trauma-Informed Care

To ensure that mental health professionals are providing individuals with Trauma-informed care, the author created a model to serve as a reminder of the therapeutic factors that foster effective treatment in play-deprived children. The acronym SAFE-T, created by the author, represents the necessary ingredients of trauma-informed care. The S stands for *safety*, a foundational principle of trauma-informed care. The environment the mental health professional provides is paramount to the therapeutic growth. The therapeutic environment should be one that is warm and inviting. The practitioner should consider paint colors that are soothing and welcoming. Another consideration is the arraignment of the furniture that is appealing and conducive to being fully engaged and present with the child. The environment should be one that is least restrictive or isolated. The A stands for acceptance. The demeanor of the therapist is crucial in establishing a therapeutic alliance. It is crucial that therapist be nonjudgmental and accepting of the client without condition. African American males who are play deprived will most likely respond well to an accepting therapist versus one who is dismissive. The third component included in the author's model for trauma-informed care is family. Unless the family is implicated, incorporating the family in the treatment is crucial. The author subscribes to a family system approach that recognizes that an issue in an individual member of the family system is indicative of issues in the entire system. The mental health professional can identify a social support system as a helpful resource for the play-deprived child. An African American male youth who is play deprived would benefit by recognizing a system of family, friends, and community resources that can provide supportive care. Parent-education on the impact of play deprivation is also an important consideration in treatment planning. This can be achieved by parental workshops, parent coaching, and resources provided for parents at little or no cost. A support system is especially indicated when there is a risk for self-harm or suicide. In the event that an individual is in imminent danger, an individualized step-by-step safety plan will be established. The support system can be crucial in maintaining the safety of the individual. The next letter, E, stands for *empowering*. Traumatized individuals have been denied the opportunity to choose; therefore, choice is a crucial component of treatment planning. The African American male youth receiving treatment should be empowered by taking an active role in goal setting throughout his treatment. Interventions that empower should be strengths-based and should avoid unnecessary labeling that may serve to debilitate the individual. Finally, trauma-informed care should not be delivered on an island but rather by a *team* of professionals. Counselors, teachers, school administrators, direct service care workers, case managers, and special service coordinators should consult and collaborate to ensure the African American male youth struggling with play deprivation can receive comprehensive care that is trauma-informed and outcome driven.

PLAY THERAPY DEFINED

Play therapy is defined by the Association for Play Therapy (APT) as "the systematic use of a theoretical model to establish an interpersonal process wherein trained play therapists use the therapeutic powers of play to help clients prevent or resolve psychosocial difficulties and achieve optimal growth and development" (2015, para. 1). The premise of play therapy is that children communicate through play. In fact, play therapy provides children the opportunity to communicate their inner world and allows them to explore feelings in the safety of the playroom. Play therapy is an evidenced-based therapeutic approach to treating children with a variety of deficits, disorders, traumas, and personal-social difficulties.

Therapeutic Benefits of Play Therapy

Play therapy is an effective means of combatting play deprivation among African American male youth. Children regain a sense of influence over their environment when they are invited into the play therapy room. In the confines of the playroom, children can explore self and can experiment with new roles. The therapeutic benefits associated with play therapy are significant. Children are intrinsically motivated to play, and this process, when nurtured, can promote self-esteem, better regulation of emotions, prosocial behaviors, and adaptive coping skills (Ray, 2011). African American male youth are afforded the opportunity to develop optimally when invited to play in the play therapy room.

Expressing and Regulating Emotions

Play therapy rooms frequently included multiple puppets and a puppet stage. Children will project their own subjective feelings onto the puppets. This allows the child the opportunity to maintain a safe distance from their emotions. The puppet becomes the "symbolic client" and the play therapist is then able to engage the child to freely express emotions. He is also given the opportunity to practice emotional regulation skills in the nonthreatening environment of the play room. If the therapist is invited to play, the therapist is able to model appropriate expressions of emotions and can demonstrate empathy. For example, if the puppet is upset or disappointed, the therapist is able to empathize with these feelings (Hall, Kaduson, & Schaefer, 2002). Play therapy is effective in reducing anxiety in children. The play therapy room provides the African American male youth a safe venue for expression of both positive and negative emotions. Puppets are also an effective means to engage a resistant child and can provide a venue for play deprived children to stimulate creativity and imagination.

Coping Skills: The Bereaved Child

Sand tray therapy is a medium of play therapy that invites the child to manipulate figures to create a subjective world. The sand tray figures represent emotions and experiences that the child may or may not have conscious awareness of. This sensory therapeutic experience gives the child permission to symbolically portray concepts like grief and loss. The child is given the opportunity to process through their individual grief and loss in a developmentally appropriate manner (Green & Connolly, 2009). Sand tray is the ideal intervention to assist an African American male youth in coping with issues of grief, loss, and trauma. The tactile nature of the sand allows the child the ability to connect to feelings and ideas surrounding the trauma. Clay has simple therapeutic properties in that it is pliable and receptive to feelings (Sherwood, 2010). In the safety of the play therapy room, African American male youth are afforded the opportunity to build a subjective world in the sand or shape his clay to represent unconscious feelings or ideas.

Social Skills

Group play therapy is helpful in practicing social skills in the confines of the playroom. Social development is enhanced and opportunities to empathize with peers are introduced (Ray, 2011). African American male youth are able to creatively practice prosocial behaviors like giving and receiving compliments, taking turns, listening, sharing feelings, assertive communication, and self-advocacy skills in the safety of the play therapy room. Through participating in school-based group play therapy, children learn about "teamwork, relationships, listening, communication, and concentration. The school benefits from improved attendance rates and a reduction in exclusions from school" (Nutall, 2013, p. 1). African American male youth are given a platform for sharing subjective experiences and are able to foster emotional intelligence. They are able to practice problem solving, refusal skills, self-advocacy skills, and empathy in the context of a therapeutic play therapy group.

Filial Therapy: Incorporating the Family in the Play Therapy

In filial therapy, first introduced by Bernard and Louise Guerney, the therapists act as supervisors and facilitators guiding the parents as they employ play therapy techniques with their own children (National Institute for Relationship Enhancement, 2015). Upon review of the research, filial therapy was recognized as an evidenced-based approach and as significant in increasing "parental acceptance, self-esteem, empathy, [and creating] positive changes in family environment, and the child's adjustment and self-esteem while decreasing parental stress and the child's behavioral problems" (Rennie & Landreth, 2000). Elianna Gil, a forerunner in play therapy practice, recognizes play techniques as a means to "engage parents and children in enhanced communication, understanding, and emotional relatedness, and can assist clinicians in their important work, and thus should be considered a viable and pivotal part of family therapy work" (as cited in Lowenstein & Sprunk, 2013, p. 42). By utilizing play therapy techniques, families are able to express emotions and broach issues that would otherwise go unresolved. Filial therapy allows the African American male youth the opportunity to build attachments and enhance relationships with parents and caregivers.

The Therapist's Use of Self in the Play

The therapeutic presence of the counselor is perhaps the most crucial agent of change in the therapeutic alliance. The counselor's skill in remaining fully present, listening intently, and receiving the child's feelings and ideas without judgment is paramount to the change process. The empathetic counselor can intuitively perceive the child's authentic self as the child shares and can support the child in reaching his or her individual potential (Crenshaw & Kenney-Noziska, 2014). African American male youth who experience play deprivation can benefit from an authentic alliance with the play therapist stimulating therapeutic gains that manifest themselves in an enhanced social aptitude, improved problem-solving skills, appropriate emotional regulation, and overall resilience when facing adverse childhood experiences.

Therapist Immersion in the Play

While utilizing effective therapeutic interventions is imperative, the therapeutic presence is perhaps the most fundamental to the child's healing journey. The play therapist must effectively determine the best use of self throughout the therapeutic process. At times, the play therapist may take an active role in the play. When invited into the play by the child, the play therapist can offer soft interpretations and facilitate the child's processing of the play. At other times, the play therapist may remain silent and only track the child's play. The play therapist's tracking of the play can insight mindfulness, building emotional intelligence in the process. The play therapist must navigate this process and ascertain how to best function in the session to facilitate effective treatment.

The Play Therapy Dimensions Model: A Model for Decision Making

Play therapists often benefit from a model to assist in treatment planning and decision making. The Play Therapy Dimensions Model (PTDM) was designed by Lorri Yasenik and Ken Gardener to guide play therapists in navigating this process. PTDM (see Figure 14.2) is based on two axes: directedness and consciousness (Figure 14.1). The play therapist considers a

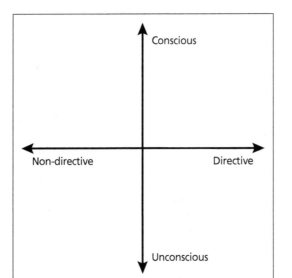

Figure 14.1 Two axes of the play therapy dimensions model. Adapted from Yasenik & Gardener (2012).

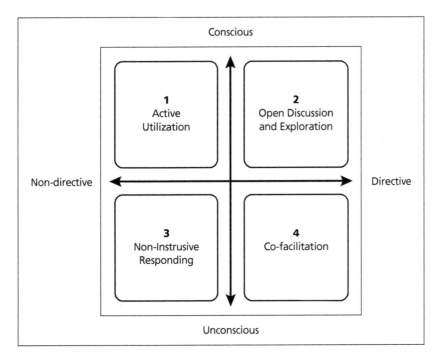

Figure 14.2 PTDM 4 quadrants.

child's level of consciousness to determine when and how often to introduce interpretation into the play. If the child has little awareness of the impact of the trauma, the child may effectively work through the issue, but much of the processing would remain in the play (Yasenik & Gardener, 2012).

Promoting Post-Traumatic Growth in Play-Deprived African American Male Youth

In an effort to promote post-traumatic growth, competent trauma-informed play therapists ensure that they are well equipped to offer quality care. The author created the acronym TRACK to provide competencies for promoting post-traumatic growth (PTG). This model is especially helpful when treating African American male youth. PTG is the concept that if compassionate care is provided and healthy coping skills are established, the client will develop the ability to flourish in spite of deficits and difficulties (Tedeschi & Calhoun, 2006). The Trauma-Informed Model Play Therapy Model developed by the author emphasizes continuing the child on the TRACK for success by employing five core competencies for trauma informed play therapists. The T represents *training*. The trauma informed play therapist should possess knowledge of the impact of trauma upon the individual's development and implications for difficulties and deficits associated with trauma. Training in evidence-based interventions is also essential in promoting post-traumatic growth. Play therapy techniques are successful in treating a variety of trauma-related difficulties and deficits in the African American male youth population. As the trauma informed play therapist provides differing levels of care, it is essential that he or she is *resourceful*. The second core competency that is essential in promoting trauma-informed play therapy is resourcefulness. The resourceful trauma-informed therapist is cognizant of the available resources or services in the community that would be helpful to the child or its family during or after the traumatic event. In an effort to prevent retraumatization, the competent trauma-informed play therapist refers to other organizations and service providers that have trauma-informed policies and procedures in place. The African American male youth receiving care may benefit and be eligible for a variety of services that will further promote post-traumatic growth. The third component of the author's Trauma-Informed Play Therapy Model, A is for *accountability*. The competent trauma informed play therapist is accountable to the immediate supervisor and peers for supervision. The dialogue between the therapist working with a child and his or her peer or immediate supervisor can ensure that trauma informed policies and procedures are being implemented. This discussion is also crucial in preventing retraumatization of the child. The fourth component that the author insists as essentially to Trauma-Informed Play Therapy is C for *culturally competent*. The culturally competent trauma informed play therapist has an awareness of cultural norms and traits of the individual they are servicing. The therapist then counsels in the context of the individual's culture and is cognizant of the family's apprehensions with the counseling process. This is especially helpful as the culturally competent trauma informed play therapist provides services for the play deprived African American male youth. The last letter of the acronym TRACK is K, which stands for "keep calm & carry on." It is essential that the play therapist who works extensively with trauma victims is practicing good self-care. If the trauma informed play therapist has poor self-care he or she may be ineffective in providing services. In an effort to prevent compassion fatigue, the author contends that a well developed plan of self-care be required for the trauma informed play therapist.

Implications for Therapists

There are significant therapeutic attributes associated with play therapy. Children are intrinsically motivated to play, and when this process is nurtured it can empower the child to greater self-awareness, improved management of emotions, prosocial behaviors, and adaptive coping skills (Ray, 2011). Adequate and ample play experiences are necessary to the optimal development of children and promote overall healthy development. In the absence of adequate and ample play experiences, devastating developmental difficulties and deficits result. Play deprivation is especially problematic among African American male youth who are materially disadvantaged. These children often lack safe and ample space to play and explore. The author contends that Trauma-Informed Play Therapy is an effective remedy to play deprivation and is especially helpful in treating African American male youth. Play therapy is an evidenced-based approach to promoting healing and resilience and is effective with this population. In the effort to combat play deprivation among African American male youth, the author contends that Trauma-Informed Play Therapy services be offered in these communities at little or no cost to the families. In addition to pro-bono play therapy services, free community after-school programs that provide safe indoor and outdoor play equipment are also essential to remedy play deprivation among this population. Awareness of the importance of play and implications for its absence should be promoted among parents and school officials. Teachers and administrators alike should be informed as to the implications of play deprivation. Schools that exist in these communities need to recognize that free play is vital and should be included as part of the child's everyday schedule. As African American male youth are provided with a safe play environment and are offered trauma-informed play therapy services, they can thrive into youth of boundless potential and can be resilient in the face of adversity.

REFERENCES

Akers, M., & Porter, G. (2015). What is emotional intelligence (EQ)? *Psych Central*. Retrieved from http://psychcentral.com/lib/what-is-emotional-intelligence-eq/

Association for Play Therapy. (2015). *Why play therapy?* Retrieved from http://www.a4pt.org/?page=WhyPlayTherapy

Brown, S. (2009) *Play: How it shapes the brain, opens the imagination, and invigorates the soul.* London, England: Penguin.

Crenshaw, D. A., & Kenney-Noziska, S. (2014). Therapeutic presence in play therapy. *International Journal of Play Therapy, 23*(1), 31–43.

Daniel Goleman's emotional intelligence theory explained. (2013). *Concordia Online.* Retrieved from http://education.cu-portland.edu/blog/reference-material/daniel-golemans-emotional-intelligence-theory-explained/

Frost, J. (2010). *A history of children's play and play environments: Toward a contemporary child-saving movement:* London, England: Routledge.

Ginsburg, K. R. (2007). The importance of play in promoting healthy child development and maintaining strong parent-child bonds. *Pediatrics, 119*(1), 182–191.

Gray, P. (2011). The decline of play and the rise of psychopathology in children and adolescents. *The American Journal of Play, 3*(4), 443–463.

Green, E. J., & Connolly, M. E. (2009). Jungian family sandplay with bereaved children: Implications for play therapists. *International Journal of Play Therapy, 18*(2), 84–98.

Hall, T. M., Kaduson, H. G., & Schaefer, C. E. (2002). Fifteen effective play therapy techniques. *Professional Psychology: Research and Practice, 33*, 515–522.

Lauer, L. (2011). *Play deprivation: Is it happening in your school?* Retrieved from http://eric.ed.gov/?id=ED524739

Lowenstain, L., & Sprunk, T. P. (2013). *Creative family therapy techniques: Play and art-based activities to assess and treat families.* Retrieved from www.lianalowenstain.com

National Institute of Relationship Enhancement. (2015). *Louise Guerney.* Retrieved from http://www.goodtherapy.org/famous-psychologists/bernard-and-louise-guerney.html

Nutall, E. (2013). Benefits of play therapy for children. *Education Space 360.*

Panksepp, J. (2005). *Affective neuroscience: The foundations of human and animal emotions.* New York, NY: Oxford University Press.

Perry, B. D. (1997). The neurodevelopmental impact of violence in childhood. In D. Schetky & E. P. Benedek (Eds.), *Textbook of child and adolescent forensic psychiatry* (pp. 221–238). Washington, DC: American Psychiatric Press.

Prescott, J. W. (1996).The origins of human love and violence. *Pre- and Perinatal Psychology Journal, 10*(3), 143–187.

Ray, D. C. (2011). *Advanced play: Essential conditions, knowledge, and skills for child practice.* New York, NY: Taylor & Francis.

Rennie, R., & Landreth, G. (2000). Effects of filial therapy on parent and child be-haviors. *International Journal of Play Therapy, 9*(2), 19–37.

Roopnarine, J. L., & Johnson, J. E. (2012). *Approaches to early childhood education* (6th ed.). Upper Saddle River, NJ: Pearson.

Sherwood, P. (2010). *The healing art of clay therapy.* Melbourne, Australia: Acer Press.

Substance Abuse Mental Health Services Administration. (2014). *Trauma-informed care, 22*(2). Retrieved from http://www.samhsa.gov/samhsaNewsLetter/Volume_22_Number_2/trauma_tip/index.html

Tedeschi, R. G., & Calhoun, L. (2006). Post-traumatic growth: A new perspective on psychotraumatology. *Psychiatric Times, 21*(4), 58–60.

Yasenik, L., & Gardner, K. (2012). *The play therapy dimensions model: A model for decision making.* London, England: Jessica Kingsley.

CHAPTER 15

WHITE RACIAL FRAMING AND ITS IMPACT ON AFRICAN AMERICAN MALE MENTAL HEALTH

Veeda Williams and Derek Wilson

Well-being is the presence of a sound mind and body, a good quality of life, and the promotion of healthy habits (Sundberg, Winebarger, & Taplin, 2002). To be healthy is to demonstrate a state of functioning that results in positive identity outcomes, healthy styles of relating, as well as the ability to cope with change. Since positive identity outcomes (and subsequent mental health functioning) require the individual/agency to engage internal mechanisms that combat negative interactions (Nobles, Goddard, & Gilbert, 2009), strategies developed for African Americans' mental health functioning must significantly take into account the negative interactions they encounter daily as a result of America's racial framing. Because traditional Western structures inherently produce outcomes that thwart the development of affirming identity traits for African Americans (Williams 2011; Wilson & Williams, 2013), appropriate therapeutic approaches for

Counseling African American Males, pages 253–274
Copyright © 2016 by Information Age Publishing
All rights of reproduction in any form reserved.

racially diverse groups must include more broadly constructed social-psychological strategies that consider the realities of diverse groups—particularly the realities of African American males, who are more likely than any other group to experience negative interactions.

Thus, this chapter broadens the discussion of mental health functioning to include the psychological implications of significant social (*identity*) processes—for African American males—which are directly linked to *outcomes*. Because African American males are disparately criminalized and dehumanized (this identity negatively constructed by and for others) within American society, *structure* confronts the Black male existence in ways that impact his ability to maintain healthy functioning—to develop healthy self concepts, to cope with daily challenges to his identity, to be mentally healthy and productive. A direct challenge to the popular notions of identity within American society, the discussion herein highlights the inability of traditional Western theory/treatment to appropriately produce positive outcomes for African Americans because these structures do not significantly consider the reality of Black identity and functioning. As a result, its theoretical paradigms—and subsequent recommendations based upon such theorizing—do not/cannot effectively evaluate or accurately reflect the reality of African American identity. Consequently, this chapter seeks to contribute to new and relevant models of interventions that counter the traditional Western approaches and significantly speak to the realities of African Americans in healthy ways.

SOCIAL FACTORS IMPACTING IDENTITY

Key elements in defining healthy identity development—systematic exposure to prejudice and discrimination (Kambon, 2014), deprived social identity (Tajfel & Turner, 1979), nonconformity to given social roles, and the inability to form healthy relationships with others (Johnson, 2013)—are shown to have important psychological implications for African American males. Umar Johnson (2013) acknowledges the challenges that Blacks face in this society in highlighting how "Blacks are forced to live within two competing worlds in this country one Black the other White, one safe and the other dangerous, the social schizophrenia that this induces can be tragi[c]" (p. 7). These factors are exacerbated for African American males navigating confrontational structures of race and identity. Encroached in the defining elements of identity, the social arrangements of American society converge in ways that negatively impact young African American males, threatening their mental health, well-being, and overall psychological functioning.

Systematic Exposure to Prejudice and Discrimination

A major challenge in examining mental health status is that the system of diagnosing health and wellness has its roots in Western theory, thought, and practice (Nobles, 2006). These constructs reflect Western cultural values of individualism and presuppose an understanding that the world is vested in the individual's mind vetting what is real or not. In America, these Western traditions take on a more dramatic impact for African Americans given the significant role of race where Black reality is rarely considered or legitimized. Because race comprises a *master* status, or status-determining trait that often overpowers other characteristics (Hughes, 1945), African Americans often incur consequences—based upon race—from all institutions within the society, including institutions of health and wellness.

The framing of American society as described by Feagin (2006) depicts how American social structures shape reality based upon race. A theme that resonates throughout Feagin's discussion of systemic racism is the notion of the perpetual oppression of people of color by Whites in America. Integral to the defining nature of systemic racism and crucial to an understanding of the persistence of these features in American society is the idea of *racial framing*. The White racial frame (Feagin, 2006), to be more specific, is "a color-coded framing of society" inherent in American structures that refers to the particular way that Whites conceive of and interpret the world. White racial framing shapes the reality of other groups as well as how these groups see themselves. This frame shapes everyday events and encounters with others and is characterized by negative images and stereotypes of African Americans, while asserting positive views of Whites and White institutions (Feagin 2006). The psychobehavioral modalities within White racial framing influences racial attitudes, ideologies, emotions, habits, views, stereotypes, images, and metaphors directed at people of color and embody the "implicit rules" as to how society is to treat people relative to race. Thus White racial framing proscribes who/what is to be valued, defining social interactions/situations and treatment of individuals based on "color" (Alexander, 2010; Goffman, 1974; Johnson, 2013).

In fact, several scholars (Alexander, 2010; Feagin, 2006; Johnson, 2013) assert that the oppression of Blacks in America is so pervasive that the discriminatory nature of these rules and meanings as well as the inequality they produce, spill over from these institutions into the everyday experiences of people of color. Keep in mind that these institutions make up the social structure of a society. Social structure defines social expectations—as developed by dominating groups—and places individuals (Black males) in groups related to institutional arrangements. These relationships become crystallized into patterns of repetition that can be predicted and expected (Johnson, 2013). Thus, within the White racial framing (Feagin, 2006) of

American society, the implicit rules and meanings associated with people of color are crystallized into regular patterns of predictable behavior. Interaction and expectations are explicitly expressed in the many racist and discriminatory acts that are commonplace within American society; these patterns create stressors in the lives of African Americans more than for any other group. They impact African Americans' ability to engage in productive activities, to cope effectively, to realize their own abilities, and to work productively to makes positive contributions to their communities (Johnson, 2013).

Evans (2013) highlights the impact of these relationships in her research of African American pilots and flight attendants in the airline industry. The work personifies how the framing plays out in the interaction between White passengers/coworkers and Black pilots where the professional status of these men are challenged in the workplace. These professionals experience the consequences of race as they are regularly referred to as boy, N1, N2, N3 (referencing the derogatory n-word characterization) as well as other negative expletives in carrying out their professional work. This work highlights how Blacks are often marginalized in White-constructed and White-controlled spaces, how they have to engage conscious, (psychological) processes in efforts to suppress personal feelings and induce proper behavior that aligns with acceptable (socially-constructed) practices—all while producing comfort for others at the expense of their own. Evan's work speaks to the *emotional labor* that African American professionals have to deal with when navigating the White spaces of the airline industry.

This is particularly problematic for African American males; their criminalization within American structures (Alexander, 2010) illuminates the impact of social forces upon psychological functioning. Before Whites are aware of the name of an African American male or anything of significance about him, they are bombarded by the social cues that convey meaning about him—who he is, his innate nature, his social and psychological predispositions—and about his value in American society. The world has watched this phenomenon play out time and again throughout American history in the beating of Rodney King, the murders of Amaduo Diallo, Oscar Grant, Trayvon Martin, Jordan Davis, Michael Brown, John Crawford, Tamir Rice, Eric Gardner, Walter Scott, and Freddie Gray as well as the countless other African American males who did not receive national coverage.

Michelle Alexander (2010) describes the pervasive, social psychological impact upon African Americans males, who are labeled as criminals in American society and are legally barred from participating in the social spaces open to all other citizens—voting, economic structures, education, jury service and other public benefits. Because the practice of labeling and discriminating against "criminals" finds legitimacy within American structures, African American males are less valued and less respected and thus, ignoring his humanity becomes normative. Experiencing legal discrimination in one system makes it easier—and more likely—to do so in others.

Denied access to the broader economic structures, African American males are thwarted from accessing legitimate means toward improving their circumstances through adequate educational access (Johnson, 2013), making a comparable living, taking care of a family, and maintaining a sense of dignity. Developed expectations and outcomes related to African American males' social status are minimal with few profitable access points. With this limited access, African American males tend to display maladaptive coping behavior as a result of systemic exposure to prejudice and discrimination, developing a pattern of psychological functioning directly derived from this social stimuli (Johnson, 2013). Thus, the racialized framing of American society imposes on African American males an identity that is antithetical to their normal and natural way of being and, as a result, establishes a controlled identity for Black males.

Deprived Social Identity and Nonconformity to Given Social Roles

A close examination of Burke's (1991) identity control theory assists in understanding how identity becomes a crystallized indication of "what it means to be who one is" (Burke, 1991, p. 837). Identity processes, as outlined in identity control theory, further illustrate how traditional Western frameworks of mental health are inadequate for examining constructs of well-being for African Americans. Because the characteristics of Black ways of being do not reflect normative values within traditional theoretical frameworks, they cannot receive affirming appraisals within these constructs, thus making the framework ineffective for evaluation of issues relating to Black behavior, identity, personality, or psychological functioning.

According to Burke's (1991) conceptualization, the identity process comprises a system in which "identity is a set of 'meanings' applied to the self in a social role or situation defining what it means to be who one is" (p. 837). He characterizes the identity process as a self-adjusting system. It is a loop consisting of various components—a *standard* or setting (the set of self-meanings), an *input* (social appraisal) from the environment or social situation (including one's reflected appraisal, i.e., perceptions of self-relevant meanings), a process that compares the input with the standard (*comparator*), and an *output* (meaningful behavior) to the environment that is a result of the comparison. This loop generates feedback from the various aspects of society in a manner that maintains a consistent operation of the identity process (Burke, 1991).

The goal of the identity process, according to identity control theory, is to maintain congruence between inputs or feedback from the social environment and the internal standard of who one believes himself or herself to be (Burke, 1991). This is accomplished when an individual, having an internalized standard of identity, engages in behavior that they believe consistent with that standard. Upon receiving feedback or appraisals (input) from others in the social environment, the individual automatically makes comparisons about the congruence of that feedback to their internal standard. If there is congruence, the standard identity is maintained and the identity loop continues as before. If there is minor discrepancy or incongruence between the input received and the standard, then output behavior is adjusted or modified to attain the desired feedback (input)—regaining congruence between internalize identity and affirmed feedback from environment. When this incongruence is small, this adjustment occurs automatically.

When, however, the discrepancy between the input and the standard "grows beyond the minimal discrepancies that are handled automatically" (Burke, 1991, p. 840), distress occurs, signaling that greater conscious control of the system is needed. When incongruence in the feedback loop becomes so much that neither the output nor the input can be adjusted enough to cause congruence between the input (appraisals) and standard, Burke suggests that it typically results in a change in the initial identity standard; the changed identity standard then serves as the adjusted output behavior in an attempt to restore congruence in the identity process. Simply stated, Blacks begin to act in alignment with an identity standard imposed by White racial structures that is antithetical to an African-centered frame of reference of being (Wilson & Williams, 2013), a standard which is negatively characterized and which entails consequences.

This theory would suggest that (a) African American (Black) identity—which has been constructed as oppositional to identity standards of Whiteness (and labeled as "criminal" for many African American males)—must adjust to negatively-characterized standards of identity in order to find affirmation/acceptance (as positive, affirming identities of Blackness are not "standard" within this construct), and (b) failure to make such adjustment is not an option; one must either adjust behavior (negatively) to conform or change one's identity standard entirely (negatively characterized) to conform. While African Americans do experience distress as a result of having to adjust behavior in social spaces that do not value the expressions of Black culture, they do not shed their thinking about who they are (Evans 2013; Williams 2011) nor change their internalized identity to embrace negatively characterized standards of who others "believe them to be."

Identity control theory—a byproduct of traditional Western schemas in academia—produces an inadequate conceptualization for capturing the realities of Black identity processes. Because it gives no consideration to the historical racial structures that have always constructed Black identity as an incongruent identity standard—incapable of yielding affirming input appraisals, no matter the output behavior—it cannot accurately reflect the processes of an identity standard that finds no consideration in traditional frameworks of being.

Furthermore, when the facts about African Americans and who they are do not fit the notions of the Western frame, the frame is not rejected, but rather the facts (Feagin, 2006). When African American males clearly do not fit the stereotypical (negative) characterization of "criminal" or other derogatory metaphors, the frame does not change, but the facts of his dignified existence are challenged. Consider the election of President Barack Obama; if the frame does not change to encompass its own values of educational, social, economic, and individual achievement for an African American, Nobel-Peace-Prize-winning leader of the free world, it certainly will not change to accommodate the average African American male within its constructs. Such identities of dignity and humanity are considered "outlier" identities for Blacks in a White racial construct.

When a person's sense of self is well established, disconfirming evidence can generally be managed in ways to preserve their self-concept (Tittle & Paternoster, 2000). For instance, "the individual might cognitively deny the response, discount the source of the reaction, ignore the reaction as aberrant, or the like" (Tittle & Paternoster, 2000, p. 449). Because the manifested racist behaviors of America's broader structures are so crystallized, when it is met with resistance, the source of that resistance (African Americans) is merely discounted, ignored, dehumanized, denied access to resources within the frame, or deemed somehow deviant and oppositional to existing social structures. So has been the case of African American males whose social characterizations are negatively charged.

Construction of the Black male as a deviant has found justification and legitimacy within American structure. It is as if America dares to shout, "This is who and what I am; tell me I am right" (Tittle & Paternoster 2000, p. 449). And the whole of American society—to include its institutions (and institutions of health)—resounds to affirm its structure and identity. Yet, when African Americans develop a positively affirming internalized identity standard of Blackness that becomes crystallized in their minds, and they dare to shout, "This is who and what I am; tell me I am right," there is no such support. American social structures do not acknowledge or encourage such an identity, but rather discount, ignore, deny access to affirming appraisals within identity processes, deny access to resources within this mainstream social structure, and deem African Americans as somehow undeserving within existing structures. Consider the recent repeal of affirmative action legislation in Michigan and California.[1] These measures—as does Identity Control Theory—assume that the same processes that Whites engage in to maintain their identity standards, Blacks are incapable of engaging in to maintain such affirming standards.

It is certainly difficult to cope with the stressors of life when (a) you are not significantly considered or included in structures that produce consequences for your life, and (b) such stressors are intentionally built into the structures that shape your life experiences. The psychological costs and challenges inherent in simply existing attests to the adaptive or therapeutic strategies to which African Americans must gain access to maintain healthy mental functioning. It is particularly challenging for African American males who are more commonly criminalized and negatively characterized when negotiating needs, access to resources, and associations with others in seeking inclusion into America's social spaces.

The Inability to Form Healthy Relationships With Others

Toni Morrison (1993) accurately describes the cultural impact and subsequent psychological (social alienation) of the White racial frame as immigrants, entering American society, negotiate associations with African Americans,

> Popular culture, shaped by film, theater, advertising, the press, television and literature, is heavily engaged in race talk. It participates freely in this most enduring and effective rite of passage into American culture negative appraisals of the native-born black population. Only when the lesson of racial estrangement is learned is assimilation complete. Whatever the lived experience of immigrants with African Americans—pleasant, beneficial or bruising—the rhetorical experience renders blacks as non-citizens, already discredited outlaws.... It doesn't matter anymore what shade the newcomer's skin is. A hostile posture toward resident blacks must be struck at the Americanizing door before it will open. The public is asked to accept American blacks as the common denominator in each conflict between an immigrant and a job or between a wannabe and status. It hardly matters what complexities, contexts, and misinformation accompany these conflicts. They can all be subsumed as the equation of brand X versus blacks. (Morrison, 1993, p. 57)

Umar Johnson (2013) further illustrated the social psychological impact of identity processes within the educational environment for Black boys when he wrote,

> Black boys are sentenced to a life of low expectations in the "Emotional Support Classroom"... is by virtue of the Black boys inability to build a satisfactory relationship with a teacher who often pays very little attention to him unless he is doing something of which she doesn't approve.... Those biases

that most White women have about black males manifest themselves in their instructional and disciplinary behavior towards their African American male students. (Johnson, 2013, pp. 23–24)

Thus, the "implicit rules" of the White racial frame play out in everyday interactions in American society, defining the meanings of what and who is most (un)desirable in social situations, shaping preferences as well as influencing identity processes as individuals socially interact with one another. However, much more than the microlevel interactions of individuals, because of the extremely historical and pervasive nature of race within this White racial framing of American society, collective definitions of Whiteness and Blackness, have become a crystallized part of a larger, structural, American identity.

Other groups entering into American society, then, recognize upon their entrance that association with Blackness entails high costs that are to be avoided—personal, physical, and psychological costs (Feagin, 2006; Johnson, 2013). Given such costs, they develop cognitive dissonance with the unfavorable characterizations of Blackness with the same fervor as they seek favorable association with the positively characterized images of Whiteness; such negotiation of *association* better positions individuals to gain greater access to resources needed to succeed in American society.

Thus, the White racial framing of American society uniquely positions African Americans as a group with which association incurs great costs. As such, the frame promotes disruptions in associations between African Americans and others entering American society, imposing identities upon all who cross its borders—making "social distancing" from African Americans seem necessary. This social alienation from others within society impedes the development of fulfilling relationships for African Americans with others and produces patterns of psychological functioning derived as a direct result of social stimuli. Absent the influence of traditional Western (racial) framing, such an imposition of identity and its resulting alienation would be less likely to occur, allowing for healthier psychological development as individuals assume more natural associations with each other.

Mental Health Disparities in Counseling

It is no wonder that Blacks represent such poor health statistics relative to Whites (see Tables 15.1 through 15.11). Given their existence in spaces where they are unwanted, unaccepted as equal, negatively-characterized, and that often work against their interests, African Americans are all too familiar with the social cues that signal "you do not belong." As a result, African Americans have to develop natural coping mechanisms for themselves

TABLE 15.1 Serious Psychological Distress Among Adults 18 Years of Age and Over, Percent, 2009–2010

Non-Hispanic Black	Non-Hispanic White	Non-Hispanic Black/ Non-Hispanic White Ratio
3.8	3.1	1.2

Source: CDC, 2012. Health United States, 2011. Table 59. http://www.cdc.gov/nchs/data/ hus/hus11.pdf

TABLE 15.2 Serious Psychological Distress Among Adults 18 Years of Age and Over, Percent of Poverty Level, 2009–2010

	African American	Non-Hispanic White	African American/ Non-Hispanic White Ratio
Below 100%	8.3	10.1	0.8
100%–less than 200%	3.5	5.5	0.6
200%–less than 400%	2.5	3.2	0.8

Source: CDC, 2012. Health United States, 2011. Table 59.http://www.cdc.gov/nchs/data/ hus/hus11.pdf

TABLE 15.3 Percent of Population With Feelings of Sadness, Hopelessness, Worthlessness, or That Everything Is an Effort, All of the Time, Among Persons 18 Years of Age and Over, 2010

	Non-Hispanic Black	Non-Hispanic White	Non-Hispanic Black/ Non-Hispanic White Ratio
Sadness	4.2	2.8	1.5
Hopelessness	2.4	2.0	1.2
Worthlessness	2.1	1.7	1.2
Everything is an effort	9.9	5.6	1.8

Source: CDC 2012. Summary Health Statistics for U.S. Adults: 2010. Table 14. http://www.cdc. gov/nchs/data/series/sr_10/sr10_252.pdf

TABLE 15.4 Percent of Population With Feelings of Sadness, Hopelessness, Worthlessness, or That Everything Is an Effort All of the Time, Among Persons 18 Years of Age and Over, 2010: Men

	Non-Hispanic Black Men	Non-Hispanic White Men	Non-Hispanic Black Men/ Non-Hispanic White Men Ratio
Sadness	3.0	2.5	1.2
Hopelessness	2.0	1.9	1.1
Worthlessness	1.8	1.6	1.1
Everything is an effort	9.2	4.9	1.9

Source: CDC 2012. Summary Health Statistics for U.S. Adults: 2010. Table 14. http://www.cdc. gov/nchs/data/series/sr_10/sr10_252.pdf

TABLE 15.5 Death Rates for Suicide, Age, Race and Hispanic Origin, 2009: Men

	African American Men	Non-Hispanic White Men	African American Men/ Non-Hispanic White Men Ratio
15–24 years	10.5	18.9	0.6
25–44 years	12.9	28.8	0.4
45–64 years	10.2	33.7	0.3
65 years and over	9.9	33.1	0.3
All ages	9.0	23.2	0.4

Source: CDC, 2012. Health United States, 2011. Table 39. http://www.cdc.gov/nchs/data/hus/hus11.pdf

TABLE 15.6 Adolescents—Death Rates for Suicide: Ages 15–19, 2009

	Non-Hispanic Black	Non-Hispanic White	Non-Hispanic Black/ Non-Hispanic White Ratio
Male	7.0	14.0	0.5

Source: CDC, 2012. National Center for Injury Prevention and Control. Web Based Injury Statistics Query and Reporting System (WISQARS) http://www.cdc.gov/injury/wisqars/index.html

TABLE 15.7 Suicidal Ideation Among Students in Grades 9–12, 2009 Percent of Students Who Seriously Considered Suicide

	Non-Hispanic Black	Non-Hispanic White	Non-Hispanic Black/ Non-Hispanic White Ratio
Men	7.8	10.5	0.7

Source: CDC, 2012. Health United States, 2011. Table 67. http://www.cdc.gov/nchs/data/hus/hus11.pdf

TABLE 15.8 Suicidal Ideation Among Students in Grades 9–12, 2011 Percent of Students Who Attempted Suicide

	Black	White	Black/ White Ratio
Men	7.7	4.6	1.7

Source: CDC, 2012. High School Youth Risk Behavior Survey Data. [Accessed 07/07/2012] http://apps.nccd.cdc.gov/youthonline

as a means of surviving the environment daily. Perhaps this explains why African Americans fail to expend significant resources toward or seek services for that which they must naturally expend energy (emotional labor) on everyday (Evans, 2013; Johnson, 2013). The Western framework of mental

TABLE 15.9 Access to Health Care—Percent of Adults Age 18 and Over Who Received Mental Health Treatment or Counseling in the Past Year, 2008

	Non-Hispanic Black	Non-Hispanic White	Non-Hispanic Black/ Non-Hispanic White Ratio
Male	6.4	10.8	0.6

Source: 2010 National Healthcare Disparities Report. Table 17_3_1.2b
http://www.ahrq.gov/qual/qrdr10/index.html

TABLE 15.10 Access to Health Care—Percent of Adults Age 18 and Over Who Received Mental Health Treatment or Counseling in the Past Year, 2008

	Non-Hispanic Black	Non-Hispanic White	Non-Hispanic Black/ Non-Hispanic White Ratio
Male	6.4	10.8	0.6

Source: 2010 National Healthcare Disparities Report. Table 17_3_1.2b
http://www.ahrq.gov/qual/qrdr10/index.html

TABLE 15.11 Percent of Adults Age 18 and Over Who Received Prescription Medications for Mental Health Treatment or Counseling, 2008

	Non-Hispanic Black	Non-Hispanic White	Non-Hispanic Black/ Non-Hispanic White Ratio
Male	3.9	9.1	0.4
Female	8.1	18.3	0.4
Total	6.2	13.9	0.4

Source: 2010 National Healthcare Disparities Report. Table 17_3_3.2b
http://www.ahrq.gov/qual/qrdr10/index.html

health embodies the ideations of this social environment; for an African American male to contribute to the social spaces that produce his stressors would be to act against his own interests (Johnson, 2013). Thus the mental health of African American males goes unguarded given the current frameworks in which it operates; their social experiences emanate from racial framing that gives little consideration to their psychological well-being.

Research data suggest that minority individuals develop expectations and outcomes related to their social status and therefore the mental health status of Black men has been limited (see Tables 15.1 through 15.11), considering the challenges they face within a society that demonstrates lack of care and concern for their well-being. The data further show that African Americans represent the worst health statistics in the United States.

According to Woods, Kling, Hanna, & Murray, C. (2012), African Americans are 30% more likely to report having serious psychological distress compared to their White counterparts and experience sadness, hopelessness, and worthlessness on average 1.3 times more than their White counterparts. Additionally, the U.S. Surgeon General found that from 1980 to 1995, the suicide rate among African Americans aged 10 to 14-years-old, increased 233% (SAMHSA, 2001).

These health disparities persist, in part, due to counseling techniques that do not effectively address the social factors that disparately impact African Americans on a daily basis, factors that have significant implications to their mental and psychological well-being. Numerous culturally relevant issues, such as disparities in the access to and availability of mental health services, homelessness, incarceration, and institutionalization (i.e., White supremacy), share equally in the strain for providing hope for addressing mental challenges Black males face. This results in Black males having higher rates of mental disorders, being less likely to receive needed mental health care or more likely to receive inferior quality of mental health services, and being underrepresented in mental health research (Alegría et al., 2009; Brach & Fraserirector, 2000; SAMHSA, 2001; Sue, Zane, Hall, & Berger, 2009). Cultural competency in dealing with these issues requires providers' understanding of their clients' experiences and lived realities. Major cultural competency skills/strategies include but are not limited to training, use of traditional healers, community health workers, culturally competent health promotion, involvement of family, cultural immersion, and administrative and organizational accommodations (Woods, King, Hanna, & Murray, 2012). It has been suggested that culturally-centered techniques theoretically can improve delivery of appropriate services to diverse populations (SAMHSA, 2001; Woods et al., 2012). Interventions with African Americans that do not involve principles of spirituality, harmony, collective responsibility, oral tradition, holistic approach, prejudice and discrimination, racial socialization, and interpersonal/communal orientation, which are often found in African American ways of being, lend to challenges in disparity of mental health care for African Americans.

In a nationally represented survey consisting of 8,762 participants, which evaluated differences in access to and quality of care between the races (SAMHSA, 2001), it was discovered that for minority groups, those who sought out treatment were more likely to receive inadequate care, with African Americans being particularly unlikely to receive quality treatment. Similar to previous research examining mental health disparities (SAMHSA, 2001; Woods et al., 2012), has shown that when patients are hesitant to seek mental health treatment, it may be due, in part, to not being culturally connected to mental health professionals, a factor likely to hinder the healing process. This recent work highlights patients' intuitive ability to recognize the limited available quality of care (SAMHSA, 2001; Woods et al., 2012) that is vested in their well-being. Experience of mistreatment and social exclusion by health care professionals, barriers to effective communication between therapists and patients, and pharmacological treatments also lend to troubling patterns within health disparities (Woods et al., 2012).

IMPLICATIONS FOR THERAPISTS AND COUNSELORS

In order to appropriately deal with the current disparities in treatment for African Americans, therapists and counselors must consider therapeutic models that counter traditional Western approaches that are largely responsible for such disparities. Absent the influence of these racially-constructed approaches, new and culturally-relevant models of interventions can produce enhanced mental health outcomes for African American males. Nobles, Goddard, and Gilbert (2009) introduced the "culturecology" model as a construct that helps to locate identity as defined by cultural agents from one cultural worldview operating in an environment from another worldview. In this work, cultural agency is the choreographed display of behavior in accordance to what is socially conforming or morally contravening in one's interactions in the world (Matsumoto, 2006). Culturecology recognizes the interaction between people and their environment (be it hostile or in harmony) as well as the ontogeny and phylogenetic survival thrust; it establishes what is normal and natural for the cultural organisms (Nobles et al., 2009; Wilson & Williams, 2014).

Wilson and Williams (2014) capture the culturecology model of Nobles et al. (2009) in noting, the person comes with an ontological cultural history imbedded with facilities, ideas, values, life practices, and expectations of pre-scripted continuous tales of survival. This survival thrust for which mental health is formed emanates for those of African descent out of a self-extension orientation in which person and environment cannot be understood in the absence of their cultural meaning (p. 519).

Nobles and Goddard (2012) state that the model recognizes that (a) "the nature of the perso" and "the nature of the environment'" are inextricably connected, (b) both the environment and human beings are cultural phenomena, and (c) the "cultural grounding" and meaning of each (person and environment) must be culturally understood (p. 221).

This recognition is necessary in order to fully understand the interactive relationship between persons and mental health. Thus, culturecology offers a unique and accurate assessment of examining identity development between agency and systems that is synonymous within tenets of social psychology.

Wilson's Ubuntu model of mental health (Wilson & Williams, 2013, 2014) prescribes that healthy functioning is generated around three main themes: connectedness, competency, and consciousness (Three Cs). Within the Ubuntu model, the primary belief is that there is an understanding of a universal process of healing that is normal and natural based on one's inherent cultural frame of reference. Ubuntu is a Zulu term that describes the essence of being human (Brooke, 2008; Hanks, 2007; Wilson & Williams, 2013). The principle of Ubuntu means we are people because of other people (Wilson & Williams, 2013; Wilson, Olubadeyo, & Williams 2015). Ubuntu helps to define the recognition of humanity as the reciprocal relationship engendered upon an I, you, and we concept: "one's humanity is made possible through the equal reciprocal recognition of the humanity of others" (Wilson & Williams, 2013; Wilson et al., 2015). From an African-centered perspective, Ubuntu espouses a system of principles that are in opposition to Western belief of humanity (Nobles, 2015). Humanity, for the European, is the need to be recognized by others without reciprocating the need to recognize others (Nobles, 2015). The Ubuntu principle of healing and intervention are not rigid in its delivery (it does not favor one racial or cultural experience over another), nor do the techniques require an overexaggeration of experiences. A multitude of entry points of intervention require unique and appropriate timing of the therapist/healer and patient/client in order for the therapist-patient to achieve a sense of harmony (connectedness). This will allow the therapist or healer to stay present in the moment, to assess the process, select the tool that can be most beneficial (competency), and become centered (consciousness) to ward off anxiety and distress.

All approaches to healing and psychotherapy have a process or protocol for intervention that is more or less formalized; most should provide options for individuals without favoring certain experiences over others in assessment/evaluative frameworks. The variability and uniqueness of the Ubuntu model of mental health (Wilson & Williams, 2013) helps the individual to locate his place and time as a healer to his personal ills (i.e., sense of self-efficacy). The Ubuntu approach to healing provides a consistent framework for intervention and a clinical road map (see model of cultural mental health in Chapter 4). While the Ubuntu themes have a clear healing process and objectives for each phase, there is freedom for implementation of specific intervention techniques. The first level of intervention is that of connectedness.

Connectedness

As it has been established, White racial framing shapes the reality of how other groups influence and appraise the way people see themselves. The everyday encounters with others, characterized by negative sentiments and interactions, assert a deleterious view of the self. Umar Johnson (2013) states,

> The Emotional and Behavioral Disturbance (EBD) classification is the most stigmatizing label used against African-American boy in America's public and charter schools.... EBD is loosely described as a disability that results from the Black boy's inability to build and maintain relationships with his teachers and peers. It also includes abnormal behaviors exhibited in school, fears associated with school, and sadness/depressed mood related to the school setting. (p. 23)

The psychobehavioral modalities within White racial framing influence how we connect with each other and the extreme ways in our efforts to connect with ourselves; for example, behaving in a punitive manner toward African Americans while showing leniency toward those of European decent. This cultural misorientation (Kambon & Bowen-Reid, 2010) or disconnect may have an effect on one's racial attitudes. Racial attitudes, ideologies, emotions, habits, views, stereotypes, images, and metaphors direct how people of color should connect with others like them and with those who do not look like them. When an African American embodies the "implicit rules" of the White racial frame as to how to treat others who look like them, a greater level of disconnect and discomfort exist. The discriminatory nature of these implicit rules and meanings are often supported by institutions and organizations that perpetuate disharmony. Thus, the primary outcomes within traditional Western approaches create a disconnect among African Americans that serves to exacerbate mental health function for African American males. The Ubuntu model allows for the individual to locate his identity in the community while placing at the forefront the need for the therapist to understand the individual's sense of self. Ubuntu portrays a spirit of oneness and harmony and offers a more functional approach to connecting to African American males.

The term connectedness is used as a fundamental principle or theme for harmony, collective responsibility, and racial socialization orientation to positive identity for African Americans (Wilson, 2012; Wilson & Williams, 2013). Connectedness relates to an individual's need to form social bonds. Within therapy, connectedness helps to serve as a psychological construct of belonging (Wilson, 2012; Wilson & Williams, 2013). The therapeutic intervention or entry point for the therapist/healer is to reconceptualize for the client the concept of connectedness. In the context of Ubuntu, connectedness is the need to be human in relation to other humans. Connectedness purports that the individual shares his experiences with others as opposed to his experiences being separate or excluded from the sources responsible for appraising or evaluating them. For example, the characterization of connectedness within an African perspective suggests that my relation with others helps me to find harmony within myself. For the African

American male, while his desire to find meaning and purpose in the world is predicated on the congruency of the personal collective values with environmental collective values, within the Ubuntu approach to mental health functioning, the collective environment does not confine his behavior to a set of homogeneous, socially constructed, and race-normative responses. As a result, he is more likely to attain such congruence between personal and environmental values and experience a sense of wholeness and validation that is most conducive to the development of a healthy identity.

Competency

While the conceptualization of the identity consists of a set of meanings applied to the self in a social role, the ability to obtain a healthy identity further requires the development of a sense of competency in the various roles they perform. Competency refers to a general repertoire of skills required for effective human functioning—oratory skills, holism, and interpersonal/communal orientation. Furthermore, competency helps to locate and determine one's level of humanity. A competent individual determines his humanity by recognizing that he must risk life until recognized. He must adopt a strategy of conquer or die to gain his humanity and not adopt a slave strategy to just remain alive by submitting to oppression for fear of losing his life. Social competency is the dexterity of moving in and out between primary culture and dominant culture (Wilson, 2012; Wilson & Williams, 2013). For the competent male, this requires responsible choices that emphasize good behavior, hard work, and fairness (Johnson, 2013). Other aspects of competency include but are not limited to future aspirations, social responsibility, role models, and healthy positive behavior.

Within the Ubuntu therapeutic process for African American males, the goal would be to examine their psychosocial competency and their belief in an ability to function effectively with others within affirming structures of support. The affirming experiences are more likely to encourage continued development of functioning skills across broader cultural and environmental patterns of social arrangements. In terms of specific treatment techniques, the objective is to engage African American males in various forms of diunital discussion, rituals, meditation, video critiques, drumming, and laughter. For example, when therapists explain that their work with teenage African American males allow them to engage with the client about his interests, revealing that he likes history, it is incumbent for the therapist to then explore aspects of history on Black male perspective and to contrast this with the client's understanding of why he enjoys history. This opens up the opportunity to share rap videos that demonstrate the history of the world through songs. This activity encourages young men to find out more about the history of

Africans and African Americans. The client's desire to seek out knowledge speaks to the shaping and honing of competency skills toward understanding himself. In contrast to Western paradigms of treatment, in which therapists build walls between themselves and the client, in this African-centered approach, the Ubuntu model requires more interaction between therapist and client. As African American males engage in these patterns of positive interactions and experiences within these treatment modalities, they begin to believe that they possess abilities and skills—a *significant something*—which garners recognition; it is through such recognition and development of competence that they gain a higher level of conscious formation.

Consciousness

One of the greatest challenges to mental health functioning is the awareness of the energies that surround you. In the therapeutic process, consciousness takes into consideration recognition of distinctions and similarities between self and others, including cognitive analyses of the social patterns or structures in which one exists. For example, one who attains recognition without reciprocating becomes the "master." One who recognizes the other but is not reciprocally recognized becomes the "slave" (Nobles, 2015). Sometimes, discrepancy occurs between sensory input from the environment and individual perceptual thresholds to manage all this input information; this discrepancy can cause distress, signaling the need for greater conscious control (Burke, 1991) to manage this sensory information. Thus, consciousness deals with the manifestations of phenomena connecting brain, culture, and physical energies (Wilson, 2012, Wilson & Williams, 2013). Williams's (2011) research noted that African and African American students acknowledged an innate level of conscious awareness of deriving from a common ancestor. In addition, this research showed that both African and African American students endorsed the notion that Black people show a lot of emotions and feelings, and express themselves with a lot of movement and body motion. This level of consciousness acknowledges that Africans and African Americans share a similar spirit (energy) and cognitive awareness of who they are and what is normative behavior within America's White racially constructed society. These results appear indicative of the salient conscious thought pattern rooted in the Ubuntu therapeutic construct and may exemplify the potential impact of this Africentric framework (in contrast to a White racial construct) in developing greater connection, competency, and consciousness—the three main themes around which healthy functioning for African American males has been structured.

Thus, while holding onto a sense of self that is well-crystallized within affirming qualities of Blackness produces distress for African Americans within constructs that do not value such an identity, it does not change "who we believe ourselves to be." Engaging structures of Blackness within America incurs costs, many psychological in nature. Consciousness allows for the individual to cope with stressors of life that place African American males at risk for (a) not being significantly considered or included in structures that produce consequences for their life, and (b) stressors intentionally built into the structures that shape their life experiences. In such cases, the therapeutic process must acknowledge the psychological challenges inherent in just simply existing. African Americans males who hold onto positively affirmed views of Black identity attest to their adaptive functioning, though this is hardly acknowledged in any formal manner. It is particularly challenging for African American males who are more commonly criminalized and negatively characterized when negotiating needs to access resources and associations with others seeking inclusion into America's social spaces. Developing a conscious therapeutic alliance with this population allows for greater challenges to place. It has been suggested that racial consciousness of identity is attributed to African American males, while unconscious manifestation of identity is attributed to European Americans (Guido-DiBrito & Chavez, 1999). Ubuntu recognizes that to be conscious is to engage in self-appraisal and to recognize the perceptions that others have relative to one's wellness.

CONCLUSION

Despite the constant challenges to identity and functioning that African American males experience within mainstream structures, it is clear that African American males have not abandoned their own reality of "who they believe themselves to be" for those constructed for them within American social structures. It just merely illustrates that mainstream theory is not an adequate framework for gauging the essence of Black identity and functioning. The traditional Western (racial) frameworks are not broad enough to accommodate racially diverse ways of being; thus, such identities are not significantly included in Western paradigms.

While Black identity must be poised to "survive" its characterizations in White racial constructs, it is likely to thrive in social spaces absent the influence of the White racial frame; that is, in spaces that gives consideration to the "authentic cultural reality . . . of the Black experience in American society" (Baldwin & Bell, 1985, pp. 61–62). African Americans, then, must continue to seek ways to construct for alternative (Africentric) structures within American society that give significant consideration to Black realities. African American mental health professionals must engage African American males in a more formalized *Afrisense* fashion to provide prescriptions and cures and explain the need for a restoration of the African self to improve his psychological functioning. It is within these structures where Black identity is positively constructed and nourished that positive mental health for African Americans will find space to flourish.

Furthermore, because the White racial paradigm lends no consideration or significance to cross-cultural patterns of behavior, particularly the Black experience that resides furthest from the White experience within the continuum, Black experiences are not taken into consideration in the construction of instruments that assess or evaluate Black identity, behavior, or personality (Baldwin & Bell, 1985). This chapter suggests the need to move in a new direction in thinking, providing therapeutic intervention that gives significant consideration to the *structural* framing of American society and its impact upon the psychological functioning of African Americans' mental health outcomes. Furthermore, utilization of a construct that is culturally specific to the Black experience (Wilson & Williams, 2013) would yield improved psychological functioning for young, African American males.

In fact, preliminary work in this area indicates that for many African American males, aged 19 to 25, social factors play a significant role in their identity development (Williams & Moreland, n.d.). Most believe that being culturally connected to mental health professionals would help, rather than hinder, their healing process and that mental health professionals who share a similar identity and are able to relate to their (consumer) experiences would provide better care to them. Furthermore, many believe that social stigma and negative characterizations play a role in thwarting efforts toward legitimate means of improving their circumstances and functioning. One young man suggested that Black identity is so stigmatizing that alcohol and drugs become a cheaper, more socially acceptable means of dealing with stressors. Such ideas exemplify how African American males develop outcomes and expectations relative to their social experience.

Social psychology approaches encompass perspectives that highlight how these significant elements of psychological functioning are influenced by specific social contexts. Clinical psychology further corroborates that what is "in the individual's mind" partly derives from what occurs outside of the individual—within his social environment. Thus, the basic tenets of the Ubuntu social psychological response to mental health functioning for African American males encompass the way in which people's thoughts, feelings, and behaviors are influenced by the real or imagined presence of other people as well as culturally responsive strategies that assist individuals' ability to gain and/or maintain balance and harmony in relation to identity formation. The Ubuntu approach counteracts the effects of White racial framing and identity control and gives consideration to innate cultural and social factors that influence the African American male's healthy mental functioning.

NOTE

1. Concomitantly, the recent mandates of HBCU's to increase their enrollments of non-Black students when Black students are being denied access to socially framed supportive White institutions speaks volumes to the support of this racial-framing construct of identity.

REFERENCES

Alegría, M., Chatterji, P., Wells, K., Cao, Z., Chen, C., Takeuchi, D. ... Meng, X. (2009). Disparity in depression treatment among racial and ethnic minority populations in the United States. *Annual Review of Psychology*, 60, 525–548.

Alexander, M. (2010). *The new Jim Crow*. New York, NY: The New York Press.

Baldwin, J. A., & Bell, Y. R. (1985). The African self-consciousness scale: An Africentric personality questionnaire. *The Western Journal of Black Studies*, 9(2), 61–66.

Brach, C., & Fraserirector, I. (2000). Can cultural competency reduce racial and ethnic health disparities? A review and conceptual model. *Medical Care Research and Review*, 57(1), 181–217.

Brooke, R. (2008). Ubuntu and the individuation process: Toward a multicultural analytical psychology. *Psychological Perspectives*, 51, 36–53.

Burke, P. J. (1991). Identity processes and social stress, *American Sociological Review*, 56(6), 836–849.

Evans, L. (2013). *Cabin pressure*. Lanham, MD: Rowan & Littlefield.

Feagin, J. R. (2006). *Systemic racism*. New York, NY: Routledge.

Goffman, E. (1974). *Frame analysis*. New York, NY: Harper & Row.

Guido-DiBrito, F., & Chavez, A. F. (1999). Race and ethnicity in development. In C. Clark & R. Caffarella (Eds.), *An update on adult development theory* (pp. 39-47). New Directions in Adult and Continuing Education, no. 84. San Francisco: Jossey-Bass.

Hanks, T. L. (2007). The Ubuntu paradigm: Psychology's next force? *Journal of Humanistic Psychology*, 48, 116. Retrieved from http://jhp.sagepub.com/content/48/1/116

Hughes, E. (1945). Dilemmas and contradictions of statements. *American Journal of Sociology*, 50, 353–359.

Johnson, U. (2013). *Psycho-academic holocaust: The special education and ADHD wars against Black boys*. Philadelphia, PA: Prince of Pan Africanism.

Kambon, K. K. (2014). *Toward the construction of a model of African self-consciousness development in Black children*. Unpublished manuscript.

Kambon, K. K., & Bowen-Reid, T. (2010). Theories of African American personality: Classification, basic constructs and empirical predictions/assessment. *The Journal of Pan African Studies*, 3(8), 83–108.

Matsumoto, D (2006). Culture and cultural worldviews: Do verbal descriptions about culture reflect anything other than verbal descriptions of culture? *Culture & Psychology* 12(1), 33–62.

Morrison, T. (1993, December 2). On the backs of Blacks. *Time Magazine*, p. 57.

Nobles, W. W. (2006). *Seeking the sakhu: Foundational writings for an African psychology.* Chicago IL: Third World Press.

Nobles, W. W. (2015). *The island of memes: Haiti's unfinished revolution.* Baltimore, MD: Black Classic Press.

Nobles, W. W., Goddard, L. L., & Gilbert, D. G. (2009). Culturecology, women, and African-centered HIV prevention. *Journal of Black Psychology, 35*(2), 228–246.

SAMHSA. (2001). *Mental health: Culture, race, and ethnicity: A supplement to mental health:* A report of the Surgeon General, Office of the Surgeon General, Center for Mental Health Services. Rockville, MD: National Institute of Mental Health.

Sue, S., Zane, N., Hall, G. C., & Berger, L. K. (2009). The case for cultural competency in psychotherapeutic interventions. *Annual Review of Psychology, 60,* 525–548.

Sundberg, N. D., Winebarger, A. A., & Taplin, J. R. (2002). *Clinical psychology: Evolving theory, practice, and research* (4th ed.). Upper Saddle River, NJ: Pearson Education.

Tajfel, H., & Turner, J. C. (1979). An integrative theory of intergroup conflict. In W. G. Austin & S. Worchel (Eds.), *The social psychology of intergroup relations* (pp. 33–147). Pacific Grove, CA: Brooks/Cole.

Tittle, C. R., & Paternoster, R. (2000). *Social deviance and crime: An organizational and theoretical approach.* Los Angeles, CA: Roxbury.

Williams, V. (2011). *Brothers of the trade: Intersections of racial framing and identity processes upon African Americans and African immigrants in America—ancestral kinsmen of the American slave trade* (Doctoral dissertation). Texas A&M University, College Station, TX. Retrieved from http://hdl.handle.net/1969.1/ETD-TAMU-2011-05-9497

Williams, V., & Moreland, D. (n.d.). *Cultural connections and mental health care: The implications of race/ethnicity on the provider-consumer relationship.* Unpublished research.

Wilson, D. (2012). Competency, connectedness, and consciousness. In V. D. Woods, N. J. King, S. M. Hanna, & C. Murray (Eds.) *"We ain't crazy! Just coping with a crazy system": Pathways into the Black population for eliminating mental health disparities* (pp. 159–161). San Bernardino, CA: African American Health Institute.

Wilson, D., & Williams, V. (2013). Ubuntu: A model of positive mental health for African Americans. *Psychology Journal, 10*(2), 80–100. Retrieved from http://www.psychologicalpublishing.com

Wilson, D., & Williams, V. (2014). Mental illness defined: Sociological perspectives. In A. Scull (Ed.), *Cultural sociology of mental illness: An A-to-Z guide* (pp. 518–521). Thousand Oaks, CA: Sage.

Wilson, D., Olubadewo, O., & Williams, V. (2015). Ubuntu: Framework for Black college male positive mental health. In W. Ross (Ed.), *African American male series, counseling African American males: Effective therapeutic interventions and approaches.* Charlotte, NC: Information Age.

Woods, V. D., King, N. J., Hanna, S. M., & Murray, C. (2012). *"We ain't crazy! Just coping with a crazy system": Pathways into the Black population for eliminating mental health disparities.* San Bernardino, CA: African American Health Institute.

CHAPTER 16

A CLINICAL DECONSTRUCTION OF THE NEGATIVE ARCHETYPES AND COMPLEXES OF AFRICAN AMERICAN MASCULINITY

O'Shan D. Gadsden and Lionel Howard

Over the past decade, the vast majority of social science research focused on African American males and Black males throughout the diaspora has emphasized pathology, exploring topics ranging from persistent academic underachievement, participation in illicit activities (e.g., drug trade, gangs, crime), depression and mental health wellness, parenting, and participation in child rearing (Kohl, Gross, Harrison, & Richards, 2015; Murry, Simons, Simons, & Gibbons, 2013; Warren, Chiricos, & Bales, 2012). Social science research studies have largely focused on crisis and deviant behaviors, and have provided little insight into the ways in which African American/Black[1] males are thriving and existing in a chronically hostile and racist world. Consequently, such research has not only contributed to but also reified

Counseling African American Males, pages 275–287
Copyright © 2016 by Information Age Publishing

misnomers and one-dimensional representations that have positioned African American/Black males as "endangered species" (Gibbs, 1988) and being in a state of "crisis" (Allen & Correspondent, 2013). These representations have often been stereotypical, presenting African American males as homogenous, violent, or otherwise unable to function in healthy and responsible ways (Powell-Hammond & Mattis, 2005; Laubscher, 1995). Even more, their lives are often framed as being expendable and of little value, and requiring militarized policing and control. Coupled with racial and racialized gender stereotypes that persist in society, as observed in social and mass media (Adams-Bass, Stevenson, & Kotzin, 2014; Jackson, 2006), the expendability of Black males' lives facilitates a normalcy and unaffected response to the loss of African American/Black males' lives.[2]

This is evident in the tragic deaths of Trayvon Martin,[3] Michael Brown,[4] Jordan Davis,[5] Eric Garner,[6] John Crawford,[7] Ezell Ford,[8] Sean Bell,[9] Amadou Diallo,[10] and countless others, whose lives were ended at the hands of White male police or White male vigilantes who refused to recognize their humanity and worth. Much has been written and debated in popular media and academic research journals regarding these criminal cases and the related deaths of unarmed African American males (e.g., Ifill, 2015). Many have wrestled with both the morality and legality of these cases, filtering these experiences through the lens of their own culture-laden lived experiences. Experiences influence our opinions regarding whether or not the deaths of these unarmed African American males were examples of justifiable self-defense or blatantly brutal killings. For example, during the investigation, arrest, trial, and acquittal of George Zimmerman, many drew attention to how fallacies and stereotypes regarding African American masculinity are mobilized in ways that criminalize and literally kill African American males. In addition, these high-profile cases highlight the ways unconscious internalization of negative stereotypes about African American masculinity undergirds how men of African American descent are both perceived and subsequently treated, resulting in microaggressions, harassment, microassaults, physical assaults, and other forms of violence.

The characterization of African American/Black males as criminal, suspect, and dangerous has not only impacted society at large, but has significantly influenced African American males' sense of self (Bryant, 2011). The internalization of negative messages and suppositions about their sense of self are believed to contribute to the onset of depression, suicidal ideation, substance use, hypermasculinity, and other attributes and behaviors that negatively impact the health and thriving of African American males (Corprew & Cunningham, 2012; Hammond, 2012; Matthews, Hammond, Nuru-Jeter, Cole-Lewis, & Melvin, 2013).

The implication of such characterizations has also been associated with negative life outcomes. For example, research has consistently shown

African American/Black males have high rates of mortality, incarceration, and discontinuity in educational pursuits (Long, 2012; Warren, Chiricos, & Bales, 2012). Additionally, inequities in hiring, and a series of recessions have removed a number of African American males from the urban employment sector (Bennett, 2014). Based on these factors and dominant assumptions (or stereotypes) about African American males, interventions that interrupt internalization of such misnomers seem warranted. Therefore, this chapter attempts to deconstruct the prevailing negative archetypes and complexes of African American/Black masculinity. We begin by briefly summarizing the predominant organizing discourse on racial identity development and socialization as it pertains to African American/Black males. The discourse provides a basis for understanding the process of identity development and socialization. Next, Jungian personality theory is explicated with particular attention to personality constructs that facilitate an understanding of the production and internalization of negative racial stereotypes, archetypes, and complexes of African American/Black masculinity. Finally, we conclude by positing clinical strategies informed by Jungian theory for supporting positive racial identity development among African American/Black males, as mediated through the development and praxis of mental health therapists or counselors.

RACIAL IDENTITY DEVELOPMENT AND SOCIALIZATION

Black males have long encountered racism and discrimination, as evident in their lynching, unequal prosecution, and exclusion from employment, for example. The vilification and subjugation of Black males has been documented and researched extensively and continues to occur, as witnessed in the tragic deaths of the aforementioned males. In response, African American/Black parents have been active and intentional in their efforts to prepare their sons and daughters for racial and gender discrimination and acts of prejudice they will likely encounter during the course of their life. Researchers have noted parenting practices and messaging focused on race and gender occurring during early development through late adolescence/early adulthood (Howard, Rose, & Barbarin, 2013; Hughes et. al., 2006). Empirical research has established the importance of racial identity development and socialization, and the protective roles these practices serve in fostering a strong sense of self, identity, and wellness (i.e., socioemotional) among African Americans and Blacks in general and males in particular (Howard et al., 2013; Neblett, Banks, Cooper, & Smalls-Glover, 2013). For example, Howard et al. (2013) found African American parents of very young boys (ages 3 to 8) provide developmentally age-appropriate race socialization messages associated with "building pride, acknowledging diversity, and [fostering a] spiritual and religio[us]" foundation (p. 227). Such messages reflect parents' purposeful efforts to establish a strong and positive racial identity within their sons, which would, presumably, facilitate adaptive functioning when encountering and having to navigate racist and discriminatory contexts.

African American/Black parents' racial socialization and identity development practices are consistent across the developmental spectrum; parents offer different age-appropriate messages, but the end goals are the same (building racial pride, etc.). Seminal research studies on racial and ethnic socialization (see Hughes et al., 2006 for a review of this research) illustrate the continuity in messaging, especially the importance of cultural socialization (i.e., teaching of African American history, culture, and heritage), preparation for bias, and promotion of mistrust. These socialization messages are communicated through direct age-appropriate conversation, as well as exposure and interaction with significant individuals (in their lives) and within various environments and contexts with the expressed purpose of countering stereotypes about African Americans and Blacks.

Race socialization is also mediated through social context and parents' own race socialization experiences. Thornton, Chatters, Taylor, and Allen (1990) argue that "the content and nature of objectives deemed important and appropriate for one's children" varies by parents and in accordance to their social context (e.g., socioeconomic status, urbanicity, and gender; p. 402). Thus, racial socialization can be further defined as "messages and practices that relate to the development of consciousness of personal and group identity, intergroup and individual relationships, and a sensitivity to one's position in the social hierarchy" (Howard, Rose, & Barbarin, 2013, p. 219). Ultimately, racial socialization is intended to support the development of a healthy racial identity.

Yet, despite African American parents' efforts to buffer their sons from the effect of racism and prejudice, the preponderance of negative social messaging and stereotyping can still adversely impact African American youth development. For example, Bryant (2011) found internalized racism to be predictive of aggressive behavior, above and beyond the effect of impulsive behavior, delinquent friends, aggressive response to shame, and drug use, all of which are most often theorized to be associated with such behavior. Bryant posits, "Negative self-concepts and characteristics inherent to internalized racism can become deeply rooted in the minds of African American youth" (p. 701). Similarly, in a review of empirical research focused on the effect of racism on the health of nondominant racial populations, Williams and Mohammed (2013) reported substantial evidence indicating that experiences of racial discrimination can contribute to adverse health conditions and alter behavioral patterns that increase health risk. Further, Williams and Williams-Morris (2000) outline three pathways by which racism can affect mental health: (a) through institutional discrimination, which restricts socioeconomic mobility; (b) experiences of discrimination as a source of stress; and (c) acceptance of the stigma of inferiority, which can lead to impaired psychological functioning. Arguably, the effects of racism may be even more pronounced among African American males, especially those males experiencing higher levels of discrimination and who internalize anti-Black attitudes.

JUNGIAN THEORY: THE INTERPLAY OF INTERNALIZATION AND SOCIETAL PERCEPTION

Carl Jung's (1913/1928/1933) theory of personality development, also referred to as *analytical psychology,* provides a robust framework for understanding how historical trends that contribute to the demonization and devaluing of African American masculinity are internalized by African American/ Black males and enacted through both micro and macro structures and systems (e.g., employment, laws and policies). Jung's theory bridges the individual and collective experience of phenomena, allowing for a psychological and sociological understanding of human behavior and condition. Accordingly, the theory posits that one's personality or psyche is comprised of three components: the *ego,* the *personal unconscious,* and the *collective unconscious.* The ego is defined as all that is within our awareness or consciousness, the part of our personality that is concerned with thinking, feeling, memory, and perception. The ego is responsible for ensuring that the functions and activities of life are carried out consistently. Additionally, it is responsible for our sense of identity as well as our sense of continuity in time.

The second component, the personal unconscious, concerns temporarily repressed or forgotten memories and experiences that give rise to *complexes.* Jung defines complexes as clusters of emotionally loaded (i.e., highly valued) thoughts, feelings, attitudes, and memories that focus on a common feeling tone. The greater the internalization of memories and experiences or emotional charge attached to the said complex, the greater the valence and influence on the individual—both cognitively and behaviorally. These complexes are organized as themes and recur over and over again within that individual's life. For example, if a White individual has a racist complex toward African American males, it will create a tone of suspicion, anger, and perhaps fear (depending on the emotional charge and valence) toward all African American males, and will impact that individual's perception and treatment toward African American males, both unconsciously and consciously. These complexes are often exhibited in the form of microaggressions, microassaults, and explicit/blatant forms of discrimination and violence toward African American males.

The third component and perhaps the deepest layer of the psyche is the collective unconscious. Concerned with humanity's collective experience of the evolutionary past, Jung (1928) posited the collective unconscious is the "deposit of ancestral experience from untold millions of years, the echo of prehistoric world events to which each century adds an infinitesimally small amount of variation and differentiation" (p. 162). Jung further posited that these ancestral experiences are internalized into the psyche, and are often characterized as racial memories, primordial images, or more commonly, *archetypes*. Accordingly, an archetype is conceptualized as an inherited predisposition to respond to certain aspects of the world. Our primitive past becomes the basis of human personality/psyche, and often leads and influences behavior (Jung, 1947). Archetypes are significant in determining our day-to-day reactions, attitudes, and values. Further, they have universal meanings across cultures and may manifest through and in dreams, literature, art, and religion.

Jung (1947) posited that archetypes are exhibited through the *persona*, which he defines as the social masks individuals present to the external world. These social mask are often quite juxtaposed from who people actually see and understand themselves to be. Personas are created consciously, integrated into the collective psyche, and developed through socialization, acculturation, and life experience. The persona is a complex system that houses both individual consciousness and the perceived needs and power of one's social community. As such, the "persona-mask" has a two-fold purpose: to make explicit impressions to others, while hiding the true nature of the self from both the self and others.

JUNGIAN THEORY: UNDERSTANDING THE IMPACT OF RACISM AND DISCRIMINATION

Application of Jung's psychoanalytic theory to understand the racialized experiences of African American/Black males affords an opportunity to more deeply interrogate the insidious nature of racism and discrimination and the implications for both White individuals and African American/Black males. Specifically, the theory provides a framework for understanding how the *collective unconsciousness* regarding African American males becomes internalized by White individuals over generations, as well as how African American/Black males have come to understand their own identity and masculinity. For African American/Black males, the collective unconsciousness includes the negative internalization of ancestral and contemporary experiences such as slavery, group discrimination, racism, and White privilege, which mediates behavior and ascription to specific archetypes. For White Americans, the collective unconsciousness presents as racialized archetypes that are informed by generational transmission of racial stereo-types, racialized values, and discriminatory beliefs. Jung refers to these types of archetypes as a "racial memory," which he defines as a memory regarding race and culture that influences our values and response to the world.

According to Jung, racialized archetypes play an important role in determining White individuals' day-to-day reactions, attitudes, and values toward African American males. For example, White individuals who hold a negative African American male archetype will hold negative perceptions of African American males, such as being dangerous, deviant, and spiritually and intellectually inferior. Collective unconsciousness is also evident in the ways in which popular and social media construct and display images of African American males; they often perpetuate and reify racialized archetypes, typically at the sociopolitical and physical expense of African American males. African American males have also developed their own distinct racial memories or racialized archetypes as a consequence of distinct historical and current life experiences, which affect their sense of self. It can be argued that such effects manifest as internalized racism, low racial identity, affinity toward Whiteness, hypermasculine attitudes and behaviors, and a host of negative psychological compensatory symptoms and behaviors.

In addition to the collective unconscious, attention to the *personal unconscious* affords an understanding of how acts of racism, discrimination, and inhumane conceptualization and treatment of African American/Black males by White individuals operates at the unconscious and subconscious realms of reality. Repressed or forgotten memories that operate on the unconscious level are reified through intergenerational transmission and exhibited through the development of complexes. Emotionally loaded feelings and attitudes, complexes, create an emotionally charged valence toward African American males that influence how White individuals treat African American males. They also inform White individuals' perceptions of African American males, reifying such archetypes as being lazy, dangerous, morally bankrupt, intellectually inferior, and socially limited. African American males are also affected by the intergenerational transmission of the effects of slavery, discrimination (past and present), micro-assaults, microaggressions, and limited mobility, contributing to the development of their own set of complexes. Such complexes include feeling hopeless, a positionality of deference toward Whites (often White males), cultural mistrust, fear and mistrust of the police, and difficulty establishing and maintaining healthy intimate relationships.

Finally, Jung's persona construct (i.e., social mask) provides insight into the effects of racism and discrimination on African American/Black males. The social masks that African American males present to the external world are often done so at the expense of their true selves and authentic feelings. They have a tremendous impact on African American/Black males' identity development and how well they are able to negotiate the stressors (i.e., racism, discrimination, White privilege) found in their external world (i.e., everyday life). Further, persona advances an understanding of why African American males choose maladaptive coping responses/strategies when attempting to make sense of and navigate the social norms of racism, discrimination, and poverty. Singer (1973) stated, "The process of adapting to society requires some compromises between authentic 'being' or natural desires, and social norms. This necessitates the construction of 'personas,' the masks which signify the roles we play in society" (p. 215). For many African American males, personas are taken on as an attempt to maintain some semblance of control, power, relevance, and humanity. Jung warns that individuals, who employ social masks, often equate them as their entire psyche. In other words, individuals actually believe who they are pretending to be and, therefore, are deceiving themselves. Embodiment or ascription to such personas can be interpreted as a form of spiritual and cultural dissociation.

When applied to the historic and contemporary context of African American males' lives, Jung's psychoanalytic theory affords us an opportunity for a deeper examination and discussion of the cognitive, emotional, and identity dissonance experienced as a consequence of taking on these social masks. Such dissonance often presents as the inability of African American males to know and understand themselves in deep and healthy ways; to develop and engage in healthy relationships with other African American males, their children, lovers/partners, and society as a whole; and to experience a full range of emotions. Similar to Dubois's construct of "double consciousness," personas may be enacted in response to racialized archetypes held by White individuals about African Americans, in general, and African American males in particular. Persona concerns both the psychological and interpersonal, and may reflect African American males' need to construct public faces—potentially at the expense of their physical and psychological well-being. Given the implications for African American males' wellness, broadly conceptualized, it is prudent to consider strategies for addressing in clinical practice.

JUNGIAN THEORY: IMPLICATIONS
FOR THERAPISTS AND COUNSELORS

As discussed previously, Jung's psychoanalytic theory of personality provides a robust framework for understanding the internalization and implication of African American/Black males' racialized experiences. While the framework allows us to understand the experiences of African American/Black males, it is equally important to consider how the framework might be: (a) used by mental health therapists/counselors to treat African American/Black male clients, and (b) used within their own professional clinical training and development. It can be argued that the mental health field has a responsibility to explore more deeply the clinical implications of racialized archetypes and complexes and how they are projected and acted out through clinical conceptualizations, diagnosis, and treatment interventions. Such projection and acting out is true for both White clinicians and clinicians of color. Accordingly, a concerted effort must be taken to mitigate such practices. These practices might include but are not limited to participation in training programs that emphasize socioculturally relevant treatment, and continuous self-development and reflexive praxis. Such practices must be considered in concert, as they are mutually reinforcing.

Socioculturally Relevant Training Programs and Treatment

It is imperative that training programs of White clinicians make an explicit commitment to begin to utilize their theoretical underpinnings and clinical skills to assist them in working toward gaining voluntary control (i.e., the healthy management of acts or behaviors by intentional action) of their archetypes and complexes, which often manifest as confirmatory biases, discriminatory and oppressive conceptualizations, diagnoses, and treatment interventions. Training programs can raise an awareness of such practices and the implications for treatment in their cultural diversity or multicultural counseling courses. Such courses should include a strong experimental component that challenges students to explore and begin to work through distorted archetypes and complexes regarding patients of differences (African American males in particular). The objectives of the experimental activities should be to promote serious inquiry and curiosity about one's positionality (i.e., beliefs, value, and attitudes) and potential bias, with the end result of making the racialized archetypes and complexes conscious. This process of inquiry and reflection would promote a more fluid understanding of an *observing ego* by assisting students (White students in particular) to develop a racial observing ego that equips them to relate to African American males (and other underserved and oppressed populations) from a position of self-examination, and not a stance of hostility and/or judgment.

Self-Development and Reflexive Praxis

White mental health therapists and counselors must take an affirmative stance to commit to utilizing and expanding their understanding of what it means for themselves individually (dimension of self-awareness) and their systems of practice (i.e., clinical paradigms, treatment plans) to more deeply understand the clinical implications of maintaining their archetypes and complexes. In order for this to occur, therapists/counselors must be open to the process of *working it through* their racialized archetypes and complexes. The psychoanalytic concept, working it through, is the process of repeating, elaborating, and amplifying interpretations made by the clinician. These interpretations are typically made about materials (e.g., written document, created art, music) patients offered as a connection or window into their unconscious mind. Thus, it is important for individuals to confront their resistance to accepting the unconscious tendencies, feelings, and cognitions that have developed into themes and pathological behaviors (Sundberg, 2001). It is believed that such working through is critical toward the success of therapy because it allows patients and organizations to involve themselves in the process of experiencing an emotional reaction without suppression. Often, when individuals and systems feel strong negative emotions about something, they will attempt to block experiencing those emotions through a number of defenses like denial, intellectualization, projection, and displacement, to name a few. It is important for therapists and counselors to begin to challenge themselves and the systems in which they work to process the emotional aspect of exploring how their negative archetypes and complexes impact the complex process of identity development, and individual, intercultural, and vocational functioning with African American males.

First, such exploration would require that the clinician's transference and countertransference related to the emotional charge of race/ethnicity be examined with his or her supervisor and/or colleagues so that these feelings and thoughts can be challenged and reified. It is only then that therapists/counselors would be equipped to assist patients, colleagues, and multileveled systems to deconstruct their own negative archetypes and complexes. This type of working through can be accomplished through specialized workshops and seminars facilitated by experts who integrate experimental elements into their curriculum, group supervision, and group consultation groups. This will allow clinicians to safely share their transferences and obtain feedback and suggestions from colleagues and teaching therapists/counselors. As a result of this working through, clinicians will be able to have direct conversations with patients of color (particularly African American male patients) about the dynamic and their feelings about working with a clinician who represents a privileged identity. The penultimate goal is the resolution and/or minimization of the power and impact of these archetypes and complexes on how underserved populations (particularly, African American males) are conceptualized, diagnosed, and treated.

CONCLUSION

The pervasiveness of racism, discrimination, and race-related fear and hostility brought to light by the recent high-profile cases involving African American males has tremendous psychological, interpersonal, and clinical implications. Therapists and counselors of all races/ethnicities (particularly White clinicians) have the responsibility to think more deeply about how their racialized archetypes and complexes negatively impact the psychological and developmental functioning of African American male patients. It is imperative that White clinicians begin to work clinically from an informed and nuanced sociohistorical and sociocultural understanding of the impact that racism, discrimination, and criminalization has on the identity development, wellness, and the self-agency of African American male patients. Mental health practitioners, in general, and White clinicians, in particular, are urged to shake off the tendency (as a consequence of racialized archetypes and complexes) to shrink away from self-evaluation and begin to shift the dialogue around issues of race and racism, on both an unconscious and conscious level. As a field, we can no longer mimic popular culture and the larger society and remain complicit by maintaining theories and clinical practices that are marred by culturally obsolete and incompetent ways of understanding and treating African American male patients. We must move beyond rhetoric to culturally competent clinical praxis. Ase!

NOTES

1. For the purposes of this chapter African American and Black will be used interchangeably. African American males refer to all males within the Black diaspora.
2. While racialized and gendered violence happens for African America/Black females (as well as Black queer and trans bodies) this chapter specifically focuses on the particularities of state and vigilante violence against Black male bodies.
3. In 2012, 17-year-old Trayvon Martin was unarmed and fatally shot in the community where he lived by mixed-race Hispanic man who claimed to be part of the neighborhood watch.
4. In 2014, 18-year-old Michael Brown was fatally shot six times by a police officer, who alleged Michael assaulted him.
5. In 2012, 17-year-old Jordan Davis was fatally shot by a White civilian male, after refusing to lower the music playing in his vehicle.
6. In 2014, 43-year-old Erick Garner, father of six, was confronted and killed by police for allegedly selling untaxed cigarettes. Police used illegal force, choke hold.
7. In 2014, 22-year-old John Crawford was fatally shot in the chest by police inside a Walmart for failing to disarm.

8. In 2014, 25-year-old Ezell Ford was killed during an "investigative stop" by police. He was shot in the back while lying on the ground.

9. In 2006, 23-year-old Sean Bell was unarmed and killed by police who fired more than 50 bullets into his car on the day of his wedding.

10. In 1999, 23-year-old, West African immigrant, Amadou Diallo was unarmed and killed by policed who fired 41 times, striking him 19 times. His wallet was mistaken for a gun.

REFERENCES

Adams-Bass, V. N., Stevenson, H. C., & Kotzin, D. S. (2014). Measuring the meaning of black media stereotypes and their relationship to the racial identity, black history knowledge, and racial socialization of African American youth. *Journal of Black Studies, 45*(5), 367–395.

Allen, F. (2013). The crisis of Black males is a national problem. *Black Voice News.* Retrieved from http://www.blackpressusa.com/the-crisis-of-black-males-is-a-national-problem/

Bennett, J. (2014). *The impact of age, race, and ethnicity on employment.* (Unpublished doctoral dissertation). Georgia State University, Atlanta, GA. Retrieved from http://scholarworks.gsu.edu/sociology_diss/79

Bryant, W. W. (2011). Internalized racism's association with African American male youth's propensity for violence. *Journal of Black Studies, 42*(4), 690–707.

Corprew, C. S., III, & Cunningham, M. (2012). Educating tomorrow's men: Perceived school support, negative youth experiences, and bravado attitudes in African American male adolescents. *Education and Urban Society, 44*(5), 571–589.

Gibbs, J. T. (1998). High-risk behaviors in African American youth: Conceptual and methodological issues in research. In V. C. McLoyd & L. Steinberg (Eds.), *Studying minority adolescents: Conceptual, methodological, and theoretical issues* (pp. 55–86). Mahwah, NJ: Erlbaum.

Hammond, P. W. (2012). Taking it like a man: Masculine role norms as moderators of the racial-discrimination-depressive symptoms associated with African American men. *American Journal of Public Health, 102* (Suppl. 2), S232–S241.

Howard, L. C., Rose, J. C., & Barbarin, O. A. (2013). Raising African American boys: An exploration of gender and racial socialization practices. *Journal of Orthopsychiatry, 83*(2), 218–230.

Hughes, D., Rodriguez, J., Smith, E. P., Johnson, D., Stevenson, H. C., & Spicer, P. (2006). Parents' ethnic-racial socialization practices: A review of research and directions for future study. *Developmental Psychology, 42*(5), 747–770.

Ifill, S. (2015). Statement by the NAACP Legal Defense and Educational Fund, Inc. before the President's Task Force on 21st Century Policing.

Jackson, R. L. (2006). *Scripting the Black masculine body identity, discourse, and racial politics in popular media.* Albany, NY: State University of New York Press.

Jung, C. G. (1913/1928/1933). The theory of psychoanalysis. In *The collected works of Carl C. Jung* (Vol. 4). Princeton, NJ: Princeton University Press.

Jung, C. G. (1928, 1947). *Relations between the ego and the unconscious in two essays on analytical psychology* (Trans, H. G. Baynes). London, England: Balliere, Tindall & Cox.

Kohl, K. L., Gross, I. M., Harrison, P. R., & Richards, M. H. (2015). Numbing and hyperarousal as mediators of exposure to community violence and depression in urban African American youth. *Journal of Child & Adolescent Trauma, 8*(1), 33–43.

Laubscher, L. (2005). Toward a (de)constructive psychology of African American men. *Journal of Black Psychology, 31*(2), 111–129.

Long, S. (2012). Reducing the Black male dropout rate. *The Journal of Negro Education, 81*(2), 175.

Matthews, D. D., Hammond, P. W., Nuru-Jeter, A., Cole-Lewis, Y., & Melvin, T. (2013). Racial discrimination and depressive symptoms among African American men: The mediating and moderating roles of masculine self-reliance and John Henryism. *Journal of Health Care for Poor and Underserved, 23*(1), 254–272.

Murry, V. M., Simons, R. L., Simons, L. G., & Gibbons, F. X. (2013). Contributions of family environment and parenting processes to sexual risk and substance use of rural African American males: A 4-year longitudinal analysis. *American Journal of Orthopsychiatry, 83*(2/3), 299.

Neblett, E. W., Jr., Banks, K. H., Cooper, S. M., & Smalls-Glover, C. (2013). Racial identity mediates the associations between ethnic-racial socialization and depressive symptoms. *Cultural Diversity & Ethnic Minority Psychology, 19*(2), 200–207.

Powell-Hammond, W., & Mattis, J. S. (2005). Being a man about it: Manhood meaning among African American men. *Psychology of Men and Masculinity, 6*(2), 114–126.

Singer, J. (1973). *Boundaries of the soul: The practice of Jung's psychology.* New York, NY: Anchor Books.

Sundberg, N. (2001). *Clinical psychology: Evolving theory, practice, and research.* Englewood Cliffs, NJ: Prentice Hall.

Thornton, M. C., Chatters, L. M., Taylor, R. J., & Allen, W. R. (1990). Sociodemographic and environmental correlates of racial socialization by Black parents. *Child Development, 61*, 401–409.

Warren, P., Chiricos, T., & Bales, W. (2012). The imprisonment penalty for young black and Hispanic males: A crime specific analysis. *Journal of Research in Crime & Delinquency, 49*(1), 56–80.

Williams, D. R., & Mohammed, S. A. (2013). Racism and health I: Pathways and scientific evidence. *American Behavioral Scientist, 57*(8), 1152–1173.

Williams, D. R., & Williams-Morris, R., (2000). Racism and mental health: The African American experience, *Ethnicity & Health, 5*(3/4), 243–268.

CPSIA information can be obtained
at www.ICGtesting.com
Printed in the USA
BVHW031927160922
647181BV00003B/20